LANDMARKS OF
LIBRARY LITERATURE
1876-1976

edited by

Dianne J. Ellsworth

and

Norman D. Stevens

The Scarecrow Press, Inc.

Metuchen, N.J.   1976

Z
731
L25

Library of Congress Cataloging in Publication Data

Main entry under title:

Landmarks of library literature, 1876-1976.

    Includes bibliographical references and index.
    1. Libraries--United States--Addresses, essays,
lectures. 2. Library science--Addresses, essays,
lectures. I. Ellsworth, Dianne J. II. Stevens,
Norman D.
Z731.L25   020'.8   75-45139
ISBN 0-8108-0899-4

CONTENTS

iii

PART IV: LIBRARIES AND THE CONCEPT OF
                LIBRARY SERVICE

PUBLIC LIBRARIES:

THE NATIONAL LIBRARY CONCEPT:

LIBRARIES AND THE YOUNG:

ACADEMIC LIBRARIES:

SPECIAL LIBRARIES:

PROBLEMS IN LIBRARY SERVICE: Librarians and
    Readers

INTRODUCTION

As every librarian knows, 1876 was marked by a number of significant events in American librarianship, so that 1976 truly marks our centennial. Two of those events, the founding of the Library Journal and the publication by the United States Bureau of Education of Public Libraries in the United States, marked a real beginning for the development of library literature in this country. Certainly much had been written before 1876 that was both important and well written. There was, however, no regular channel of communication for the profession, such as Library Journal--and the enormous number and range of library journals that have come in its wake--was to provide; nor was there a standard of quality, such as Public Libraries in the United States and the early issues of the Library Journal were to provide.

In the 100 years since 1876 a large number of articles, books, journals, reports, and other documents have been published. Some of them have been very good, many of them have been very bad. As Eric Moon indicated, "There are articles a-plenty around in librarianship ... but the majority of them say nothing, or say what it is no longer necessary to say because it has been said so often, and most of them say it ... incredibly badly."[1] But Moon is only one of the most recent critics of a literature that probably has been maligned more often that it has been praised. The best critique, by Ralph Beals, is, unfortunately, all too well hidden in the papers of the Sixth Annual Institute of the Graduate Library School of the University of Chicago which was held in 1941. In that essay Beals characterized the library literature as comprising three types: glad tidings, testimony, and research.

> Glad tidings, which comprise a somewhat large proportion of the periodical literature of librarianship are of two kinds: speculative essays about what might, could, would, or should be true of ... librarianship, and announcements, more or less un-

1

varnished, of something about to be done or very
recently undertaken. Glad tidings, like the apostle's
faith, are the essence of things hoped for--the substance of things unseen. The point of view is an-
ticipatory and optimistic.... A second and still
more numerous class of professional publications
falls in a category that may be called testimony--
testimony not in the legal sense, but in the sense
commonly associated with religious sects: retrospective accounts of something done, of benefits con-
ferred. Testimony is often, though not invariably,
cast in the first person plural: We have thought;
we have tried; we have accomplished this or that.
Even when this formula is not employed, the implications are nearly always personal and, hence, likely to be idiosyncratic.... Now experience is the
sole source of error as well as of truth; and in a
substantial part of the published testimony about
... librarianship one wonders whether the process
of winnowing has been carried far enough to yield
wholly trustworthy results.... [Testimony, it may
be noted, is what later observers, most notably
Ralph Shaw, have come to characterize as "How I
Run My Library Good" literature.] A third source
of evidence comprises publications that may, with
some propriety, be described as research. This
class is not limited to statistical studies, nor do all
statistical studies, as such, necessarily fall within
it. ... [2]

These and other criticisms have not prevented the publication of numerous anthologies of library literature designed
to bring together what one editor or another has felt are the
best or most useful articles in one area of the field or another. So many anthologies have been published that criticism of anthologies is virtually a field in its own right. If
the publisher of this volume may be cited as a critic of the
literature, perhaps one of the editors may best be cited as
a critic of anthologies. "I am increasingly dismayed," he
wrote, "by anthologies, generally designed to serve some
poorly defined purpose, in which all of the material is readily available in any decent library and for which, therefore,
a solid bibliographical article might well suffice and might,
indeed, be even more useful since it could cover a wider
range of material. Such anthologies only contribute to what
can best be described as information pollution. They might
have some value as a supplementary textbook in a course but

they have relatively little other value. "3   Here again, though,
this is only one of the most recent criticisms of anthologies.
Ralph Beals may also be cited as an earlier, and more literate, critic of this aspect of the library literature as well:

> I should not wish for a moment to propose that any
> librarian who has not already committed the indis-
> cretion of an anthology should straightway set about
> doing so.   Our shelves already sag under the weight
> of far too many anthologies covering about the same
> ground, put together in about the same way, and
> intended to serve about the same purpose. 4

If the quality of library literature is as bad as it is
made out to be, and if we are inundated by anthologies, why
then this book?

The criticism of the literature is, it must be conceded,
a general one designed to apply, perhaps, to the majority of
our writings.   As librarians committed to the preservation
and use of written records we recognize that there has been
much that has been written and published in our field in the
past 100 years that is extremely important and significant.
Surely the written word has had a major impact on the theory
and practice of librarianship.   This anthology is intended to
identify and present those contributions that represent true
landmarks for our profession.

This anthology is thus intended to draw together, for
a general professional audience, a number of articles which
taken as a whole provide a reasonable perspective on the kind
of writing and thinking that has shaped the state and mind of
our profession over the past century and has helped it to arrive, for better or for worse, at the point that it now is.
All of us, it is to be hoped, can gain in our thinking as we
try to solve present day problems from the experience of
reading and examining, as a package, these essays.

In many ways a bibliographic essay might have been a
better approach, for space limitations have precluded our including it in this anthology many items that ought to constitute a part of such a review.   Unfortunately, a bibliographic
essay on this broad topic, as fine as it might be, is not
likely to motivate even librarians to turn to their shelves to
read all of the items cited.   A few librarians might read a
few of the items cited but that is the best that one could hope
for.   This bringing together in one place of essays that reflect

the growth and development of American library thought provides a ready opportunity for librarians, and others, to read
a broad series of essays that reflect American library efforts
and concerns over the past 100 years.

                         *   *   *

     We hope that those who review and read this anthology
will disagree with our selection of articles and will find glar-
ing omissions. Such a process will show that they have not
only read but have thought about what they have read. In
order that they may better understand what we have left out,
we are including the following brief description of our methodology.

     Apart from personal recollections and a concept of the
literature as gleaned from past study and reading and research
efforts, a variety of approaches, designed to bring about a
broad initial familiarity with the literature, were used. We
cannot guarantee that our immersion in the library literature
of the past century was as total as it might have been, but
we can testify that we did nearly drown under the volume of
what we did examine. Available biographies and biographical
sketches of American librarians were examined to see what
comments had been made on their writings. A wide range
of full-length works on library history, in the broadest possible sense, were read or at least examined very carefully.
Cannon and Library Literature were scanned for appropriate
items. As topics and individuals were thought of and discussed, journals, indexes, and other sources were reexam-
ined. Mention of the project in several library journals
brought only a limited, and largely unproductive, response.
Correspondence with approximately 75 library leaders, selected for their interest in library history and their long association and personal experience in the profession, brought
replies, which furnished a variety of interesting and useful
suggestions, from about half of those contacted. Finally, as
seems always to be the case, serendipity played a significant
role in our gathering processes.

     We began with some broad criteria. Those were:

     1) Articles that caused a great deal of discussion at
the time of publication or which otherwise clearly had a significant impact on American librarianship (e. g. , Osborn's
"The Crisis in Cataloging");
     2) Articles by distinguished librarians that presented

their philosophy or views exceptionally well (e. g., Shaw's "From Fright to Frankenstein");

    3)   Articles, comments, editorials on notable topics or themes (e. g., Kunitz's editorial, "The Spectre at Richmond");

    4)   Articles that were exceptionally well written, whatever the impact or topic or whoever the author (e. g., Shera's "On the Value of Library History");

    5)   Notable documents or reports (e. g., Public Libraries in the United States).

The assembling process brought together no end of material. All of it could not be used and much of it, obviously, did not warrant inclusion. The selecting processes involved both some broad decisions and, ultimately, some individual ones.

As an initial, and admittedly very arbitrary, decision it was concluded that to attempt to handle in this volume book-length material, or even selections from such items, would not be feasible. Thus Munthe's American Librarianship from a European Angle, Rider's The Scholar and the Future of the Research Library, and other equally important works which are indeed landmarks, were reluctantly dropped. For this material a bibliographical essay might well be in order and we would recommend it as a deserving project.

Next, we concluded that although they were often significant, works written by committees or groups should be excluded because we felt that this volume should deal with the contributions of individual librarians. Thus the Library Bill of Rights and The Freedom to Read Statement, and other similar items were excluded. Here again, a volume of documents of American librarianship from 1876 to 1976 would seem to be worthwhile.

Often there seemed to be several good articles on the same subject and it was difficult to decide how to deal with them. We decided that we should try to achieve some balance as to subjects represented. This meant that where we had several good articles on the same subject, we tended to pick only one, in order that other topics could be represented.

Another problem was in trying to distinguish between articles that had impact or importance and articles that described events of happenings that had impact. Thus we debated the question of including an article by Metcalf that described the development of the Lamont Undergraduate Library at Harvard, but concluded that it should not be included because, while the development of that library was a significant event, Metcalf's article simply described what had taken place.   It was the development of the library that was significant, not the article.

Finally, we tried to exclude articles that appeared upon examination to be too specialized or to describe in too much detail projects or events.   Many seemingly promising articles were dropped when examination showed that they were too chatty or drew conclusions based only on their authors' personal experience discussed at length.   Thus, by a process of natural selection, most of what Beals characterized as "testimony" was omitted.

Perhaps what we have largely included are "glad tidings" (although Osborn on cataloging and Mason on computers could hardly be described as "glad"), largely of the first category of "speculative essays about what might, could, would, or should be true of ... librarianship. "   This, it seemed, was the area in which the articles that were truly significant and should be cited as landmarks do fall.

Finally, of course, it became, as it always does, a matter of individual judgment.   A thorough rereading and reconsideration of the many articles which we had collected, a screening and winnowing of those articles, and an arrangement and rearrangement of those articles led to the selection of what is here presented.

We hope that these articles do indeed represent the most significant that have been published in the past 100 years.   We hope that they will be of more than passing interest and that they will, in this selection and arrangement, contribute something to our understanding of the thoughts and ideas that have helped make our profession what it is and what it may become.

NOTES

1.   Eric Moon.   "The Library Press, " Library Journal 94: 4104, 1969.

2.   Ralph Beals.   "Implications of Communications Research for the Public Library, " in Douglas Waples, ed. Print,

Radio, and Film in a Democracy.   Chicago: University of Chicago Press, 1942, p. 19.

3.   Norman D. Stevens' review of William E. Hug's Strate-
gies for Change in Information Programs, in College
& Research Libraries 35:376, 1974.

4.   Ralph Beals.   "The Librarian as Anthologist, " DC Libraries 12:19, January 1941.

PART I

LIBRARIANS AND LIBRARIANSHIP

Introduction to Part I

LIBRARIANS AND LIBRARIANSHIP

A provision of endless apparatus, a
bustle of infinite inquiry and research,
may be employed to evade and shuffle
off real labor--the real labor of thinking.

                --Sir Joshua Reynolds[1]

    The basic role of the librarian in American society is
a topic that, perhaps more than any other, has occupied "Our
Profession" through these first one hundred years.   For that
reason alone it seems appropriate to begin this anthology with
those articles which have been most significant in the discussion of that fundamental concern.   Unfortunately, too little
of the discussion of this important topic has shown evidence
of the real labor of thinking which should constitute our essential work.   Much of the writing in this area reflects the
insecurity and uncertainty of a quest for a standing to be
awarded by someone else rather than earned by ourselves.
Paradoxically, some of the best writing of librarianship is
also to be found in articles--those with a positive tone based
on a clear understanding of the real value of libraries--deal-
ing with the same basic issues.   In no other area that we
considered is the disparity in the quality of thought and ex-

---

1.   The quotation at the head of this introduction, and of the
chapter introductions that follow, are all taken from D. W.
Krummel's A Librarian's Collacon: An Anthology of Quotations and Aphorisms Reflecting the Moral Philosophy of the
Library Profession (Urbana: Illini Union Bookstore, 1971).
The nearly 900 quotations by other than professional librarians that Krummel supplies in that "anthology of quotations
and aphorisms reflecting the moral philosophy of the library
profession" make a splendid complement to this anthology of
the writings of librarians on the library profession.

pression so great. Of the many excellent statements on librarianship as a profession, we have chosen as a starting
point for this anthology four which most clearly addressed
the major aspects of the issue in the American perspective
and which most clearly have affected all librarians.

Except perhaps as a classroom exercise, there is little question but what librarianship now can be considered a
profession. Many attendant questions relating to how those
professional attitudes and goals can be put into practice effectively do remain unresolved. Many of the articles in this
anthology will touch on one aspect or another of those attendant questions. The second section of this chapter, in particular, looks in more detail at some of the basic problems of
putting professionalism into practice. A wide range of subjects and articles were considered for inclusion here but ultimately some important subjects (e. g., faculty status for
academic librarians) with a narrower focus were dropped in
favor of those which deal more fully with the broader issues
of what it is that we, and ultimately our users, should expect from librarians and how the work of librarianship should
be shaped.

OF THE LIBRARIAN'S PROFESSION*

Archibald MacLeish

Nothing is more difficult for the beginning librarian
than to discover in what profession he is engaged. Certain
professions define themselves. Others are defined by those
who practise them. The librarian's profession is of neither
nature. A librarian is so called not for what he does, as
the farmer who farms or the lawyer who laws, but from the
place in which he does it. And the definitions of the librarians, though they are eloquent in describing the librarian's
perfections, are reticent in saying what the librarian's perfections are for.

Hugo Blotius, the sixteenth-century librarian of the
Hofbibliothek in Vienna, defined his profession by saying that
a librarian should be learned in languages, diligent, and
quiet--adding by way of reminder to his master, the Emper-
or, that "if not of noble blood he should be given a title to
enhance the dignity of his office." Cotton des Houssayes told
the general assembly of the Sorbonne in 1780 that when he
reflected "on the qualifications that should be united in your
librarian" they presented themselves to his mind in so great
a number, and in such character of perfection, that he dis-
trusted his ability not only to enumerate but even to trace a
true picture of them. Pressing himself to the point, however,
the learned orator (who spoke, it should be noted, in the
Latin tongue) supplied the following description of the office:
"Your librarian should be, above all, a learned and profound
theologian; but to this qualification, which I shall call fundamental, should be united vast literary acquisitions, an exact
and precise knowledge of all the arts and sciences, great
facility of expression, and lastly, that exquisite politeness

*Reprinted by permission of the Houghton-Mifflin Co. from
the Atlantic Monthly 165:786-790 (June 1940).

which conciliates the affection of his visitors while his merit
secures their esteem. "

One gathers that M. des Houssayes thought well of the
librarian's office, but beyond that, and a certain conviction
of personal inadequacy, one is little wiser than before.   To
be at once a profound and learned theologian, the possessor
of vast literary acquisitions, the exact and precise master of
all the arts and all the sciences, a facile writer and a charm-
ing gentleman possessed of that exquisite politeness which
wins heads as well as hearts, is to be an unusual and admirable human being--but even to be all these things at once is
scarcely a profession.

And yet it is largely in the vein of the orator of the
Sorbonne and the librarian of the Hofbibliothek that the profession of the librarian is presented.   Modern librarians--
perhaps because they do not speak in Latin--have never been
as eloquent as Cotton des Houssayes, but even modern librarians write as though the profession of the librarian had
been defined when the scholarly attainments and linguistic
achievements of the, perhaps, ideal librarian have been described.

The consequence is that the beginning librarian is
thrown upon his own resources, upon the dictionary, and upon
the familiar sentences of the great founder of the Bodleian
Library at Oxford.   From Sir Thomas Bodley, besides learning that a librarian should not be "encumbered with marriage
nor with a benefice of cure" and that he should be "a per-
sonable scholler and qualified, if it may be, with a gentle-
manlike speeche and carriage ... able to interteine commers
in aswel of other nations as our owne, with meete discourses
for the place, " the apprentice librarian will learn that a librarian is a Keeper of a library.   From the dictionary he
will learn that a library is "a large collection of books, public or private. "   And by his own resources he will attempt
to deduce what the Keeper of a large collection of books, public or private, may, in actionable and intelligible language,
be.   Keeper, but how a keeper?   Of books--but what, then,
in this context is a book?

It is not an altogether simple question, and for this
reason.   There are two meanings of the word "book" and
two relations, therefore, between a book and the man entrusted with its keeping.   There is one meaning which signifies a physical object made of certain physical materials in a

physical shape. There is another meaning which signifies an
intellectual object made of all materials or of no materials
and standing in as many shapes as there are forms and bal-
ances and structures in men's minds. The two meanings
overlap and are confused. Readers associate the intellectual
book with the physical book, thinking of Plato's vision of the
world in terms of dark green linen with a gilded name. Collectors associate the physical book with the intellectual book,
imagining that because they possess a rare edition of a poet's
work they somehow have possessed the poem. But the two
meanings are nevertheless distinct. The physical book is
never more than an ingenious and often beautiful cipher by
which the intellectual book is communicated from one mind
to another, and the intellectual book is always a structure in
the imagination which may hang for a time above a folio page
in ten-point type with a half-calf binding only to be found thereafter on a different page above a different type and even in another language.

When it is said, therefore, that a librarian is a keeper of books, it must be determined first of which of these
two books he is the keeper. Is he, for one example, the
keeper of the small, clothbound object of 110 pages of text
and vi of front matter manufactured by Macmillan and Co.,
Limited, in London in 1928 and called The Tower by W. B.
Yeats? Or is he the keeper of that very different object created in many men's minds before, and now in yours, by this
--these words, these symbols, images, perceptions:--

> That is no country for old men. The young
> In one another's arms, birds in the trees,
> --Those dying generations--at their song,
> The salmon falls, the mackerel-crowded seas,
> Fish, flesh or fowl, commend all summer long
> Whatever is begotten born and dies.
> Caught in that sensuous music all neglect
> Monuments of unaging intellect.

It makes a difference whether the book is the cloth
and paper or the intellectual image. If it is the physical
book of which a librarian is keeper, then the character of
his profession is obvious enough. He is a custodian as all
keepers of physical objects are custodians, and his obligations
are a custodian's obligations. He is a sort of check boy in
the parcel room of culture. His duty is to receive the priceless packages confided to him by the past and to redeliver
them to the future against the proper stub. To perform that

obligation he must be reliable, orderly, industrious, and clever. He must devise infallible and complicated ticket systems to find the parcels on the shelves. He must read the notations of origin and ownership in a dozen tongues. He must guard the wrappers from the risks of time and theft and matches and men's thumbs. He must be courteous and patient with the claimants. And for the rest he has no duty but to wait. If no one comes, if no one questions, he can wait.

But if it is not the physical book but the intellectual book of which the librarian is keeper, then his profession is a profession of a very different kind. It is not the profession of the custodian, for the intellectual book is not a ticketed parcel which can be preserved by keeping it from mice and mildew on a shelf. The intellectual book is an imagined object in the mind which can be preserved only by preserving the mind's perception of its presence. Neither is the librarian's profession the profession of the check boy who receives and guards and redelivers,--receives from the past, guards against the present, and redelivers to the future,--for the intellectual book is not a deposit of the past which the future has a right to call and claim. The intellectual book is a construction of the spirit, and the constructions of the spirit exist in one time only--in that continuing and endless present which is Now. If it is the intellectual book rather than the physical book of which the librarian is keeper, then the profession of the librarian is not and cannot be the neutral, passive, negative profession of the guardian and fiduciary, but must become instead the affirmative and advocating profession of the attorney for a cause. For the intellectual book is the Word. And the keepers of the Word, whether they so choose or not, must be its partisans and advocates. The Word was never yet protected by keeping it in storage in a warehouse: the preservation of the Word is now, as it has always been, a cause--perhaps the greatest--not, I think, the least in danger in this time.

It makes a difference, therefore,--a very considerable difference in the understanding of the librarian's profession, --which of these two meanings of the book is taken. Both are held. The librarian who asserts that the sole and single strength of his profession in a distracted world is its disinterested objectivity--meaning its negative and custodial detachment from the dangers which beset the Word--thinks of the book necessarily as a physical object on his shelves for which, in its intellectual aspects, he accepts no share of risk or credit. The library trustee or the moralizing editor who demands of librarians that they stick to the job of pasting on the labels and handing out the loans accepts, but with less honesty, the same assumption--less honesty because he speaks, not from love of the librarian's profession, but from hatred of the Word, and fear of its persuasions.

Those who love the power of the Word and who defend it take the opposite position. Shortly after William Dugard was released, through the efforts of John Milton, from Newgate prison, he published two letters by John Dury, deputy keeper in 1649 of the King's medals and library, which put the case with eagerness and passion: "For if Librairie-Keepers did understand themselves in the nature of their work, and would make themselves, as they ought to bee, useful in their places in a publick waie; they ought to become agents for the advancement of universal learning.... The end of that Imploiment, in my conception, is to keep the publick stock of Learning, which is in Books and MSS, to increas it, and to propose it to others in the waie which may bee most useful unto all. His work then is to bee a Factor and Trader for helps to learning, and a Treasurer to keep them, and a Dispenser to applie them to use or to see them well used, or at least not abused."

As between these two conceptions of the profession a man can choose only for himself and not for those who practise the profession with him. But there are, notwithstanding, certain considerations which even a novice among librarians may propose. The chief of these considerations is the nature of the times in which men live. In a different time from ours--such a time as men a generation ago considered natural and normal--it made relatively little difference whether a librarian behaved himself as a custodian of volumes or as a "Factor and Trader for helps to learning, and a Treasurer to keep them, and a Dispenser to applie them to use." A generation ago the Word, the life of the mind, the Monuments of unaging intellect, were not under attack. It was agreed by all civilized nations, by all governments in power, that the cultural tradition was a common treasure, that truth was an end to be sought equally by all men, and that the greatest glory and final justification of human life was the creativeness of the human spirit. In such a world the librarian who considered himself a custodian, who devoted himself to the perfection of his catalogue and the preservation of his bindings, and who waited for the calls of those who had business with his collections, was not only prudent but

entirely wise.   There was no need for him to advocate the
cause of learning or to assert the supreme importance of the
contents of his library, for no one doubted the one or challenged the other.   The librarian who presented himself in
the years before the Great War as a champion of culture
would have received the ironic welcome he deserved.   What
was required of him then (and what he practised) was discretion, dignity, and a judicial calm.

But the world in which we live is not that world.   The
world in which we live is a world that world would have believed impossible.   In the world in which we live it is no
longer agreed by all governments and citizens that truth is
the final measure of men's acts and that the lie is shameful.
There are governments abroad and there are citizens here to
whom respect for truth is naïve--governments and individuals
who, when it is proved they lie, have not been shamed "either in their own or in their neighbors' eyes."   In the world
in which we live it is no longer agreed that the common culture is a common treasure.   There are governments abroad
and there are citizens here to whom the common culture
which draws the peoples of the West together is a common
evil for which each nation must now substitute a private culture, a parochial art, a local poetry, and a tribal worship.
In the world in which we live it is no longer agreed that the
greatest glory and final justification of human history is the
life of the human mind.   To many men and many governments the life of the human mind is a danger to be feared
more than any other danger, and the Word which cannot be
purchased, cannot be falsified, and cannot be killed is the
enemy most hunted for and hated.   It is not necessary to
name names.   It is not necessary to speak of the burning of
the books in Germany, or of the victorious lie in Spain, or
of the terror of the creative spirit in Russia, or of the hunting and hounding of those in this country who insist that certain truths be told and who will not be silent.   These things
are commonplaces.   They are commonplaces to such a point
that they no longer shock us into anger.   Indeed it is the essential character of our time that the triumph of the lie, the
mutilation of culture, and the persecution of the Word no longer shock us into anger.

What those who undertake to keep the libraries must
consider--or so it seems to me--is whether this profound
and troubling alteration of the times alters also their profession.   Granted that it was not only possible but desirable for
the librarian to think of his profession in negative and cus-

todial terms in the quiet generations when the burning of
books was a mediaeval memory, is it still possible for librarians to think of their profession in these passive terms
in a time in which the burning of the books is a present fact
abroad and a present possibility at home?

Granted that it was not only prudent but wise as well
for the librarian to admit no positive, affirmative duty to the
cause of learning in a time when learning was universally
honored and the works of great art and great scholarship
were admired monuments, is it still wise for librarians to
admit no positive duty to learning in a time when governments abroad ignorance instead of knowledge to their people,
and fanatical and frightened citizens at home would, if they
could, obliterate all art and learning but the art and learning they consider safe?

In a division which divides all men, because it is a
division drawn through everything that men believe, can
those who keep the libraries--those who keep the records of
belief--avoid division? In a struggle which is truly fought,
whatever the economic interpreters and the dialectical ma-
terialists may say to the contrary, across the countries of
the spirit, can those who hold those countries remain neutral? In an attack which is directed, as no attack in history
ever was directed, against the intellectual structures of the
books, can those who keep the books contend their books are
only objects made of print and paper?

I can answer only for myself. To me the answer is
not doubtful. To me the changes of the time change everything. The obligations of the keepers of the books in such a
time as ours are positive obligations because they have no
choice but to be positive. Whatever the duty of the librarian
may have been in a different world and a more peaceful generation, his duty now is to defend--to say, to fight, and to
defend. No one else--neither those who make the books nor
those who undertake to teach them--is bound as he is bound
to fight in their behalf, for no one else is charged as he is
charged with their protection. No one as much as he must
say, and say again, and still insist that the tradition of the
written word is whole and single and entire and cannot be
dismembered. No one is under obligation as he is under
obligation to meet the mutilators of the Word, the preachers
of obscurantism, the suppressors--those who would cut off
here and ink out there the texts their prejudices or their
parties or their churches or their fears find hateful. And

these obligations are not obligations which are satisfied by
negatives. The books can be protected from the preaching
demagogues and the official liars and the terrorizing mob
not by waiting for attack but by forestalling it. If the cultural tradition, the ancient and everpresent structure of the
mind, can still be saved, it can be saved by reconstructing
its authority. And the authority of art and learning rests on
knowledge of the arts and learnings. Only by affirmation,
only by exhibiting to the people the nobility and beauty of their
intellectual inheritance, can that inheritance be made secure.

Some years before his elevation to the bench, Mr.
Justice Brandeis referred to himself as "counsel for the situation. " The librarian in our time, or so it seems to me,
becomes the counsel for the situation. His client is the inherited culture entrusted to his care. He--he more than any
other man--must represent this client as its advocate. A-
gainst those who would destroy the tradition he must bring the
force of the tradition. Against those who would mutilate the
monuments he must bring the beauty of the monuments. A-
gainst those who would limit the freedom of the inquiring mind
he must bring the marvels of the mind's discoveries.

Keepers of books, keepers of print and paper on the
shelves, librarians are keepers also of the records of the
human spirit--the records of men's watch upon the world and
on themselves. In such a time as ours, when wars are
made against the spirit and its works, the keeping of these
records is itself a kind of warfare. The keepers, whether
they so wish or not, cannot be neutral.

THE PROFESSION*

Melvil Dewey

The time has at last come when a librarian may, without assumption, speak of his occupation as a profession. And, more, a better time has come--perhaps we should say is coming, for it still has many fields to conquer. The best librarians are no longer men of merely negative virtues. They are positive, aggressive characters, standing in the front rank of the educators of their communities, side by side with the preachers and the teachers. The people are more and more getting their incentives and ideas from the printed page. There are more readers and fewer listeners, and men who move and lead the world are using the press more and the platform less. It needs no argument to prove that reading matter can be distributed better and more cheaply through lending libraries than in any other way, and we shall assume, what few will presume to dispute, that the largest influence over the people is the printed page and that this influence may be wielded most surely and strongly through our libraries.

From the first, libraries have commanded great respect, and much has been written of their priceless worth; but the opinion has been largely prevalent that a librarian was a keeper only, and had done his full duty if he preserved the books from loss, and to a reasonable extent from the worms. There have been noble exceptions to this rule, but still it is a modern idea that librarians should be more than this. It is not now enough that the books are cared for properly, are well arranged, are never lost. It is not enough that he can, when asked, give advice as to the best books in

*Reprinted from Library Journal Vol. 1, No. 1 (Sept. 30, 1876).

his collection on any given subject.   All these things are indispensable, but all these are not enough for our ideal.   He
must see that his library contains, as far as possible, the
best books on the best subjects, regarding carefully the
wants of his special community.   Then, having the best books,
he must create among his people, his pupils, a desire to
read these books.   He must put every facility in the way of
readers, so that they shall be led on from good to better.
He must teach them how, after studying their own wants,
they may themselves select their reading wisely.   Such a librarian will find enough who are ready to put themselves under his influence and direction, and, if competent and enthusiastic, he may soon largely shape the reading, and through it
the thought, of his whole community.

The time is come when we are not astonished to find
the ablest business talents engaged in the management of a
public library.   Not that we have less scholarship, but that
we have more life.   The passive has become active, and we
look for a throng of people going in and out of library doors
as in the markets and the stores.   There was a time when
libraries were opened only at intervals, and visitors came
occasionally, as they come sometimes to a deserted castle
or to a haunted house.   Now many of our libraries are as
accessible as our post-offices, and the number of new libraries founded has been so great that in an ordinary town we no
longer ask, "Have you a library?" but "Where is your library?" as we might ask where is your school-house, or
your post-office, or your church?

Shares Educational Responsibility

And so our leading educators have come to recognize
the library as sharing with the school the education of the
people.   The most that the schools can hope to do for the
masses more than the schools are doing for them in many
sections, is to teach them to read intelligently, to get ideas
readily from the printed page.   It may seem a strong statement, but many children leave the schools without this ability.
They can repeat the words of the book, but this is simply
pronunciation, as a beginner pronounces another language
without getting any clear idea of the meaning.   Could the
schools really teach the masses to read, they would be doing
a great work.   The children of the lower classes have to
commence work at a very early age, and it is impossible to
keep them in the schools long enough to educate them to any

degree.   The school teaches them to read; the library must
supply them with reading which shall serve to educate, and so
it is that we are forced to divide popular education into two
parts of almost equal importance and deserving equal attention: the free school and the free library.

It is in the interest of the modern library, and of
those desiring to make its influence wider and greater, that
this journal has been established.   Its founders have an intense faith in the future of our libraries, and believe that if
the best methods can be applied by the best librarians, the
public may soon be brought to recognize our claim that the
free library ranks with the free school.   We hold that there
is no work reaching farther in its influence and deserving
more honor than the work which a competent and earnest librarian can do for his community.

The time was when a library was very like a museum,
and a librarian was a mouser in musty books, and visitors
looked with curious eyes at ancient tomes and manuscripts.
The time is when a library is a school, and the librarian is
in the highest sense a teacher, and the visitor is a reader
among the books as a workman among his tools.   Will any
man deny to the high calling of such a librarianship the title
of profession?

LIBRARIANSHIP AS A PROFESSION[1]

Pierce Butler

Our modern library system is a classic example of the way in which a new cultural institution originates and develops within a civilization. Here the adjective "new" is no misnomer. Our library is a new thing. There were book collections which we call "libraries" in earlier periods, but the library, as we have it, is something previously unknown. The public libraries of imperial Rome, the monastic and cathedral libraries of the Middle Ages, the princely and municipal libraries of the Renaissance, and the national, state, and university libraries of the Enlightenment were forerunners rather than ancestors of the modern library. That is of comparatively recent origin. It began less than two centuries ago, when certain people, desiring more books to read than they could buy individually, pooled their funds in an informal private corporation. In most instances the co-operating persons were laymen interested only in general literature, more rarely physicians, lawyers, or merchants in need of vocational books and periodicals. But, in any case, since the causes were similar, the same general procedure was adopted spontaneously and independently in many different places in Europe and America.

In each instance, as the practicability of such a book collection became manifest, more and more people wished to share in the benefit. Hence a strong tendency gradually arose to extend membership privileges until ultimately the whole community was included. Various devices were successively adopted to achieve the expansion--public subscriptions, lotteries, private benefactions, state subsidy, and,

This article is reprinted by permission of the University of Chicago Press from Library Quarterly 21:235-247 (October 1951). Copyright 1951 by the University of Chicago Press.

finally, tax support.   Naturally, in America, where frontier
conditions, geographical expansion, and population increase
imposed a tradition of book scarcity unknown in Europe, the
development of the modern library has been most extensive
and consistent. [2]

The modern library, then, has come into existence,
spontaneously and almost inadvertently, by a cumulation of
immediate empirical procedures, without anyone planning or
foreseeing very far ahead.   But this is characteristic of
every normal cultural evolution.   So also is the way in which
the intellectual content of librarianship has gradually emerged.
Theory followed practice instead of leading it.   As the library system was forming itself, librarians were becoming
ever more aware of the larger significance of their office.
Librarianship, figuratively speaking, was becoming self-conscious.   The movement, however, was gradual, not sudden.
Indeed, three separate phases may be distinguished in the process.   During the first, particularly in the 1850's, the librarian became increasingly aware of his scholarly responsibilities.   He thought less of the janitorial and custodial duties
of his office and more of the intellectual and literary.   In
short, he discovered himself as a bookman.   Next (roughly
speaking, in the 1870's), a new age set in.   American librarians, in spontaneous unanimity, began to pay closer attention to their manipulative operations.   They recognized
ever more clearly that a book stock, however rich or extensive, becomes a library only when it is systematically arranged, conveniently stored, and completely inventoried.   So
the librarian came to know himself as being a technician as
well as a bookman.   And, finally, a third enlargement of his
self-consciousness occurred.   Since the turn of the century,
Americans, like Europeans, had been becoming ever more
"socially minded," as they called it.   And by the early 1920's,
librarians generally had extended the new concepts to their
own vocational activities.   Here, as elsewhere, the first
emphasis fell on the individual; but later it shifted to the community, so that the particular gave place to the general and
description could pass into explanation.

By such processes as these (which here, of course,
are vastly oversimplified), American librarianship has attained its present intense self-consciousness, particularly during the last quarter-century.   Today librarians, as never before, are aware of their cultural environment.   Where formerly each ordinarily confined his attention within the particular
institution where he worked, they now all think freely of inter-

library cooperations and co-ordinations. Where once they regarded schools, clubs, and factories mainly as possible
sources of readers, they now consider them as recipients of
library influences. Where once they saw publishers and booksellers chiefly as suppliers of library material, they now perceive them as fellow-distributors of reading matter. Where
before they were inclined to fear photograph records, films,
and radio as rivals to the book, they now welcome them as
alternative mediums of public communication. In fact, librarians presently think and talk about such things as the library
and the community, the library and scholarship, the library
and world affairs. So, also today's librarians are striving
earnestly to define the library, formulate its objectives, and
appraise its responsibilities and accomplishments as never
before. In short, they are now seeking a philosophy of librarianship in the broadest and truest sense of that much-
abused term.

In the quest, however, they are hampered by a lack
of self-consciousness in another direction. Although they
recognize the triple character of their activities, their recognition remains empirical. As yet they do not perceive clearly how these three elements are integrated into the organic
unity of a profession, although they constantly so name it.

For we all do believe that librarianship is a profession. We have long since come to feel that it belongs in
the same category as do such vocations as medicine, law,
and engineering. But our belief here is an emotional conviction rather than a rational conclusion. We can adduce
neither evidence nor argument to justify our opinion. Nor
shall we be able to do so until we clarify our ideas about
what the essential nature of a profession is.

Our present vagueness in this matter seems to be due
very largely to semantic confusions. At present, the word
"profession" and its derivatives are omnibus terms that carry all sorts of different meanings. For example, we commonly apply the same adjective "professional" to thieves who
will steal anything, plumbers whose work is reliable, golf-
players who have lost amateur standing, musicians to whom
music is more than an avocation, and chemists who possess
a theoretical as well as a practical knowledge of chemicals.
We can use the word thus indiscriminately because in each
instance the context will indicate whether we refer to the
morals, the competence, the wages, the talent, or the scholarship of the persons designated. The term always requires

some such specific identification, for it carries no single common meaning through all its uses. [3]

For most purposes, the ideological diversities of the term may be ignored; but, when we need to free our general idea of "a profession" from any specific implications, we must overcome our semantic confusion, lest we mistake verbal for factual identities. Here, as always, the cultural history that lies behind etymological development will prove illuminating. Originally, the word "profession" meant an acknowledgment or declaration and referred to the vow taken by the cleric or monk. Thus the word is a linguistic fossil from the age when religion was the only profession. The same idea still prevailed as medicine and law slowly freed themselves from ecclesiastical connections: the neophyte physician took the Hippocratic oath, and the beginning lawyer a similar one as a barrister. Then, finally, as purely secular professions emerged in ever increasing variety, the emphasis of the term shifted from the initiation of the practitioner to the cultural function that he performs. And today this differentiation has gone so far that we now have not one adjective "professional" but many. They sound alike and look alike, because they have a common derivation, but they have entirely different meanings. Certainly, the professionalism that we think we recognize in librarianship is unlike the professionalism of a craftsman or an artist but like that of a physician, a lawyer, or an engineer. Accordingly, henceforth in this essay we shall use the word "profession" with a corresponding, though unexpressed, limitation.

But the librarian's self-identification has been retarded by another error. Persuaded of his own professional status, he has always been inclined to imitate the outward forms of the other professions before attaining the corresponding internal development. This tendency has undoubtedly been a factor, though by no means the only one or the strongest, in many of the past departures of American librarianship.

This certainly happened when education for librarianship was inaugurated. The main purpose of the founding fathers was, of course, to provide vocational training. But, undoubtedly, they were also influenced by the idea that librarianship should have its professional schools because the other professions have them. These early library schools, however, did not produce the effects that their founders hoped for. They did help some individuals on their way toward professionalism, but they did it almost inadvertently--by their

associations rather than by their teachings. Unfortunately,
they were founded in an age when librarians thought too exclusively in terms of library technology.   Library education
was, therefore, conceived as primarily a training in the
niceties of cataloging and classification.   Consequently, a
core curriculum was then crystallized which even today re-
sists dissolution and makes educational reforms more difficult than they should be.

In the same fashion and for a similar reason, injury
as well as benefit resulted from the premature organization
of librarians. Here again the leaders were animated by mixed
motives.   Their chief purpose was to secure the benefits of
common counsel, but they also hoped to assert the dignity of
librarianship by assuming the external shape exhibited by older and more mature professions.   The American Library
Association was established in a library age of formal rather
than functional definition.   For the purposes of membership,
anyone who worked in a library or was interested in libraries
was regarded as a librarian.   Hence the organization has always been what the American Medical Association would be
if it enrolled druggists, nurses, and hospital clerks as well
as physicians, gave them all an equal vote, and evaded ill-
advised majority decisions by political manipulations.   Unquestionably, our association has done much good for librarians and for libraries.   Yet it is more a labor union than a
learned society.[4] Its chief virtues are its weight as a pressure group and its dexterity in vocational propaganda--both,
be it said, invariably exercised on the side of the angels.
But its massive centripetal force is deadly: it captures and
reduces to standardized regularity every new movement in
librarianship, however particular and special.   And, at the
same time, its centrifugal force is disruptive: it has pro-
liferated subdivisions to the point that the recent regional
fragmentation was inevitable.   Today the American Library
Association is national in name only: its only unity consists
in a vacuous set of honorific titles (cursus honorum) and a
central bureaucracy.

Still another departure in librarianship grounded in a
mistaken conception of professionalism is the recurrent clam-
or for certification.   Hitherto, this movement has been comparatively innocuous because it has been unsuccessful.   Here,
again, an imitative measure is advocated on delusive presup-
positions.   Even though the practice of medicine, law, and
engineering is rightfully limited to those who can pass a qualifying examination, it does not follow that the same restriction

should at present be imposed upon librarians.   In all those
other professions a distinctive and almost esoteric scholarship has long since been developed and is universally recognized.   But the same thing is not true of librarianship.
Here, if a group of experienced practitioners were asked to
enumerate the necessary qualifications, there would be almost
as many prescriptions as there were prescribers.

But, most portentous of all, perhaps, is the appearance among librarians of the scientistic delusion.   This is a
mistaken assumption that librarianship is a profession only in
so far as it is a science.   Though of recent origin, the fallacy has spread so far that now many librarians say "library
science" whenever they refer to librarianship. [5]   The trend
of thought behind this verbal usage is, however, not peculiar
to librarians but is characteristic of our period.   For a long
time now, science has been conferring so many benefits upon
humanity that many people have come to look upon science as
mankind's sole possible benefactor.   But this inference is
wholly unrealistic, for it belies at once both the nature of
scientific thought and the character of human experience.   In
the library itself, as in every other field of man's activity,
innumerable intangibles appear that cannot be reduced to objective, quantitative, and predictive terms, although they can,
nonetheless, be rationally observed, described, classified,
and evaluated.   To cite but one example, the effect of Shakespeare's genius upon a reader cannot be isolated, measured,
or anticipated, although it is no less a reality of experience
than the physical book that contains Shakespeare's writings.

To say all this is not to belittle the importance of
science but merely to deny the extravagant claims made in
its behalf by fanatics.   Probably the highest intellectual
achievement in librarianship during the last thirty years was
the establishment of library science on a sound basis in a few
areas.   Anyone who participated in the movement may well be
proud of it.   And every librarian must sincerely hope that
the new science will speedily be extended to every other
phase of librarianship that is amenable to scientific investigation.

This hasty and, no doubt, superficial survey of modern library history would seem to suggest that the librarian's
failure to attain complete self-consciousness has been chiefly
due to a single cause: hitherto he has thought too much of
the formal and too little of the functional characteristics of
both his own and the other learned professions.   Accordingly,

he might do well to embark upon a new line of thought and
first endeavor to discover the general functional pattern that
runs through all these other erudite vocations.   Then, if he
can identify the same pattern in his own activities, he may
believe that he has demonstrated its professional character.

Taking medicine, law, and engineering, then, as typical professions, we must first discover what the physician,
the lawyer, and the engineer have in common.   Obviously,
the only "objective" things (to use current jargon) are the
framed documents that hang in their offices.   Each professional has two of these--an academic diploma and a license.
The first certifies that its owner has pursued successfully a
relevant course of study, and the second that impartial ex-
aminers have found him permanently proficient in its subject
matter.   Hence the double inference follows that the essence
of any profession is a special scholarship and that the validity of this scholarship is a matter of grave public concern.
Or, to move from fact to function, we may define the professional as a person who, by means of his special intellectual equipment, does something that is important to other
people.   Both these statements are platitudes.   As we all
know, the most intelligent layman will work havoc at any professional task; yet any moderately intelligent layman can be
turned into a professional by a few years of special training.
And, similarly, we all know that without such things as modern medicine, modern democracy, and modern machinery
Western civilization would speedily revert to a lower standard,
if not to actual barbarism.

But let us examine the matter of professional scholarship more closely.   Any scholarship, general or special, is
a system of ideas--facts, theories, and opinions that a people has accumulated and uses in the routine of living.   It
therefore represents the intellectual element in its culture and
consists of a rationalization of its past experience.   Hence
any scholarship, to be complete, must embrace the whole
ambit of the experience to which it is related.

This principle, however, is constantly ignored in modern thought because we habitually think of scholarship in
terms of its processes--research and education--instead of
in those of its cultural function.   Actually, of course, the
latter alone is significant; man is a thinker for exactly the
same reason that he is a tool-user and a social being--to
exploit the human possibilities of his environment.   Therefore, culture, the routine of exploitation dominant in any

period, is necessarily an organic integration of a scholarship,
a physical equipment, and a social organization.   In other
words, scholarship is the intellectual content of culture, and
its pattern conforms to the pattern of the cultural activities
to which it is related.   Hence, as the following considerations
will show, the basic pattern of scholarship must be an endless series of triple branchings--or, to put it more pedan-
tically, a sorites of trichotomies.

Any human act that is more than a physiological re-
flex involves three simultaneous awarenesses--of the material, of the process, and of the motive.   This principle holds
true whether the activity is that of a prehistoric American
chipping an arrowhead or that of a present-day citizen casting
his ballot in a national election.   In both cases each of the
awarenesses is of a distinctively cultural nature.   The Indian
did not discover for himself the peculiar properties of flint,
he did not invent a process for flaking it, or decide on his
own initiative to supplement his vegetarian diet with the flesh
of animals slain for the purpose.   All these intellectual accomplishments had been slowly but progressively accumulated
by innumerable generations of his predecessors and transmitted to him in their present perfection.   And, as a matter
of fact, he had probably so assimilated all this toxologic
scholarship that he did not raise his mineralogical knowledge,
his operative lore, and his alimentary purpose to the level
of consciousness, as he labored.   Indeed, his immediate motivation may have been no more than a recognition that his depleted quiver ought to be replenished as a matter of routine.
And exactly the same things are true of his intellectual state
in every other cultural activity.   In every case he had complex and systematic rational familiarities of the material, the
process, and the purpose of his labor.   From this it follows
that his scholarship--the total intellectual content of his cul-
ture--was of a triune character, including a science, a technology, and a humanistic discipline. [6]   The science dealt with
the properties of the relevant materials, the technology with
the processes by which they could be exploited, and the humanity with the motives, reasons, purposes, or ends for
which the science had been accumulated and the technology
invented.

The scholarship that an intelligent American citizen
uses when he votes in a presidential election likewise contains a science, a technology, and a humanity.   He knows
theoretically the facts and principles of democratic government.   Through the exercise of graphic skills he reads and

marks his ballot so as to register his vote correctly. And, at the same time, he is conscious of reasons for his choice among the parties and candidates. But the rational origins of his decision are entirely different from those of his political science and his literacy. Yet they are definitely intellectual and not merely emotional or spiritual. A vote dictated by partisan enthusiasm or personal feeling is irrational, but so is one based on ethical or theoretical grounds alone. [7] Yet, though every political problem requires a decision from the citizen, the data upon which he must form his opinion are, for the most part, indeterminate: they involve unpredictable personalities and unrevealed facts of the future. Hence the vote of even the most intelligent and best-informed citizen in a major election is a venture into the unknown, with only what we sometimes call "worldly wisdom" to guide him. But so also is every other decision concerning human conduct, past, present, or future. Yet every human being is constantly required to make such decisions concerning both himself and his fellows in their personal and their corporate activities.

Now this worldly wisdom is no weird intellectual faculty that exists by itself and is amenable to no training or discipline. Though it deals with imponderables, works only by argument, and attains no more than possible or probable opinions, it is grounded in knowledge and controlled by logic and rationality. Hence this branch of scholarship--the rationalization of human motives no less than of those that deal with the materials and the processes of culture--must, in civilization, be consciously recognized, systematically investigated, and explicitly communicated. This was formerly done in Western civilization; but more recently the humanities, both in formal education and in popular thought, have become atrophied or, worse yet, displaced by pseudo-sciences. [8]

One reason for the present distortion of our thought is obviously the prevalence of academic specialization. For practical reasons and with great profit in both research and education, we subdivide our scholarship and study each portion as a separate discipline. But, in so doing, we commonly forget the artificial character of this process. Since culture is a complex of routines and scholarship is the intellectual component of culture, the pattern of scholarship will conform to the pattern of the routines. Accordingly, the natural unit of scholarship will be determined by the unitary cultural routine to which it is related. Furthermore,

since, as we have seen, every routine involves a triple
awareness, every natural unit of scholarship must contain a
science, a technology, and a humanity.   But we do not observe this principle in our academic practice.   There we
subdivide by the form instead of by the content or function of
scholarship.   Consequently, such studies as mathematics,
sociology, and poetry are not typical examples of scholarship,
though we commonly so regard them.   Indeed, for our present purpose they are only misleading categories of abstraction and, as such, should be disregarded.   The only real
unit of scholarship is one in which scientific, technological,
and humanistic elements are organically integrated by their
relevance to a specific cultural routine.

In these latter days the nature and function of technology and science are so universally understood that further
discussion of them here would be superfluous.   But this is
not the case with humanity.   For nearly a century, Western
thought was increasingly neglectful of humanistic facts and
ideas.   Indeed, the shift of intellectual interest went so far
that for a while the neglect was commonly justified by one
argument or another.   Many people claimed that, in the
presence of a sound science and an efficient technology, the
matter of motive would take care of itself--mere logic and
common sense would dictate humane conduct automatically.
Others, however, took a more theoretical position.   They
denied the threefold character of scholarship and insisted that
it is of one kind only: technology is only applied science,
and the so-called "humanistic disciplines" mere survivals of
pre-scientific thought that would ultimately be brought to scientific order.

But, in the present period of cultural catastrophe, our
former intellectual complacency has been shaken.   Both the
empirical and the scientistic dismissals of the humanistic
problem are rapidly losing their popularity.   People generally are groping for a reorientation of their motivations.   Yet
in this quest few of them seem to notice that the clearest
presentation of the problem occurs not in the university divisions, where they usually look for it, but in the professional
schools.   Here alone scholarship on its highest level has resisted academic fragmentation and retains its organic unity,
and here alone is the humanistic branch unmistakably an essential component of the whole.

For our purpose we may define "humanity" as the
study of motivations.   These occur in every human activity,

even if it be mere observation of what is happening. But in
any vocational activity the motivation assumes a double character. Whatever his calling may be, a worker has a personal reason for working, which, quite commonly, is that of
earning his livelihood. But over and above this he is also
impelled by an impersonal motivation. This is immediately
imposed by the conditions of the job, but these, in turn, are
determined by the requirements of the culture in which the
activity forms a constituent organic function. Whether a man
shovels coal or practices medicine, there is a cultural as
well as a personal reason for his work. But there is also a
great difference between their relative importance in the two
jobs and in the degree to which the cultural motive must be
consciously apprehended.

The vocational hierarchy of civilization exhibits, along
with other variations, a regular gradation in the intellectual
content required at the various levels. At the bottom, un-
skilled labor requires little rational control. The economic
and industrial organization of culture sets the task, recruits
the workers, and integrates their combined performance automatically. The knowledge and skill required of the laborer
are of a general character--equally pertinent to innumerable
other jobs--and his personal motivation--the exchange value
of his wages--has no relationship whatever to the cultural significance of the work.

But at the top of the vocational hierarchy, in the professions, all these conditions are exactly reversed. Here a
special science and a special technology are indispensable,
and both are of such an abstruse nature as to be unintelligible
to a layman. The humanity also is esoteric. Even the personal motivation is different. The predominant reason why
any individual enters a profession and continues to practice
it as long as he lives is seldom monetary. It is, instead,
a personal predilection for the work that is more intellectual
than emotional. This is why in so many cases the candidate
will undergo great hardship to obtain his education and will,
with equal devotion, live in semipoverty thereafter, while in
other cases men of wealth will work just as hard as though
their livelihood depended on it.

Correspondingly, in the professions the cultural motivation differs from that on the lower vocational level. Here
it must not only be conscious and explicit, but it must be
developed intellectually to the point that it becomes a specific
humanistic discipline, just as distinctive and esoteric as the

co-ordinate professional science and technology. Today, however, the reality and the specificality of these professional
humanities are so generally misunderstood that in each case
it will be worth while for us to identify them.

The cultural motivation of medicine is, obviously, the
promotion of health in the individual and in the community.
But the very idea of health is humanistic and has no meaning
for science whatever. The only appraisal that a biologist
can make concerning an organism or a reaction is to decide
whether it is typical or otherwise. This, however, is a statistical observation instead of an evaluation. To science
everything, including disease or monstrosity, is normal to
its circumstances. Now this, of course, is the attitude of
the physician as a scientist. But he is also a humanist.
As such he extends his rationality into a realm of values
where health is the generic good. But health includes a
whole series of intermediate values, such as longevity, im-
munity, and comfort. The physician's thought is (if we may
again oversimplify) dominated by three imperatives: to keep
his patient alive; to cure his ills; and to do both without undue disturbance of his normal cultural activities. Moreover,
the physician must pursue these ends not singly but together.
In so doing he assumes an attitude that often seems irrational to a nonmedical observer, because this attitude can be attained only through a special intellectual discipline. It requires more than common sense and general knowledge, because it involves all sorts of special considerations. Where
the layman may merely feel, the physician must know and
act. To be merciful as a doctor, he must often be pitiless
as a man. He must personalize his patient just as certainly
as he generalizes the disease. In short, the physician must
face with mental clarity and emotional poise--without laughter
or tears--the whole tragedy and comedy of man's biological
existence. Consequently, the personality of a good physician
is suffused with an intellectual humanism. Yet, rather curiously, the special scholarship that supports it ordinarily remains unconscious and implicit, an unformulated humanistic
tradition transmitted through generations of doctors by personal association. [9] This is possible because medical students
spend a longer time in training and, in clinical instruction
especially, in closer contact with their teachers than those
of any other profession.

The law[10] also has its humanity no less than its science and technology. Its cultural motivation is the promotion of justice, a term which summarizes the optimum atti-

tude of men to each other and to the community. In the interests of justice the lawyer performs at least three major
functions: he preserves the integrity of society by enforcing
the rights of property and person; he conserves civic decency
by promoting law-observance and penalizing its infringement;
and he maintains the dignity of both state and citizen by protecting the self-respect and reputation not only of the innocent but of the guilty, except at the points where the law
condemns them.

These things do not occur in nature. They remain
mere cosmic potentialities until man calls them into actuality.
Hence science can regard them only as peculiarities in the
behavior pattern of the zoological species that it names Homo
sapiens. To the anthropologist savagery and civilization are
merely different; neither one is better or worse than the other. To the sociologist a street gang and a church congrega-
tion belong to the same order; both are groups of like-minded
people voluntarily organized for a common purpose. To the
political scientist a tyranny and a republic are but variant
forms of government. And to a historian the hero and the
villain, if equally influential, are indistinguishable from each
other. [11]

Accordingly, the cultural motivation of the lawyer cannot be comprehended in his science but requires a special intellectual discipline if it is to go beyond the normal impulses
of the ordinary citizen--as it must. For the lawyer has to
recognize and pursue the ends of justice in situations so complicated that the layman is completely lost. He must perceive
concurrently and in due proportion the general and the particular in any case. In the interests of his client he cannot
infringe the rights of others or the state. To maintain the
compromises of civilization, he must be able to identify behind concrete details a juristic principle. Hence the lawyer's
chief qualification is skill in a special dialectic.

In legal education, therefore, far more time and attention are given to the professional humanity than to either the
science or the technology. Indeed, the student is taught not
so much what the law is as how to find out what it is as
occasion arises. Yet legal bibliography and the technicalities
of pleading occupy but a small segment in the professional
curriculum. For the most part that is devoted to incessant
drill in generalizing from particular cases--i. e. , in studies
of a definitely philosophical character. [12]

With respect to its intellectual content, engineering
seems, at first glance, to stand quite apart from medicine
or law and to consist of science and technology alone.   The
distinction, however, is delusive and arises from the character of the cultural motivation involved.   The end pursued by
the engineer is utility, which, despite its more homely nature, belongs to the same category as do health and justice,
for civilization depends no less on its physical equipment
than on the vitality of its citizens and the civic order.

Again the scientist, as such, knows nothing of the
canons of efficiency, economy, and convenience that dominate
the thought of the engineer.   Yet these qualities, being mechanical and hence quantitative, assume a scientific and technological guise that conceals their essentially evaluative nature.   An engineer measures the performance of his machines
by physical instruments, their economy by his balance sheet,
and their convenience, less exactly, by their sales volume.
Quite understandably, then, the theory of utility, as such, is
ordinarily given no place in the professional education of the
engineer.   It is presented, without specific identification,
along with the science and technology. [13]

There is, however, a larger humanistic significance
in engineering than immediate utility.   Every major invention in human history, from the bow and arrow to television,
has brought about profound cultural changes.   But these,
being mass and long-term effects, are dealt with by historians and publicists rather than by the engineers themselves.

On the basis of this analysis of older and more mature professions, we may now turn to librarianship and inquire whether--and in what degree--it exhibits the same characteristics.

The intellectual content of librarianship undoubtedly
consists of three distinct branches.   It deals with things and
principles that must be scientifically handled, with processes
and apparatus that require special understanding and skills
for their operations, and with cultural motivations that can
be apprehended only humanistically.   The crucial question,
however, is whether this triune intellectual content is so abstruse as to become a special professional scholarship.

The whole course of library history hitherto seems to

imply that it is not. Our library system has come into existence by the automatic processes of cultural development.
Librarians always have operated, and still do, with an empirical rather than a theoretical attitude toward their problems.
Their techniques are so matter-of-fact that a layman can
quickly learn them on the job. Apparently, the practitioner
animated by personal motives alone does just as well as one
who thinks also about cultural objectives. And, even now,
the majority of library workers have never attended a professional school.

        Yet many considerations suggest that among librarians
the development of a complete professional scholarship is retarded rather than unnecessary. In many particulars the findings of scientific research during the last quarter-century
have already demonstrated the futility of our former empiri-
cism. The apparent simplicity of library technology depends
on two facts that are commonly ignored: the layman who becomes a librarian overnight is already an experienced bookman and library user; and he always enters a going concern
manned by experienced operatives. And, finally, the absence
of an explicit humanistic discipline is undoubtedly the cause
of two distressing characteristics that have always marked
librarians as a group--their ancillary attitude and their fad-
dishness. Lacking an awareness of a distinctive cultural
function of their own, they tend to think of themselves as
mere handmaidens to other cultural agents. And without a
theoretical recognition of the humanistic peculiarities of their
vocation they are always inclined to adopt enthusiastically innovations which, however useful elsewhere, are irrelevant to
the library.

        The cultural motivation of librarianship is the promo-
tion of wisdom in the individual and in the community. Wisdom, like health, justice, and utility, embraces a whole hierarchy of supporting qualities, such as understanding, judgment, and prudence. Knowledge in itself is meaningless.
Unless it is personally assimilated and its implications comprehended, it has no human value. There is such a thing as
a learned fool. Similarly, rationality, like experience itself,
is always synoptic. It requires a concurrent awareness of
many things and a simultaneous recognition of their relativities.
And, to be wise, a man must also have prudence. He must
survey all the effects of any action, weighing advantages
against disadvantages, achievements against disturbances, progress against confusion, and immediate benefit against ultimate cost.

Librarianship is not, of course, the only profession devoted to the promotion of wisdom. To name but two others animated by the same cultural purpose, education and journalism may be mentioned. But in each of these three callings the whole situation is distinctive. The teacher deals with a single subject area and with a homogeneous group of students, whose attendance is compulsory. Yet the time has long since passed when any graduate of a curriculum was deemed competent to teach it. Indeed, today every professional candidate must be trained not only in the science and practice of pedagogy but also in its history and philosophy.

The editor faces entirely different conditions. His subject matter is imposed upon him by the course of events, and his treatment of it by the kind of public to which he addresses himself. The attention of his readers is, theoretically at least, purely voluntary. But the most outstanding peculiarity of journalism in contrast with teaching and librarianship is its commercialism. Hence, in the past, journalism, like engineering, had little explicit humanism. Indeed, the tradition among newspapermen runs in the other direction: they dramatize themselves as cynical and disillusioned. But, with the rise of professional schools in this area, an explicit recognition of the cultural motivation is developing rapidly.

From one point of view the librarian's promotion of wisdom seems merely to supplement that of the teacher and the journalist. The library assists the school and imparts information not included in the formal educational curriculum. And it supplies readers with current periodicals and files of previous issues. But these marginal contacts are only casual and incidental to the chief function of the library. This is to communicate, so far as possible, the whole of scholarship to the whole community. The librarian undertakes to supply literature on any and every subject to any and every citizen for any and every purpose. He does this not so much for the immediate value of the knowledge imparted as on the theory that, in the long run, the process will sharpen the understanding, judgment, and prudence of the readers and thus sustain and advance civilization.

For many reasons, the librarian needs an explicit theoretical understanding of his cultural motivations even more than does the teacher or the journalist. He is concerned with the whole encyclopedia of scholarship and with every cultural activity. His program is not prescribed by a curriculum or the course of events. The whole world's liter-

ature in space and time falls within his jurisdiction. And because he is singularly free from any control or supervision,
except in budgetary matters, his responsibility is the greater.
Accordingly, if he lacks the humanistic discipline relevant to
his office, he will easily fall captive to extraneous movements
and, with the best of intentions, sacrifice his primary function to them. For example, when a fourth-rate novel, that
he himself would not deign to read, falls under local censorship, two lines of thought are open to him. Thinking as a
layman, he may recognize only that the freedom of the press
has been invaded and in protest fight for the circulation of
that particular book, thereby perhaps bringing himself and his
library into a frustrating disrepute among many members of
the community. Or, thinking as a librarian, he may regard
as paramount the attitude of particular civic leaders and the
public toward library censorship in general and so endeavor
to improve the occasion by circulating literature that will
promote a sensible, discreet, and prudent attitude toward
this highly controversial subject.

From this and from innumerable other instances that
might be cited it should be apparent that the librarian, no
less than the physician or the lawyer needs a specific humanistic perspective. He must always be vividly aware that
everyone who enters the library is impelled to do so for both
personal and cultural reasons. In dealing with those who approach him, the librarian must bring more than good will
and sympathy to the meeting. His attitude must be more intellectual than emotional, for he must be able to generalize
the reading need at the same time that he personalizes the
reader. And it is only by explicit study and discipline that
he can thus exploit the humanistic possibilities and probabil-
ities of his office.

The activities of a working librarian are of almost infinite variety. The world of books in which he operates is of
terrifying magnitude. The cultural benefits he mediates are
nearly as numerous as the individuals he serves. The social
groups and institutions with which he co-operates are inex-
tricably interrelated and overlapping. And most of the forces
to which he must respond lie beyond his control. Yet somehow the librarian must manage to maintain a sense of direction and perspective amid this chaos of thought and activity.
He does this in part by devising instruments and processes
for doing things effectively, economically, and conveniently.
He does it in part by reducing his experience and problems
to objective, quantitative, and predictive order. And he does

it in part by raising sentiment in himself and others to the
level of realistic, rational, and normative wisdom.

In short, the librarian can be a librarian only in the
degree that his scholarship becomes truly professional. [14]

NOTES

1. The following paper is an interim summary of ideas
    that the author still hopes some day to present
    more systematically in an "Introduction to Librarian-
    ship." As now projected, this volume should con-
    tain four major sections: librarianship as a tech-
    nology; librarianship as a science; librarianship as
    a humanistic discipline; and education for librarian-
    ship. Here only the first three topics are discussed;
    the fourth will be treated in a later paper.

2. In this connection, it is significant that in Germany,
    where prewar book wealth has become postwar book
    poverty, a trend toward approximating the Ameri-
    can library system is now unmistakable.

3. At first glance, the idea of "livelihood" may seem the
    basic meaning in the instances cited above, but
    this is delusive. There are millionaire kleptomani-
    acs and perhaps even journeyman plumbers. And,
    certainly, it is more than avarice that keeps so
    many athletes, artists, and scientists in profession-
    al practice long after their financial future is as-
    sured.

4. In the recent reorganization, the one change that has
    most incensed the members at large is the aboli-
    tion of the Placement Bureau, i. e., a free labor
    exchange for librarians.

5. Their predecessors in the technological age were al-
    most equally addicted to the term "library econ-
    omy."

6. To apply these terms to a low culture is an exaggera-
    tion, just as the definitions that follow are under-
    statements in a high one. In civilization, for ex-
    ample, science goes far beyond mere observation
    and description to generalization and explanation.

7. In one sense, our system of government might be de-
    scribed as ultimately amoral and nonrational.   It
    requires loyal co-operation from the citizen even
    in a course of action against which he voted and
    that he still believes to be wrong and foolish.   This
    is not because everyone ought to be intellectually
    diffident, i.e., realize that, when so many believe
    otherwise, he is probably mistaken.   Neither is it
    because of any mystical democratic principle that
    a majority decision is a divine revelation (vox popu-
    li, vox Dei).   The real reason is that culture, the
    ultimate public concern (res publica), must tran-
    scend all other considerations for the individual
    when he acts in his civic and not in his personal
    capacity.   If every minority should virtually secede
    from the community, civilization would be impos-
    sible.

8. A comparison of current scholarly literature on Hamlet
    with that published even fifty years ago will illus-
    trate the character and the extend of this displace-
    ment.   The modern scholar makes the philology,
    which his predecessor used only instrumentally, the
    end of his labors and ignores the humanistic prob-
    lem completely.   That problem, of course, is to
    identify and explain the effect of the play upon the
    attitude of a sensitive reader toward certain phases
    of human conduct.

9. Rarely is the great physician temperamentally philosophi-
    cal and didactic; but, when he is, medical human-
    ism becomes readily articulate.   A supreme exam-
    ple of this is the volume Counsels and Ideals from
    the Writings of William Osler (Boston, 1929), a
    book that might well be read by students of any
    other profession.

10. The law is cited here as a typical specimen of the pro-
    fessions that deal with the official regulation of
    men's social relationships.   Therefore, the term
    here refers to legislators, administrators, and
    statesmen as well as to attorneys.

11. These statements are, of course, only theoretically
    true.   In practice, every student of human affairs
    remains himself a human being and, despite all his
    efforts to the contrary, always tempers his science
    with humanism.

12. Even bad lawyers may be good philosophers. As extreme examples, two former jurists, known to
everyone, may be cited: Clarence Darrow, by completely identifying himself with his client emotional-
ly, subverted justice to anarchy, while Oliver Wen-
dell Holmes, in his passionate devotion to an ideal
of personal freedom, sometimes projected it into
utopia. Yet each, with a dialectic skill that reached
genius, could always justify his sentimentality by
irrefutable argument.

13. Perhaps this peculiarity of engineering springs from the
fact that the values it mediates are so direct and
obvious. A machine is, in itself, conspicuously
desirable in a way that a drug and a lawsuit are
not.

14. The group of assumptions underlying this whole inquiry
might be called "culturalism." Here it is developed
only philosophically, i.e., in an attempt to view a
typical segment of human experience as a whole and
in the widest possible perspective. Whether or not
it carries ontological, epistemological, and axio-
logical implications concerning what lies behind that
experience is a metaphysical problem which does
not arise in the present connection.

PROFESSIONALISM RECONSIDERED*

Mary Lee Bundy and Paul Wasserman

Librarians, like many in other marginal or maturing professions often spend considerable time being concerned about whether or not they are truly professional; much effort sometimes goes into reassuring themselves that they are indeed professional and that they should therefore enjoy the recognition and rewards of professional status. Such preoccupation manifests itself in a wide range of activities common to all such upward-mobile and self-conscious aspiring groups. They conduct public relations programs designed to create a favorable image of their craft. Being much concerned about status differences, they discuss endlessly means of differentiating the professional worker from the lesser educated.[1] They establish and seek vigorously to strengthen their occupational associations; they promulgate a code of ethics and establish internal means of controlling members who violate it. They frequently turn to legislation to control entry into practice. Concomitantly, there is a striving toward the identification of a philosophical and intellectual base for practice. Ultimately their educational efforts find a place in the universities where they come eventually to seek academic parity for their instructional programs by meeting university standards of scholarship.

Many early claims of professionalism and early activities to attain it tend to be suspect since they are often a mélange of the real and the fanciful, in which pious longings are often confused with reality. A field's recruitment publicity is thus often based upon ill-conceived sloganeering or

---

*Reprinted by permission of the American Library Association from College and Research Libraries 29:5-26 (January 1968).

44

myths which sometimes turn out to be nearer to what the
discipline and those who practice in it would like to be than
what they really are.   The ethic presented by the group can
be so vague as to defy relation to the realities of practice. [2]
The educational preparation, or training as it is more frequently termed, conducted by the professional school, is
sometimes offered by instructors who are displaced, or perhaps misplaced, from practice, and it tends heavily to the
practical, the mechanical, and the ritual.   Only very gradually and very subtly does the university influence manifest itself in reorienting course content, so that a grudging tolerance for conceptual and theoretical issues comes to find its
place alongside the pragmatic.

Even within firmly established professions the ethic
may be more pious hope than reality.   Carlin's findings in a
study of the legal profession suggest that a group may so
frequently and flagrantly overlook malpractice that it in effect condones it. [3]   The widespread abuses of the Hippocratic
oath by the medical fraternity in such instances as fee split-
ting and the proprietorship of pharmacies and optometry
houses, attest to its hypocritical abuse. [4]   It is doubtless true
that professions discourage their members from making public disclosures of undesirable practice, acting only after
there has been a public scandal.   Certainly, much of the effort of professional groups seems to stem more from self-
interest than from a true regard for their responsibilities. [5]
Many groups which claim to be professional have never had
a sense of community responsibility.   Intra-group rivalry
goes on within professions, while at the same time fields
strenuously resist encroachments from other occupational
groups through the use of political and economic mechanisms,
and they strive to reassign less glamorous tasks to others.
Conditions of actual practice in virtually every profession de-
part in important measure from the professional ideal.

These disparities, however, do not mean that the professions do not have well-established traditions of service or
commitments to standards, nor does it mean that they are
not committed to the advancement of knowledge and the practical art of their fields.   It is to these ends that the attempt
to achieve professional status for librarianship appropriately
addresses itself.   All established professions have an awareness of the conditions of practice required for a professional
to grow and develop.   They have frequently struggled to protect practice from political or other influences which would
corrupt or misuse or down-grade, and on balance they must

be viewed as a force for orderly progress within the democratic tradition. The more advanced professions, although
their practice may remain imperfect, provide traditions,
ideals, models, and directions for emerging professions.

Librarianship appears to be in the midst of a serious
shortage of personnel. In order to attract from the limited
reservoir of talented people who are sought and competed for
by each of the professions, it must be possible to offer potential recruits rewarding and satisfying careers. To do so
implies a speed-up in the process of professionalization. In
order to fulfill their original mandate of serving as guardian
of society's information needs and in order to influence positively the forward motion of progressive information development in a time of competition with other emergent information-
oriented disciplines, librarianship must more fully take on the
responsibilities and substance as well as the forms of a profession. Without such commitment, librarians may ultimately find themselves left only with custodial tasks while the intellectual aspects, as well as the more active forms of information service, are yielded to other groups.

Some in library education place all their hope in the
next generation of librarians. In effect, they would write off
most of those now in practice as essentially and permanently
semi-professional. This attitude is unrealistic. It ignores
the fact that during the next two decades, which may well
prove to be most critical for determining whither (or whether)
librarianship, the major decisions influencing variations and
adaptations in information services will be made by those who
are already in practice. Furthermore, such a view tends to
be over-sanguine about the real advances of present educational programs over those of the past. Viewed in historical
perspective, the library schools may be seen to have been a
decisive influence in whatever degree of professionalization
has been achieved thus far. They have succeeded in placing
their programs, at least in a formal sense, at the graduate
level. Nevertheless, one may remain skeptical of the capacity of library education, and of library educators (except for
certain isolated institutions and, regretfully, isolated individuals) to be fully transformed along the drastically variant
lines which contemporary technological, societal, and behavioral advances clearly require.

Many librarians are without doubt best suited, either
by temperament or through the remorseless habituation of
long experience, to performing super-clerical tasks. In some

instances they may even be hostile to or suspicious of efforts
to upgrade the intellectual demands put upon them in their
practice, but it is not necessarily because they are uninterested or opposed to intellectual effort.   Frequently they are
highly literate, intelligent people who remain satisfied with
or resigned to spending major portions of their working lives
performing at a nonintellectual level.   It is simply that the
acculturation process in library education or in practice, or
both, have been so devoid of genuine intellectual content that
they have come to identify their roles, and the role of librarianship generally, as pedestrian and uninspiring.   For them,
as for many similar types in other humdrum fields which do
not call forth the breadth of their imagination or the finest
quality of their minds, there is sublimation in the form of
home pursuits, hobbies, and travel.   For them the battle is
over.   Library work is a nine-to-five routine--the best comes
only on long weekends, extended holidays, travel, and early
retirement.

The field also has many competent and thoughtful people (mostly in the earlier years of service and not yet ground
down by the weight of experience and bureaucratic indoctrination) who are deeply disturbed by the disparity between what
they believe constitutes professional practice and what most librarians now do.   Many were and remain deeply disgruntled
about the calibre and content of their educational preparation
and are strongly motivated to improve practice in the field.
It is to this group, uneasy and unfulfilled by their present
roles, to whom this article is primarily directed, in the hope
that it may contribute somewhat to enlarged understanding of
what professional practice in librarianship involves and what
needs to be done to advance this field toward such a goal.

Professionalism will be viewed here not in abstract
academic terms but rather in the real world in which librarians practice, through a comparison of the behavior of librarians with what is customarily considered to constitute professional behavior.   The central thesis is that it is in terms of
three major relationships--with clients, with the institution
where he performs, and with the professional group--that the
decision as to whether one is or is not a professional is decided.

The Librarian-Client Relationship

The client relationship is the central role of any pro-

fessional whether the client be an individual or, as is frequently the case in the practice of law, a company or other
institution.   It is his raison d'être, his justification for the
claims he places on individual institutions and on the society
generally, even though not every professional works directly
with the client.   For even with the increasing institutionalization and bureaucratization of professional activities and the
consequent lessening in the degree and frequency of client relations, the ultimate purpose remains service to the client.
In an ideal and unambiguous relationship, the client relies
upon the professional for the expertise which his problem or
situation requires.   The professional, by virtue of his training, experience, and specialized knowledge, offers the client
the counsel, service, or prescription which he views to be
appropriate whether or not this is precisely what the client
wants or thinks he wants.   The professional's guidance may
not always be followed, but the judgment and recommendation
of the professional are not open to question or debate by the
layman.   The professional knows.

When cast in this context, how does the librarian-
patron relationship measure up?   Generalizations are always
fraught with risk, particularly when they attempt to characterize a practice stretched across a continuum as wide as
that of librarianship.   Yet, in spite of the hazards, perhaps
some broadly relevant observations can be advanced here.
In general library situations, that which is requested by or
offered to the patron is ordinarily just not complex enough
to be considered a professional service.   The service provided would not overtax the capacity of any reasonably intelligent college graduate after a minimum period of on-the-job
training.

This is not necessarily because librarians do not wish
to serve (although some do not and have developed a practiced
hauteur which quickly suggests to all but the doggedly perse-
vering client that they are thought to be intruders or igno-
ramuses).   Yet, in spite of this element and despite allega-
tions that the collecting function takes high precedence over
the service function, American librarianship has for the most
part enjoyed a proud tradition of service.   Perhaps in the
past however, and even into the present, library work has
had a decidedly feminine cast.   That is to say, librarians
achieve intrinsic satisfaction from the very act of serving
and are content to perform in minor and inconsequential capacities.   This can also manifest itself in other ways.   Like
the doting mother shoveling spoonfuls of food into the mouth

of the child and joyful at the sight of consumption, the librarian may be too frequently insensitive to the limits of the information user's appetite, to the preciseness of his need or to the particularity of his taste. The willingness to play an inexpert role may well have been reinforced by the fact that the librarian has had some little knowledge about many things but not very much genuine understanding of anything. This portrait is not drawn to suggest that it is only the very most complex problems with which a librarian must concern himself, nor, to use a medical analogy, that the general reference librarian is any less consequential than the general practitioner. It is to suggest only that the druggist should not be confused with the doctor.

An apparently related phenomenon is the essential timidity of practitioners, clearly reflected in the widespread, deep-seated, and trained incapacity or high degree of reluctance to assume responsibility for solving informational problems and providing unequivocal answers. The problem may be viewed at two levels of service, each interrelated. At the general level, it is reflected in the extinction of the reader's advisor, that breed of librarian who could, would, and did actively channel readers along rational and productive lines by making concrete recommendations and introducing taste and discrimination into such choices. The reluctance to be assertive may be as much a function of insecurity born out of fears engendered by the limits of the modern librarian's mind to cope with the complexities of an ever broadening spectrum of knowledge, or awe of the growing sophistication of middle class readers among whom higher educational preparation is now widely characteristic, or because of the confusion which attends a set of objectives for library service which tolerates light diversion with intellectual development as equally viable missions: It is the client then who always determines his wants, and it is only the most iconoclastic librarian who suggests alternatives either by making precise recommendations or by skewing client choices through close control of the content of collections to reflect excellence. Perhaps, in this sense, it is the children's librarians who are the most professional. Not only are they experts in their literature who share commitment and high purpose, but they also presume to advise and direct their clients readily and to influence the client's independent choices by maintaining careful quality control over the composition of their collections. (It is of course easier to assume this posture with the child than with the adult.)

This problem is also seen at the general level in the
conduct of reference librarians who balk at offering judgments about the quality of material or, at times, even at
making comments upon the relevancy of material to particular informational problems.   Rather than straightforwardly
and self-assuredly advising a patron which is the singular or
which the most promising sources, reference librarians appear to be most comfortable when providing numerous works
or voluminous bibliographies.   Moreover, it seems characteristic of the librarian's psyche to recoil from giving out
straight answers.   Instead, it is invariably the printed source
in which the information is to be found that is offered.   What
may have been an appropriate rationale for such an approach
in an earlier period seems less relevant in 1967.   Whether
a service which relies solely upon a book stock as the only
true source of information is congruent with contemporary
realities (except for such isolated cases as law or medicine)
is subject to serious doubt.   In a time of abundant and oftentimes more realistic alternatives to searching on printed pages,
it is anachronistic for librarianship to remain so heavily committed to and dependent upon published sources to the exclusion of other possibilities.   Viewed in solely economic terms,
hours spent searching the literature for potential data which
may no longer be current seems far less rational than employing alternative approaches, as for example, telephoning
and asking someone who knows, even if the knower is five
hundred miles away.   While training and temperament have
geared librarians to fact finding from published sources, by
setting such a limit on the approach they circumscribe their
role, and in the process, their professional value.

For the most part librarians remain medium- rather
than client-oriented.   In clinging tenaciously to the information container of another age, and as they continue only to
acquire and stock and shelve books, they resist the idea that
the more fundamental commodity of modern times is information and that it takes myriad forms.   They will meet the client's requirements if it can be done with a book and only
with a book.   For the clientele the vehicle is beside the
point, the point is the information sought.   By concentrating
exclusively on the book and by resisting alternatives, the librarian remains comfortable and unpressured, while the client finds other avenues of access to information because of
the librarian's default.

As part of this same syndrome, we find large-scale
collection building seen as the expression of the librarian's

expertise rather than rapid uncomplicated access to intelligence. Yet, the most effective client service may well be enhanced when the librarian concentrates his efforts upon careful discrimination in choice of acquisitions rather than in fiercely competitive and feverish collection building. [6] Ultimately, means become ends; libraries are measured in terms of the size of their collections while the more significant measure, the quality and nature of the service they render, is ignored.

Viewed from another angle, catalog conventions, codes, policies, and procedures are also divorced from their ultimate purpose--service to the client. Detachment from clientele permits cataloging personnel to remain dedicated exclusively to the book literature, while ignoring or avoiding less conventional forms and media. As a consequence, these remain outside the control of the library and the patron dismisses the library as a source for any but the traditional published forms. The full potential of a very powerful tool to support clientele service is unrealized.

At another level of service, the library and the librarian functioning within the framework of a specific subject discipline, many of these built-in constraints are absent. Librarians here are typically more prone to deal with and give specialized treatment to nonconventional sources, and they are prepared to go further in pursuing information requests. Where there is lack of assurance on the part of the librarian or limits on the reliance which the client places on his expertise, it will most frequently stem from the inadequacy of the librarian's educational preparation in the substantive field. To function in a science setting without the requisite orientation in the science disciplines or in a financial environment without understanding a balance sheet or the working of the financial markets serves only to reinforce the tenacity of the librarian to cling to card catalogs and book titles rather than to venture forth upon the precarious ground of substantive information; it reaffirms in the client's view the belief that the level of sophistication to be expected as an aid in problem-solving from library personnel is minimal. In either case, the effect is far from the most efficacious ideal for the professional-client relationship.

The remedy here may be to close the chapter on that phase of library history which tolerates, as one example, the well-meaning English major who gravitates into medical librarianship. Granted the need for organizational skill, the service ideal, and technical grounding in information handling, it will only be when the client can respect the subject competence of the librarian that he will accept him and respect him for his professional competence in the meaning employed here. Now this is not to say that the subject librarian need be a highly trained and advanced student of a narrow and specialized discipline to perform effectively, but rather that there must come to be a better match than has yet existed in typical cases between his preparation and his field of practice. Under such terms, someone without rudimentary grounding in the biological and chemical sciences would be discouraged from medical library service and someone without economics and financial study from business librarianship. Of course, this would call for a reorientation in recruitment patterns away from the more traditional and disproportionately heavy reliance upon those trained in the humanistic disciplines and toward the sciences and the social sciences. With the increasing role of the federal government in the support of graduate study, as reflected in such programs as those of the Office of Education and the National Library of Medicine, such a prospect is less remote than when there were no incentives to offer library students and at earlier stages when library work was less related to information services and more to a predominantly custodial function.

Two prototypes of this professional ideal suggest themselves. One is the subject-expert special librarian. He is epitomized in the law librarian with a law degree, the fine arts librarian trained in fine arts, or the music librarian with substantive preparation in music. In the university setting, some but not all departmental and college librarians fall into this category. More recently the subject bibliographer has come to be found increasingly in the universities. Such an individual plays the role of subject collection builder and librarian. Sometimes drawn from the particular field of scholarship, sometimes from librarianship, he enjoys the respect of his clientele for his subject competence. It may well be that the next stage in the educational preparation of librarians will call for a fundamental modification, to build into the educational preparation of librarians a planned and programed sequence of enhancing the subject competence of its students, for there can be little doubt that when the librarian is comfortable, both in the subject matter of the field in which he serves and in the substance of librarianship, he is far more strongly equipped and so more likely to achieve fuller acceptance as a professional in his role relations with clients.

Pushed one stage farther, under these terms the librarian can move from a fundamentally passive to a more aggressive role in information prescription. At home in the subject field, he will be less reliant upon published bibliographic sources, and he will far more readily generate for himself the bibliographic and reference aids for his clientele, for they will grow naturally and logically out of his work in a subject area in which he is not alien. Because bibliographic organization and imaginative informational approaches to subject matter in burgeoning fields are so much sought by clienteles, here is an obvious path to improved clientele esteem.

The responsibility for a lack of aggressive professional service in problem-solving terms must be laid at the door of professional education for librarianship. For the schools, with only rare exceptions, have failed to breed an appreciation for the subtleties or the potentialities of the professional role. Where individual librarians have assumed significant information responsibilities for their constituencies, it has resulted from a combination of their own inherent and intuitive perception of their clientele commitments with imaginative application of bibliographic expertise and subject competence.

What the schools have produced is several generations of librarians committed zealously to the pattern of general service. While the library school student may have been exposed to a smattering of philosophy, and berated with and perhaps inspired by librarianship's service commitments and yearnings, nowhere was this likely to have been translated beyond the bounds of a vague service concept and on into the terms which might correspond with truly professional practice. Reference instructors (typically generalists themselves who rely on the descriptive terms of bibliography, simplistic isolated fact-finding exercises, or vague problems of reference administration) might seek to rationalize their offerings by suggesting that general, mechanistic, totally book-slanted orientations are intended for only the beginning stages of practice. This indoctrination, however, appears to have conditioned most librarians to perform throughout their careers at no higher level of attainment than that of this beginning practice. In learning a set repertoire of responses to meet only narrowly defined client requirements, librarians have not been provoked to consider the alternative of undertaking more demanding or new and differing responsibilities for their clienteles.

It would be naive for any occupational group to believe it could establish its professional role independently, for the ability of any professional to perform and the capacities in which he functions are in many respects circumscribed and influenced by external factors. This may be particularly true for librarianship, which has been a relatively passive pursuit. Since this has been so, it is not surprising to find that the librarian's role has come to be influenced by the expectations of the library's clientele and community which, in many instances, correspond to the minimal attainment level which he has set for himself.

A professional certainly cannot assume a professional role with a client without the client's acceptance of him in the role of expert. Varying factors have tended to prohibit such acceptance of librarians. One has been the conditioning of clienteles to view the librarian in negative stereotyped terms with a consequent reluctance to enlist him as an active ally in the information seeking process. On non-literary matters, the average person simply does not expect--and his experience reinforces this view--that the librarian would be able to help him. The unlettered may hesitate to seek help for fear of revealing their presumed ignorance to someone who appears so all-knowing and bookish and who would tend only to reinforce their feelings of inadequacy in an alien environment. The research scholar, reluctant to relinquish to another the tasks which he has performed unaided (except in the university, to graduate assistants who function under his guidance, and who as a consequence have the subject background to understand fully the nature of the work upon which he is engaged), requests only minor assistance from librarians.

These barriers do not appear to present insurmountable obstacles to professional performance. If the librarian succeeds in developing skill and finesse in reducing the hesitancies of those not accustomed to use libraries, larger numbers who genuinely require information may be expected to turn to them. [7] And as career preparation for librarianship came to comprise substantive preparation beyond the solely bibliographic, so would the disposition of the client change to place heavier reliance upon him for assistance of a more professional calibre. No ultimate wresting of control from the client is involved, for as in every other instance in which a professional is employed, the choice of whether or not to use the service, and then to accept or reject its guidance if it is found to be unreliable or inexpert, is retained by the client.

The immediate institution in which the librarian performs may also have decided and frequently dysfunctional influences upon the client relationship. These institutional constraints will occupy us in further detail hereafter. Just as
the wider environment influences the library, it also determines to a considerable degree the professional role of the
librarian. The clientele group, in the aggregate, exerts its
influence, for libraries, like other service institutions, tend
to accommodate to those who use them. And such external
forces have characteristically tended to perpetuate traditional
roles for the institution and in the process for the professional role. Several examples shall be cited.

At a time when the population composition has shifted
radically in virtually every older core city, the public library
essentially retains its cultural orientation to the middle class,
and this results in an institutional role and a concept of client service which corresponds with the strivings, literary
tastes, and values of a middle class clientele which often is
no longer present. The community typically is indifferent to
this incongruity. In a university during the period when it
seeks to develop its graduate and research programs (and this
is the present state of a large proportion of American institutions of higher learning), the undergraduate service requirements continue to preoccupy the library as the influence of a
longer history of undergraduate programs continues to hold
sway, while the graduate and faculty constituencies are neglected. This situation often persists until the research
faculty succeeds in exerting its influence upon the university
and upon the library's administration. Not only are the libraries inclined to be biased in favor of one constituency over
another, but in each instance the community expects only
minimal forms of service. Public library patrons tend to
settle for recreational fare. In the university a classroom
appendage, the reserve reading room, is too often confusedly
equated with the entire library by administrators who do not
understand the nature of a library and by librarians who do
not understand the nature of either.

In the school library, client service is often a victim
of the conflict between the ideal of service to support the individual student's intellectual growth and development, and to
the curricular requirements of the school. Moreover, many
school libraries carry out functions which bear no relation to
either objective, as reflected in such activities as librarians
substituting for teachers, or in the use of the library as a

study hall or for class disciplinary purposes. There may be
some fundamental question and ambiguity about who the client
really is--the school, the teacher, or the student--and this
only further compounds the conflict inherent in the situation.

In each of these instances, accommodation is to requirements which are not reinforcing of professional-client
relationships, but are rather the contrary. Where service
expectations are minimal from the community, and as these
are furthered through the institutional orientation of the library, whatever the aspirations of the librarian, he is restricted from enhancing his professional role. The point is
that this role is of course, to a considerable extent, conditioned by the public image of the library and the function of
the librarian which is in need of drastic modification, if the
professional ideal is to be furthered.

The client relationship has been dealt with thus far as
a primarily individual matter, but it seems relevant also to
consider it in its community context, and in comparison with
other similar fields. To take two illustrations, let us consider public health and social welfare. Energetic clientele
effort conceives of its role as embracing more than only the
existing consumer, but also reaching out and functioning as
a professional service in improving the community as regards
such affairs. For public health, this would include preven-
tive measures in a program designed to reduce the incidence
of disease, and in social service, the organization of activities committed to a reduction in the frequency of need for
welfare assistance. The counterpart for library service
could be found only through commitment to constituencies not
now viewed as the library's responsibility--for the public library, the marginally literate and other non-users of traditional services; for the academic library--the devising of new
forms and methods of information service beyond the passive
collection function; for the school-library--a commitment to
building collections and services to influence the teacher in
his continuing education and his effectiveness to perform.
Such a perspective of the revised professional commitments
for library service is not in conflict with the views of progressive elements in the library profession. Yet, far more
persistent and far more pervasive is the widely shared consensus that libraries basically are for those who use them
and that it is no part of the library's or the librarian's responsibility to shift in the direction of those who do not.
The implementation of far-reaching, innovative, or imaginative approaches to professional/clientele services seems only

remotely possible, or likely to develop in only isolated instances, when viewed against the general level of current
commitments and current practice.

Institutional Relationships

Client relationships are importantly conditioned by the
bureaucratic setting within which librarians function. As is
equally true of other types of professionals who practice in
formal organizations, librarians are faced with conflicts inherent in the incongruence between professional commitments
on the one hand, and employee requirements on the other.
Professionals view the freedom to function independently, the
exercise of discretion, and the formulation of independent
judgments in client relations based upon their own standards
and ethical views, as essential to professional performance.
The professional resents institutional authority which attempts
to influence his behavior and performance norms, preferring
control by colleagues. These requirements for independence
are met to varying degrees in the institutionalized professions,
and in librarianship, scarcely at all.

Librarians do perform in their direct client relationship with remarkably limited review or supervision, and
stated conversely, with perhaps equally limited direction or
training. The reference librarian is typically free to set his
own limits on how or whether to deal with patron inquiries.
He will, in fact, often spend more time on those questions
which interest him or upon which he feels confident. Or, he
will perhaps determine the relevance of an inquirer's need
based upon his assessment of the prestige, the authority, the
personality, the appearance, or the presumed social, economic, or intellectual stratum which the patron represents.
Despite the democratic ethic upon which library service is
founded, the human tendency to choose to deal with individuals
or situations which do not threaten, or to cater to those presumed to be most important, remains unbridled.

It is not so much that the institution tolerates such
personalized judgments of the relative merits of a quest by
the reference librarian out of deference to his expertise or
evaluative acumen, as much as that the encounter does not
appear to be viewed as critical or crucial enough to warrant
inspection (as compared, for example, with preparing cards
for a catalog which can be assessed as a permanent record
of the success or failure of performance). If administrative

pressure is exerted, it will most typically be directed toward
expediting or handling of more requests so that larger numbers of patrons can be accommodated. In some large systems there may even be a deliberate striving for anonymity,
with new staff members cautioned against trying to build a
personal following.

While the institution may not directly interfere in the
client encounter, in addressing himself principally to satisfying immediate client needs the professional inevitably runs
counter to the system which is designed not to maximize client service, but for the over-all good of the largest number,
even if this is only a most modest good. And since rigid
adherence to bureaucratic ritual (rules and regulations) permits
of practices which may be efficient in terms of the organization's requirements, in any given instance professional service to clientele may be sacrificed. 8 Ultimately, the bureaucratic routine imposes procedures which may be in conflict
with the very goals of the organization--the dialectic is complete, means have become ends, and the intellectual and professional design is sacrificed upon the altar of economic and
efficient work procedures.

This is not to suggest that there is not a need for
order and control in organizations which traffic as heavily in
stock and records as do libraries. With the growth in size
and scale of activity, the need for procedural consistency is
accentuated. Nevertheless, such regularization means that
perhaps ironically in the very largest libraries with the greatest resources and thus the greatest potential for professional
service, the tolerance for individual needs will be most sharply curtailed, the client service minimized, and the professional values most seriously threatened. The role of the library,
as Walton has so concisely put it, is to find that precise balance which introduces only enough routine to keep order and
record-keeping integrity, but not so much as to impair the opportunity to afford clientele convenient and unhampered access
to resources. 9 Finding this balance may be seen as the task
of the creative administrator. It is clearly not to be found
in imposing burdensome ritual which may serve to stultify
the opportunity for professional behavior and practice.

It is for this reason and to act as a countervailing
force to the pressures for economy which would reduce standards of service that it is essential for professionals in organizations to assume decision-making responsibilities in relation to goals and standards of service. 10 Yet, with only rare

exceptions, libraries fall into that class of organizations in
which goal decisions are tightly controlled by the administrative hierarchy. They are consequently often at the mercy of
other tendencies of bureaucracy which run counter to professional aspirations and responsibilities. While professional
spirit and zeal thrive most in an atmosphere which tolerates,
even furthers, freedom of inquiry and pronounced license for
unrestricted thought and action, the hierarchical system by
its nature protects and perpetuates itself through its demands
for submission, obedience, and acceptance. Since the hierarchical structure is reinforced when it withstands any pressure for rapid change, it tends to be organized in such a way
as to inhibit the stream of ideas within the organization which
might ultimately culminate in variations in organizational arrangements or practices. One consequence is that libraries
tend not to advance beyond the levels of minimal service, for
the organizational structure strives to reinforce the status quo.
While there may be tolerance for procedural improvement,
particularly when there is a universal climate provoking such
modification (automation of circulation procedures may be a
case in point) resistance to any more fundamental change such
as goal modification remains as staunch as ever.[11]

Compliance of professionals is achieved through a reward system which distributes benefits and higher incentives
for loyalty to the institution. While the professional presumably addresses his fundamental loyalty to the societal responsibilities of his calling and therefore to the commitments
and responsibilities to the clientele which this engenders, the
institution recognizes only organizational loyalty. As the professional seeks institutional rewards, security, and status, he
pays for them with compliance and conformity at the expense
of his professional obligations. The professional who retains
a fundamental identification with clientele commitment is inevitably forced into a position of conflict with organizational
requirements.

Bureaucratic structure clearly imposes restraints, yet
these tendencies which are contrary to professional requirements are not necessarily irreversible processes or insurmountable barriers. Even so, librarians continue to tolerate
and perpetuate conditions of practice which fall short of the
professional ideal. Perhaps this stems from the lack of understanding on the part of many librarians as well as administrators of what the issues are. In many library situations,
a librarian viewing his primary commitment as essentially to
client service, rather than to institution, would be considered

disloyal, uncooperative, or otherwise suspect, even among
his peer group--fellow librarians. May this not perhaps be
the case of the new breed of subject bibliographer being
spawned in the academic library, forced to choose between
allegiance to library or to subject discipline, and gravitating
away from the rigid bind of bureaucracy and toward the more
free flowing current of his scholarly company? By many librarians he is seen as a prima donna, impatient with necessary work routines, unwilling to help out in emergencies, a
waster of time spent in idle conversation with his clientele
about their work--renegade and spoiled.

Administrators in other comparable fields (particularly
when they are drawn from the professional ranks as is true
of most library administrators), are sensitive to professional
needs, values, and aspirations, and as a consequence, strive
to bend the bureaucratic limitations in order to accommodate
to the working requirements of professional and other specialists in their organizations. Library administrators sometimes view operational constraints to be of such overbearing
importance that they are exaggerated through their administration. Too often the administrator (not infrequently one who
blows the horn of professionalism loudest), has not a minimum understanding of the proper climate within which professionalism is cultivated. He will view professional standards
from the standpoint of internalized organizational standards,
see the products of graduate study as so many replacements
for the firing line without regard for their needs or their immediate or ultimate aspirations. Under these terms, librarians are treated like interchangeable parts serving where and
when needed. Librarians man desks and meet schedule commitments, and in the process, deny and are denied the opportunity to care, to grow and to act professionally.

Nor is the library administrator always sensitive to
the changing requirements of the external environment within
which his organization functions. In the academic milieu, the
storm warnings have long been out to alert the administrator
to the fact that for important elements of his clientele their
information requirements are simply not being met effectively
and that only dramatic modification of the library's role will
alter things. Where the problem is economic, and this will
typically be only a minor symptom of a more fundamental
disorder, the library administrator does both his library and
the larger institution a disservice when he accepts only the
crumbs from the organizational table. Indeed, library administrators sometimes make a virtue of such martyrdom when

they might better recognize that there are times and issues
for which one must stand up and be counted, even if this implies putting one's job on the line. In the public library, the
central issue relates to the basic role of the library during a
period when social needs, modern technology, and other dramatic factors should be influencing a re-evaluation of the conventional middle-class and book orientation which was seen as
appropriate for another time and under different circumstances.

     People and institutions ultimately get the form of ad-
ministration which they seek. If so, why during a period of
drastic personnel shortages, have librarians tolerated forms
of administration which deny them the opportunity for full expression? As the administrators do not often understand the
nature of professional commitment--or are short-sighted
enough to sacrifice it--so librarians come to assume that professionalism may simply be a slogan, or that administration
may be the only professional practice. Since there is no
basic commitment to clientele, or awareness of what is being
sacrificed, they succumb easily to an authoritarian structure.
In doing so, they need no longer assume more responsibility
or undertake differing tasks, carry the burden of professional
commitment, or take risks which put them in conflict with the
process, their submissiveness lends further credence to the
bureaucratic ethos which holds that people need to be led for
they are not mature enough to lead themselves. It is not
simply that some librarians do not resist bureaucratic entrap-
ment, nor that library leadership sometimes diabolically ex-
ploits the very individuals who must be inspired to adapt and
to innovate rather than to be smothered in stale ritual, but
that the environment created by library administrators and
closing in the practicing librarian is diametrically at odds with
the independence of action and freedom from restriction which
most characterizes truly professional service.

     Part of the difficulty in libraries is undoubtedly re-
lated to improper utilization of personnel. In recent years,
a greater number of individuals who carry out so-called professional library functions have benefited from formal academic preparation for librarianship. Yet it is undoubtedly true
that libraries have not tended to analyze systematically their
position structures and requirements, and as a consequence
disproportionate numbers of librarians are employed in capacities which do not call for their full range of preparation
and expertise. Too many librarians are under-utilized in
roles which call for lesser skill or training, with the result
that there is much zealous guarding of the few cherished in-

tellectual tasks from those with less formal preparation, if
equivalent competence to perform.   It is true that if a professional were to continue to perform at a concentrated peak
level of strenuous intellectual effort all through the day, the
strain would be intolerable.   This is one reason why professors do not lecture forty hours a week, or social workers
spend a full work day in case interviews.   But, the problem
in librarianship appears rather one of a need to attempt to
reach equilibrium closer to the other end of this scale.

At precisely the same time when administrators be-
wail an abundance of unfilled positions, accurate analysis of
working environments for members of these very staffs would
all too frequently identify the sharp limits on opportunities
for the expression of imagination and creativity--the burdens
and ritual of desk covering, the routine and menial tasks
more economically delegated to lesser paid employees.   Im-
balance in the proportion of time spent by professionals on
chores which may be tiring, energy sapping, but professionally shallow and devoid of importance, may be quite widespread in libraries.   The dignity and respect which might be
accorded to professional, rather than to administrative pursuits, is too often denied.   Exuberant professional spirit,
high ideals, zeal, and commitment to innovation and experimentation are so often suspect and misunderstood that enthusiasm is ultimately thwarted by the bureaucracy until even
the idealists succumb to the nine-to-five mentality or find
other outlets for their creative aspirations.

Librarians are alert to and much concerned with the
need to re-allocated certain routine chores to others less
qualified; this is laudatory.   But they do not as often recognize the fact that time spent in administrative work is also
time spent in non-professional practice.   And in this they
have much in common with those in other disciplines who
look schizophrenically toward the twin goals of administrative
aspirations and professional satisfaction.   Perhaps because
the utility of administrative accomplishment is more clearly
understood, and is so often attributed a higher value in a
bureaucracy and in the culture, and because the goals of professional practice in librarianship are so confused and ambiguous, librarians more readily assume such administrative
responsibility without remorse.   And it may be for this reason that the assumption of administrative role is so often
equated with success.   It naturally follows that the highest
professional performance is seen as administrative activity,
and that service to clientele through direct or indirect per-

formance, comes to be viewed merely as a way station on
the high road to the assumption of administrative responsibility.

It would be misleading to convey the impression that
problems would be solved if only work assignments were to be
better distributed, or if more dignity and stature were accorded to professional performance in libraries.   Given the
organizational propensities of librarians, personnel reclassification might lead only to more tightly circumscribing the
librarian's role, if albeit at a higher level.   What appears to
be required is a more fundamental administrative reorientation toward an institutional climate which advances the professional spirit and yields organizational responsibilities to the
professional group.   Nor is this to propose democratic administration or a human relations approach as an end in itself,
but rather that the decisions about the future of libraries and
of librarianship itself may well hinge upon the extent to which
professionalization is furthered.

As long as professionalism remains so weak and so
ill-understood, libraries will remain unable to solve not only
their immediate and pressing problems, but they will be un-
prepared and so unable to make the radical adaptations necessary to meet the rapidly shifting and growing requirements
put upon them.   Under these conditions outside intervention
will come to influence the changes required, either by direct
action upon the library or by fashioning new alternative forms
of information service.

This may be what has happened in a number of university libraries where top library administrators have been relieved of their responsibilities or where outside insistence has
resulted in the addition of more expert personnel to the staffs
of the libraries.   Perhaps administrators have served as the
whipping boy for the limited level of professional attainment,
when all who would aspire to professional standing should
stand in the dock together.   It may be that as some administrators charge, the majority of librarians are simply unpre-
pared to assume mature responsibilities, although perhaps
this is more a consequence of the bankruptcy of administrative leadership than of inadequacies among librarians.   Nevertheless, to the degree that administrators countenance, if not
foster, a set of organizational conditions less than appropriate
for even minimal professional practice, it is they who are in
greatest jeopardy and it is they who must beware.

The Professional Group

Why is the record for professionalism in individual libraries so weak, and why has librarianship failed to move
more rapidly toward maturity as a profession? In order to
answer this question and thus better to understand the nature
of the professional commitment, it is necessary to consider
the wider grouping of which the librarian is a part as well as
the nature of his professional relationships. In these terms,
the professional group--the associations and societies--as
well as the less formal personal identifications and group
affiliations, are seen to be relevant. Through these relations are derived many of the patterns of the librarian's behavior and his continued professional growth. The process
of acculturation into the group is begun during the educational sequences when the initiate is not only inducted into the
field and affairs and is introduced to its intellectual substance,
but is also indoctrinated in its commitments, its value orientation, and the standards which ultimately guide his practice.

Although the library-school tie may be securely attached,
and while the bond may grow stronger as the nostalgia of each
passing year adds further romance to old associations, the
indoctrination process of the schools in feeding fuel to professionalism has been remarkably weak. The mystique, the
induction rites, the salute to service concepts, the glorifica-
tion of its heroes, the reinforcement of the field's sense of
its own importance and accomplishments, all these have been
present as long as one remembers. But, the substantive
content, the body of significant professional knowledge, the
theory, the philosophy and the ethic, these have evaded the
field's grasp except in rare and isolated instances. Why
should this have been so?

Perhaps the answer may in part be found in the role
which library education has assumed in orienting its program
so markedly to the requirements of those who come either
while heavily engaged, or during the brief respite from practice after a period of past involvement. Many such students
view library education grudgingly, as only a necessary intru-
sion, to be managed dextrously and conveniently, and to be
related as much and as directly as possible toward reinforcing the operational skills which they have already gained on
the job. The schools, perhaps seeing their role in much the
same manner, conscious of the need to placate their clients,
and having no firm philosophical orientation and commitments
either, have provided institutionalized accommodation to precisely such requirements.

What is more, because the professional schools have
tended toward weakness and have followed the more active
vanguard in the field of practice, they have allowed the special interest groups--public, school, special libraries--to influence them in orienting their course sequences toward the
presumed needs of particular areas of practice.[12] In the
course of pursuing such a fragmented approach, librarianship
has been divided rather than unified around a common theme,
philosophy, or professional commitment. By offering technical courses for specific types of libraries, it is as if to
suggest that the process of administration or organization of
materials or informational problem-solving is fundamentally
variable by type of library. Cross-fertilization is thereby
reduced; school librarians see themselves as something apart
from public librarians, and academic from special librarians.
To suggest only one serious dysfunction, the ultimate end of
this process is to reinforce the institutional barriers to co-
operative and imaginative planning, and seriously to impede
the logical next step in the evolution of library service--the
invention and organization of regional and interinstitutional
information systems.

Perhaps the most searing indictment of all, however,
is that while library education has evolved to the graduate
level in the university, when its content is measured against
the honest yardstick of its intellectual contribution there is
room to doubt whether its claim to professionalism has not
been a ploy by those in library education who simply seek to
rationalize their own roles as professionals. For if library
education is not truly professional education, what then is
the self image of the field's educational and administrative
leadership?[13] This is not to say that library education is
incapable of advancing to the stage where it is more centrally
concerned with ideas, issues, theory, concept, and less with
routine, description, procedure, and method, more with why
and less with how, more with what for and less how to. But,
the transition from description and homily and routine has
only grudgingly given way to scholarship. There are still
hundreds of students in graduate library programs memorizing
names of famous modern librarians, committing to memory
large sections of classification schedules, cluttering their
minds with details of whether certain books have an index and
table of contents or not, and taking superficial cultural romps
through the various fields of knowledge to learn such things
as the fact that Margaret Mead is an anthropologist, instead
of studying the reasons for contemporary trends in societal
information developments, the logic of comparative systems

of classification, the structure of bibliography and information agencies as resources for problem solving, or the personal, organizational, and social group determinants of information need. To the extent that the details have overshad-
owed the more fundamental issues, so has education been
routinized and stripped of its potential for embodying a content that is intellectually viable.

Part of the problem is one of the certification of mediocrity. At a time when the accreditation process in library
education (jealously and zealously guarded as the prerogative
of one national organization) should be strengthening the fiber
of the educational product, it is accrediting and reaccrediting
programs of doubtful merit thereby giving its imprimatur to
schools very distant from any ideal or even advanced attainment. A truer service to professionalism would be to submit each program to ever more critical test, to encourage
experimentation. The perspective of other organizations
might well be sought (representation from SLA and ADI as
illustrations), if only to encourage library education programs
to foster timeliness and consideration of alternatives to their
conventional fare. Present accreditation of graduate library
education is in danger of fostering a negative standard--like
the way in which a hack writer is encouraged when he watches
an inferior television program and is sure he can do that
well himself. Of course, the prescription of an absolute
standard would be absurd, but it must certainly be time for
graduate level programs to aim higher. In a period so crucial for librarianship's future, when excellent students present themselves in abundance, to tolerate and certificate
mediocrity and worse is a disservice to professionalism and
to the students who are being prepared.

The relatively painless acquisition of the association's
seal of approval may, however, be only symptomatic of a
more fundamental ailment. Education for librarianship may
simply not have succeeded in attracting to the scholarly dimension of librarianship the theorists and researchers competent to build the concepts and the knowledge base upon
which to construct an intellectual basis for professional practice. Drawn predominantly from, and committed almost over-
whelmingly to, humanistic disciplines (when not to educational
methodology), faculties in librarianship have failed or refused
to see in library service a scholarly pursuit. Analytic insight is uncommon. Descriptive and historical orientations
abound. Doctoral study has remained predominantly an academic exercise, serving either as the springboard to admin-

istrative advance or as the terminal research effort, short on
methodological rigor and long on detail and bibliography.

Like the practicing librarian who bemoans the overload of clerical demands and busily perpetuates a role which
tolerates the condition, academics accede to excessive course
loads, teaching commitments in subject matters alien to their
background and preparation, and wistfully lament the lack of
time for genuine research and scholarship. But, the fact of
the matter may simply be that they have not had the imagination or the conceptual orientation, the scholarly and intellectual footing to do more than remain a lap or two behind practice in their classrooms. For they seem to have almost universally failed to identify the basic problems or even to ask
the most interesting questions, and so ultimately what they
have taught proves to be irrelevant to contemporary requirements.

Lacking a conceptual base, typically barren of the analytical skills of the social or hard sciences, what scholarly
effort is carried on by library faculties tends most frequently
to center upon historical study or the applied survey. Where
research has been fostered it has remained largely irrelevant
to the educational offering, and even doctoral study has been
characterized by a sterility and detachment from the fundamental issues in a way that is remarkable for a field so much
at the center of societal concern. The link-up first forged
with the social sciences at Chicago in 1930's and 1940's has
slipped away, and now information science seems the only
serious intellectual issue to be engaging the attention of more
than a handful of library scholars. Yet, there is danger in
this that the technological issues and applications will so
overwhelm the scholarly company in librarianship that alternative issues, with all of their behavioral, political, and organizational ramifications, will be swept aside and once more
pragmatic means rather than philosophical ends will engage
the attention of the field's most inquiring minds. 14

Just as the schools provide or fail to provide the basic intellectual orientation and the body of knowledge fundamental to the claims of professionalism, the wider professional grouping acts to support professionalism in practice
purely because it is a vehicle for wider personal recognition
and reward. Within the scholarly disciplines, the source of
recognition and prestige tends to be the peer group of colleagues rather than the local institution. Success and the
achievement of career satisfactions are most often accorded

only following distinctive attainment among the scholarly fraternity, even while there may be some degree of ambiguity
and conflict between local and cosmopolitan orientations. 15
In the professions, career advancement proceeds differently.
Except for the relatively small number of individuals engaged
in research, writing, or other scholarly pursuits, the path to
wider recognition through the channel of publication tends to
be closed. 16 Perhaps for this reason librarians sense that
they must concentrate so energetically upon purely local demands and requirements, since without having achieved profession-wide visibility, the route to advancement locally or
laterally into other organizations is equated with recognition
within one's own organization of the effectiveness of his performance.   But, in a time of almost unlimited opportunity,
the truer barrier to advancement may be the restriction upon
mobility which handicaps the individual.   While it is uncertain whether career advancement within libraries is promoted
by profession-wide contribution (except in the case of academic libraries where such recognition is more common),
the process of professionalization might be furthered if this
were to be the case more generally.   This is not to suggest
that the goals of librarianship would necessarily be enhanced
by a spate of ill-conceived and poorly executed articles, but
rather that an institutional tone which honors such external
commitment becomes a stimulus to professionalism, just as
the converse may be equally true.

        Librarians can and frequently do achieve visibility.
It is also clear that professional involvement is often prelude
to career advancement.   While it is unquestionably true that
some few in librarianship have adroitly identified the political
utility of organizational engagement as a device leading to
career opportunity, it is equally true that for many, many
more, professional affiliations and participation serve as the
tool of improved practice.   This may be best illustrated by
the special librarian's reliance upon professional colleagues
in other institutions to expand the scope of his expertise, for
as he draws upon his fellow librarians as external access
points to information, he in the process expands the confines
of his limited collections.   In so doing, he reinforces im-
measurably the professional contribution which he can make
to his own organization.

        We suspect that a significant hallmark of the librarian
who functions as a true professional is reflected in the nature
of his relationships.   The professional constantly expands upon
his circle of contacts and reinforces and strengthens existing

colleague relations, pursuing an active role by continuing his growth through self-study and associating himself with the local and regional and national activities in librarianship and in other special disciplines with which his work puts him in contact. For him, keeping up with professional trends and advances through the journals and monographs is a matter of fact. To lose touch with current affairs would make him feel as uncomfortable and ill-equipped professionally as to remain out of touch with broader societal affairs would render him uneasy as a generally aware person in his culture. This is in contrast to the librarian who confines his relationships to those which are merely comforting, reassuring, and reinforcing of his prejudices and limitations.

Nor is this to suggest that all so-called professional activity is desirable. Those who have participated in groups in which meetings consist of members explaining why they have failed to complete assignments or committees which deliberate weightily the means for perpetuating themselves instead of considering their purpose or program, or still others which consume hour after hour preoccupied with minutia, need no reminder of this. It is likely that many energetic and imaginative librarians have been repulsed and disenchanted from professional engagement by participating in precisely such exercises in frustration. The associational excesses of the ritual, the routine, and the social do not characterize only the local groups; as a consequence the participation of some of the most thoughtful and committed of librarians has been shunted off.

It is interesting to speculate whether identification with professional norms and values may be impeded, enhanced, or otherwise affected by practicing in large libraries, compared to the situation of the librarian in the special library or the school, where he is functioning apart, and associating more with a distinct clientele or discipline. In theory, professional ties should be reinforced through daily interaction with professional colleagues. Yet, close colleague associations with other librarians seem also to foster undesirable aspects of professionalism. Professional values may be more strongly reinforced through interaction and identification with clientele. This would clearly be the case in those instances where such undesirable or negative manifestations as a strong alliance in defense of the status quo or a tendency to band together in common disregard if not active resentment of the clientele, were to be found. [17] While librarians working in concert may be better able to impose their standards and

values on the institution, frequently they tend rather to reinforce and tolerate minimal service expectation.

If recent events in New York City libraries are a har-
binger, more militant group solidarity when it takes shape
may more likely be found in efforts to organize as collective
bargaining agents rather than as professionally goal-oriented
groups. While proponents of unionization reason that unions
are fully compatible with professional goals and objectives, 18
in view of the emphasis in organized labor on such matters
as seniority rights and employee benefits it remains to be
seen whether the effect may not be a reinforcement of the
very rigid authority structure of libraries which serves now
as an impediment to innovation and furtherance of service
commitments.

There are certain issues which require of professionalism that their proponents stand up and be counted. While the
library profession supports an ethic with regard to intellectual
freedom that calls for librarians to resist censorship pressure, the Fiske study documents the ways in which many librarians practice forms of self-censorship. 19 It is equally
true that librarians do not always resist or are not always
successful in resisting external censorship pressures. Whether or not the practice varies from the ideal, the ethic is viable. More librarians will stand up for it than if it did not
exist and unless it were to be so flagrantly disregarded as
to become a mockery, society will ultimately come to know
and respect it and the group which supports it. 20 But, censorship is the most dramatic issue, not necessarily the one
most central to professionalism. Librarians need equally to
be militantly vocal about meeting minimum standards of excellence in such terms as the conditions, the support for,
and the resources necessary for them to perform by acceptable standards.

In theory, if a professional cannot win minimum conditions for practice, he leaves. In actuality, he usually does
nothing of the sort, for a variety of reasons good and bad.
Many librarians are married women and hence immobile.
Librarians frequently rationalize that it is better to remain
and so offer some level of service while seeking to influence
change for the better, much in the same manner as the optimistic woman whose life mission is to reshape some unde-
serving and unsuspecting male. There is perennial hope
that conditions will improve. In these matters, librarians
do no worse than faculty members of academic programs in

which all who seek admission enter and everyone who enters
ultimately graduates.   No pat formula is at hand to describe
whether in a given situation at a given time the conditions are
irremediable, or must remain intolerable.   It is only to be
hoped that decisions may come to be made more frequently in
terms of the professional commitment and the zeal for improved conditions, rather than the naive wish or the longing,
and that aggressive professionalism will become a more widespread standard than patience and hope.

It will never cease to be an embarrassment to those
who aspire to professionalism to find library situations in
which the fiercest partisans for improvement are not the librarians themselves, but rather some outside or community
group such as faculty members or teachers who struggle
tenaciously for improved resources and conditions of operation.   It is precisely here, in the passiveness or aggression
of its commitment to the ideals and goals of library service,
that those who practice it are assessed.   Librarianship has
not yet reached the stage in its development where it exerts
the type of influence over its members which requires them
to stand up and be counted on important issues or to refuse
to practice in situations where resources are inadequate to
do a minimal job.   It therefore continues to countenance
forms and levels of service which fall short of adequate
standards.   It has been conditioned by a national and educational leadership attuned to the acceptance of the modest and
unassuming prospects of the past when resources were scarce
or unattainable.   In these more affluent times, librarians
have still not been aroused to demand the conditions for effective performance which are typically far more readily within their reach now if only they will aspire to them.

For much of the history of American librarianship,
the professional associations remained forward of practice.
But, in many ways the one primary national organization
now no longer speaks with authority for all the elements in
librarianship.   Information activity under various names is
shifting dramatically and incorporating new forms and new
paths to entry into practice.   Libraries as they have traditionally functioned must either respond to contemporary requirements, or lose to competitive agencies and technologies.
While the principal national association has been influential
in many ways, its primary focus has been and remains political rather than professional.   It has identified predominantly with the public library, and in the process lost touch with
many of the most significant developments which should be

influencing the library profession. Through its overly modest
position on accreditation standards for graduate education, its
non-existing role in the accreditation or certification of libraries, and by concentrating its zeal most strenuously upon
aggrandizing the scale of its size, its political influence, and
its economic power, it has contributed little to professionalization and tended, by default, to perpetuate inadequacy.

Like the libraries which it reflects, the American Library Association is a bureaucracy with the same built-in
vested interests. To the extent that its key posts are held
by those in administrative positions in librarianship, and that
power in the organization is wielded by a relatively small
coterie, it is less a professional association than an administrative confederation. Like other oligarchical organizations
of large size and wide geographical dispersion, it proves less
capable than it should be of attracting younger, innovating
elements into its higher councils. By concentrating its efforts on improving only the most underdeveloped situations
in librarianship, it frequently misses being in the vanguard
of new or imaginative directions for librarianship. By assuming unto itself a wide range of national, international,
research, and societal responsibilities, for which it is less
than ideally equipped, it purports to do more than attain the
political ends at which it is most successful. Conventions
and meetings which appear designed in greatest measure to
reassure the rank and file that problems are under control
by reinforcing outmoded traditional approaches, are of only
limited service to a profession in a rapidly changing world
posing new demands.

Viewed against the perspective of history, librarianship can be seen to have made only slow and gradual evolution as a profession and exists now as only a marginal entry
in the competitive race for professional status. The conditions of modern times, however, are such that if librarianship does not move much more rapidly forward toward enhanced professionalism, the field will not only decline rapidly, but ultimately face obsolescence. Already, traditional
and conventional libraries are being replaced as new agencies
and new practitioners respond more appropriately to changing
requirements for information and professional service.

Progress in librarianship is made by only a relatively
small number. Innovation remains on trial when it should
be encouraged. The field stands conservatively and deeply
rooted in the past at a time when such a stance exposes it

to danger.   Fundamental to advancement is the need to forge
a new professional identity founded upon some of the characteristic elements which have been treated here.

NOTES

1. Hence the term "professional librarian. "   One might
    question parenthetically whether there could be such
    a thing as a nonprofessional librarian.   And would
    it be comparable to such a thing as a nonprofession-
    al lawyer, nonprofessional doctor, nonprofessional
    dentist, etc. ?

2. Or, as in the case of the library code of ethics, grows
    from a lack of understanding of what the nature of
    a professional ethic really is, emphasizing as it
    does the "employee's" obligation.

3. Jerome E. Carlin, Lawyers on Their Own: A Study
    of Individual Practitioners in Chicago (New Bruns-
    wick, New Jersey: Rutgers University Press,
    1962).

4. For recent documentation of such practice among oph-
    thalmologists see the testimony of Dr. Marc An-
    thony, of Spokane, Washington, reported in the
    New York Times, February 1, 1967, p. 43.

5. Adam Smith had some comments to make about the prac-
    tices of merchant groups which may not be too tan-
    gential to be relevant here.   "People of the same
    trade seldom meet together, even for merriment
    and diversion, but the conversation ends in a con-
    spiracy against the public, or in some contrivance
    to raise prices.   Though the law cannot hinder the
    people of the same trade from sometimes assem-
    bling together, it ought to do nothing to facilitate
    such assembling, much less render them necessary. "
    From The Wealth of Nations (New York, Dutton,
    [1937]).

6. This point is elaborated in Paul Wasserman, The Li-
    brarian and the Machine (Detroit: Gale Research
    Co. , [1967]), p. 50ff.

7. Although, at least in the public library, a fundamental

modification of objectives is required for this to
be the case.   The alternative is to have the information responsibility assumed by others.   A recent monograph suggests the establishment of a national information system at the community level.
See Alfred J. Kahn, et al., Neighborhood Information Centers: A Study and Some Proposals (New
York: Columbia University School of Social Work,
1966).

8.   As for example, in following such a policy as that in a
       number of university libraries which specifies that
       a librarian will not carry out extensive literature
       searches for any faculty member since the library
       could not be expected to provide such service for
       all who sought it.

9.   John Walton, "The Administration of Libraries," Johns
       Hopkins University Ex Libris, November 1957.

10.   For a fuller consideration of authority structure in li-
        braries as an influence upon decision processes,
        see Mary Lee Bundy, "Conflict in Libraries," CRL,
        XXVII (September 1966), 253-62.

11.   In many instances concentration upon automation may be
        viewed as an administrative strategy for diverting
        attention from more basic problems and thereby
        forestalling the necessary fundamental reassess-
        ment of goals and services.

12.   One manifestation which illustrates such influence may
        be seen in the meeting on library education for
        special librarianship convened each year by the
        SLA Educational Committee during the annual con-
        ference.   While the subject matter of the discus-
        sion varies from year to year, the common theme
        is the attempt to arrange for a dialogue between
        special librarians and library educators about the
        educational requirements for practice in the special
        library.   See for example, Special Libraries, LVII
        (January 1967), for a report of the Second Forum
        on Education for Special Librarianship.

13.   This issue is elaborated in Bernard Barber, "Some
        Problems in the Sociology of the Professions,"
        Daedalus, American Academy of Arts and Sciences,
        XCII (1963).

14. In a way that may be analogous to that of the weak library which concentrates its zeal on automating its processes rather than in building client services and timely information access.

15. See, Alvin Gouldner, "Cosmopolitans and Locals: Toward an Analysis of Latent Social Roles, Part I," Administrative Science Quarterly, II (December 1957), 281-306.

16. There is one important yet subtle difference between a professional society and a scholarly discipline in the way in which recognition and prestige are awarded to its membership. Prestige in the professional society typically comes from office holding and work for the organization, while in a scholarly discipline, prestige more usually follows upon academic productivity as reflected in the form of articles and monographs. This may relate very essentially to the difference between librarianship and some of the more scholarly disciplines with which it is sometimes compared.

17. Whether such characteristics tend to be more pronounced in academic libraries because of their unique status problems when compared with other types of libraries, would serve as the basis for an interesting line of inquiry.

18. "... It is true that a union of professional people, whether they are researchers in an industrial laboratory or college professors, will be substantially different from that which you would find in an industrial organization of plant workers. But, the fact that they have joined a union doesn't change the fact that they still have professional standing, professional competence," in "How to Negotiate with a Professor's Union" (an interview with Dr. John McConnell) in College Management, II (January 1967), 25.

19. Marjorie Fiske, Book Selection and Censorship; A Study of School and Public Libraries in California (Berkeley: University of California Press, 1959).

20. See for example, the "Freedom to Read" statement prepared by the Westchester Conference of the Ameri-

can Library Association and the American Book
Council in 1953, ALA Bulletin, XLVII (November
1953), 481-83. It is important to recall that at
this very time other prestigious national societies
assumed a position of studied silence. This was
the case of the American Political Science Association, to cite only one of a number of such bodies,
which might be viewed as having an important concern with the issues of censorship and political
freedom.

THE PROFESSION AND ITS PROBLEMS

THE NEXT FIFTY YEARS*

Louis R. Wilson

The celebration of the fiftieth anniversary of any individual or organization is always an occasion which may
profitably be used to review the past and to attempt to forecast the future. On this occasion, Dr. Bostwick has dealt
very interestingly with many phases of the Club's first fifty
years. My part in the celebration is to point out changes
which members of the Club, in common with librarians generally, will witness in librarianship within the second fifty
years.

I have always been stirred when I have contemplated
the objectives which the early members of the American Library Association set themselves in 1876. They decided they
could profit from the organization of a professional association. Without loss of motion they founded the ALA. They
further decided they needed a medium of communication, a
source of standardized supplies and equipment, a classification system and body of cataloging rules, an additional major
bibliographical tool, and a library school for the training of
competent personnel for the direction of libraries. In rapid
order, the Library Journal was established, the Library
Bureau began to produce supplies and equipment, the Dewey
Classification and the Cutter Cataloging rules were published,

---

*An address delivered at the fiftieth anniversary of the New
York Library Club, February 20, 1936, this is reprinted by
permission from Library Journal 61:255-260 (April 1936).
Published by R. R. Bowker Co. (a Xerox company). Copyright © 1936 by R. R. Bowker Co.

the American Catalog began publication, and the first library
school at Columbia was projected.

Here is a record of action, of achievement. The philosophy of librarianship, however, on which Dewey and Cutter and Bowker and Leypoldt based this action, has not been
recorded with equal clarity and directness. If you wish to
know why they acted with such despatch and unanimity, what
they thought and believed about libraries, you will not find it
clearly stated in what they said.

Philosophy of the Library

As we celebrate the fiftieth anniversary of this club,
a number of whose charter members were also charter members of the American Library Association, I am conscious of
a distinct demand on the part of younger librarians to know
more exactly what this fundamental philosophy of the library
was. Three young librarians who have recently had the dar-
ing to record their views on the subject have ascribed the
rise of the public library in America to three entirely different causes. Borden, with a penchant for philosophic statement and an outlook that is distinctly social, finds that the
influences which brought the library into being were largely
democratic, educational, and social. The library grew out of
America's demand for educational opportunity and the necessity of training citizens for effective participation in a democracy. Wellare, a keen observer from England, and influenced
somewhat by the possibly different causes leading to the establishment of libraries in that country, associates the development of the American public library with the growth of
philanthropy and the reform movement which undertook to improve the general lot of the laboring class. Orman, younger
than the other two, and looking at the question from the distance of the North Pacific Coast, sees the American public
library springing from an economic demand--the desire on the
part of an economic order to secure a body of workers trained
in part by the library who could produce goods effectively, a
desire, he contends, that has grown more feeble in the past
decade and is reflected in smaller support to libraries now
that the machine has been brought to such a degree of perfection that it is no longer necessary to make special provision for the education of the worker through the library.

I am not prepared to say which of these views is correct. None of them may be. But during the next few decades

these young members of the library profession, or others,
are going to set forth systematically in clear perspective the
philosophy underlying the activities of Dewey and his co-
workers so that future librarianship may be able to chart its
course in the light of this philosophy.   They maintain that
American librarians must have a philosophy of librarianship,
just as an individual must have a philosophy of life, if he is
to make the most of himself.   Consequently, they are going
to find out what this philosophy of the library was.   This
constitutes the first important change in the field of librarianship which I expect to see take place.

Objectives of the Library

        The demand of these inquiring juniors, however, will
not stop at this point.   They are also demanding that librarians shall know more exactly than they have in the past what
the objectives of the library in present society are, and how
the library of today and tomorrow is to be maintained so that
it may perform its legitimate function.   Not only are their
futures at stake, but they are convinced that the effective
development of the library cannot be achieved unless its objectives are clearly defined and the place of the library in
society is clearly understood.   They insist, and I find myself
in agreement with them, that if the library is to serve the
public in such way as to win enlarged support, it will have
to formulate and define its objectives more sharply, it will
have to make them primarily educational, and it will have to
bring librarians and the public generally to a widespread and
clear understanding of them.   If democracy is a way of life,
its appropriate functioning can be achieved only by the training of members of society which will enable them to adapt
themselves successfully to this way of life.   On this assumption, the school today receives support from local and state
resources and is universally considered in America as a legitimate and necessary charge against the state.   As society becomes more complex, as the period in which men must adjust themselves to the mode of life which a democracy makes
necessary becomes longer and the proper administration of a
democracy becomes more involved, it will become increasingly imperative that society, represented both by the locality
and the state, shall make provisions for those types of education which will prepare society for democracy.

        I expect to see the library, therefore, go consciously
educational in the broad sense and take those steps in the re-

adjustment of its organization, equipment, and personnel
which will enable it to meet the educational needs of groups
as well as of individuals and to serve society in a fundamentally educational way. If it undertakes this wholeheartedly,
if, like the English libraries, it places the entire coordinated
book resources of the nation at the service of individuals and
groups interested in educational advancement, if it becomes
skilled in its administration of this service and fits it nicely
to the needs of the public, I expect to see library service
adequately supported by both locality and state. But if it
does not do this, the school, the forum, the agricultural extension organizations in the rural areas, or some other
agency or agencies, are going to take leadership in this field.
The clarification of the objectives of the library and the adjustment of its service to the educational needs of society
constitute the second change to which I look forward.

Recently, the University of Chicago was given $1,000,-
000 by the Spelman Fund for a building for seventeen national organizations associated with it, which are concerned with
the improvement of various forms of local, state, and national government. The gift was made in order that they might
be better equipped to carry on their work. From time to
time I overhear the discussions of those who are in charge
of these organizations, and I constantly study their publications. In both discussions and publications, these experts in
government insist that public officials must know what the
functions of their offices are and how to test and measure
their performance in the light of carefully designed standards.

Measures of Performance

Today, the American Library Association has standards for public libraries with which we are familiar. These
experts, however, consider them inadequate for the purposes
which they are intended to serve. They insist that these
standards do not reveal the exact unit costs of different activities, that they cannot be used effectively in measuring efficiency of operation, and that they do not greatly aid the library administrator in shaping and directing the policies of
his library, or in understanding the interests and meeting the
needs of individuals and special groups. Furthermore, they
say they do not enable the taxpayer to know whether the services provided through the library are worth what they cost.
What they actually mean is that libraries do not have devices
at present by which they can accurately measure their admin-

istrative effectiveness or social significance. The next ten
years will witness the development of a body of costs and
measurements for various types of library service which will
meet these adverse criticisms and enable the library to justify its support upon a basis of substantial facts, rather than
of unproven assumptions. To a philosophy of action and specific objectives will be added accurate measures of per-
formance--all of which are essential to sustained progressive
achievement. This will constitute a third fundamental change
in librarianship.

The fourth change which I foresee relates to training
for librarianship. This change will be evidenced in several
ways.

Training for Librarianship

First of all, the professional training of the librarian
in the future will be relatively less concerned with technique
than it is today. I say relatively less concerned with technique. The amount of training of a technical nature which
librarians must possess will always have to be sufficient to
carry on library processes effectively and economically. It
will also place greater emphasis on the principles or theories
which underlie the various subjects embraced within the curriculum, and it will present the subjects constituting the entire curriculum in a more systematic perspective. The present graduate of the library school knows how to classify
books, how to catalog them, how to develop bibliographies,
etc. In the future he will be more familiar with the fundamental principles which underlie these important processes.
He will not only learn how certain things are done, but he
will understand more fully why they are done, and when confronted with a difficult problem which calls for the application of principles or for relating the activity in question to
the appropriate division of the general field of librarianship,
will move with a greater degree of assurance to its proper
solution. In these respects, education for librarianship will
more nearly approximate education in other professional fields
in which knowledge of subjects and principles are fundamental, and where knowledge of the application of principles may
be acquired in part on the job. The multiplication of textbooks and staff manuals and the development of a system of
internships and examinations will greatly facilitate this change.

In the second place, the librarian of the future will

acquire a more extensive knowledge of society, of social
trends, and of the social significance of the library as a
social agency. He will know the causes which gave rise to
the public library. He will know the library's major objectives. He will know more concerning the relation the library
bears to other public or private agencies operating in the
same field, the methods by means of which the education of
the public in socially significant ways can best be effected,
and how to measure the library's educational and social effectiveness.

Specifically, the library school student will know far
more than he does today concerning the extent the public
reads and the effect of reading upon the public. It will be
taken for granted that he will know who constitute the reading
public or publics with which he is to deal, how extensively
this public reads materials of various kinds secured from
various sources, and the part which the library plays in the
dissemination of these materials. He will know more about
the difficulties which different groups of readers find in understanding print, how these difficulties may be minimized
or overcome, how extensive reading increases the range of
vocabulary and power of comprehension of an individual, and
how speed in reading increases the competence of people at
different educational levels. And it should not be too much
to expect that as this field is developed by the psychologist,
the sociologist, the librarian, and other students of society,
he will know more than is known today of how reading shapes
the attitudes and influences the behavior of the reader generally.

It should not be too much to hope that some library
school may unite scholars from many departments and schools
in some university in attempting to determine what the socially significant effects of reading are and how they may be
multiplied. When that is done, the work of the library will
be clarified, and the prospective librarian will be able to take
up his work not only with a better understanding of books and
the technical procedures of making them available to the public but also of the effects of reading and how to employ books
in behalf of society in a genuinely helpful way.

In the third place, the library school of the future
will see to it that the contributions which a great university
can make to the prospective librarian are focused upon and
integrated with his technical and professional training. It
will see to it that his professional knowledge, which should

serve as the spearhead of his equipment, is thoroughly re-
enforced with a sound knowledge of some specific subject and
an extensive body of supporting information drawn from related and contributory fields.   Otherwise, the training of the
college and university librarian, of the librarian of the great
public, reference, or scientific library, of the heads of major departments and of those in charge of special collections,
cannot be depended on to give its possessor mastery of his
field or to carry him successfully through the difficult and
complex situations which he may expect to encounter in future library service.   It can hardly be supposed that the
questions of academic status and professional rank, which are
so acute with the college librarian, can be answered satisfactorily on the basis of training that extends only one year
beyond the baccalaureate degree.   It is taking far too much
for granted to assume that the university librarian will be
able to understand the objectives and administrative procedures of the university, that he will be able to appreciate the
points of view of scholars with respect to advanced studies
and research, and that he will be able to fit the library to
the needs of all its patrons, without having specific training
in these fields.   Nor can it be assumed that the public library administrator will be able to find his way through the
complexities of municipal government and finance or that he
can relate the activities of his institution successfully to the
programs of other social agencies or contribute effectively to
the formal and informal education of the community at large,
unless he has acquired a thorough understanding of these subjects which at present are often not embraced in his founda-
tional or professional training.

     In the fourth place, investigation and experimentation
in the library schools, particularly those giving advanced degrees, will receive greater emphasis than they do today.
This does not mean, as some may fear, that the candidate
for the Ph. D. will be trained solely as if he is to become
a lifelong investigator, rather than a practicing librarian;
that he will so concern himself with analysis that he will
overlook the importance of relationships and synthesis.   It
does mean, however, that if he is to be charged with the direction of a social agency, such as the library is, he will
be able to understand the concepts and procedures which are
generally employed in studies which deal with highly complex
social situations.   It means that he will be trained to recognize, define, and limit for the purposes of study the problems which arise in the various fields of library science.
Inasmuch as many of these problems lie outside the fields of

classification, cataloging, and bibliography, it means that he
will be trained to use the tools and methods, singly or in
combination, which scholars in all subjects have found may
be most appropriately utilized in attacking and solving problems in their fields or in experimenting with some new aspect of a subject with reasonable prospect of being able to
handle the experiment scientifically and successfully.

As I foresee the development in the field of education for librarianship, I am convinced that the librarian of
the future will not only have to know how certain things must
be done, and why they must be done, but that he will have
to know what the needs of society are and how to apply an
extensive body of special knowledge and methods of analysis
and synthesis in meeting them. The library in America today, with its vast and highly specialized collections and its
varied and extensive clientele is not the simple thing it was
when this Club was founded. The fact that librarians have
not determined the causes which gave rise to the public library, that they have not formulated the objectives of the library clearly, that they have largely muffed the opportunity
to define the relationship of the library to the organized adult
education development of the past decade and to increase the
educational effectiveness of the library in that field, that they
have produced comparatively few major reports on library or
educational or other social subjects of wide social significance
--I say these facts may be attributable in large measure to
the limitations which have marked the training of the librarian
in the past, but which are being removed at present and
should largely disappear in the future.

In the fifth place, library schools will become more
substantially supported so that they can carry out a more adequate program of instruction, experimentation, and research.
It must be remembered that the oldest library school is less
than fifty years old and that it was just ten years ago that
the major movement of library schools to university campuses
began. Similarly their incomes are beginning incomes, as
contrasted with the accumulated resources of longer established departments and schools. As a matter of fact no library school giving advanced instruction has an income of
more than approximately one per cent of the total income of
the university with which it is associated. The average is
more nearly half of one per cent, and funds for loans, schol-
arships, and fellowships, such as the New York Library
Club is providing here, are just beginning to accumulate.
Likewise, except for the fellowships made available to librar-

ians through the educational foundations, little assistance has
been provided as yet for members of library school staffs
and student bodies through the national research organizations
whose resources for this purpose amount to more than
$1,000,000 annually. As schools become longer established,
as they develop more extensive experience, as they revise
their curriculums in accord with changes in service and
methods of teaching, as they integrate their work with that
of supporting departments and become more accustomed to
the procedures of investigation and experimentation, I expect
to see them more substantially supported financially so that
they may more effectively prepare the prospective librarian
for his future task. These various changes in the education
of the librarian and in the support of the library school,
comprise the fourth important development in librarianship
I foresee in the next fifty years.

Two other changes which I foresee relate to the selection of library personnel and the greater use of mechanical devices in library service.

Selection of Personnel

Getting properly equipped people to enter the library
profession is, of course, fundamental to library advancement.
The problem is how to select the right kind of people. This
problem is being attacked in a number of ways. Dr. C. C.
Williamson has recently released statistics showing that academic accomplishment at the undergraduate level gives an
excellent basis for the judging of the probable scholastic effectiveness of a student at the professional level. Miss Har-
riet E. Howe has studied the results of special tests of prospective library school students as to vocabulary range and
reading competence. The personal interview has long been a
means by which the determination of fitness has been attempted. More recently, the procedures of the Occupational
Conference have been studied as they have been applied to
the rehabilitation of workers displaced in industry, and the
experience of organizations employing large numbers of
trained persons, such as the American Telephone and Tele-
graph Company and the Tennessee Valley Authority, has been
brought under review.

For the past two years a member of the Department
of Psychology at the University of Chicago, who has achieved
decided success in determining the effect of movies upon chil-

dren, has been carrying on an investigation from which further assistance may be expected.   He has undertaken the isolation of what he terms primary abilities of personality.
Through an extensive battery of tests he has secured an extensive body of information concerning each member of a
group of two hundred individuals.   If the information concerning an individual is properly broken down, he is convinced
it will reveal a number of these primary abilities.   To date
he has isolated five and he foresees the day when he will be
able to determine what special abilities a person possesses
with something like the accuracy that the chemist determines
the various elements which may be present in a chemical
solution.   Gradually through the total information which academic record, personal interview, special tests, and experience drawn from other fields make available, the problem
which now confronts directors of library schools of choosing
the right person for library work will be greatly simplified.

Mechanical Devices

          In an extremely interesting article in a recent num-
ber of the Library Journal,[1] Miss Ethel M. Fair has conclusively shown that the manufacturer of the machine has not
extensively discovered the library.   Possibly it might more
properly be said that the library, concerned principally with
books and readers and staffed largely with people from the
conservative liberal arts college, whose training has been
largely literary and historical rather than scientific or experimental, has not drawn upon the manufacturer of the machine for the simplification of many of its operations.   In
the future, I am convinced there will be marked change in
this particular.   More librarians will be recruited from the
fields of the social, natural, and applied science, whose concern is with the present and future as well as the past.   The
photostat, the camera, the projector, and the reading glass
will be the commonplace equipment of the library of tomorrow.   Once an idea is reduced to manuscript, through the
process of photography and mechanical means of reproduction,
it can be forever kept in print.   It will be possible to issue
editions of one or two copies at approximately the same cost
per copy of editions of one-hundred or more.   And the physical equipment of the library for the use of these devices and
for the storage of photostats and films will undergo significant
changes.   Not only will this revolution in service to the scholar take place, but it will be accompanied by the perfection of
devices for the multiplication of bibliographies and catalogs,

and the analysis and recording of loans. Through the use of
book cards and registration cards punched for tabulating machines, the library will be able to secure at a minimum expense a daily analysis of the population served and the different types of materials and kinds of assistance which have
constituted the total service to the public. Through the use
of mechanical devices, the library administrator will not
only be able to cut down the cost of resources for research
and the daily operation of his plant, but he and the taxpayer
will be able to measure with greater assurance the social
significance of the performance of the library. This is a
change which is already knocking at the door.

Use of Library Resources

        A final change which I wish to point out is that of
cooperation and coordination in the use of library resources.
Thirty years ago in North Carolina the main emphasis of the
State Department of Education was the establishment of local
tax school districts and the building of small schoolhouses.
The formation of such districts and the building of a school-
house a day were set up as major objectives. Within the
past ten years, those objectives have been discarded and the
county as a school unit, consolidated schools, and centralized
state support have taken their place. A similar transition in
thinking about libraries and library support is to be noted in
many parts of America. There are many who have come to
the conclusion that the library in the small town, which maintains an entirely independent existence, cannot provide as adequate service as it could through cooperation with similar libraries in nearby communities. They have decided that the
one-room library, like the one-teacher school, is not an economical and effective library unit.

        Some day, and I hope it may not be in the too far
distant future, I expect to see the rugged individualism of
communities yield in respect to library service to the extent
that neighboring libraries will supplement each other's resources and that many libraries now serving individual communities will be developed as county and regional libraries
beyond the limits of the communities in which they happen to
be located. I have in mind the town and city libraries of a
state like Illinois. The state contains 102 counties, ninety
of which have one or more libraries. One contains eight.
Many have sufficient wealth to support adequate county-wide
service, but only one does so. Service and cooperation,

rather than ownership, will be emphasized, and when this happens, the ability of the library to play a significant role in preparing people for effective participation in democracy as a way of life will be tremendously increased.

What is to be the New York Library Club's part in effecting these changes, in multiplying the effectiveness of the library as a social and educational institution? I leave that question with you. Here is America's greatest concentration of population, of wealth, of library workers, of library resources, and of potential library users. Here is also the greatest concentration of publishing houses and organizations engaged in the direction of adult education, occupational rehabilitation, and the extension of knowledge of the useful and fine arts. It is a laboratory par excellence in which to investigate and experiment and create in the development of metropolitan library service. I cannot conceive of its doing less in meeting this challenge than the charter members of this club and the charter members of the American Library Association did in meeting the challenge of fifty and sixty years ago.

NOTE

1.   Library Journal 61:47-51 (January 15, 1936).

CRITIQUE OF LIBRARY ASSOCIATIONS IN AMERICA*

Ralph E. Ellsworth

The relationship between a practicing professional and his or her national association is not always easy to understand, nor does it remain constant from decade to decade, nor can it be divorced from the factor of size, nor can it escape the consequences of the impact of personalities or specific events. Several specific incidents in my connection with the American Library Association, which began in 1931, will illustrate all these points.

In fact, the American Library Association began to have serious problems the year I joined it--1931. I cannot claim responsibility for being the cause of these problems, though I flatter myself by thinking I contributed my share, but it does seem to me that the American Library Association has been in a state of crisis ever since.

Experiences with ALA

1931 was the year of the Waples-Thompson debates on the question of a science of librarianship. The Carnegie Corporation had just given the University of Chicago a large grant to establish the Graduate Library School. In choosing a dean and a faculty the new school encountered difficulties with the ALA over the question of the kind of school it should be and the kind of faculty it should recruit. The ALA wanted none of the "science" business. It wanted the school to be run by people who were library-school graduates and who

*Reprinted by permission of the University of Chicago Press from Library Quarterly 31:382-395 (October 1961). Copyright 1961 by the University of Chicago Press.

would be practical.   The University of Chicago wanted to
bring scholarship to the profession and it found little or none
among the practitioners.   So it went outside the profession
and selected a dean and a faculty, most of whom had not had
the benefit of a library-school training--George Works, Douglas Waples, Pierce Butler, Louis R. Wilson, etc.   The ALA
resisted and protested.   I do not have access to the records
of correspondence and conversations (although I am sure I
could have if I wished).   However, I know that the American
Library Association Bulletin and the Library Journal were
full of angry letters of denunciation.

        Yet those of us who had the benefit of instruction and
association with that first generation of outsiders know that
the ALA was wrong.   Why was it wrong?   Because it was
dominated by thinking that did not understand scholarship, and
because it was afraid and hence emotional in its approach to
the problem of library education.

Devil in the Machine

        A second incident took place about 1936 when Douglas
Waples was in his heyday with his many studies of mass-
reading behavior.   Harper E10 was full of clacking Monroe
calculating machines and crews of National Youth Administration workers being managed by a few graduate students.
Billy Haygood had been working at ALA headquarters on some
statistical project that required the use of a calculator.   His
comments on the reaction of the ALA staff to the machine
were somewhat as follows: "Why, those women really thought
there was a devil in the machine.   They gathered around me
and were filled with awe and wonder as I ground out percentages."   They reacted much as you and I do when we visit
Mortimer Taube's Washington Ramacs at work storing bits
of knowledge.

        What's my point?   Cultural lag.

National Problems

        A third incident took place in the Drake Hotel on the
stage of a general session of the ALA during the early years
of the war.   The association was concerned about war issues.
Carl Milam leaned over to me and whispered that he had just
had a telegram from the State Department stating that Presi-

dent Roosevelt was having trouble with Congress on a matter
of our sending supplies to our Allies and needed help, and he
asked if I would introduce a resolution to indicate the association's backing of Roosevelt's position.   I did, and it was
approved and transmitted to Washington.

The point of this incident can be interpreted in several
ways.   A cynic could say that a professional association has
no business expressing its views on matters outside its professional competence.   Others could say that a national association is exactly the right organ through which professional
men and woman should express their views on national problems.   In recent years, the ALA has done little of this.

Appointment of A. MacLeish

A fourth incident occurred when President Franklin D.
Roosevelt proposed Archibald MacLeish for Librarian of Congress.   The issue was not MacLeish's competence but the
fact that he was not a professional librarian.   Although I was
not present and hence did not actually hear the statement,
the records show that at the San Francisco meeting the president of the ALA made some public statements (surely with
the blessings of the executive board) that were most unfortunate and that have embarrassed the profession ever since.

Religious Pilgrimage

A fifth and more important incident took place just before the war in the lobby of the Drake Hotel at an ALA mid-
winter meeting.   Robert Lester, then secretary of the Carnegie Corporation, Errett W. McDiarmid, and I were sitting
in the lobby watching the parade of females.   I made some
comment to the effect that it seemed pretty silly for all those
poorly paid librarians to spend their own money and time
coming to the association's meetings to sit through endless
committee sessions talking about the same old problems and
going home broke and tired.

Mr. Lester replied with a comment that revealed his
wisdom and understanding.   What he said was something like
this: "Yes, but you must understand that the American Library Association meetings are a kind of religious experience
to them.   At home they work hard, are unrewarded, not appreciated, and they feel they aren't getting any place.   They

come here in the spirit of a religious pilgrimage. They pay
25 cents for a cup of coffee, and they listen to the big shots,
and they decide things in their committee meetings, and they
feel that they have done things. The process becomes a thing
of importance in itself. " And he was right. In our time,
participation in a national association provides for many a
substitute for the kind of participation previous generations
were willing to give to the church.

The person of the executive secretary is a kind of religious symbol that proves this point. Carl Milam--able,
handsome, gray haired, strong and articulate--was a perfect
father symbol for his time. John Cory--equally able and
vigorous--probably looked too young. David Clift--equally
able and strong but not so handsome or gray haired--prob-
ably is just the right symbol at a time when the idea of the
organization man is so prominent.

I suppose one could make a good case for studying the
religious significance of the role of the headquarters. First,
in modern times, the ALA was housed in a suite of rooms in
an office building; then in a brownstone Victorian mansion;
and now, at last, symbolizing the fulfillment of the profession,
it is to have a glass and air-conditioned building of its own,
located, as always, in the geographic center of the nation
where every librarian can stop off on his way to or from a
foreign assignment or Washington where he has applied for a
grant to Verner Clapp, the Eastern Archbishop of the association.

Acting--Not Planning

A sixth incident also took place in the early years of
the war when Malcolm Wyer was president of ALA. Reflecting perhaps the influence of the New Deal years, our committees were fervently engaged in "Planning. " President Wyer
announced that we should now move into action. So all the
committee labels were changed to imply that we were "Acting. " Yet it seemed to me that we kept right on doing exactly what we had been doing under the banner of "Planning. "

The point of this incident, I suppose, is that a membership association, as we call ourselves, fulfills the needs
of its members when it is doing, or working out its destiny,
and it is the process of working-out that is the essence. Results are secondary. How else can one account for our willing-

ness to spend a large share of our time on committee assignments that go over and over the same problems, mostly with
little to show for our time? The first major task an incoming president of the association or one of its divisions faces
is making committee assignments. He tries to draw in new
blood and give everyone something to do. His second, and
final, task is to make progress reports and annual reports
of committee work. The hierarchical executive secretaries
spend most of their time spotting new names for the committees and then passing around and filing the committee reports.
The process itself becomes an end in itself.

Proof of Innocence

The seventh and last incident I shall report occurred
two years ago, when John C. Hervey, adviser to the American Bar Association Section of Legal Education and Admissions to the Bar, sent a letter about law-school libraries to
the deans of all approved law schools. In response, the Association of College and Research Libraries (ACRL) set up a
committee to look into the problem raised by Mr. Hervey's
letter and asked me to serve as chairman. What I learned
about professional associations while looking into this problem cannot be crammed into this paper, but perhaps some
of the implications can.

It has been the policy of the Association of Law
Schools (made up of deans of law schools) that each university is free to decide for itself whether law-school libraries
shall be administered as part of the university library system or as an autonomous unit directly under the dean. However, Hervey's letter, dated March 10, 1958, representing
the views not of the Association of Law Schools but of the
American Bar Association Section of Legal Education and
Admissions to the Bar, said:

> At the meeting in New York last July the Council
> determined that sound educational policy requires
> that the law faculty have autonomy over the Law
> School Library. A committee on draft was ap-
> pointed. The committee made its report at the
> meeting in Atlanta last month and the Council has
> adopted the determination following: 'The use of
> the library is an integral component of the educa-
> tional process of the law school. To assure maxi-
> mum contribution to this process it should be ad-

ministered by the Law School as an autonomous unit, free of outside control.   Exceptions are permissible only where there is preponderance of affirmative evidence in a particular school, satisfactory to the Council, that the advantages of autonomy can be preserved and economy in administration attained through centralizing the responsibility for acquisi- tion, circulation, cataloging, ordering, processing, or payment for books ordered. '

In other words, a university that wished to administer its law-school library as part of the university library sys- tem would have to prove, to the satisfaction of the council, its ability to do so.   You must be able to prove your inno- cence; the council does not have to prove your guilt.

This reversal of traditional concepts of handling inno- cence and guilt, coming as it did from lawyers, intrigued our committee and in this spirit we tackled the problem. As a first step, I sent to the committee a proposed draft of a statement that I thought we might send to university presi- dents explaining the nature of the problem and putting it in its proper setting.   Somehow this draft letter reached Mr. Hervey and also Dr. William K. Selden, executive secretary of the National Commission on Accrediting.   Dr. Selden and I then exchanged friendly letters in which I learned of the ef- forts of the National Commission on Accrediting to arbitrate matters of this kind among American universities.   I was in- vited to meet with Dr. Selden and members of the American Bar Association Council on Legal Education and some mem- bers of the section.   We did so in the main dining room of the Mayflower Hotel in Washington, and, after a round or two of refreshments, there occurred a session that probably will long be remembered by the waiters in that dining room --for the volume of sound, at least.

Law, Medicine, and Architecture

The American Bar Association Council on Legal Edu- cation--not the Association of Law Schools--had spoken on a matter of internal management in higher education.   But the council was composed of men who were not, with one excep- tion, in universities.   What I learned later was that there is a kind of Dr. Jekyll and Mr. Hyde relationship.   When the Association of Law Schools wants to apply pressure they some- times do so in the name of the American Bar Association.

The pressure device is the bar examination. Before one can join the American Bar Association he must have been admitted to the bar of one of the states in the United States. To be admitted, an individual must first pass a difficult written examination given by the state bar. The American Bar Association exercises considerable influence on the standards of these examinations. The state bar associations can, of course, disbar a lawyer as well as admit him to practice.

So here you have an example of a national association that has developed a method of imposing its will on local institutions and people by means of a state licensing agency whose standards and practices the national association can control. The quality standards of the legal profession are thus fairly well nationalized.

The American Medical Association has developed a similar pattern of control. No doctor can practice until he has been licensed by a state board. To become a recognized specialist he must also pass his national board examinations, which are controlled at the national level by the specialists in each field.

In both cases there are also special associations--the American Association of Law Schools and the Association of Medical Colleges--working on problems of professional education, and each has a great deal of power of influence in its own right, including the power of accreditation. In both the American Bar Association and the American Medical Association one finds the same inner conflicts between type of activity and form of organization that plague the American Library Association.

A third national association--the American Institute of Architects--should be considered. It consists of members and Fellows. The latter are elected, presumably on the basis of special competence or achievement. An architect cannot practice without being licensed by a state board, after a rigorous written examination. Schools of architecture are accredited not by the Institute itself but by a quasi-independent organization called the National Architectural Accrediting Board. Its members come in part from the members of the American Institute of Architects. A school can operate without this accreditation and its graduates may be licensed if they can pass the state examination, but the going is tough and every school tries to win accreditation.

The recognition of a special category of elite practitioners--the Fellows--gives a character to the American Institute of Architects that tends to emphasize special achievement. This character is almost entirely lacking in the ALA. Whatever awards we have to offer are given by special committees operating from the top of the association and thus they tend to be recognitions for length of service rather than for special merit. Nominations for Fellows of the American Institute of Architects, on the other hand, originate from a local chapter and are accompanied by careful documentation. Politics enter in, but the selection process is about as rigorous as can be imagined. The ALA's selective process, on the other hand, seems capricious and erratic and unresponsive to real demonstrations of merit.

These three national associations--the American Bar Association, the American Medical Association, and the American Institute of Architects--serve as examples of strong national organizations that possess considerable power through their state licensing boards and their national accrediting agencies. They also exert considerable influence in many other ways. Two of them--medicine and architecture--recognize special competence with appropriate titles of distinction.

In a broad spectrum, other national associations operate with varying degrees of power and influence. Power always comes from the ability to accredit schools and the ability to control admission through state agencies. Influence is exerted in a variety of ways, well known to all of us.

Universities and the Associations

Universities have long been troubled by the efforts of national associations to control the training of the professionals. For years the American Association of Universities worked on this problem through a special committee. Dr. R. G. Gustavson, when he was chancellor of the University of Nebraska, attempted to curb the power of professional accrediting bodies through the American Association of Universities. Dean Dayton McKean stated the problem well in a recent article, "Who's in Charge Here? The Universities or the Professional Associations?"[1] Until recent years no effective curbs have been developed.

The National Commission on Accrediting, created by the members of the American Association of Universities, exists for the purpose of trying to teach national associations how they can best get the results they want without at the same time harming the freedom of universities to run their own shows. The commission has no power, except the power of persuasion and education. My experience with them on the law-library problems taught me that the process of educating national associations is a long, slow exercise in patience and tact, especially with those that appear to be dominated by people who are not directly connected with colleges and universities. The ALA, I judge, would be thought of as one of the more reasonable national associations on the problem of professional education. But what can be said on a recent resolution passed by the Pennsylvania Library Association?

Recognizing that an effective educational program at the college level requires intelligent and efficient use of a variety of educational materials to meet curricular demands, be it resolved:

That the Executive Board of the Pennsylvania Library Association request the Middle Atlantic States Association of Colleges and Secondary Schools and the Library Education Division of the American Library Association to recommend that library orientation, covering formal instruction in the use of books and libraries, be required of all freshmen; and further that credit be given for such a course. [2]

Problem of Diverse Interests

Let us return now to the problem of what I learned about national library associations from the law-library experience. Many attempts have been made over the years to bring all library associations into one national library association under the name of the American Library Association. I have attended more than one meeting in which representatives of the various associations tried to exchange views, but I had not really comprehended what the ALA looks like to others until I had worked with the law librarians.

Naturally, in a group of libraries as large as the American Association of Law Libraries one finds all kinds of people and all shades of views. I was surprised and pleased to find so many who would like to be a part of the ALA. But to my amazement, they felt that the ALA was

now so complex and bureaucratic and so involved with processes they they could not possibly establish a base within it.

The Association of Research Libraries

This is not a new complaint. The Association of Research Libraries (ARL) was established long ago, when the
ALA was relatively small and simple, because the libraries
of large universities and other research libraries did not
want to waste their time and efforts with the machinery of
the ALA. The lure of having a small exclusive club may
have been a factor, but, I am convinced, that was not the
major reason for the separation of the Association of Research
Libraries.

In fact, at the time of the last Cleveland meeting of
ALA and ARL in 1950 I tried very hard to persuade ARL to
realign its structure, membership, and operations so that it
would no longer drain off talent and monopoly on certain
problems in such a way as to weaken the Association of College and Research Libraries. But many of my colleagues in
the ARL (and on this point Frank Lundy has spoken bluntly
and truthfully)[3] told me that I was wrong, that it was a waste
of time to work through the ACRL and the ALA and that a
smaller group of men with common problems could do more
with less wasted effort outside these two associations.

My experiences with various projects--the dissertations
publications plan and the Committee on Resources--have prov-
en the validity of their claims. When ARL wants to work on
a project, they can pick the right men, go at the problem directly, and get the job done. But when the Committee on
Resources goes at a job (the publication of the 1952-55 segment of the National Union Catalog, for example), it must
first get approval through the ponderous machinery of the
ALA. This takes time and effort that few busy men are
willing to expend. Actually, our resources committee gets
its job done by going underground, so to speak, and acting
as part of the ARL. Eventually, to everyone's embarrassment, the ALA's approval comes along. The ARL can keep
continuity of committee membership, but the ALA cannot. It
must pass the work around. Major problems that the ARL
thinks worth tackling cut across ALA divisional lines and the
provinces of executive secretaries, and the process of thread-
ing the maze is more time-consuming than most of us like
to admit.

Thus I found that the members of the American Association of Law Libraries feel that it is impossible to establish a home within ALA without at the same time losing their identity or wasting their time. They do not feel that they are any better than school or public libraries, but their interests are different and they feel uncomfortable in the presence of so many other kinds of librarians.

This, of course, is what has bothered members of ACRL for so many years as a group within ALA. At the time of the Buffalo ALA, when Blanch McCrum was president of the Association of College and Research Libraries and when Charles Brown, Errett W. McDiarmid, and I were members of a committee that was leading a revolt (which came within an inch of succeeding) our argument was that ACRL could never thrive as long as its headquarters staff had to do its work through the ALA's central staff. We thought the executive secretary of ACRL should be located in a university where he and his staff could keep close to the actual operations of a library. We were not uninterested in, or unsympathetic toward, the common problems of all librarians--freedom of speech, federal legislation, international relations, and the welfare of libraries as such--nor were we unwilling to work in the name of ALA for these major issues and for other issues that were important to other types of libraries, but we did object to the inevitable dilution of our own special kind of organization. We felt such dilution could not be avoided if our headquarters were at ALA headquarters and if control of our own affairs were, in part, in the hands of other kinds of librarians.

Time has, I think, proven that we were right. The ALA's last attempt to reconcile the elements of type of library and type of activity might have worked twenty years ago; but today, partly because of the size of the organization and partly because of the temper of the time, it has had the effect of magnifying the importance of type of activity at the expense of the integrity of type of library. This is fatal because it will not only prevent the bringing of other types of libraries--for example, law and special libraries--into the ALA, but it is creating a mood which may drive some types out of the association. School libraries are on their way, and college and university libraries are exceedingly restive.

Enlargement of ARL

A new matter has recently come up that bears on this

point.   The ARL has made a practice of reviewing its composition and nature every five years.   A special committee
usually studies the problem and reports to the association
at the end of each fourth year of the five-year span.   The
report to be submitted this year at Cleveland reads as follows:

> During the course of these meetings [with the Na-
> tional Science Foundation] it became evident that
> ARL as now constituted--both because of limited
> membership and operational restrictions--cannot
> speak for research libraries.   In short, ARL does
> not at present fill a need that is being expressed
> with greater frequency as government, foundations,
> and the scholarly world become ever more aware
> of the need for unbounded access to organized
> knowledge.   It is clear that there is no other na-
> tional organization which can adequately or properly
> represent the large research libraries of the coun-
> try....
>
> Evidence of recent years affirms the fact that the
> Association of College and Research libraries is
> primarily an organization of individuals rather than
> of institutions.   It is inherently restricted in pro-
> gram development since it is one of many units of
> a larger organization.   The voice of research li-
> braries must be forceful and direct.

To meet this need the committee recommends that
ARL expand its membership, establish a full-time secretari-
at, accumulate a larger budget, and go to work.   If this is
done, then ACRL will find that its University section will be
weakened and it will become a group that has nice programs
at ALA meetings, and that's about all.   It is my judgment
that if the plan I am going to propose had been adopted years
ago, ACRL could have become the national spokesman for
research and other interests of higher education.

Complex Organization

As incoming president of the Association of College
and Research Libraries, I have had the opportunity this year
to read the correspondence of past presidents and of the work
of ACRL's executive secretary.   There is simply too much
machinery to be worked, too many people to consult, too many

reports to be made, too many boards to be convinced. It
just is not worth the struggle, nor is it worth the cost.

Worse, this kind of complex organization provides a
fertile breeding ground for the type of organizational man who
will think up projects like the little folder--prepared for National Library Week--which on the cover had a picture of a
red arrow pointing from the page of a book to the mind of a
reader to his heart. This kind of symbolism is not very
different from the motto of the Nazis who said: "We think
with our blood." It may be good public library promotion--
though I doubt it--but for academic librarians it is anathema.
It has become a symbol for the watershed over which, I think,
our thinking will split.

Some of us thought Schulz in his Peanuts cartoons expressed the situation pretty well. As you recall, one day
Charlie Brown said that he always takes out a book during
National Library Week "because it does something for the
morale of librarians. Librarians like to feel needed." The
next day Charlie Brown said, "I took out a book from the
library. The librarian was so excited. She kept shuffling
through all those cards on her desk, and then she'd move
her ink pad back and forth and she stamped everything in
sight. I feel that for at least one librarian I have made National Library Week a complete success."

The same kind of thinking happened with the draft of
the Code of Ethics for Librarians that was proposed this
year. It was unacceptable to the ACRL's Board of Directors
because it was sentimental and sloppy. It was the inevitable
result of a national professional organization that has lost
its sense of national purpose, not because the people who
make it up have lost their senses, but because the very structure of the organization puts them in relationships that prevent them from speaking sensibly.

The Council of National Library Associations has been
an organization that most of us could not take seriously. It
seemed to meet somewhere in the East once a year and to
appoint committees that issued wordy and ponderous reports
signifying nothing. One of the traditional horseplay jokes in
ARL has been the annual appointment of a delegate to the
council. Yet, I found, much to my surprise, that some of
the law librarians felt that they could more easily establish
a base in the council than they could in ALA.

Others besides the law librarians have felt more comfortable outside the ALA. Although I have never been a member of the Special Libraries Association, I am not unaware of the fact that they have generated a sense of professional cohesion and purpose that the ALA lacks. That is certainly true in the Denver area.

The Problem Is Size

Now we must be careful not to become confused and to place blame where it does not belong. We should, first of all, take a hard look at the factor of size. Universities with student enrollment of 20,000 are quite different in terms of their allegiances from universities that have 10,000 students.

I suspect that the American Library Association may be trying to pretend that it can be the same kind of organization it was when it had not 25,000 but 10,000 members and when the spirit of specialization was much less strong than it is today. I know that attending an annual ALA conference now so large that it can meet in only a few cities (and then on a very dispersed basis) is quite different from what it was when the ALA was only half as large. I know that filling out an ALA election ballot now when a majority of the names are only names--not people I know--is a frustrating and unhappy experience--one that breeds disrespect for the organization. If each of us had to vote for the senators and representatives in all the states I venture to predict that our federal government would cease to exist as we know it today. To be sure, we can all vote for the president and the vice-president because we can personalize this act.

We are pleased that there are so many librarians and we hope the ranks will increase in size and quality, but this should not blind us to the need for modifying our pattern of organization so as to retain the quality of our personal relationship to the national organization. Size creates problems of personal involvement. Nor do we think we can escape the influence of size by shifting the emphasis to state or regional chapters, although that may be a good thing to do for its own sake. For some kinds of libraries, and I imagine this would be true of law, medical, and university libraries, local associations are less important than are national ones because our problems are national in nature. There are local problems to be solved, and it is at the local level that we can best appreciate the interdependence of all types of libraries; but we cannot solve our big problems at the local level, for we need contact with our colleagues all over the country, not just the ones we meet all year. The regional associations may be strong in some parts of the country, but in the Rockies they constitute just another annual convention we think we ought to attend just to be good joes.

Professional Maturity

The second factor--professional status or maturity-- also needs examination. I mentioned earlier that several of the national associations were strong in part because they could control admission and practicing at the state level by licensing--the associations of physicians, lawyers, architects, for example. But we librarians have not been able to persuade all state legislatures that possession of a library-school degree is essential. How can we do this when it is obvious to all that some of our best college and university librarians have never attended a library school--Archibald MacLeish, Fred Wagman, James Babb, Charles David, William Dix, to mention only a few. In fact, unless I am mistaken, the dean of one of our library schools, Jack Dalton, has no library-school degree. This is not to say that professional library training is bad, or unnecessary. Our Robert Millers, Herman Fusslers, Lawrence Powells, and Robert Vospers prove that it is valuable. Nor is it to say that the Fred Wagmans would not be better librarians if they had had library-school training. But in the presence of such various preparations--among college and university libraries, at least--it is hard to make a case for airtight accreditation or licensing.

School and public librarians have, in their respective areas, been able to go further in licensing. The school librarians, by working through the regional accrediting associations for schools, have been able to do the most.

It can be argued that the ALA through its accrediting power over library schools has, during the last twenty-five years, raised the level of librarianship and I would agree. But do not forget that the same group fought the establishment of the kind of school the University of Chicago Graduate Library School became. Although I do not see how one could prove it, it seems obvious to me that it has been the Graduate Library School, through the influence its graduates

have exerted, that has been the major factor in raising the
quality level of library education in the United States, not
the ALA.

Likewise, I would argue that it was the dynamic action of Archibald MacLeish, who quickly focused national attention on the salaries of the Library of Congress staff, who
started the salary levels upward (plus the influence of infla-
tion and the laws of supply and demand since World War II)
--not ALA's Board on Personnel.   At best, the role of the
ALA in this respect has been minor.   And that should surprise no one.

Under the heading of status and maturity one would
have to mention the influence of studies, such as the Public
Library Inquiry.   Unfortunately, there is no way of evaluating
the effect of such studies.   Coming as they did at a time
when all community services were expanding, it is impossible
to judge their relative influence.   It would be best to assume
that they did have a positive effect, but not to give them too
much credit.

But would one argue that advances in medical care in
the United States came about as the result of the American
Medical Association?   Indeed not!   In fact, a good case
could be made for the argument that the American Medical
Association has held back the progress of some kinds of
medical care and is still doing so.   It should be obvious
that it has been the results of research in the medical sciences and of better teaching in the medical schools that have
been primarily responsible for advances in medical care, not
to mention the fact that we Americans have had the money
to pay for it.

And in the field of architecture, would you say that it
was the influence of the Institute, or the fact that we have
had an influx of European architects plus some good ones of
our own, that has given us some good architecture lately?

And, come to think of it, isn't it true that most of
the important new ideas in academic librarianship have come,
not from the ALA, but from the ARL or from the minds of
imaginative individuals?   The Farmington Plan, the Midwest Inter-Library Center, centralized processing, microphotography, modular planning, undergraduate libraries are a
few examples.

Or, would it be better to say that the ALA, as an organization, is primarily an expression of the public library institution in the United States?

Positive Contributions of ALA

Let us turn now to the positive contributions the ALA has made and see what can be learned from these.

First, I would point to the defense of intellectual freedom. Here the record is clear, brilliant, and important. It is also too well known to require enumeration. This was an ALA contribution. Carl Milam and his successors in the office of executive secretary deserve the most credit. The ALA membership wanted to defend intellectual freedom, and it did so through its national organizations and its committees.

Second, I would point to the activities of ALA on the international front. Again, the wisdom of Carl Milam and his predecessors and successors led them to stress this work. I should imagine that they deserve the credit for convincing our government to establish information libraries all over the world and for seeing to it that all kinds of American influence and help were given. The role of the two Librarians of Congress, MacLeish and Evans, in office during the war years, was also important.

Third, I would point to federal relations. This too is clearly an accomplishment for ALA.

Fourth, I would point to the promotion of the public library as an adult-education agency as an example of an activity that would not have been carried out without a national organization such as the ALA.

Fifth, we can all be proud of the fact that ALA has a fine record on lack of racial discrimination. The Jew has had a better break in the field of librarianship than he has had in the field of teaching. ALA's position on racial discrimination has been a good one and the association's leadership has made this possible.

Future Role of ALA

How then can we generalize about the role of the asso-

ciation as a national organization representing the profession
of librarianship? It has not succeeded in representing all
librarianship. It is not the single spokesman for librarianship. But it shares this weakness with many of the other
professions--like higher education and medicine. What would
it have to do to become a truly national spokesman? It is
my opinion that it would have to change its nature, point of
view, and organizational structure and that it would be wise
to do so now before time runs out.

A Federation

First, the ALA would have to become a true federation of library organizations--such as the Council of National
Library Associations is in name. It should keep the name
"American Library Association" but should become the central holding company for a series of already existing associations of types of libraries--public, school, academic, special,
law, medical, private, etc., etc. It should force the dissolution of the organizations that represent types of activity and
it should force the subordination of these activities into the
types of libraries where they belong.

It should encourage the independence of the national
associations of types of libraries in all ways possible--phys-
ical, financial, and operational. The collective governing
officers of these associations should be the policy-forming
and governing body of ALA. The dues collected by the associations making up the association would provide it with the
funds it would need to carry on the types of over-all activities,
mentioned above, that the association can perform successfully for all librarianship.

In this kind of an organization, each and every librarian could give his allegiance to his type of library association knowing that by so doing he was a part of the over-all
national library association. No library association would
need to remain out of the ALA for fear of losing its integrity
or of being uncomfortable.

The Council of National Library Associations could be
dissolved. Possibly the ARL could become a nice cozy club
devoted to the pleasures of the cup, the plate, and the comfortable chair.

Academic librarians would not need to be worried about

being dominated by public libraries, or vice versa, because each would be autonomous. If the Public Library Association wants to promote National Library Weeks and to publish brochures asking people to cultivate their minds through their hearts, well and good. If the ACRL wants to be stuffy, well and good. If the American Association of School Librarians wants to affiliate with the National Education Association, let it do it. If some types of libraries want to establish various categories of membership based on achievement, let them do it.

They would all want to remain as part of that kind of an "American Library Association" because they will believe in the association's doing the kinds of things they will ask the association to do and they will therefore be willing to pay for the carrying out of these functions. Such an "American Library Association" is the kind of national organization I think all librarians want the American Library Association to become.

Points of Emphasis

Second, ALA has succeeded in exerting considerable influence on national policy in certain areas--intellectual freedom, racial discrimination, international exchange of information, and federal aid to libraries and adult education-- by intelligently applying effort and talent and by setting a good example. These things the ALA could continue to do if it were organized in the manner I described just as well as it can today.

Third, it has succeeded in winning the emotional allegiance of librarians in certain types of libraries--primarily public--but not all types. If the ALA were to become the kind of organization I outlined, it would not lose any of the emotional attachments it now has, and it would stand a good chance of drawing into its influence several types of library associations that now will have nothing to do with the ALA.

Fourth, leadership in several areas that were once closely mothered by the association--such as library education and professional achievement--have now matured and have passed into other hands. The library schools themselves are generating the new thinking that is giving vitality to library education. Professional ideas of merit do not come from the ALA any more but from the large number of able and imagina-

tive practitioners like Ralph Shaw, Mortimer Taube, Jesse
Shera, John Cronin, Fred Wagman, and Herman Fussler--to
mention only a few names in the field of academic librarianship.

In fact, the ALA personnel has become preoccupied
with the machinery of the association. David Clift never has
time any more to raise his eyes above the brawling of his
brood to contemplate the directions of actual libraries. The
various executive secretaries in the association are busy with
ALA business, most of which is self-generating in nature.
Symbolic of this attitude is the statement of the May, 1961,
ALA Bulletin in the memorandum to members section. "The
Council on Library Resources, Inc. has recently announced
a grant of $210,652 for the continuation of the Library Tech-
nology Project through April 30, 1962. These funds will
permit the addition of three new positions to the project staff
and will also make possible a move to larger quarters in the
vicinity of the Headquarters" (italics mine). As though the
permitting of the addition of new positions and the making
possible a move to larger quarters were the purpose of the
grant! Of course, I know that was not the intent of the statement, but that's the point. It is the subconscious levels of
thinking, or the real assumptions, that I am talking about.

Radical Surgery

I have serious doubts of the wisdom of letting a national association get into this kind of a fix. It can only become more complex and more bureaucratic and further removed from reality if it is allowed to go on as is. Radical
surgery is called for. The whole complex, interlocking nonsense of council and executive board operations could be replaced by a simple governing board consisting of the collective officers of the constituent library associations.

Disperse the executive secretaries and house them in
real libraries, and they will learn to cut out meaningless activity.

The remaining essential central secretariat--even including the central publication office might not need to occupy
more than a few of the offices in ALA's new headquarters.
The rest could be rented to other associations that have not
yet learned the wisdom of simplicity.

The radical surgery need not result in the killing of the kinds of activities my analysis shows that an organization like ALA is capable of performing. These things--sponsoring federal legislation, publishing, international projects, intellectual freedom, etc.--would continue to be done both at the central headquarters and in the headquarters of the constituent library associations, some of which could be at ALA quarters and most of which would be located elsewhere.

Much of the sound and fury which we mistakenly think of as the American Library Association would dry up and never be heard from again, because it is nothing more than the clanking of the machinery of the association.

The other noises we might begin to hear would be the sounds of librarianship--teachers, researchers, catalogers, reference librarians, children's librarians, administrators, documentalists, etc.--all hard at work. That would be the true sound of the American Library Association.

NOTES

1. Colorado Quarterly, VII (1958), 395-408.

2. College and Research Libraries, XXII (May, 1961), 261.

3. Personal letter from Lundy to Ellsworth.

DO WE WANT A LIBRARY SCIENCE?*

C. Seymour Thompson

Many times in the last few years I have asked myself a question which I have usually answered with a negative-- Have we a library science? Apparently many others have been entertaining the same doubt. In 1928 Mr. Roden, in his presidential address before the American Library Association, referred to the two library schools which were planning "to devote a major portion of their time to--extensive research into the principles, if any, that underlie our practice."[1] In the first number of the Library Quarterly Dr. Williamson tells us that the new school at Columbia was named a "school of library service," rather than a school of library science, to evade the question whether library work can be accurately called a science.[2] Dr. Waples, in the same number of the Quarterly, shows that it is the fixed intention of the Graduate Library School of the University of Chicago to develop for us a science of librarianship, but warns us that many years will be required for the full achievement of this ambition.[3] It seems that we have become pretty well agreed that we have not now a library science, but we are apparently determined that we will have one; like the newly rich who was told that he had no savoir faire, and immediately said "I will get one, I don't care what it costs." Yet I must confess, I fear, to a perverse disposition. As I have pondered over the course which we seem now to be following, I have added to my original question another--Do we want a library science?

Dr. John Dewey says: "Science signifies, I take it,

*Reprinted by permission from Library Journal 56:581-587 (1931). Published by the R. R. Bowker Co. (a Xerox company). Copyright © 1931 by R. R. Bowker Co.

the existence of systematic methods of inquiry, which, when
they are brought to bear on a range of facts, enable us to
understand them better and to control them more intelligently,
less haphazardly and with less routine."[4] But unless we take
these words in a much broader sense than their context indicates the author intended, as to both the "systematic methods of inquiry" and the "range of facts," they provide only
for applied science and not for the theoretical. Such a concept would exclude, for example, the fundamental, most vital
elements of political science. Our definition of science should
be reasonably exacting, yet moderately conservative; not restricting the field to the exact sciences, but confining it to
those subjects which are characterized by scientific qualities,
as the word scientific is commonly understood in the intellectual world. Chief among these qualities, I think, are patience and thoroughness in investigation and study, and a constant habit of systematic, logical thinking and reasoning.
We must expect of a science that it shall not merely give
evidence of a bit of scientific method here and there, but
that its entire work shall be performed in a manner which
can be properly termed scientific. We must expect that the
principles on which it is based and the knowledge which it
has accumulated shall have been methodically formulated and
systematized. But we should remember that sound, fundamental principles, no less truly than minute facts, can be
scientific; that scientific method may rely upon careful study
and correct thought, without employing the microscope or any
system of exact measurement.

     That we have developed in the library profession a
considerable body of knowledge, or rather, of technique and
opinion, there can be no doubt. How much of this can be
classed as science is open to argument. For classification
and cataloging, I believe we can justly claim at least a hum-
ble place among the sciences; we may speak of the science of
classification, the science of cataloging. Can we say as much
for our administrative system in general? It has some scientific aspects. It is controlled very largely by a few fundamental principles which have been widely accepted, have
demonstrated their soundness, and are no more subject to
change than are the principles of other sciences, such as
medicine, supposedly much more exact. Yet a very large
part of our practice is based on haphazard experimentation;
much of it has resulted from hasty, superficial consideration,
rather than from precise thought; too much of it is governed
by local conditions or by tradition or whim or accident; much
of it has been somewhat methodically formulated, but mainly

in a pragmatic fashion which shows little resemblance to a
rational system. We may have a good foundation on which a
science can be built, but it can hardly be said that in our
administration and service as a whole we have yet developed
a science.

Hitherto, with or without science, I think we have done
exceedingly well, but in the future we must do even better.
Before we rashly conclude that our present shortcomings are
due to empirical methods, let us become introspective, for
I believe it is scientific to diagnose the cause of an ailment
before prescribing a remedy. What is the most important,
basic qualification for librarianship? Dr. Waples thinks no-
body will deny that librarianship is "primarily a social enterprise."[5] But everything is social; and I think it is more accurate and more salutary to consider it as primarily an educational enterprise, even though in some phases the sociological element may be predominant. If librarianship is primarily an educational profession, its fundamental and dominat-
ing purpose must be educational; if its principal purpose is
educational, the most important qualification for a librarian
must be--education. More specifically, for education is a
broad word, our purpose is what Mr. Jewett described in
1853 as "the diffusion of a knowledge of good books, and enlarging the means of public access to them."[6] Does it not
follow, then, that the most important qualification for librarianship, the qualification that must underlie all others, is "a
knowledge of good books," with the high standards of education which that presupposes?

The report of the A. L. A. Survey in 1926 showed that
in the large public libraries less than 24 per cent of the professional employees were college graduates, and in the large
college and university libraries less than 58 per cent.[7] In
1927 the Bureau of Public Personnel Administration gave this
summary--eloquent in its brevity--of the conditions its study
had revealed:

> In many of the smaller libraries, and particularly
> in the public libraries where only one, two, or
> three persons are employed, the library workers
> as a rule do not have the education, library train-
> ing, library experience, and other qualifications es-
> sential for the effective performance of the duties of
> their positions. In the large and in many of the
> medium size libraries--there [are] very few library
> workers engaged in professional work with less than

a high school education, many with college training
or technical library school equipment, or both, and
a low proportion with a college education including
or supplemented by a technical library course one
or two years in length. 8

At the very point where we should be strongest, we
seem to find our greatest weakness.   I do not forget that the
very small public libraries and extension agencies are doing
work of such a nature that to talk of high educational attainments and extensive knowledge of books would be absurd.
But these form only a single phase of library work, and it
is not belittling their importance to say that they cannot be
considered as typical in estimating the nature and the needs
of librarianship in the United States.   Nor do I forget the
goodly number of men and of women in the profession to
whom the following statement does not apply.   But, considering the field as a whole, we librarians, as a class, are not
possessed of sufficiently high educational attainments; we are
not, as a class, distinguished for a knowledge of good books.
That is a statement, I believe, which we cannot deny, if we
are honest and candid; and if we are conscientious, we shall
earnestly and unremittingly seek a remedy.

Low salaries cannot be considered the only cause of
the fact that our educational standards are not higher, and
we will do well to cease attributing all our deficiencies to
inadequate compensation.   The underlying, ultimate cause is
the fact that we ourselves have too generally undervalued educational qualifications.   We have, indeed, held pretty stead-
fastly to the high purpose which was so well expressed by
Mr. Jewett, and that, to me, is the most encouraging fact
in American library history.   But because of the rapidity and
the practicality of our growth we have not always retained a
correct sense of values; we have too often esteemed quantity
above quality, and have allowed secondary purposes and secondary qualifications to assume primary importance.   In developing a body of administrative method adequate to meet
the needs of the new ideals of service, for a long period we
placed an exaggerated emphasis on technique and routine,
from which we have not yet entirely recovered.   In developing service of more practical value to practical people--which
made a good slogan for initial experiments in publicity--and
in trying to prove that we were of actual dollars and cents
value, we lost much of the older admiration for the cultural
value of the library, for we did not succeed in adding the
new ideal to the old without displacing some of the former.

Then came the day of "efficiency" in business, and we rallied to the cry for efficiency in library administration. This,
too, was well, for everyone will admit that our libraries
must be efficiently administered, but it had an unfortunate
by-product. To prove that our administration was efficient
and business-like, we had to prove that we ourselves were
keen, efficient executives, engaged in a business of no small
importance. The fear of being called academic increased.
We had plenty of admiration then, and we have today, for
the small number of scholars in our profession, but not the
kind of admiration that inspires emulation. The men most
emulated were, and are today, the successful business men,
the men of executive genius, the men who do big things, --
the live wires. Yes, our libraries must have efficient, business-like administration; but I hate to think of a librarian
being known chiefly as a live wire. It is not good for an
educational profession; for one that likes to call itself a
learned profession.

The chief need of the library profession, in my opinion, is a revival of the bibliothecal spirit. This can be
brought about without sacrificing anything that we have gained
in perfection of method, in practicality of service, in efficiency of administration. I believe that one most desirable
means to this end is a distinction, as clear-cut as it can be
made, not only between the clerical positions and the professional, but between the clerical duties which cannot be divorced from the professional positions and what we call their
professional duties. Other measures which have been proposed and tried for increasing our educational efficiency, I
cannot discuss here. The chief remedy lies, I believe, in
cultivating a proper conception of the primary purpose of
our work and the primary qualifications. Let us cease trying to be what we are not, what we are not supposed to be,
and what we cannot be with any noteworthy degree of success.
Let us be content to be librarians--as business-like and efficient as possible, an active influence in community life, but,
above everything else, librarians. There is no danger that
the pendulum may swing back too far toward the point from
which it has come. And if every member of the ALA became convinced that his or her success as a librarian depended, more than on anything else, on improvement in educational equipment and in knowledge of books; that, although
these alone are not sufficient, and must be supplemented by
many other essentials, they still remain primary and fundamental, we should have no cause for concern whether librarianship is or is not a science.

But there are many who will not agree with me in this. Many eminent authorities are saying that empirical methods have done well enough, perhaps, in the past, but have carried us as far as they can. Dr. Williamson, for example, tells us that "empirical thinking and empirical methods--are not scientific and are rapidly being discarded in every other important field of knowledge and service"; that "--in education, in business and industry, in social service--everywhere except in the library field--extensive programs of research are being carried out, highly organized and well financed"; and that "if the library is to rise to its opportunity as a social institution and educational force it must--begin very soon to attack its problems by a thoroughgoing application of the spirit and methods of research that are being found so effective in every other field. "9

With the very highest respect for the learning and the ability of Dr. Williamson, I find it impossible to accept this view of the question. Regardless of what may have been accomplished by the new research in other fields, the entire argument by comparison with these other vocations seems to me somewhat fallacious. Our problems, our circumstances, and, particularly, our aims and purposes, differ so greatly from those of business that the analogy here is not trustworthy. And I question the reliability of the comparison with education, closely akin to teaching as our work may be, for the kinship is one of educational purpose alone, and not at all one of problems, conditions, or methods. Furthermore, I am not convinced that scientific research in education has yet demonstrated its value conclusively enough to serve as a model. Certainly in a very large number of the research studies that are being published every month it is difficult to recognize even a potential value. I will cite only one example, which may be of special interest to librarians. A scientific study was made of "the specific illegibilities found in the writing of Arabic numerals. " It demonstrated two things: that both children and adults frequently make illegible figures, and that some figures are made illegible more frequently than others. One remedial procedure was suggested: that the figure 5 should be written with one stroke of the pen; and the author naively states "there is a possibility that this method is used by certain librarians" since the handbook of the New York State Library School, more than thirty years before this scientific study was made, had contained a direction that all figures should be made without lifting the pen. 10 Much good may have been accomplished, and more may be accomplished in the future, by educational research, but the

science, if it is a science, is still in a crudely experimental
stage. Shall we not wait, at least until it has emerged a little further, before we accept the argument that we must copy
its methods?

Even less convincing is an argument advanced by Dr.
John Dewey, on behalf of scientific methods, and cited approv-
ingly by Dr. Waples in relation to librarianship. Dewey says:

> The existence of scientific method protects us also
> from a danger that attends the operations of men of
> unusual power; dangers of slavish imitation partisan-
> ship, and such jealous devotion to them and their
> work as to get in the way of further progress. Any-
> body can notice today that the effect of an original
> and powerful teacher is not all to the good. Those
> influenced by him often show a one-sided interest;
> they tend to form schools, and to become impervi-
> ous to other problems and truths; they incline to
> swear by the words of their master and to go on
> repeating his thoughts after him, and often without
> the spirit and insight that originally made them sig-
> nificant. [11]

Are we going to be frightened by a bugbear like that?
Of course, we do not want slavish, uncritical acceptance of
any man's ideas, but in this iconoclastic, skeptical age the
danger of this is surely insignificant. The argument is specious and factitious; unworthy of a scientific mind, altogether
unworthy of acceptance by the library profession. Has the
world been the worse for Socrates and Plato and Aristotle?
For Pestalozzi and Herbart and Froebel and Spencer? Apply
it to the library profession. To what extent have we suffered
from "slavish imitation partisanship?" Did "jealous devotion"
to Melvil Dewey and his work "get in the way of further
progress?" Have we been the worse for Cutter and Green
and Poole, to mention but a few of the pioneers? Or for
John Cotton Dana, to mention one who has most recently left
us? Yet we shall soon, probably, have a scientific study,
culminating in a doctoral thesis, on "The Dangers Inherent in
the Presence of Great Men in our Midst. "

Something of the nature of the proposed science of librarianship can be learned from the list of "problems under
investigation at the Graduate Library School, University of
Chicago. " Some of these problems, I gladly admit, are excellent, but they are mainly those listed under the heading

"historical," rather than those which seem to be most representative of the school's principal purpose. From most of
the studies thus far announced little good can come, so far
as I can see, to the library profession,--certainly not enough
good to compensate for the harm they will do. In considering
the following "research projects," remember the statement
made by the director of the school, that the student's individual research on his chosen problem "is the nucleus" of his
"entire program."[12] "Evaluation for interest of topics discussed in contemporary magazines by representative groups
of adults." Assuming, rashly, that reliable and significant
data can be compiled which will prove that certain classes
are more interested in some of the topics than in others, in
what way will this increase the value of our service? "Comparison of actual reading in non-fiction with interest in non-
fiction topics for representative groups." If it is discovered,
by some scientific process not yet known by ordinary librarians, that the non-fiction which people read relates to topics
in which they are not interested, what are we going to do
about it? "Comparative study of costs of books in various
classes of literature represented in small college libraries."
When it is demonstrated that books in some classes of literature cost more than books in some other classes, shall we
"stock" more heavily in the cheaper classes and discontinue
the other "line?" This would, indeed, be a unique contribution to the principles of book selection, which the empirical
librarian would not have produced in a long time. "Comparison of professional activities performed by school librarians
with activities performed by teachers for corresponding grades,
evaluation of activities for importance, and consensus to estimate appropriate responsibility of teacher and librarian in respect to each type of activity." This seems to imply--but no,
I will not undertake to elucidate it. "Measurement of vocabulary difficulty in ALA subject headings for representative
groups of public-library patrons." Quite palpably this was inspired by the thought that since vocabulary-difficulty studies
have become popular, and undoubtedly useful, in the teaching
of languages, there should be a place for them in library science, and that the place must be found.

More concrete evidence of the aid which scientific research promises to bring to librarianship is found in an article entitled "Propaganda and Leisure Reading: a method by
which to identify and offset propaganda in students' leisure
reading,"[13] written by the Director of the Graduate Library
School in Chicago and based on data collected by one of the
students. Its thesis is that a college should do everything

possible to protect the student against the insidious and powerful propaganda which assails him from novels, plays, moving
pictures and other popular media--propaganda involving sex,
militarism, crime, business ethics, personal ideals, and other problems. "In order to identify types of sex situations
presented in plays, novels, and moving pictures, respective-
ly," an analysis and classification was made of 266 recent
plays, 226 novels, and 122 films. Twenty-seven "typical situations" were ferreted out and divided into three groups--
Unconventional, Conventional, and Unclassified. Among the
"unconventional" situations are divorce, bigamy, social ostra-
cism, secret marriage, and ten even less pleasant forms of
departure from what the scientists regard as conventional.
The "conventional" group includes only three "situations"--
love, conventional marriage, and chivalry. "Situations"
which appear as "unclassified," since the investigators were
uncertain whether they are conventional or unconventional include marital unhappiness, broken engagements, jealousy,
relatives' interference, vamping, and flirtation. A table presents, in percentages, the frequency with which each of the
twenty-seven "situations" appears in plays, in novels, and in
moving pictures, and the "median frequency" is established.
But no mere abstract can do justice to the scientific method
by which all this is done. The conclusions reached are more
important than the methods followed. Dr. Waples says:

> The problem of supplying deficiencies in the infor-
> mation obtained by students from casual sources is
> almost entirely a problem of providing material for
> the students' leisure reading. It is thus a problem
> for college librarians to take seriously. --A solution
> would consist of three steps: first, preparing
> through faculty cooperation a list of the personal
> and social issues [such as flirtation, jealousy,
> bigamy, and divorce] that immediately concern stu-
> dents and which are not specifically treated by one
> department; second, analyzing the elements of each
> issue as presented in popular media--plays, novels,
> story magazines, films, and radio--to determine the
> relative emphasis given to each element with a view
> to selecting the elements omitted or insufficiently or
> improperly represented; and third, providing on dis-
> play shelves in students' reading rooms or the col-
> lege library such fiction or interesting non-fiction
> as may be found to present such elements adequate-
> ly.

Further studies of the presentation of sex are in progress at Chicago, and it is hinted that similar studies may
be made later of other issues.   How these researches will
revolutionize the selection of books!   To fight propaganda
with propaganda, for, notwithstanding Dr. Waples' disclaimer,
this is what his article advocates.   To base our open-shelf,
best-book collections, not on the purpose of cultivating appreciation of books and broad acquaintance with literature in all
its branches, as we have hitherto done in our happy, unscientific fashion, but on the idea of promoting the reading of
books which present certain elements of sex or crime or business ethics or what not, which we consider "omitted or insufficiently or improperly represented" in other propagandist
media.   In such ways would scientific research promote "the
diffusion of a knowledge of good books."

This article may be taken as typical of the research
studies which, in a few years, when we have enough trained
scientists and doctors of philosophy, will fill our library periodicals.   Each one will be written in the same keenly analytic style; bloodless and utterly de-personalized; as cold and
unsympathetic as the case records of a hospital; appreciative
of nothing but minute facts, or supposed facts, their analysis
and presentation under the guise of science.   This is a conception of science and of librarianship which, if unrestrained,
will stifle all true appreciation of books and of people, the
two things which make library work a joy and an opportunity,
and will develop a generation of librarians who will perceive
not the opportunity and cannot know the joy.   Dr. Waples says
that the problem of propaganda is one which the college librarian must take seriously.   I maintain that all librarians
must take seriously the entire, larger problem of introducing
this idea of scientific research into the profession of librarianship.   We should hear, from all sides, an earnest, emphatic,
serious protest against this new conception of librarianship
which is being thrust upon us.

"Do we want a library science?"   This question involves far more than the intrinsic value of a few specific
studies.   It involves the fundamental purpose of the endeavors
to develop a science of librarianship, and the effect these endeavors will have on the profession.   Dr. Williamson predicts
that the day may come when readers' advisers will "when requested administer scientific intelligence tests, aptitude tests,
comprehension tests, etc., and on the basis of scientific findings prescribe a program of reading"; when "for many adult
patrons the public library will have on file psychological and

other personal data as complete and as scientifically prepared
as any to be found in the records of hospitals or social service clinics."[14] I believe, and I most earnestly hope, that
this day will never come. Is the child of the future to be
robbed of the delight and the education of finding his own way
in a well selected collection of good books, with no other in-
trusion than helpful, friendly advice--which is not an intru-
sion--such as hundreds of children's librarians are not giving
to children every day? After he has been tested and measured
and psychoanalyzed in school, shall he come to the public library, there to be tested and measured and psycho-analyzed
again, and given a prescription for reading, "to be taken as
directed" until the time comes for new tests and measurements and a new prescription? Is the adult to be likewise
treated, whenever we can persuade him--for it is reluctantly
recognized that we cannot force him--to submit to psycho-
analysis and other scientific tests? Any purpose of this sort
is radically wrong. Our universities, I think, are beginning
to rebel against the doctrine that every boy and every girl
should be given a college education even if that education has
to be dragged down to the level of every boy's and every
girl's intelligence. Let us likewise abandon the idea that
every man, woman, and child in every community is a potential reader of books, and cease to fit our service to the lowest intellectual capacity. Unlimited improvement, far beyond
our present ability, is still needed in our service to readers
who can and will derive benefit from books without being subjected to examination and treatment in a literary psychopathic
ward.

The attempt to make librarianship a science of this
sort is wrong in purpose and will be almost totally unproductive of good. It will have, moreover, a most disastrous effect on the profession as a whole, not confined to the few librarians who may seek advanced training and the doctor's degree. This, as I see it, is its most lamentable feature; yet
this, apparently, is exactly what the advocates of scientific
research desire. Dr. Williamson says that "the great weakness of the readers' adviser service is its total lack of scientific basis."[15] A recent number of the ALA Bulletin[16]
contains the adult education slogan "Every Library Worker a
Readers' Adviser." Everything seems to indicate that the
scientific school would have us accept both of these ideas,
resulting in the slogan "Every Library Worker a Scientist."
Dewey's Sources of a Science of Education is frequently
quoted as an unimpeachable authority, and many of his sentences have been paraphrased to make them applicable to the

library and the librarian as well as to the school and the
teacher. Let me paraphrase a little myself. Dewey says:
"A constant flow of--reports on special school affairs [library
affairs] and results is needed. ... The contributions that
might come from class-room teacher [library assistants] are
a comparatively neglected field. ... It is unnecessary to point
out the large extent to which superintendents and principals
[chief librarians and branch librarians] have been drawn into
the work of studying special problems and contributing material relative to them. It is to be hoped that the movement will
not cease until all active class-room teachers [library assist-
ants], of whatever grade, are also drawn in."[17]

So we must assume that every librarian and every assistant will be expected, at least, to become acquainted with
the results of all research studies that are made, and, if
possible, to make contributions of their own. What will be
the effect of this insistence that librarians must adopt the
methods of scientific research; that training in those methods
is essential for one who desires recognition? It will set up
false ideals. It will divert the attention of the profession
still further from the need of better educational equipment
and greater knowledge of books. It will inspire large numbers of librarians and ambitious assistants with a desire,
not to become better librarians in the sense that has been
honored by long and praiseworthy tradition, but to become
known for a bit of scientific research. It is folly to say that
we can develop a sufficient number of well equipped librarians
at the same time that we are in hot pursuit of our sister profession, education, in attempts to prove that our work is a
science. We have made good progress, and it is possible to
make still further progress, toward the improvement of our
educational statue, but we cannot develop in the library profession a body of scientists; we can develop only a body of
dabblers in imitation science. Admit if you will--though I
shall never admit it myself--that the scientist who is held
up for admiration is a finer fruit than the older type of bibliothecal librarian for whose continued existence I am pleading. But remember Sir William Temple's friend, who succeeded well in growing plums where he could never have
grown peaches and grapes; and remember Sir William's dictum that "a good plum is certainly better than an ill peach."

In an article entitled "Yes, But Religion Is an Art!"
Harry Emerson Fosdick says: "It still remains true that the
loveliest things in human experience are not adequately covered by the word 'scientific.' We have been hood-winked and

hypnotized by the prevalent insistence that everything must
be subsumed under this one category, whereas art, music,
poetry, love, religion [and, I should like to add, libraries]
can never be crowded within its limits.   They belong as well
to the realm of beauty....   To be sure, all realms have
somewhere an aspect on which science can speak with authority. --[But], while music [for example] has a scientific aspect,
it is an art.   We have been so bulldozed by the question, 'Is
it scientific?', that, as Paderewski [has said], 'those who
would come in contact with art are obliged to live on what
the great masters of the past left us.'   Important as the service of science has been, the persistent pressing of the question 'Is it scientific?' into every realm has depleted our living; and our hard-headed factual thinking, with its hard-headed and often hard-hearted factual results in a highly mechanized and commercialized civilization, is proving to be starva-
tion diet. "18

     When it was first announced that the dream of a gradu-
ate library school was to become an actuality, I rejoiced, for
I assumed that this would bring into the profession more of
the elements which it so urgently needs; that, without detract-
ing at all from the wonderful contributions which America has
made to the development of the popular library and to library
administration, it would enable us to make a larger contribution than we have hitherto made to bibliographic studies; that
it would develop a larger number of librarians well equipped
to advance the cause of scholarship; that their influence would
restore to the profession as a whole something of the older
ideals which we have unfortunately lost.   "Do we want a library science?"   My answer is, Yes, if our conception of
science conforms in general with that which I tried to define
at the beginning of this paper.   But if we can have a science
only by adopting the psychosociological laboratory methods
that are being urged upon us, my answer is, No, we do not
want librarianship to be a science.   Let it be an art; a Fine
Art, --untouched by science.

                              NOTES

1.   American Library Association Bulletin, 22:315 (Septem-
       ber, 1928).

2.   Library Quarterly, January, 1931, pp. 5-6.

3.   Ibid., January, 1931, p. 33.

4. Dewey, John. The Sources of a Science of Education,
        pp. 8-9.

5. Library Quarterly, January, 1931, p. 30.

6. Norton's Literary Register, 1854, p. 57.

7. American Library Association, A Survey of Libraries
        in the United States, I:136 and 263.

8. Bureau of Public Personnel Administration, Proposed
        Classification and Compensation Plans for Library
        Positions, pp. 7-8.

9. Library Quarterly, January, 1931, pp. 3 and 8.

10. Newland, T. Ernest. "A Study of the Specific Illegibil-
        ities Found in the Writing of Arabic Numerals," in
        Journal of Educational Research, March, 1930, pp.
        177-185.

11. Dewey, op. cit., pp. 11-15.

12. Library Quarterly, January, 1931, pp. 28, 34-36.

13. Waples, Douglas, in Journal of Higher Education, Feb-
        ruary, 1930, pp. 73-77.

14. Library Quarterly, January, 1931, p. 14.

15. Ibid., p. 8.

16. January, 1931, p. 36.

17. Op. cit., pp. 46-47.

18. Harper's Magazine, January, 1931, p. 130.

DO WE WANT A LIBRARY SCIENCE?
A REPLY*

Douglas Waples

Mr. Thompson first sets up his own definition of science whereby science becomes an unlovely thing with which the less any one has to do, the better. He then assumes without any justification whatever that certain studies, for which I am personally responsible and which fit his definition of science represent the character and scope of the work of the institution that employs me. Third, he ridicules the studies, one by one, and declares them harmful to the profession I am attempting to serve. On each of these three points I have certain facts and counter suggestions to present. On certain other points, I am in close agreement, as for example, that librarianship has won an honorable place for itself without particular attention to research on the part of the profession as such; that it is incumbent upon librarians to be well-read persons, and that it would be a catastrophe leading to chaos if all librarians were to become investigators. On this last point, Mr. Thompson, in his own person, furnishes highly convincing evidence. In short, I strongly approve a revival of the "bibliothecal spirit" and believe it can be more promptly revived if we can find out more precisely what it is.

Concerning his definition of science, Mr. Thompson represents the not unusual academic type that cherishes a positive dread of modern science and its methods. Where these fears are present, his descriptive terms, his irony, and his choice of illustration all betray a frank antagonism.

*This article, written in response to the preceding one, is reprinted by permission from Library Journal 56:743-746 (1931). Published by R. R. Bowker Co. (a Xerox company). Copyright © 1931 by R. R. Bowker Co.

He seems to feel that to examine men in the mass is to belittle the human dignities; that to distinguish a group with
certain traits in common is to deny the worth of personality.
Inevitably his distrust has given rise to theories correspondingly hostile.

In his zeal, Mr. Thompson often misrepresents positions which he himself docs not accept.   He ridicules what
he cannot refute.   He cannot understand how other men with
a different type of experience as a background, but with
ideals as high as his own, should try to advance professional
achievements by methods whose validity he distrusts.   He ad-
vises librarianship to forego all use of a whole set of processes that have proved their efficacy in solving certain problems to the satisfaction of competent scholars, only because
he contradicts flatly the consensus of modern opinion.   He
explicitly denies the findings of educational research, and
seeks to discard it by burlesquing a single unworthy example.
Mr. Thompson's arguments would call for no formal reply if
they revealed clearly the extent of his departure from ordinary standards of rationality.

Yet for all this he has been the first to express an
irritation at fundamental studies that many members of the
library profession have doubtless felt.   This irritation is
largely explained by the fact that the more definitely a piece
of research is restricted, other things being equal, the better it is.   Hence the results being small are likely to seem
trivial to any one who does not see them in relation to other
items of established evidence.   The irritation is moreover
justified by the abundance of sloppy thinking that passes for
research.   Yet even a large number of stupid biologists or
sociologists can have no effect upon the potential human worth
of biology and sociology.   Scientific work like any other work
must be judged in the light of its purposes, and judged by persons whose experience with various methods of accomplishing
the purposes has qualified them to pass on the validity of
results.   Whether we like it or not, society has always made
its intellectual progress by an accumulation of small gains,
systematically achieved.   Doubtless it always will. The right
spirit is not enough.

My next concern is to make plain the fact that the issue raised by Mr. Thompson concerns me personally and not
the Graduate Library School of the University of Chicago.
While he imputes what he dislikes about science to the School
as a whole, my particular field of adult reading is the only

one he specifically attacks.   That I have thus far been allowed to study the problems of adult reading as I please,
need not mean that the School as such ascribes any value
to such studies.   It does mean, however, that the Library
School is faithful to the tradition of the University of Chicago
which, in religion, philosophy, economics, political science,
sociology, the natural sciences, and any other field, regards
freedom of investigation as the essential condition of productive scholarship.   Since the territory which graduate studies
in librarianship may cover is almost as wide as scholarship
itself, it is obviously silly to call the whole region sterile
just because some seed falls on stony ground.

Whether my studies to date constitute an abuse of this
freedom is doubtless a question which neither Mr. Thompson
nor I can answer until there has been time to note their effects upon the principles and practice of American librarianship.   Thus far their effect has been nil, for the excellent
reason that no applications to library administration have yet
been attempted.   In playing the role of a professional Paul
Revere, Mr. Thompson has spread the alarm prematurely.
The enemy may be advancing, if it is the enemy, but he's
a long way off and he is not numerous.

My next topic concerns the harmful effects of the particular studies to which Mr. Thompson refers.   Since his
misconstruction of their purpose is deliberate and somewhat
clever, I shall attempt to suggest certain values of each problem.

Problem I.   To find the relative interest of representative
             groups of readers in a list of contemporary sub-
             jects.

The results of the first two years' work on this problem were published in a widely advertised volume[1] before Mr.
Thompson's broadside went to press.   The volume contains
its own answer to the questions Mr. Thompson raises, an
answer which no less a literateur than Henry Seidel Canby
was quick to catch in his Saturday Review editorial.   Whether the findings will benefit librarians or not depends, of
course, upon how much librarians choose to apply them.
Some members of the profession tell me that it would be easier to purchase books acceptable to readers if we knew more
about the interests of readers of different types.   To attain
such knowledge, much more work will be necessary.   In the

course of the investigation many other important factors in
book selection may be made available to librarians. If so,
the library should attract and satisfy readers that do not now
visit the library. But the fact must be stressed that we do
not yet know how far the library can benefit the public.
Hence the excitement of the quest. Librarianship in any
case has much to gain and nothing to lose.

Problem 2. Comparison of actual reading on non-fiction
topics with the readers' interest in the same
topics.

Mr. Thompson here asks, "What are we going to do
about it if it is established that people do not read on the
topics of most interest?" Any librarian sincerely concerned
with the social efficiency of his institution should want to know
the reasons for its failures. He must strive to remove the
conditions that prevent people from reading on the subjects
they wish to know more about. Our present results in this
investigation go straight to the center of the question--is the
library accomplishing its advertised purpose of serving the
public? If it is not, there are many things we can do about
it. We might proceed to discover in respect to non-fiction
(a) what literature is accessible to people who do not read
on their preferred subjects? (b) does this literature include
material on such subjects? (c) how does the reading on interesting subjects differ from reading on uninteresting subjects? (one would naturally expect reading on uninteresting
subjects to be explained by an unusually attractive style, by
greater accessibility, and by wider advertising, among other
differences), (d) what do format, price, appearance, shelving,
and other conditions have to do with the amount that is read
on given subjects? and especially (e) how does the relationship between reading and subject interest vary among groups
who read much and groups who read little? Answers to such
questions can scarcely fail to help the librarian, publisher,
and others to remove conditions that now prevent large numbers of adults from reading authentic material upon the subjects of most concern to them. Such studies should magnify
the educational functions of the library in the direction Mr.
Thompson advocates.

Problem 3. Comparative studies of costs of books in various
classes of literature represented in small col-
lege libraries.

Here Mr. Thompson asks ironically whether the idea
is to buy more widely in the cheaper classes of literature.
While it is unpleasant to parade the obvious, the facts are
that few small college libraries have enough money to buy
the books they need in each field or department. Furthermore, they are accustomed to apportion funds among the various departments according to the number of students enrolled,
or the number of instructors, or according to the proportion
of the fund allotted to each department the previous year.   It
is therefore important in drawing a departmental budget to
know which departments can get relatively more for their
money than other departments, owing to differences in the
average cost of books.   The departments having to pay relatively more per book are not being fairly treated unless they
receive correspondingly larger appropriations.

Problem 4.   Comparison of professional activities performed
              by school librarians with activities performed
              by teachers.

This one Mr. Thompson "will not undertake to elucidate. "   The point of the study is to discover what, if anything, the library contributes to the enrichment and range of
reading on the part of school children, and this in terms of
differences between what the teacher and the school librarian
actually do with books and with children.   Our present inability to distinguish clearly the duties of the school librarian
from those of the teacher in the same type of school is largely responsible for the present controversy as to what the
school library is worth and what sort of preparation the school
librarian should receive.

Problem 5.   Measurement of vocabulary difficulty in ALA sub-
              ject headings for representative groups of public
              library patrons.

This problem should appear sensible to any one who
believes that the library catalog should use the terms that are
familiar to the readers who consult it.

Problem 6.   "Propaganda and Leisure Reading. "

A whole page of the Library Journal is given over to
the last of the projects which Mr. Thompson burlesques.   In

that space he succeeds in concealing the nature of the study
so completely that I can only refer any open-minded reader
to the original article. In a discussion of student reading
the article introduced some evidence gathered for a purpose
entirely unrelated to library interests. The article closed
with a recommendation which Mr. Thompson has "doctored"
by inserting highly misleading examples. His process is only
slightly less effective than the technique used in An Expur-
gated Mother Goose.

Any honest reader will, I think, find nothing amiss in
the conclusion Mr. Thompson finds so preposterous; namely,
that college libraries should have well-balanced collections,
and that it is possible by the methods described to find out
how well-balanced they are with respect to highly controversial issues not covered in the regular college curriculum.

The individual studies mentioned in the foregoing para-
graphs may be less impressive than the negations expressed
so emphatically by Mr. Thompson. Hence the following confession of faith may be appropriate:

1. The library profession is under an obligation to
society to acquire whatever knowledge serves to justify public
confidence.

To call a profession learned is to say that it may safely be practiced only by those who have more knowledge than
the ordinary layman can acquire. Such a profession must invite and receive from its public an attitude of trust and confidence. In return for this confidence, no other assurance
may be offered than ceaseless research, a diligent checking
of factual observation, and a constant striving to discover
new and better tests of service efficiency.

2. Librarianship has won and justified public confidence to the extent, as Mr. Thompson says, that librarians
know and provide "good books."

This means that librarians have been able to supply
the individual reader with books that meet his particular and
various needs, in so far as such books are available, whether the needs be cultural, recreational, vocational, civic, or
whatever.

3. The recent phenomenal increase in the total output of printed matter has made it vastly more difficult than
formerly to select the best.

During the past twenty years, the amount and variety of reading matter has greatly increased. In this increase, books form an ever-diminishing proportion. The librarian, perhaps, will never be greatly concerned with supplying to the public the new forms of ephemeral reading matter. But even if he confines his attention to books alone, it becomes more and more difficult for him to distinguish good from bad. None but the most casual and amateurish judgment of a book can stop short of the questions "good for whom?" and "good for what?" It is thus necessary to study readers and readers' purposes before one can tell what books serve certain purposes best for certain readers. Such books are "good books."

4. The studies herein mentioned must simplify to some degree the problem of selecting good books.

If this statement is questionable, one may point out that bibliography and the "bibliothecal spirit" at best tell little more than what books there are and what the books are about. To tell what the books are worth one must know for what purposes the books have been or might be used. Such purposes can only be learned by study of readers who differ widely in respect to the many conditions (such as sex, age, and occupation) that are known to influence reading needs.

There is thus opened to the librarian an opportunity to extend his professional horizon by acquiring an acquaintance with readers comparable in system and adequacy to his present knowledge of books. As the bibliographer looks to the specialist in the given field of literature for sources and for methods of investigation, so the librarian concerned with a definition of readers' needs should look to the social scientist for equivalent sources and methods. I fail to see wherein this analogy is not perfect.

5. The studies may be justified by their contribution to theory even if practical applications are not yet apparent.

It has been said that the individuals concerned with the particular studies under discussion are ultimately concerned with the improvement of practical librarianship. The fact can not be over-emphasized. However, the scientist who identifies a new disease bacillus is not less practical than the physician who saves lives before and after the discovery. The bacteriologist and the physician play different but supplementary roles.

So with librarianship and with schools for the training of librarians. There is need for both specialist and general practitioner. Of the two, the general practitioner is the less dispensable. If I were compelled to vote for one or the other of two types of library schools, one devoted to specialized research and the other to the training of young people to operate libraries according to present methods, I should vote without hesitation against the research school and for the library school which teaches the conventional processes.

But we at Chicago and the professional representatives who established our school believe there is a place for both types of school; that with due tolerance and the requisite amount of hard work our current studies will eventually bear directly upon vital problems of library administration; and that, in the meantime, both the specialist and the general practitioner should pray to escape the reptilian view of the field which confines the best interests of the profession to what one happens to know most about.

In concluding this comment on Mr. Thompson's article, may I express the hope that the issue may not be allowed to drop. It is perhaps the most significant issue confronting the profession today. Much clarification should result if many others are moved to discuss it from the standpoints of their chosen fields of specialization. To this end I have exercised a commendable self-restraint in ignoring the more personal elements of the Thompsonian tirade. Honi soit qui mal y pense!

NOTE

1. What People Want to Read About, ALA, 1931.

THE PLACE OF RESEARCH
IN LIBRARY SERVICE*

C. C. Williamson

Research: What attitude does the word evoke in the
young library-school graduate? Is the emotional state produced pleasant or unpleasant, or a mixture of these two elementary reactions? If by means of some delicate instrument,
or by some subtle skill, I could have the answer to that question at once, I should perhaps know whether to persist in following the manuscript I have prepared or whether I am likely
to accomplish more for library service by throwing it aside
and talking about anything that comes to mind. But I have
not the delicate instrument nor the requisite skill, so well
are your emotional responses controlled and directed. In
other words, so hardened are you to occasions of this kind
that you may even get some pleasure from the consciousness
of doing your duty and seeing the thing through. Psycholo-
gists tell us that the unpleasant emotions are slower of arous-
al than the pleasant. If your emotions are of the former class
I can only hope that they may be inhibited completely or that
they will not produce the withdrawal response for at least
thirty minutes.

I affect the language of the psychologist to confess at
the outset that I have had some doubts as to the interest you
may have in this subject, or, rather, in my ability to interest you in it--no doubt at all as to its importance. Just as
I was thinking I ought to make some such confession as this
my eye chanced to fall upon a few lines in the recently published volume of Stephen Crane's Collected Poems which are

*Reprinted by permission of the University of Chicago Press
from Library Quarterly 1:1-17 (January 1931). Copyright
1931 by the University of Chicago Press.

so appropriate that I must quote them.

> There was a man with tongue of wood
> Who essayed to sing,
> And in truth it was lamentable.
> But there was one who heard
> The clip-clapper of this tongue of wood
> And knew what the man
> Wished to sing,
> And with that the singer was content.

I shall be content if when I am through a few of you know or think you know what I have been trying to say.

In my talking and writing about library service and training for library service I have sometimes been accused of being dogmatic. Perhaps there is ground for the accusation, but I am inclined to adopt Chesterton's defense of being dogmatic. "The human brain," he says in his Heretics, "is a machine for coming to conclusions; if it cannot come to conclusions it is rusty," and he goes on to relate the story that somebody complained to Matthew Arnold that he was getting to be as dogmatic as Carlyle. "That may be true," said Arnold, "but you overlook an obvious difference. I am dogmatic and right, and Carlyle is dogmatic and wrong."

By the very nature of my daily occupation I am forced from time to time to try to evaluate the library profession and to compare its future with that of other professions. Young men and women are constantly asking, "What is the future of library service?" "Will it offer me a satisfactory career?" My answers to these questions are optimistic, not always positive, and, I hope, never dogmatic.

I think we have made some progress in the last decade, but it would be easy to overestimate both its amount and its significance. Development it seems to me has been too largely of a quantitative rather than of a qualitative character. Statistics of use and of financial support of libraries show gratifying growth. Much has been heard of programs of adult education and of "reading with a purpose," but I am in some doubt as to whether libraries are doing their job much better than they did before the Great War. It is difficult to detect improvement in the professional status of the librarian. The demand for so-called trained assistants has increased notably in volume. The number of library schools and other training agencies has increased rapidly. Salaries, and at the same

time the prestige, of the more important administrative positions have increased in a significant way, but for the rank
and file little progress seems to be made in remuneration
and in other evidences of satisfactory professional status. No,
I do not find it easy to believe that libraries, with the exception perhaps of certain highly specialized types, are doing
their jobs much better than they did ten or even twenty years
ago; at all events not enough better that anyone should wax
enthusiastic about the future.

If the library is to rise to its opportunity as a social
institution and educational force it must, it seems to me, begin very soon to attack its problems by a thoroughgoing application of the spirit and methods of research that are being
found so effective in every other field. In the natural sciences as well as in the humanistic and social sciences, in
the applied sciences, in education, in business and industry,
in social service--everywhere except in the library field--
extensive programs of research are being carried out, highly
organized and well financed.

Everyone is familiar with the great advances being
made through scientific research in medicine, in aviation,
in wireless communication, and in all lines of engineering.
In business, research has come to be regarded as one of
the most important factors of successful management. Large
business corporations have their research departments as a
matter of course. Personal qualities of intelligence, courage,
and initiative are no longer a guaranty of business success.
Efficiency of administration and quantity and quality of output
are under the constant scrutiny of the research laboratory.
Research programs are a most important consideration in the
evaluation of corporate securities.

Mr. Edward A. Filene, of Boston, one of the leading
merchants of the country, holds that American prosperity has
been due largely to research--"to an application of the same
scientific methods in the conduct of business as have been so
successful in medicine, biology, physics and astronomy."
American business, according to estimates quoted by Mr.
Filene, is spending more than $200,000,000 annually on re-
search--$70,000,000 through government and $130,000,000
through commercial concerns, the largest of them employing
thousands of scientists, engineers, statisticians, and other
research workers. The modern business man no longer looks
upon research with contempt.

In education as in business, research is playing an increasing role. Every large school system has its research department. Dr. John W. Withers, dean of the school of education of New York University, in a recent article asserts that

> research service should be maintained for every
> school system regardless of its size. Scientific
> study is necessary everywhere in present day edu-
> cation. Mere personal opinion, however expert and
> experienced, is no longer sufficient. It is impos-
> sible to maintain an efficient modern school system
> without the aid of research and no American public
> school, urban or rural, should be without service
> of this kind. [1]

Cities of 75,000 population or over he thinks should spend $12,000 to $100,000 a year on their own standard research organizations. For the smaller communities bureaus of research should be maintained in state departments of education, in colleges of education, in state universities, and in state normal schools and teachers' colleges. And these should be supplemented by similar bureaus in privately endowed colleges and universities.

This is not a mere dream. Something approximating Dean Withers' proposal is already in existence, as most of you know. Many journals are devoted to research in education. Books and monographs are published by the thousand, reporting the results of research. Perhaps it is being overdone. Perhaps the scientific and practical value of some of the output is not very great. Nevertheless, the net result of the whole movement is of tremendous significance.

What about research in the library field? A little sporadic work here and there by individuals that may possibly be classified as research. No organized or co-operative plans, or only the beginnings of such in two or three university library schools. No money appropriated anywhere, so far as I know, specifically for research in library service. Not a single person employed anywhere by a library or a library system to study problems of library service. No research fellowships. No research professorships.

Incredible? Yes, but true. Not a book or even a pamphlet devoted specifically to research in the field of library service. No journal in which reports of research studies

can be published, except in brief and popularized form. One
of the most hopeful indications that this condition may soon
be remedied is the fact that the Carnegie Corporation has recently appropriated $25,000 to assist in starting a new library
journal to be edited and published at the Graduate Library
School of the University of Chicago. Will there be enough material worthy of publication to keep a quarterly journal going?
In the years that the project has been under discussion it has
been freely predicted by leading librarians that there will not
be enough.

For the last three years I have asked the students in
a second-year class in a library school to go systematically
through the files of our professional journals for a long period of years and report any material which seemed to them to
meet the minimum requirements of contributions to knowledge
through original research. The paucity of such material has
been startling. I am not condemning our professional journalism. In the main it seems to provide what the profession
desires--current news of persons and events, a sprinkling of
gossip, scraps of bibliographical and literary information,
and addresses and papers sometimes interesting, sometimes
informative, but almost never reporting results of scientific
study.

Not infrequently I have been pessimistic enough about
this situation to wonder whether there is any justification for
using the term "library science." When the new library
school was started at Columbia four years ago we evaded the
question by calling it a "school of library service." That
there is such a thing as library service no one can doubt,
and personally I do not doubt that it ought to be based on a
library science, but I wish the scientific character of our
professional activities and of our professional literature were
more obvious.

Is there or can there be such a thing as library science? The answer will depend on our definition of science.
Frederick Barry in his Scientific Habit of Thought, essaying
a definition of science, says:

> ... We classify business management, pugilism and
> medicine together as sciences because, though as
> occupations they are only incidentally related, they
> are all characterized by the practical, methodical,
> and so far as is humanly possible, the rational
> utilization of knowledge for the attainment of definite
> results. ...

> Any concern or occupation sufficiently important,
> purposive, practical, explicit and rational, which
> is based on knowledge or its pragmatic equivalent,
> is Science. This knowledge ... may be the knowl-
> edge of natural phenomena either mechanical or
> vital, of emotion, will and thought, of human affairs;
> of ways and means, methods and procedures, of ab-
> stract relationships; of God. [2]

In point of subject matter Barry would allow us a library science. On the basis of scientific attitude of mind I
have a grave doubt as to whether we can at the present time
claim to have anything more than an embryonic science. And
my doubt is only made stronger as I read a little book by
John Dewey entitled The Sources of a Science of Education,
a careful reading of which I heartily recommend to you all.
Try substituting "library science" for "science of education"
in paragraph after paragraph and you will find you have an
illuminating and inspiring treatise on the scientific basis of
library service. He says:

> Clearly, we must take the idea of science with
> some latitude. We must take it with sufficient
> looseness to include all the subjects that are usual-
> ly regarded as sciences. The important thing is
> to discover those traits in virtue of which various
> fields are called scientific. When we raise the
> question in this way, we are led to put emphasis
> upon methods of dealing with subject-matter rather
> than to look for uniform objective traits in subject-
> matter. From this point of view, science signifies,
> I take it, the existence of systematic methods of in-
> quiry, which, when they are brought to bear on a
> range of facts, enable us to understand them better
> and to control them more intelligently, less hap-
> hazardly and with less routine.
>
> No one would doubt that our practices in hygiene
> and medicine are less casual, less results of a
> mixture of guess work and tradition, than they used
> to be, nor that this difference has been made by
> development of methods of investigating and testing.
> There is an intellectual technique by which discov-
> ery and organization of material go on cumulatively,
> and by means of which one inquirer can repeat the
> researches of another, confirm or discredit them,
> and add still more to the capital stock of knowledge.

Moreover, the methods when they are used tend to
perfect themselves, to suggest new problems, new
investigations, which refine old procedures and create new and better ones. [3]

I very much fear librarians do not qualify as scientists,
whether we adopt Barry's criterion of "rational utilization of
knowledge" or Dewey's "method of dealing with subject matter" and "intellectual technique." Barry[4] notes in this connection William James's famous classification of men into two
types, the tough-minded and the tender-minded. The first

comprises those who find their greatest satisfaction
in the prosecution of affairs: industrial and commercial, political, ecclesiastical or scientific. The
other type constitutes the bulk of humanity, who discover in emotional appreciations--crude or refined,
ingenuous or subtle, commonplace or exalted--a
greater joy than in the exercise of the practical
reason. This type finds its extreme representatives
among adventurers, journalists, artists and musicians, prophets, poets and religious devotees...
[and, I am tempted to add, librarians].

In common speech [to quote Barry a bit further]
all tough-minded people (or better, perhaps, all
people when they are tough-minded) are scientific;
but not all, certainly, are scientists. This designation is reserved for those who make the search
for new knowledge not only their business, loosely
speaking, but strictly their profession and often
their sole pre-occupation. [Their habit] provokes
the investigation of facts alone and compels an ever-
increasing development of rational acumen and un-
emotional detachment. The knowledge which it yields,
rid of all its accidental characters, is now commonly called science. Even when these words are
used carelessly or in error, they signify the belief
or pretension that whatever is thus designated is,
in fact, the outcome of rational and dispassionate
investigation.

Another way of expressing a mild skepticism as to the
genuineness of library science is to say that on the whole we
tend to be empirical in our thinking rather than scientific. I
use the term "empirical" not perhaps in its strictest philosophical meaning, but to describe any action guided solely by

experience. In the practice of medicine, for example, we
may call a treatment empirical when we find it is followed
because it has been found (or believed) to have been successful, although the reason for its efficacy is not known.

In this sense much of our library science is purely
empirical. The average librarian is an empiricist, not a
scientist. Most administrative practices and technical procedures are followed because they have been tried somewhere
and have been found to work. What psychological or other
principles are involved is unknown. The librarian's relation
to his patrons has only an empirical basis. He has only an
empirical knowledge of the attitude of readers toward library
service, of why certain classes do not use the library, of the
motives which bring people to the public library. The great
weakness of the readers' adviser service is its total lack of
scientific basis. I fear most teaching in library schools promotes rather than diminishes the empirical tendency. Quantitative studies are its greatest enemy, but probably not one
librarian in a hundred has ever had training in quantitative
methods.

I am not condemning empirical thinking and empirical
methods. I am merely pointing out that they are not scientific and are rapidly being discarded in every other important
field of knowledge and service. Dewey says in his little classic on scientific method, How We Think, that empirical thinking

> is fairly adequate in some matters, but is very apt
> to lead to false beliefs, and does not enable us to
> cope with the novel, and leads to laziness and pre-
> sumption, and to dogmatism.

The disadvantages of purely empirical thinking are
obvious.

> 1. While many empirical conclusions are,
> roughly speaking, correct; while they are exact
> enough to be of great help in practical life; ...
> while, indeed, empirical observations and records
> furnish the raw or crude material of scientific
> knowledge, yet the empirical method affords no way
> of discriminating between right and wrong conclu-
> sions. Hence it is responsible for a multitude of
> false beliefs. ...

... Empirical inference follows the grooves
and ruts that custom wears, and has no track to
follow when the groove disappears.... "Skill enables a man to deal with the same circumstances
that he has met before, scientific thought enables
him to deal with different circumstances that he has
never met before." ...

... Mental inertia, laziness, unjustifiable
conservatism, are its probable accompaniments.
Its general effect upon mental attitude is more serious than even the specific wrong conclusions in
which it has landed. Whenever the chief dependence
in forming inferences is upon the conjunctions observed in past experience, failures to agree with the
usual order are slurred over, cases of successful
confirmation are exaggerated.... 5

Now let us revert for a moment to the conclusion we
reached above, that practically no research is being devoted
to the problems of library service, in which respect it stands
alone among the so-called sciences. What is the reason?
You may infer from what I have just been saying that I attribute the absence of scientific research to the fact that librarians lack the scientific attitude, are tender-minded rather than tough-minded, think empirically rather than scientifically. No, that is not my conclusion. Both, it seems to
me, are the results of a third fact. And what is that?

Can it be that there are no problems in library service that call for scientific research? Nothing more to learn?
No unsolved problems? It is to be classed with--what shall
I say?--the activities of the street-car conductor, the waiter,
the clerk? I cannot compare it with salesmanship, or the
mechanical industries, or mining, or farming, for they have
all been subjected to research and profoundly modified thereby. No, if library service does not need scientific research,
cannot benefit from it, it must stand alone among the so-
called professions and be on a much lower plane than I have
always supposed. No, if I thought for a moment that this is
the reason we have so little scientific research, I would lose
no time in transferring myself to some activity where growth
and improvement are possible.

A second possible reason that there is so little research in the field of library service is that if it is a science
at all and not an art, it is only an applied science and that

the necessary research is therefore carried on in the underlying sciences--psychology, social science, political science,
etc. True it is that to a large extent library science is an
applied science, but so are education and engineering and agriculture.

To my mind the real reason that there is so little scientific study of the problems of library service is that practically no librarians have been trained in scientific methods.
Added to this, of course, is the fact that the unit or organization has been too small to make possible the necessary degree of specialization. Moreover, there has been, and still
is, I believe, a deep-rooted prejudice among library workers
against subjecting their activities to scientific scrutiny. Intelligence, common sense, hard work, devotion, and an admirable spirit of service have given us a library service of
which we are not ashamed. We do not want less of these
qualities, but the time has come for a scientific examination
of many underlying assumptions and for the application of
methods of inquiry which have proved fruitful in so many
fields.

I think there is in their development a very close
parallel between library science and the science of education.
Twenty or twenty-five years ago education stood where library service stands today. The great strides that have been
made in education have been due almost entirely to scientific
study of its problems. Scientifically determined facts are taking the place of empirical judgments, guesswork, and individual opinions.

We may, I think, dismiss the idea that library service
offers no field for research. We hear it said now and then
by librarians of long experience and high position that there
is not sufficient content in the field of library science to justify programs of study leading to the degree of Doctor of
Philosophy or even to a Master's degree. There might be
some ground for this view if one were to consider only the
slender body of technique that is peculiar to library management. It certainly overlooks completely the fact that the librarian, like the engineer, the teacher, the physician, is not
primarily a technician but is applying to the solution of his
problems many sciences with which it is axiomatic that he
must be familiar if he is to apply intelligently what they have
to contribute.

One year too much for the training of a librarian who

has to be a psychologist, a sociologist, an expert in the world
of books, or a specialist in some field of science or the humanities! How absurd! To produce a Doctor of Philosophy
regarded as fit to teach elementary psychology to college
Freshmen at least three years of intensive graduate study and
research are considered the minimum. So in sociology or
any other of the academic disciplines.

We hear nowadays of a science of administration or
management. I suppose it is in the main only an application
of the principles of psychology, but has it nothing to offer to
the librarian who has to organize for the production of a service and to sell that service to his public? We are still
handicapped by the widespread idea that the successful administrator is born with all the necessary qualities and that all
he needs is experience. There is not time to speak of the
demands made upon reference and research librarians, and
upon those who conduct special services in various fields.
The public library must be more than an efficient business
organization; it is a social and educational agency. Social
science and education should figure largely in training for
public-library service.

It seems to me incredible that anyone acquainted with
the facts should doubt that there is enough a librarian needs
to study to keep him busy three years--the minimum period
which seems to be generally agreed upon as necessary to
achieve a reasonable degree of mastery of some general subject and complete and publish a significant piece of original
research in some special phase of it. Take note of the fact
that it is not only, and not primarily, knowledge and information that needs to be acquired. Nothing short of a life-
time is sufficient to learn all that a librarian needs to know!
The important thing is training in scientific methods of attacking and solving problems, the cultivation of the scientific
spirit and attitude. As soon as this is recognized and acted
upon, library science will become a reality. Until that time
librarians, no matter how many facts they carry in their
heads, will be looked upon as clerks and routinists.

The fear of a dearth of problems for research in library service in itself unmistakably reveals the lack of scientific training and the scientific attitude. "The scientist," says
Dewey, "advances by assuming that what seems to observation to be a single total fact is in truth complex."[6] He proceeds to break up the gross fact into its elements. Those
who see no field for research in library service or need of

advanced training for librarianship simply fail to recognize
the fundamental complexity of library science.   To most librarians, as to almost all others, it presents an entirely
false appearance of simplicity.   May I emphasize my point
as to the essential complexity of library science by quoting
a short paragraph or two from Dewey's The Sources of a
Science of Education, substituting "library" where he uses
the word "education," as I recommended doing a little while
ago with the whole book, and also using the word "service"
where he uses "instruction."

> ... We have become only recently alive to the com-
> plexity of the library process and aware of the num-
> ber and variety of disciplines that must contribute
> if the process is to go on in an intelligently direct-
> ed way.... Not merely inert conservatives in the
> general public but many professors in other lines
> in universities have not been awakened to the com-
> plexity of the library undertaking.   Hence, such
> persons regard the activities of those in library
> schools as futile and void of serious meaning.
>
> ... There is no subject-matter intrinsically marked
> off, earmarked so to say, as the content of library
> science.   Any methods and any facts and principles
> from any subject whatsoever that enable the prob-
> lems of administration and service to be dealt with
> in a bettered way are pertinent....   It may be
> doubted whether with reference to some aspect or
> other of library service there is any organized body
> of knowledge that may not need to be drawn upon to
> become a source of library science.... 7

If library science has no important content of its own
but draws when and to the extent necessary upon all other
fields, why provide for librarianship independent training in
research?   Why not consider the librarian merely an executive who calls upon the psychologist, or the sociologist, or
the architect, or the engineer when he is needed?   The answer is, in the first place, that the mere executive librarian,
not recognizing the complexity of the problems he has to deal
with, will not know when to call in the outside expert.   And,
in the second place, the outside expert sees the problem only
from his own narrow point of view.   We may bring in the
psychologist to study a library problem, but he is merely a
psychologist, and so the sociologist, the statistician, the engineer, and the bibliographer.   The scientifically trained li-

brarian is all and none of these. Their attitudes, their
skills, and their points of view are fused and unified in him
into a new product. This is why, as I see it, we must have
people trained for research in library science. The psychologist cannot do the librarian's job; the sociologist cannot
do it. Nor can experts in any of the other fields which must
be familiar to the librarian so that he can draw upon them for
his facts and methods when necessary. It might easily take
five or six years of graduate study instead of three to train
a librarian worthy to hold the degree which signifies the appropriate and thorough scientific training.

     If there were time it might prove interesting and
profitable to point out some of the difficulties of taking over
bodily into library science the applications of underlying sciences which have been made in other fields. We should find,
I think, that the scientific problems of the librarian are, in
many cases at least, more difficult and complicated than
those of the so-called educator. The librarian no less than
the school man has need of training in psychology, for he
too must be a close student of human behavior. However,
the librarian's clinical and laboratory material is rather
more elusive and uncertain. Research work in education has
concerned itself very largely with the development and application of tests--tests, first, to determine the existing capacities of the individual, on the theory that an understanding
of present behavior is essential if behavior is to be changed.

     Let us assume, though it may be contrary to fact, that
the librarian is not concerned with the psychology of learning
--that is, the process of learning. He nevertheless is concerned with the effect of what is learned through reading upon
the developmental of traits, interests, habits, and mental and
social attitudes, in short with the effect of reading on behavior. Why does he not need as much as the educator to
have an accurate knowledge of the individual's behavior before
the modification took place?

     But here the research worker in education has a great
advantage over his colleague in library service. In formal
education the subject--or victim if you prefer--is under complete control. He cannot refuse to take any test that the educational authorities see fit to administer. That is a tremendous advantage which educational science has over library
science and over the social sciences in general, except perhaps in the field of social pathology. The student of education can treat his material much as does the chemist and

biologist. He can put it under the microscope or in the test
tube or in the animal cage or on the operating table, and
subject it to almost any experimental conditions desired while
observing the results and accurately measuring them.

Unfortunately (fortunately, too, perhaps) the library
researcher has no such degree of control over his human
material. He cannot put his readers like guinea pigs in
cages and experiment with their diet, or like dogs on the
operating table and with or without anesthetic explore the
mysteries that only the scalpel will lay bare. What he does
he must do, for the most part, with the subject's consent.
Consequently, the process of accumulating the necessary data
is longer and more difficult. This of course one reason we
have always proceeded so largely by empirical, rule-of-thumb,
and guesswork methods and procedures.

How much use the librarian may eventually make of
tests and measurements I do not venture to predict--much
more, I do believe, than is commonly assumed. I can see
no inherent reason why the future reader's consultant should
not when requested administer scientific intelligence tests,
aptitude tests, comprehension tests, etc., and on the basis of
scientific findings prescribe a program of reading. The time
may come when for many adult patrons the public library will
have on file psychological and other personal data as complete and as scientifically prepared as any to be found in the
records of hospitals or social service clinics.

In the meantime, the librarian must confine the study
of his human material to problems for which the appropriate
techniques and procedures seem to be less inquisitorial, to
involve less baring of the inner and secret chambers of the
reader's life and personality. One such approach, psychological in its nature, is a study of attitudes. In the practical work of a librarian, attitudes are a most important fac-
tor--his own attitudes, the attitudes of the staff, of the patrons, and even of the non-reading public. How can he
measure and analyze correctly, how can he understand and
modify, the attitudes that condition his success? This is one
of the challenges that library service makes to scientific psychology. The librarian may find the testing and measurement
of attitudes as fundamental in his work as mental measurements have come to be in formal education.

I had hoped to have time for a few words about the
bearing of what I have been saying on advanced training for

librarianship.   At what point should training in methods of
scientific research begin?   How much of a student's time
should be devoted to research and how much merely to learning what is already known and easily accessible in print?
That is, what proportion of time and effort should go to growth
and what to maintenance of the status quo?

I am far from assuming that the research product of
students in training will be of very great value.   In other
fields no product of importance is expected until after the
period of training represented by the doctorate.   The Guggen-
heim and other fellowships having serious research as their
prime object are of the post-doctorate type.   But after all,
only a small percentage of our graduate students will ever go
on to the doctorate or engage in scientific research for its
own sake.   The value of introducing a certain amount of research into the graduate curriculum is found in the by-products; and these accrue to all, not merely to the few who show
special aptitude for it and go on to make their contribution in
the research field.

And what are these valuable by-products?   First of
all, I think I would say, the better, or more scientific, habits
of thinking, which ought to result.   I imagine that most teachers who have had experience with graduate students at the beginning of their work, particularly if their college courses
have been predominantly literary rather than scientific, would
agree with Professor Truman L. Kelly, of Harvard University, who finds that average or above-average students are
unable ordinarily to observe, infer, and make generalizations
about phenomena. 8   And the reason, he thinks, is that they
have never had even the simplest training in these processes;
that, in fact, they have "probably had training antagonistic to
these things."   Dr. J. Christian Bay, the accomplished librarian of the John Crerar Library, recommends training in scientific method for librarians.   He says:

> Science, as everybody knows, grows by observation
> and experiment....   The art of seeing, and seeing
> correctly, is common among scientists.   The skill
> of correct observation need not be foreign to the
> librarian....   If a chemist tries his hand at librar-
> ianship, he will carry his laboratory habits with
> him.   A good knowledge or skill gained in a spe-
> cial field of work or research will mean a gain to
> library science if applied to its domain. 9

It should not need to be pointed out that the librarian who is to have any responsibility for the service of research libraries should have training not only in the spirit and methods of research in general but special training in the field covered by his library. Even though the librarian may not himself engage in serious research, he should be able to grasp readily and appreciate the significance of scientific studies made by others. Moreover, when scientific research comes into its own in the library field, as I am confident it will, the research worker will have to depend on the cooperation of those who are carrying on the services subjected to study. Any findings of value that go back into improved service will have to go through them. They should certainly be more than mere inert "channels of reception and transmission. "

There is one more by-product too important to pass over without mention--the vitalizing of teaching that results from research. Contrary to a view widely held, I believe that the best and most inspiring teaching is closely tied up with genuine research. The idea is well expressed in a passage quoted by Professor Frederic A. Ogg in his survey, Research in the Humanistic and Social Sciences:

> Without the attitude of mind toward his [the professor's] subject that comes from the constant employment of research methods, the edge of his analysis will become dulled and a disposition to accept and impart the old will be substituted for an inner compulsion to question and re-examine--a compulsion which the teacher should feel if it is to be communicated to his students. 10

If your time and patience permitted, we might indulge in some speculation as to the steps by which research is likely to come to occupy its rightful place in library service, but that must be left to some other time and occasion. It is pretty safe to conclude that the process will not be unlike that which has gone on in many other fields, education probably offering the closest analogy.

NOTES

1.   "The Scientific Method in the Study of Education, " Journal of Educational Research, March, 1930, p. 212.

2. Op. cit. (New York: Columbia University Press, 1927),
    pp. 5, 7.

3. Op. cit. (New York: Horace Liveright, 1929), pp. 8-9.

4. Op. cit. , pp. 8, 11.

5. Op. cit. (Heath), pp. 146-49.

6. Ibid. , p. 150.

7. Pp. 49-50, 48.

8. Scientific method (Ohio State University Press, 1929),
        p. 126.

9. The Sciences in the training of the librarian (1928), pp.
        12-13, 17.

10. Op. cit. (Century, 1928), p. 21.

PART II

THE HISTORICAL VIEW
OF LIBRARIANSHIP

Introduction to Part II

THE HISTORICAL VIEW OF LIBRARIANSHIP

Those who cannot remember the past
are condemned to repeat it.
--George Santayana

In an anthology devoted to reproducing the historical landmark statements of librarianship, statements on library history itself obviously cannot be overlooked. An historical view of librarianship is not only essential to the interpretation and resolution of historical problems but is also, and perhaps more importantly, helpful in aiding us to see a little more clearly where we have been and where we might go.

Many of the writings on library history, while useful, are inconsequential in that sense, primarily because they deal with the specific details of the history of individual libraries, of the history of library development in a particular area, of the life of an individual librarian, or of the factual details of a specific historical event. Too seldom have these writings sought to place the events and their details into the kind of historical perspective and social context that enables us to make sense out of them.

That all of the items that are included in this chapter are relatively recent is an indication of the recent maturity of library history. As in so many other areas, it was the work done at the Graduate Library School of the University of Chicago in the 1930s that first brought about significant research and writing in library history. The synthesis of individual library histories, biographies of individual librarians, and factual historical writing into interpretive historical writing had its genesis there. Subsequently Jesse H. Shera, a product of Chicago in the 1930s, through his leadership in library education as well as through his own voluminous writing has brought to us, perhaps more than any other individual

151

a sense of what library history can and ought to be. It is
heartening to note that within more recent years the work of
writers such as Phyllis Dain, Dee Garrison, and Michael
Harris, not all of whom could be represented here, is bringing to the study of library history the kind of creative and
imaginative scholarship that Pierce Butler and Shera so elo-
quently called for.

ON THE VALUE OF LIBRARY HISTORY*

Jesse H. Shera

Librarianship, as we know it, can be fully apprehended
only through an understanding of its historic origins.... It
is obvious that the librarian's practice will be determined in
part by his historical understanding.... Unless the librarian
has a clear historical consciousness ... he is quite certain
at times to serve his community badly. "[1] Thus wrote Pierce
Butler almost two decades before the Public Library Inquiry
sought to assess the American public library through the application of the most approved techniques of sociological analysis. At first blush, Butler's insistence on the importance of
historical awareness for an understanding of the role of the
library in modern society might seem to be little more than
an impassioned outcry of a spirit in protest against an age
that has rejected the values of history--against a world which
has come increasingly to believe that it, like Lot's wife,
would suffer disaster if it were to pause, even briefly, for
a retrospective glance. It is indeed true that, when Butler
so emphatically enunciated his belief that librarianship could
not fulfill its highest social destiny if librarians remained
ignorant of the historical development of the library as a
social agency, he was contradicting the popular trend. In
the early 1930s American librarianship was striving, as it
still is today, for professional respectability. There was a
growing faith that librarianship had, or could be given, an
intellectual content, and that content was sought in an ever
growing corpus of principles and techniques for the manipulation, operation, and administration of library materials.
This was the day of glory for the technicians in their white

*Reprinted by permission of the University of Chicago Press
from Library Quarterly 22:240-251 (July 1952). Copyright
1952 by the University of Chicago Press.

aprons, and everywhere attention was concentrated on process
rather than on function.

In opposition to this excessive preoccupation with the
techniques of library operations, Pierce Butler wrote his Introduction to Library Science. In this credo not only did he
set forth a philosophic frame of reference within which librarianship could be seen as an integral part of the contemporary
culture, but he argued strongly for a recognition of history
as basic to an understanding of the library in relation to its
coeval culture. Not only did he reveal that a knowledge of
history is essential to the librarian's complete intellectual
equipment, but he showed history itself to be the logical
starting point for almost every inquiry into the nature and
function of the library as a social agency.

This struggle to win for history a recognition of its
importance as a constituent element in the emerging scholarship of library research has not yet been won; it has, in
fact, lost ground with the increasing tendency to adopt, for
research in librarianship, the methods of investigation of the
other social sciences. In the rush of librarians to apply the
form, if not the substance, of social science research to library problems, means have often been mistaken for ends,
techniques have been employed without thought of their appro-
priateness, results have been hastily interpreted, and the historical method has been all but trampled underfoot.

The purpose of the present essay is, therefore, threefold: (1) to examine again the contribution which history can
make to an understanding of the role of the library in society; (2) to identify and isolate, if possible, the reasons for
the decline in the importance of history as an aid to the better understanding of the library as a social agency; and (3)
to indicate the future course which research in library history should take, if it is to justify the time and effort spent
in its pursuit.

The Social Value of History

Before one can make a case for the justification of
library history as an essential part of the intellectual content of librarianship, one must first attempt to determine the
social utility of history itself. The writing of history is one
of the oldest major forms of human literary activity, if not
the oldest. This very fact of survival for so many centuries

is in itself eloquent testimony of its social importance. Yet
it is only within the last century or two that scholars have
begun seriously to speculate about the specific values that history has to offer. Not content with the easy assumption that
history, like virtue, is its own reward, many scholars have
devoted countless hours to the re-examination of history, in
the hope of extracting from it an apologia, an adequate justi
fication, an answer to the question "What is history for?"

In the final analysis, all arguments in support of the
social utility of history derive from the analogy between the
memory of the individual and history as the collective memory
of the group. An awareness of one's past is, for the individual, an essential part of the reasoning, or thinking, process.
John Dewey, indeed, held that "thinking is a reconstructive
movement of actual contents of experience in relation to each
other."[2] Admittedly, societies lack the capacity of the individual for the automatic recall of past experience, and, in
the absence of an organic memory that can store experiences
and reproduce them when needed, the society must create its
own group memory. Thus the habit of recording in some
graphic form the accounts of past experience appears even
among primitive societies. As this utilitarian history was
developed and refined, it gave rise to a new kind of creative
narration, in which concern with accuracy was united with the
pleasure of knowing the past and retelling it for the benefit
of others. "The general verdict of our Western civilization,"
writes Crane Brinton, "has been that a knowledge of history
is at the very least a kind of extension of individual experience, and therefore of value to the human intelligence that
makes use of experience. And certainly the kind of knowledge
we have called cumulative--natural science--is committed to
the view that valid generalizations must depend on wide experience, including what is commonly called history."[3]

But the purpose of history is more than recall. Memory is not enough. The simple narration of past events is
insufficient unless it is supplemented with an active understanding that can draw from this reconstruction of the past
a synthesis, a series of generalizations, that not only will
give the past a living reality but will make of it a medium
for the better understanding of the present. Without such
interpretation, history degenerates to an empty antiquarian-
ism pursued for its own sake. The late R. G. Collingwood
supplied possibly the clearest explanation of the true purpose
of history, when he wrote:

> What is history for? ... My answer is that history
> is 'for' human self-knowledge. It is generally
> thought to be of importance to man that he should
> know himself: where knowing himself means know-
> ing ... his nature as man.... Knowing yourself
> means knowing what you can do; and since nobody
> knows what he can do until he tries, the only clue
> to what man can do is what man has done. The
> value of history, then, is that it teaches us what
> man has done and thus what man is. [4]

Thus he derives his complete definition of history as

> ... a science, or an answering of questions; con-
> cerned with human actions in the past; pursued by
> interpretation of evidence; for the sake of human
> self-knowledge. [5]

History, then, is a social science in the broadest
sense, and the methods it employs are identical with the
methods of the social scientists in so far as they can be
practicably applied to the available historical data. The use
of social science techniques in historical research is limited
only by the peculiarities that inhere in the data of history itself.

But Clio is no mere stepchild of the social scientist;
she is, in fact, a social scientist in her own right. The increasing attention which historians are directing toward the
growth of institutional history--the history of business corporations, for example--the history of economic phenomena,
and the historic impact of urbanization all testify to the historians' use of generalizations contributed by the other social
sciences. The historian, in turn, contributes to the social
sciences a check on such sociological generalizations. As
Gottschalk has pointed out, the historian can serve the other
social scientists in three ways: (1) by discovering historical
cases that will illustrate and support social science generalizations, (2) by discovering cases that will contradict such
generalizations, and (3) by applying social science generalizations to historical trends or series of similar or related historical trends or series of similar or related historical events
to test the validity of the former. [6] Hence "finding contradic-
tions in and exceptions to social science generalizations is
one of the ways the historian can best contribute to an understanding of society."[7] Not only, then, does the historian provide the other social sciences with data derived from his in-

vestigations, but his work supplies a check on the validity of
their concepts.   The social scientist who rejects as inconsequential the findings of history is as unscientific as the historian who pretends to write about past social phenomena or
social behavior without knowing the findings of the social scientists in relevant fields.

The Social Utility of Library History

        The writing of library history in the United States be-
gan, as was inevitable, with the long, tedious, and often uninspiring narration of the events, personalities, and circumstances surrounding the formation, growth, and development
of individual institutions.   These largely antiquarian biographies of libraries and librarians were an essential prerequisite to generalizations concerning the emergence of the library as an institutional form.   Roughly three-quarters of a
century was devoted to this kind of minute exploration of library history,   years which brought forth such notable works
as Quincy's The Boston Athenaeum, Mason's The Redwood Library, Johnston's The Library of Congress, Wadlin's The
Boston Public Library, Lydenberg's The New York Public Library, and a host of less ambitious works.   Biographies of
librarians were less numerous and, on the whole, less successful; but here one might well mention Garrison's John
Shaw Billings, Kingdon's John Cotton Dana, and the half-
dozen useful little volumes in the "American Library Pioneers"
series.

        By the 1930s there had accumulated a sufficient body
of these historical data to enable a few individuals to discern
the broad general outlines of the emergence and development
of the library as a social institution, to relate it to its contemporary social milieu, and to identify, in a general way,
the forces that brought the library to its present state of development and shaped its institutional form.   Thus Arnold
Borden's speculations on the sociological beginnings of the
American public library and Lowell Martin's observations on
the public library as a social institution were carried forward in the more comprehensive investigations of Ditzion's
Arsenals of a Democratic Culture and the writer's Foundations of the Public Library.   At the same time, the antiquarian approach was not entirely abandoned, and factual studies
of individual libraries continued to be produced, many of
them limited to unpublished theses sponsored by and carried
out in the several library schools.   Research in library history

is, of course, far from exhaustive (it can, in fact, never really attain completion), but the available syntheses show the major lines of development that characterized the growth of the American public library and reveal it as a part of the process of institutionalization that is characteristic of our culture. One may, therefore, appropriately inquire into the value of these investigations and their true bearing on the practice of librarianship.

What is the real value of library history? Perhaps such a question can best be answered by describing certain situations in which a disregard of library history has resulted in confused thinking and much misdirected effort, consequences which eventually are professionally disastrous and socially re-grettable.

The Adult Education Movement of the 1930s

A quarter of a century ago librarians, inspired by the plans of the American Library Association for an "expanded program" of activities and eagerly seeking a promising cause with which they might ally themselves, seized with mission-ary ardor upon the newly invented term, "adult education." Though the phrase was new, the idea was at least as old as Benjamin Franklin's Junto. The social libraries of the eight-eenth and nineteenth centuries were voluntary associations of adults eagerly seeking "self-improvement." But the mortality rate of these organizations was high, in spite of the initial enthusiasm of their founders. The nineteenth century brought with it the lyceum movement, the mechanics' institutes, the literary societies, the associations for the education of the merchants' clerks, and the Chautauqua movement.

In 1925 William Jennings Bryan died in Chattanooga, Tennessee, within the very shadow of the unhappy Scopes af-fair, and with him went the Chautauqua movement, to which he had contributed so much of his vitality. By this time, too, the old Chautauqua Literary and Scientific Circle was, for many people, little more than a childhood memory; Acres of Diamonds had become almost legendary; and even the par-ent-institution, "simmering in the tepid lakeside sun," would hardly have been recognized by its founders, Vincent and Miller. Already the motion picture, the automobile, and even the radio were making the village get-together less and less important in American community life.

The death of the traveling Chautauquas in the last mag-
nificent gesture of the Jubilee Year may have accentuated the
rapidly changing pattern of American culture, but it did not
mean that the popular urge for "self-education" had disap-
peared. If the brown tents of the Chautauqua had been stored
away for good, their place was soon to be taken by the American Association for Adult Education and its forums, discussion groups, adult education councils, and directed reading
programs.

All the aberrant manifestations of the urge for the intellectual growth of the adult directly or indirectly stimulated
a temporary interest in the growth of library book collections.
Many of the movements actively included libraries and library
promotion as important segments of their operating programs.
But even at a time when the public library was itself expanding rapidly in both number and size of collections, every attempt to associate the library movement with that of adult
education met with conspicuous lack of success. Virtually
every library that owed its existence to the initiative of the
lyceums, the Chautauquas, or the literary circles died with
the demise of the movement itself.

Yet this eagerness of librarians to ally themselves
with a social movement so obviously less stable than their
own reappeared with renewed vigor in the 1930s. In this
recrudescence of the cultural urge the librarians were, as
they had been in an earlier day, the willing, eager, and often
misguided disciples. Everywhere librarians began the establishment of readers' advisory services, the formation of
forums and discussion groups, the promotion or encouragement of adult education councils, the preparation of selected
reading lists for "adult beginners. " The American Library
Association sponsored "Reading with a Purpose, " and all
turned to the "A Cube E" for hope, guidance, and inspiration.
In scarcely more than a decade, the tumult reached its highest pitch when Alvin Johnson published his The Public Library
--a People's University. Extremists even went so far as to
argue that, if libraries were to play their proper part in
adult education, they themselves would have to publish books
especially suited to its needs. [8]

No one reflected that the very arguments advanced by
Johnson, which then seemed so convincing, were almost identical with those employed a century earlier by Henry Barnard,
Horace Mann, and others seeking to promote an incipient public library movement. No one turned back the pages of his-

tory to discover that for decades such arguments had fallen
on ears that were almost totally deaf to such appeals. No
one recalled that every attempt to associate the library with
universal "self-improvement" had been conspicuously unsuccessful. No one reflected that attempts to associate libraries
with Franklin's Junto, the lyceum movement, the self-help
associations of mechanics' apprentices and mercantile clerks,
the Sunday-school movement, and the literary and scientific
reading circles had all failed to achieve permanence. The
fact that the library has none of the attributes of "a people's
university" bothered no one. In short, there was a universal
unawareness of the fact that this entire program was a serious distortion of the historic role of the library in society.

Today the adult education movement, if not dead, is
certainly suffering a lamentable malaise; but the popular faith
in the self-education of the adult still persists, and, if there
has been disillusionment concerning the efficacy of "reading
with a purpose" and the generosity of Andrew Carnegie, faith
has found restoration in the "American heritage" and the
benevolence of Henry Ford.

The Public Library Inquiry

When Robert D. Leigh and his associated experts in
the social science disciplines began their "appraisal in sociological, cultural, and human terms of the extent to which
the [public] librarians are achieving their objectives" and set
out to assess "the public library's actual and potential contribution to American society."9 they unquestioningly accepted
the time-honored assumption that "the major objectives of the
American public library are ... education, information,
aesthetic appreciation, research, and recreation,"10 and it
was within this frame of reference that the Inquiry staff conducted a wholly unscientific procedure, but the Inquiry did
not stop here. It made further assumptions which Mr. Leigh
has stated as follows:

> From their official statements of purpose, it is evi-
> dent that public librarians conceive of themselves
> as performing an educational task. The library,
> however, may also be thought of as a constituent
> part of public (or mass) communication: the ma-
> chinery by which words, sounds, and images flow
> from points of origin through an impersonal medium
> to hosts of unseen readers and audiences.... And

the public library's services to its patrons are in
direct, though often unacknowledged, competition
with the commercial media. One clue, then, to the
discovery of the public library's most appropriate
role in contemporary society is to see it against the
background of the whole enterprise of public communication. [11]

Following this line of reasoning, Campbell and Metzner surveyed, for the Inquiry, the use made of the public library by the adult population in eighty selected communities.
Their conclusion was that the public library is "failing to a
considerable extent as an agency of mass communication and
enlightenment. "[12] It is their opinion that "the library suffers
from being a quiet voice in an increasingly clamorous world"
and "there is reason to believe that through broader services
and a more active information program this fraction of the
population (which it now serves) could be considerably increased. "[13]

Mr. Leigh and his staff of social scientists must have
taken some passing notice of the history of the American public library. In fact, Oliver Garceau devotes the opening chapter of his The Public Library in the Political Process to a
historical consideration of "The Foundations of Library Government. " But they could not have read this history with
much care or thoughtfulness. Even a cursory examination of
the history of the American public library would have made
unmistakably clear that the public library never has been,
and probably never was really intended to be, an instrument
of mass communication. The public library, as we know it
today, came about through the effort of small and highly literate groups of professional men--scholars, lawyers, minis-
ters, and educators--who sorely needed books for the performance of their daily tasks and who, through their efforts,
convinced their respective communities of the social utility of
supporting a public library. Even George Ticknor, who,
more emphatically than most, argued for the public library
as an agency of popular culture, helped fill the shelves of the
new Boston Public Library with titles that more properly be-
longed in the study of the man of letters.

If one learns anything at all from library history, it
is certainly that the public library has never evinced any of
the attributes of a mass-communication agency. It has never
had a "captive audience"--not even an "elite" captive audience.
Similarly, the librarian has never been a "manipulator" who

seeks to win the agreement of as large a part of his captive
audience as possible to his particular aims. Furthermore,
in the library the initiative has always come from the library
patron, never from the librarian. The librarian has never
been able to bend his patron to his purpose as has the radio
commentator or the newspaper columnist. Thus any attempt
to study the public library as a segment of the existing system of mass communication ignores history, and the Public
Library Inquiry, in so doing, may have committed a costly
and disastrous blunder.

The Problem of Definition

The misconceptions that underlie both the adult education movement and the Public Library Inquiry derive from the
same fallacious definition of the "educational" function of the
library. The concept of the library as an educational agency
is a direct transfer to librarianship of nineteenth-century faith
in the education of the masses, a faith that had its roots in
the eighteenth-century Enlightenment and the belief in the
idea of progress and the perfectibility of man. Through the
influence of nineteenth-century educational leaders, this dogma of human perfectibility was transformed into a general
conviction that the intellectual improvement, i. e., the education of the young, was a universal social responsibility--and
thus began the ever expanding movement for free, tax-supported public schools.

But this new urge for universal education was met by
two opposing forces. The first came with the realization that
men are not created intellectually equal and that there are
great masses of the population incapable of assimilating the
traditional classical scholarship, which in previous centuries
had been restricted to the few who could profit from such
rigid mental discipline. Hence popular education was expanded, through such instruments as the Morrill Act, to include training in the agricultural and industrial technologies,
partly because the basic acceptance of popular education was
thereby extended and partly because there was in our increasingly technological culture a growing need for people trained
in these skills.

The second counteracting force came with the discovery that our cultural pattern was not singular but dual, that,
in addition to the Greco-Roman culture which had up to this
time dominated popular education, there was an independent

folk culture which was not derivative but had its roots in the hearts, minds, and experiences of the masses of the people.

These opposing forces, then, brought schism to the educational world, but the librarians continued to cling tenaciously to the traditional nineteenth-century concept of education as an attempt to impose upon the public the traditions of classical scholarship and to translate popular culture into "elite" terms. Thus many librarians view their institutions as bulwark against an encroaching flood of cultural mediocrity and seek to explain away their failure to "educate" the masses. This unrealistic infatuation of the librarian with his educational responsibilities arises in part from a desire to share in the prestige that the professional educator has long enjoyed in American culture, but it is in large measure the result of the deterioration of the definition of education itself. During the last few decades the term "education" has been so broadly and loosely applied that it has now very nearly lost all meaning. Today almost every human experience has been described at one time or another as "educational," and even the advertiser who discourses at length on the deleterious effects of certain tobaccos upon the membranes of the "T-Zone" has come to think of himself as a missionary of popular enlightenment.

Such absurdities force a return to the original definition of "education," as derived from the Latin educere, "to lead forth." The educator, then, is a leader, one who conducts the student from a world that is familiar to a land that, at least for the student, is unexplored. The librarian, by the very nature of the responsibilities which he has assumed, cannot function effectively as such a leader. Only in a few isolated instances has personal contact between patron and librarian made possible the student-teacher relationship; yet from just such exceptions has grown a whole myth concerning the "educational" role of the librarian in society. So long as the social responsibility of the librarian remains the collecting, organizing, servicing, and administering of the graphic records of civilization and the encouragement of their most effective utilization, he cannot be an educator in the proper sense. To superimpose upon his established functions these irrelevant tasks will certainly confuse his objectives, if it does not actually destroy the true purpose for which the library was created.

This does not imply that the librarian must resign himself to a passive role in society, that he must continue to

be "a quiet voice in an increasingly clamorous world. " To
be sure, the world would doubtless profit from an increase
of vocal restraint. The librarian is at complete liberty to
promote his services with all the intensity and drive that he
deems desirable; but his vigor, if misdirected, can result
only in frustration and eventual failure. Nor does this argument suggest that a social agency cannot attempt to change,
even drastically, its function in society; but the proponents
of such alteration must be aware that the course which they
are proposing is counter to the historical trend and may well
involve grave risks. To reason that, because educators and
librarians both make use of books and ideas, librarians are
therefore educators is equivalent to saying that Old Dutch
Cleanser is a food merely because it is usually kept in the
kitchen and used by the cook.

Reasons for the Neglect of History

        Though one may grant that an understanding of the
past is of major importance to those engaged in the social
sciences, either as practical workers or as scholars, it still
remains true that the uses and limitations of historical study
have long been debated. As Crane Brinton points out, "there
have always been individuals to whom the study of history
seems unprofitable, even vicious, a limitation on the possibilities of soaring that the human spirit not dragged down by
history might have. "[14] There are a number of reasons for
this growing lack of interest in history that is so strikingly
characteristic of the historian's colleagues in the other social sciences, even though the popular appeal of history still
remains relatively strong.

        With the maturation of the social sciences as a recog-
nized field of scholarship has come the development of a
whole new constellation of techniques for the isolation, analysis, and investigation of social phenomena. In past centuries
man turned to history alone, as today he turns to the entirety
of the social sciences, for an understanding of man's social
behavior. Then history was the only key to an understanding of man as man. But today history no longer provides the
sole textbook for the study of human social, psychological,
economic, and political behavior; and, with the evolution of
specialized techniques in each of these branches of social
science, there has arisen not only a diminution of the prestige of the historian but a concurrent distrust of his methods.
Thus social scientists generally have come to consider his-

tory, if not actually a sterile and fruitless field of investigation, at least an academic adornment, to be pursued only for
its own sake, with little or no thought to practical utility.
In short, they would challenge Collingwood's defense of history that "the only clue to what man can do is what man has
done" and that the "value of history, then, is that it teaches
us what man has done and thus what man is. " That the social scientists, in following this line of argument, are pursuing a dangerous path has been suggested in the illustrations
above.

The second argument that has been so successfully
used against the historian arises from the belief that an increasingly complex pattern of social behavior denies the predictive value of history. If there have been those who have
clung to the belief that history does not repeat itself, it is
only because they subscribe to the popular adage that even a
donkey will not stumble over the same stone twice. In this
the social scientists have been strongly supported by the historians themselves, who have been eternally timid in defending the predictive value of their craft even when they must
have known that a donkey will stumble over the same stone
not only twice but many times. The Bourbons never learn.
The great powers of the world relentlessly precipitate wars,
fight them, win and lose them, and then go about the business of fomenting future conflicts with policies and practices
almost identical with those that brought on earlier international strife. The cynical aphorism that "man learns nothing
from history except that he learns nothing from history" is
too often true. But man does sometimes learn something
from history--though not so much as he should--and the real
question is: Does his wisdom increase with sufficient rapidity to avoid catastrophe?

But the third and basic reason for the decline of history may be charged directly to the historians themselves.
When Leopold von Ranke first enunciated his conviction that
the task of the historian was to re-create the past "wie es
eigentlich gewesen ist, " he inaugurated a new era of scholarly accuracy in historical writing. At the same time he
shackled historians for generations to come to a blind devotion to the fact per se, and from this bondage the historians
have even yet been unable to free themselves. The result
has been that synthesis and interpretation have been forsaken
in the mad scramble to re-examine all history in the light
of the new Rankean methodology. Thus has arisen a widespread belief that the true historian busies himself with the

minutiae of historical detail, having little or no regard for
the significance of the factual remains that he is able to un-
cover.

Such a criticism does not imply that the Germanic influence in historical scholarship is to be disparaged.   The
historical documents which Von Ranke found stood in need of
just such searching criticism and analysis as his methods
could give, and the school of historical writing which he
founded merits all the credit given to it.   No history can
rise above the level of the accuracy in factual detail upon
which it rests.   But historians have often forgotten that syntheses and interpretations are also facts and that their truth
to reality is often more important than the lesser values of
their constituent elements.   Truth itself is absolute, not relative, but the importance of truth can display an infinite degree of variation.   Robert Maynard Hutchins has said:

> Philistines will ask, what is truth?   And all truths
> cannot be equally important.   It is true that a fi-
> nite whole is greater than any of its parts.   It is
> also true, in the common-sense use of the word,
> that the New Haven telephone book is smaller than
> that of Chicago.   The first truth is infinitely more
> fertile and significant than the second. ...   Real
> unity can be achieved only by a hierarchy of truths
> which shows us which are fundamental and which
> are subsidiary, which significant and which not. 15

Similarly, the question of whether or not General Cus-
ter disobeyed the orders of General Terry and of which man
was more responsible for the disastrous massacre of the
Seventh Cavalry at the battle of the Little Big Horn is less
important than the whole fact of governmental stupidity in
dealing with the problems of the American Indians.   Yet an
excessive amount of historical scholarship has been chan-
neled into establishing the truth or falsity of the insignificant
trifles, and, for all its good intentions and lofty motives, it
has in many ways rendered history a real disservice.

The Reorientation of Research
In Library History

If the writing of library history is to realize its fullest possibilities, it must be subjected to a drastic reorientation that will bring it into conformity to an underlying philoso-

phy respecting the social function of the library itself.   During the last two decades the earlier writing of library history has been severely criticized because of an excessive preoccupation with antiquarian detail and a provincial point of view. This charge that the authors of library history saw the library as an isolated and independent agency existing in a social vacuum was a thoroughly justified and wholesome criticism, and it promoted some useful exploratory thinking about the relation of the library to its coeval social milieu.   But it did not go far enough.   Even those writers who tried to present the library in sociological terms confined themselves to its institutional structure and form.   They described, with a reasonable degree of success, how the public library assumed its present institutional pattern, but they did not question the current underlying assumptions about the function of the library in society, and hence they failed to explain why it came to be the kind of public agency it now is.

This failure of library history completely to come to grips with the problems of interpreting the social context from which the library arose may be explained in another way.   "Man," says Pierce Butler, "is 'a thinker ... a tool-user, and a social being,' and therefore his culture is trichotomous--'an organic integration of a scholarship, a physical equipment, and a social organization.'"16

Valid library history, then, can be written only when the library is regarded in relation to this tripartite division of culture, a phenomenon which not only has physical being, is formed in response to social determinants, but finds its justification as a segment of the totality of the intellectual processes of society.   The library is an agency of the entirety of the culture; more specifically, it is one portion of the system of graphic communication through which that culture operates, and its historic origins are to be sought in an understanding of the production, flow, and consumption of graphic communication through all parts of the social pattern.

One may properly conclude, therefore, that the historical emergency and development of the library as an agency of this process of graphic communication must be viewed in a framework of effective investigation into the whole complex problem of the trichotomous culture, a study of those processes by which society as a whole seeks to achieve a perceptive or understanding relation to the total environment--the physical, the social, and the intellectual.

So long as the process of communication was personal,
direct, and immediate, the problem of transmission was a
simple and local matter.   But as it became possible to extend the communication process to ever greater dimensions
through space and time, as the pattern of culture became increasingly complex, and as the informational needs of society
became more divergent and even conflicting, an understanding
of the historical development of the several aspects of culture
becomes mandatory.   Although the ultimate aim of such a
study is effectively to order our communication processes to
the end of greater benefit to society, it cannot proceed toward
any valid conclusions without first answering such questions
as: What have been the respective roles of the "personal
carrier" and of the graphic record in the communication process?   How did the main stream of graphic communication
grow to its present flood proportions?   What tributaries fed
its turbulent waters, and how and to what extent did it irri-
gate the surrounding wastelands of human ignorance?   What
is the real contribution of libraries to this enrichment of the
culture?   What can be known of the past that will promote
the exploitation of truth and the avoidance of error?   What
hope is there for the future ordering of graphic communication for the benefit of mankind?   Even the mere listing of
such questions reveals the depth to which their answers must
be rooted in an understanding of the past.

The limitations of the present discussion preclude the
possibility of describing in detail a research program in the
history of librarianship and bibliographic organization that
would contribute to the answering of such questions.   But a
few topics for investigation may be suggested that should ex-
emplify the kind of historical inquiry which the writer has in
mind.

It would seem to be a truism that the history of the
library is related to the history of book production itself and
that the two should be investigated in relation to each other.
Yet we do not know what state of complexity a literature must
achieve before society demands libraries of varying degrees
of structural intricacy or subject specialization.   The profession already possesses a series of histories of individual
"special" libraries in medicine, business, industry, commerce,
and the like; but all these, placed end to end, do not present
a useful history of the special-library movement in this country.   No history of special libraries has yet been written that
will answer such questions as the following:

1. What kinds of special libraries appeared first?

2. What was the structure of the business or industry at the time the special libraries for that particular enterprise developed?

3. What was the "structure" of the literature of that particular field, i. e., was it largely contained in books, in periodicals, or in special reports?

4. What were the basic informational needs of the enterprise, and what kinds of publications were essential to the meeting of these needs?

5. What was the maturity of the bibliographic organization for the particular field to be investigated; were its materials well organized bibliographically, or were there few bibliographies, guides, and indexing or abstracting services?

6. In all these respects, how does one field compare with another or one period with another in the demands that it makes for library and bibliographic resources?

Such an intensive analysis, not only for the special library but for the public library, the large research library, and the other bibliographic services that have been stimulated by our increasingly complex system of graphic communication, would contribute substantially to our understanding of the place of the library in our society.

Without such a "clear historical consciousness," is the librarian likely "at times to serve his community badly"? Indeed, without such an understanding, he is in constant danger of not serving his community at all. The degree of his success will be largely determined by the extent to which practical considerations are founded upon historic truth. To paraphrase the words of a German writer on archeology, library history is the concern of every librarian, for history is not an esoteric or special branch of knowledge but a synthesis of life itself. When we busy ourselves with library history, librarianship as a whole becomes our subject. History is not an occasional or partial affair, "but a constant balancing on the point of intersection where past and future meet. "[17]

NOTES

1. Pierce Butler, An Introduction to Library Science (Chi-
    cago: University of Chicago Press, 1933), pp. 81,
    89-90, 101.

2. John Dewey, Essays in Experimental Logic (Chicago:
    University of Chicago Press, 1916), p. 176.

3. Crane Brinton, Ideas and Men (New York: Prentice-
    Hall, 1950), p. 19.

4. R. G. Collingwood, The Idea of History (Oxford: Clar-
    endon Press, 1946), p. 10.

5. Ibid. , pp. 10-11.

6. Louis Gottschalk, Understanding History (New York:
    Alfred A. Knopf, 1950), p. 252.

7. Ibid. , p. 253.

8. James Truslow Adams, Frontiers of American Culture
    (New York: Charles Scribner's Sons, 1944), p.
    230.

9. Robert D. Leigh, The Public Library in the United
    States (New York: Columbia University Press,
    1950), p. 3.

10. American Library Association, Committee on Post-war
    Planning, A National Plan for Public Library Ser-
    vice (Chicago: American Library Association,
    1948), p. 107, summarizing from the committee's
    Post-war Standards for Public Libraries (Chicago:
    American Library Association, 1943), pp. 19-24.

11. Leigh, op. cit. , pp. 25-26.

12. So interpreted by William S. Gray, "Summary of Read-
    ing Investigations, July 1, 1949 to June 30, 1950,"
    Journal of Educational Research, XLIV (February,
    1951), 403.

13. Angus Campbell and Charles A. Metzner, Public Use of
    the Library and Other Sources of Information (Ann
    Arbor: Institute for Social Research, University of

Michigan, 1950), p. 45.

14. Brinton, op. cit., p. 19.

15. Robert Maynard Hutchins, The Higher Learning in Amer-
     ica (New Haven: Yale University Press, 1936), p.
     95.

16. Pierce Butler, "Librarianship as a Profession," Library
     Quarterly, XXI (October, 1951), 240.

17. C. W. Ceram [pseud.], Gods, Graves, and Scholars
     (New York: Alfred A. Knopf, 1952), p. 20.

THE SOCIOLOGICAL BEGINNINGS
OF THE LIBRARY MOVEMENT*

Arnold K. Borden

Although next to the public-school system and the press
the library exercises the greatest educative influence in the
state, it rarely appears to be given much weight in the de-
liberations of sociologists and political scientists. Perhaps
the wisest and most searching analysis of American life ever
made was that by Viscount Bryce in his American Commonwealth, yet the two volumes of that work contain no more
than a passing allusion to libraries. Similarly, the more
contemporary study by Professor Beard disposes of the library movement in the sentences, "Wholly apart from such
utilitarian ends, a sheer quest for wisdom evoked thousands
of lectures, either free or at nominal cost, and whole libraries of easy guides and handbooks."[1] And it is not clear
that the author has in mind much more than publishers' series.

Even more remarkable is the consistent failure of librarians to inquire into the economic and social beginnings
of the library movement in this country. An exhaustive history of it has not been written, much less one which applies
to it the principles of sociological and historical research.
From a strictly contemporary point of view the sociological
study by W. S. Learned[2] is illuminating but does not aim to
be retrospective.

Suppose, for instance, one entered into the reasons
for the great expansion of library facilities in America between 1850 and 1890. In 1850 there were about 100 libraries

*Reprinted by permission of the University of Chicago Press
from Library Quarterly 1:278-282 (January 1931). Copyright
1931 by the University of Chicago Press.

of 5,000 volumes or more aggregating something like 1,000,-
000 volumes.   In 1890 there were 4,000 libraries containing
27,000,000 volumes.[3]   In this period the first library convention was held (1853), and the American Library Association, the State School at Albany, and the Library Journal
were founded.   Surely the causes for this phenomenal growth
must lie sufficiently deep to call for more than superficial
investigation.

Not the least important factor in bringing about this
sudden rise of libraries to a position of power in the community was the impetus given by the work and example of
the federal government.   Contemporaries and subsequent writers have been more or less aware of this fact.   Pre-eminent
was the work of the Smithsonian Institution and the United
States Bureau of Education.   The first undertook to become
a center of bibliographical information by inviting libraries
to send printed catalogues of their possessions, supplied libraries with government publications, and instituted a system
of international exchange with foreign governments and learned
societies.[4]   The most potent stimulus to the library movement, however, was given by the United States Bureau of
Education.   Beginning with its first annual report in 1870, it
regularly assembled information and statistics and gave the
library a place of prominence in the educational work of the
government.   Especially efficacious in this direction was the
publication in 1876 of the special library report, of large dimensions.   This was a great codifier of existing procedure
and sought by calling attention to progress in other countries
to stimulate interest and emulation.   There were quotations
in the Introduction, for instance, from the librarian of the
University of Freiburg to the effect that library science should
have a common organization, a uniform system of cataloguing,
a professorship to give instruction it, etc.   As a result of
the work of these two governmental bureaus, then, of the distribution of public documents and the publication of a catalogue of the Library of Congress, the federal government deserves a great amount of credit for library progress.

Supplementing the work of the government was the initiative of many private individuals.   Ticknor's efforts in Boston illustrate the effectiveness of such.   Names like Pratt
and Lenox recall the part philanthropy played in making many
great library establishments possible.

But when one has reviewed all the accomplishments of
government and individuals, the reasons behind the rapid li-

brary expansion in the latter half of the nineteenth century
remain unexplained. Was the government then of the philoso-
pher-king type, perceiving the educational needs of the nation
and proceeding to their fulfillment? Political scientists, however, would hardly allow the virtues of a benevolent despo-
tism to the American government of that period. There is
no question, of course, that individuals saw that the success
of a democracy depended upon the education of its citizens,
and it was these individuals who became champions of such
causes as the library movement. But in the final analysis
the educational progress of this period received its incentive
from below rather than from above, from sociological forces
then at work rather than from the government which played
its part by giving intelligent aid and direction.

In the first place the library movement was intimately
associated with the establishment of free public schools.
Logically, it would seem that the public school was a necessary prelude to the library, that a body of people capable
of reading must be created before the library could perform
a significant function in the community. The public school
did in fact precede the library by a decade or more. In
Massachusetts, where the first library legislation for free
public libraries was passed in 1847 and where in a few years
libraries were widespread throughout the state, the public-
school system had long before taken definite shape. Horace
Mann had done most of his work before 1850. The first
American high school was established in Boston in 1821, and
the first law requiring the establishment of high schools was
passed by the Massachusetts legislature in 1827. By 1852
children were compelled to attend school. The story is substantially the same in New York and other states, with library legislation following close on the heels of the public
school.

The people of the period saw more or less clearly
the need of supplementing the school with the library, and
many of the libraries then instituted were in conjunction with
schools. Massachusetts, New York, Michigan in 1837, and
Rhode Island in 1840 passed school laws containing library
provisions. Ticknor spoke of the library as "the crowning
glory of our public schools."[5] Horace Mann and Jevons
(Methods of Social Reform) spoke of it in a similar way. A
report of the Boston Public Library in 1875 stated this view
very emphatically.

Another antecedent condition favoring the growth of

public libraries was the increased voting strength of the people. In the years before 1850 universal manhood suffrage was achieved. Having the power, the people also had the will to have funds voted out of the public treasury for the foundation and upkeep of public libraries. It will be recalled that in New England, in some parts of which the public library early flourished, the governing body was still a pure democracy. In New England and elsewhere the people felt sufficiently the need of enlightenment to tax themselves not only for schools but for libraries.

Attendant upon the increase of wealth resulting from the establishment of the factory system and the exploitation of the natural resources of the country was the increase of leisure demanded by labor. The creation of surplus wealth itself was a necessary prerequisite to the establishment of expensive school systems and libraries, but it was not until the working classes demanded a greater share of their product that the use of leisure became a subject of importance. "The period from 1820 to 1850 may rightly be named the Awakening Period of the American Labor Movement."[6] There was considerable legislation during the middle decades of the nineteenth century which shortened the hours of labor. Ten-hour-day laws were passed in New Hampshire in 1847 and Pennsylvania in 1848, and by 1868 eight-hour laws had been passed in Connecticut, New York, Illinois, Wisconsin, Missouri, and California. The opposition of "vested interests" and courts, however, precluded any great advances until after the bargaining power of the labor unions became strong enough to assert itself and until after the formation of the American Federation of Labor. By 1890 higher wages and shorter hours were the order of the day.

The great increase in leisure among the most populous classes of society made the public library a necessity. By and large the rapid multiplication of libraries between 1850 and 1890 was synchronous with the labor movement and the achievement of shorter working hours. Whether or not the connection between the two movements was visible to the people of that day, it appears clear in retrospect that such a connection existed.

Students of library history, therefore, must not look upon the library as an isolated phenomenon or as something which has been struck off the brains of individuals in moments of philanthropic zeal. The universal emergence of the library as a public institution between 1850 and 1890 suggests the presence of common causes working to a common end. From the point of view of history as well as from that of contemporary conditions the library needs to be studied in the light of sociology, economics, and other branches of human knowledge.

NOTES

1. C. A. Beard, Rise of American Civilization (New York, 1927), II, 796-97.

2. The American Public Library and the Diffusion of Knowledge (New York, 1924).

3. W. I. Fletcher, Public Libraries in America (Boston, 1894), p. 115.

4. George B. Goode (ed.), Smithsonian Institution, 1846-1896 (Washington, 1897), pp. 815-22 (article by J. S. Billings).

5. G. Ticknor, Life, Letters, and Journals (Boston, 1876), II, 300 ff.

6. J. R. Commons, Documentary History of American Industrial Society (Cleveland, 1910-11), V, 20.

PART III

THE SOCIAL RESPONSIBILITIES
OF LIBRARIES

Introduction to Part III

THE SOCIAL RESPONSIBILITIES OF LIBRARIES

> We have physicists, geometricians, chem-
> ists, astronomers, poets, musicians and
> painters in plenty, but we have no longer
> a citizen among us.
> --Jean-Jacques Rousseau

The idea of librarians taking a stand on social issues
is not, of course, a new one; nor is the idea of the librarian
as an agent of social change new. To the extent that librarians have been, and are, an intrinsic part of the educational
and social structure of American society, and librarians dis-
seminators of ideas and not merely caretakers of books,
many of these issues have been inescapable. While, as this
chapter should make clear, attention has been paid to these
issues for some time, it was the 1960s that saw the real
development of concern by librarians about their social responsibilities. Even a brief survey of the literature of the
past decade and a half will confirm the outpouring of concern,
often articulate but more often merely fervent, over the relationship of the librarian, and of libraries, to society. Social consciousness is now, and probably will continue to be,
an important concern of our profession.

It is not the intent of this chapter to debate the relative merits of the social issues that have concerned librarians
for the past one hundred years, nor to give a comprehensive
survey of all of the issues which could be subsumed under
the heading of social responsibilities. Rather, we have sought
to include outstanding articles dealing with some of the more
challenging issues that have occupied us for some considerable time and which still occupy and concern us.

First and foremost, of course, is the ever-present
issue of censorship which, more than any other social issue,
is of direct and immediate concern to librarians. The re-

sponsibility of providing the library's public with information
and of somehow selecting what information is to be available
is one of our central roles. Often that role places the librarian in the sensitive position of having to make critical
judgments about material on which feelings run high. Selection inevitably brings with it the prospect, whether real or
imagined and whether by others or ourself, of censorship.
Here we have included two of the strongest positive statements
on the issue, by Leon Carnovsky and Margaret Monroe, that
have been made.

Other social issues, although they have not always
loomed so large as the issue of censorship, and although they
have, for the most part, only more recently come to the fore,
also deserve attention. Foremost among these is the question
of who is to be served, and open access as an ideal of library service. At a time in the early 1900s when many librarians were seeking to make their collections and services available to the flood of immigrants entering the
United States, it was only a few Black leaders, such as
W. E. B. DuBois, who were raising questions about segregated library facilities in the South. Not until Kunitz so
forcefully raised the question of segregation in 1938, and
called upon the American Library Association to take a
stronger role on the issue as it affected libraries and librarians, did this important social issue begin to become
of concern to American librarians. Little real action
took place, however, until the social ferment of the 1960s
when Rice Estes, E. J. Josey, A. P. Marshall and others began so clearly, and for the first time with support,
to speak out. Much has changed but much remains to be
done before the ideals of open access and equal service to
all users are realized.

The problems of the role of women in librarianship
and of discrimination against women within the profession is
another issue that has been articulated by many over the
years. As women came to dominate librarianship numerically, leaders such as Salome Cutler Fairchild, Caroline Hewins,
and M. S. R. James, among others, expressed concern over
the role and status of women as librarians. Here again,
though, it has only been since the developments of the 1960s
that writers, such as Anita Schiller, have forcefully and effectively addressed this issue.

The resolution of social issues is not an easy task.
Librarians are as diverse in their ideas and opinions as the

public which they serve.   A commitment to the free exchange
of ideas and the possibility that we can act if we so wish are
perhaps all that one can hope for.   As librarians our roles
in these social issues are not always clearly defined but, in
the end, it is our concern for humanity and not our professional credentials that is important.

QUESTIONS OF A POLITICAL SCIENTIST*

Carleton B. Joeckel

The temptation is strong to begin this governmental
view of the public library by observing that the political scientist and the expert in public administration have only very
recently discovered the library.   The presence of Dr. Tol-
man as our introductory speaker makes it impossible for such
a statement to pass unchallenged, since he has been a part
of the government of our greatest state too long and knows its
distinguished library record too well to permit such liberties
with history.   In his article for the January Bulletin, he al-
ludes to the establishment of a system of public libraries in
New York nearly a hundred years ago.   Indeed, it was in
1827 that a practical political scientist, Governor De Witt
Clinton, first suggested this system of tax-supported libraries
connected with the schools.   Another statesman-administrator,
who was several times governor of Massachusetts--Edward
Everett--played an important part in the founding of the Boston Public Library, speaking of the library as "the finishing
hand in the system of public education."   And coming down to
December, 1932, many of you have doubtless noted that a recent governor of New York, in a widely commended plan for
the reorganization of the government of the city of New York,
has duly provided places in his Department of Education for
the three public library systems of that city.

And yet, in spite of these and numerous other examples which time does not permit me to cite, it is in a very
real sense true that students of government, both theoretical
and practical, have given surprisingly little attention to the
functions and objectives of public libraries.   When a textbook

*Reprinted by permission of the American Library Association
from ALA Bulletin 27:66-70 (February 1933).

of almost six hundred pages on municipal administration, used
in the training of future municipal officials devotes less than
one page to libraries and when a long and detailed survey of
social problems and social planning, published in 1932, discusses at length the subject of adult education and the proper
use of leisure time without once mentioning the word, "library," one may be permitted to wonder what their authors
really think about libraries.

But we are safe in saying that this situation is rapidly
changing; more and more the political scientist is including
the library in his view of government.   Permit me to venture
the opinion that his analysis of the library is likely to be
more penetrating, more critical, and more discerning in
vision and in imagination than is that of most librarians.
These professors of political science and of public finance,
the steadily growing group of trained experts in public administration, will not fail to appraise the library with competent
analytical judgment.   They appreciate more clearly than the
librarian why the library's back is against the wall; they know
better than he the real significance of the boycott against
government which the library world is feeling so definitely.
They have a broad and comprehensive understanding of the
acid test of necessity and achievement to which every governmental activity is now being subjected.   It will not take these
honest but friendly critics long to discover both the strength
and the weakness of the library as a part of the governmental
structure.

Almost instinctively, these men tend to ask certain
questions about libraries.   It is my task today to suggest
what some of these questions may be.   It is more than likely
that librarians will spend much time in answering many inquiries similar to these in the next few years.

Evaluating the Library

The first and most fundamental question is not new,
but in recent years the librarian has rarely been obliged to
answer it.   Better for him, perhaps, if he had!   Briefly, it
is this: Is free public library service really a proper and
necessary function of government?   We are today in the midst
of an interesting, but difficult, stage of speculation about the
relative importance of the various governmental services.
Lincoln Steffens has recently described this as a "cycle of
self-examination."   Apparently no wholly logical and workable

formula for the comparative evaluation of the functions of
government is going to be found, and it is likely to be the
old story of "devil take the hindmost," with great variation
in results in different communities.

Just where and how the public library will come out
in this inevitable struggle for existence will often depend on
the cleverness of library boards and librarians in rough-and-
tumble argument before city councils and other appropriating
bodies, as well as on the public support which may be rallied
around the library banner. This very Trustees' and Citizens'
Day, sponsored by the American Library Association, is a
natural attempt to organize such support. But right here the
librarian finds himself face to face with a fundamental difficulty. He needs a thing which he does not have--namely, an
adequate appraisal of the results of the service he is rendering. Such an appraisal, if it could be presented in a form
at once authoritative and interesting, would probably be the
best argument for continuing library service at its recent high-
water mark. Unfortunately, the existing tests, the so-called
standards, of the effectiveness of library service seem to the
political scientist almost entirely quantitative and lack the
qualitative meaning he would prefer.

Any thorough attempt at a real appraisal of the results
of library service in a typical American community probably
seems to the average librarian a task of such difficulty and
such magnitude as to be almost hopeless. Yet such surveys
and appraisals are fairly common in other fields; one of
them, Middletown, is known to all librarians. If a similar
survey could be made in a single well selected city, it might
serve as an example which could be used by all libraries a-
like. Is it not possible for this Association to find a library
Robert and Helen Lynd and funds to finance them?

Has the Library a Platform?

The second question will probably be this: Has the
public library a real platform--a definition of its purpose and
of its vital necessity so brief and so simple that it will appeal to citizen and administrator alike? Some of you in this
audience may know the answer to this question, but certainly
the average librarian of the average American public library
does not. I doubt very much whether ALA Headquarters
knows it, and I freely confess that I do not. It is true, but
not particularly helpful, to say that the library has been swept

along so rapidly and so easily by the great and rapid expansion of governmental functions that the formulation of such a platform has seemed unnecessary. The result is that the day of the library's first great testing finds members of the American Library Association still debating whether the library is for all the people or only for some of them, whether it shall supply books of ephemeral interest to its readers or leave such books to the tender mercies of the rental libraries, and so on. Am I going too far when I say that I doubt whether any other activity of government is as vague, as indefinite, and as generally inarticulate in defining its purpose and its proper field of service and in telling the world at large about its achievements as the public library? For some reason, the librarian seems much less sure of his ground than the school superintendent, the police chief, the city engineer, the public health officer, the director of public recreation, or almost any other municipal officer one might name.

To sum up on this point, the great need of the library is a brief and appealing platform which may be used over and over again in the daily press, in municipal journals, in talks before clubs and organizations of all kinds, and in public and private discussion in every city and town throughout the country.

Next, there is the eternal question of finance. It will not require much research to disclose the fact that many librarians are not interested in financial statistics; rather, they are inclined to feel that the quality of their work is tainted and contaminated by too much analysis of costs. The modern administrator, on the contrary, likes figures and uses them regularly as one of his administrative controls. Naturally the financial expert will have many questions to ask about libraries--questions which the librarian will often be unable to answer.

Why a Separate Tax Levy?

The basic question here, however, is not one of detail, but of policy. One hears it over and over: "Why should the public library be protected by a separate tax levy, distinct from the general municipal levy?" The librarian will be ready with many answers to this question, but his best arguments will leave the financial administrator cold, because he is striving earnestly for the centralization of budget-making and tax-levying powers. With the whole general property

tax system apparently crashing about our heads, the financial
expert will hazard the opinion that the librarian is fighting a
losing battle both as to the correctness of the theory of such
separate taxes and as to their practical utility as producers
of revenue.

Again, the financial expert is keenly interested in the
possibility of putting the library on a service cost basis.
Can the library be run like the city water department, the
street railway, the telephone company, or the gas and electric company with all costs paid for by the actual users of
the service?   At least one expert has seriously suggested
this way out for the library, and a number of public libraries are already experimenting with the idea in a partial way.
This plan is so attractive that it seems only fair to warn the
librarian that he must endeavor to understand its full significance.   He must be prepared to meet the suggestion boldly
and with complete statistics at hand as to its effect on his
library.

One other financial matter must be mentioned in summary form.   Up-to-date officials spend much time in analyzing governmental costs--not merely the complete costs of
certain services, but more particularly the unit costs of doing
specific kinds of work.   In this respect the library offers an
almost virgin field.   Obviously the librarian must be prepared
to answer questions about unit costs; if he be wise, he will
be forehanded with his data.

Finally, the political scientist comes to a group of
questions affecting the governmental organization of the public library.   Just where does the library belong in the structure of local, county, or state government?   Here again the
political investigator encounters the traditional desire of the
librarian for independence from the rest of government.   Very
much as in the case of separate taxation, this attitude of
aloofness will not meet with much sympathy from the student
of government.   As a matter of fact, is it not somewhat
curious that the public library, a democratic institution if
there ever was one, should seem so fearful of democracy in
its legally constituted form?   In this era of experiment and
change in the forms of government, perhaps the best defense
of the library will not be found in continuing its struggle for
separate and preferential treatment, but rather in so thoroughly demonstrating the value of its service that its position
will be secured by the weight of public opinion.

One of the most significant and interesting phases of present-day experimentation in governmental organization is the proposal to reduce the number of units of government and consequently to increase their size. This question is being studied and agitated in many states and with respect to many public activities. The library is not too well prepared, either with respect to existing laws or with respect to the genuine interest of librarians in the question, to play its part in the changes of this sort which are surely coming. True, there are county library laws in most of the states, but county libraries will not solve the problem of enlarging the unit of library service in all cases, by any means. The typical public library unit is still so small and so weak as to be seriously lacking in administrative efficiency, and the area it serves is unnecessarily circumscribed. Moreover, the typical librarian is not as vitally concerned as he should be in changing the situation. I will not say that the librarian has been selfish in this respect, but rather that he has been so absorbed in the library problems of his own town or city that he has overlooked the fascinating possibilities of expansion of the units of library service. Unless I am greatly mistaken, there is going to be plenty of opportunity for unselfishness, perhaps also for the sacrifice of personal ambitions, when libraries begin to take really advanced ground in this vitally important question of enlarged units and equalization of service. Sweeping changes in the complicated structure of local government are being recommended on all sides. The public library must adapt itself to them.

In conclusion, let me remind you that I have been trying to present the point of view of the political scientist; I do not say that my own views as a librarian would always coincide with those I have suggested. Nevertheless, I am convinced that the librarian has much to learn from the student of government and that the two are likely to find a common ground of mutual understanding and interest. When some of the apparent conflicts have been thoroughly explored and adjusted, it seems reasonable to believe that there will still be a place for the public library as a part of government, perhaps a better place than we imagine possible in these evil days.

THE OBLIGATIONS AND RESPONSIBILITIES OF THE LIBRARIAN CONCERNING CENSORSHIP[1]*

Leon Carnovsky

I have never met a public librarian who approved of censorship or one who failed to practice it in some measure. In some cases the practice was resented and adopted only in response to assumed or actual pressure; in others, it was accepted as proper and was justified on the score that no library can provide all books and that, just as most books which have been published cannot be found in any single library, so a library is forced to practice censorship in effect, if not in name, by failing to acquire the thousands and millions of books which it passes up for reasons of money, space, community interest, or whatever cause.

First of all, I should like to clear up the confusion behind this conception; it is a confusion between book selection and censorship. Though the result may be the same in both --nonprovision of a book--the reasons are different and should be clearly recognized. Assume a typical public library in a middle western town of ten thousand, run by a librarian doing the best he can to provide a wide assortment of literature. The librarian sees a review of a history of Persian art, priced at $25.00, but he quickly concludes that this book is not for him, a decision obviously based on sound reasoning. The elements in his reasoning are lack of potential interest, cost, possession of other books on the same general subject, and the relative importance to the accomplishment of his objectives of this book as compared with half-a-dozen others that he can buy for $25.00. Then he sees an announcement

*Reprinted by permission of the University of Chicago Press from Library Quarterly 20:21-32 (January 1950). Copyright 1950 by the University of Chicago Press.

in Publishers' Weekly of a new book by Faith Baldwin, but
he has always felt that the literary standards of his collection required a better quality of fiction; therefore he does not
even seriously consider the book, much less order it.   Next
he reads about a book entitled Studs Lonigan.   It is well reviewed, widely publicized, inexpensive, and a lot of people
ask for it.   Yet the librarian decides not to buy it.   Though
all three books are thus denied the potential borrower, one
would have to employ a highly specious logic to conclude that
a censorship was operative in all three cases.   We must
clearly distinguish between identical effects that result from
altogether different causes, and we shall never face the censorship problem squarely and honestly until we see that book
selection (which implies book rejection) and censorship are
not identical.

        Censorship is defined in the Encyclopaedia of the So-
cial Sciences as "the policy of restricting the public expression of ideas, opinions, conceptions and impulses which have
or are believed to have the capacity to undermine the governing authority or the social and moral order which that authority considers itself bound to protect."[2]   It is a conscious
policy and may be enforced without the assent of the majority;
indeed, it may be instituted by a small group or even by an
individual who feels strongly concerning a certain issue.
Though such issues may fall in any sphere of human interest,
the practice of censorship has been most frequently invoked
in three areas, namely, politics, religion, and morals, and
therefore it is in these areas that the problems of censorship as they impinge on library administration are most often
encountered.

        The theory of free speech in the political realm has
been so thoroughly discussed that it seems a little strange
that it should need a defense in 1949.   Clearly and forthright-
ly expressed in the First Amendment to the Constitution,
copied and incorporated in some form in our state constitutions, strongly supported by court decisions of the most re-
spected and honored members of our judiciary, it still remains an ever present issue to plague and puzzle us.   The
reason is that freedom is not and can never be an absolute.
My freedom to make noise is directly contrary to your freedom to enjoy quiet.   Nor can there be absolute freedom of
speech; society itself imposes limits upon it, and it becomes
the business of the courts to determine whether the limits
have been transgressed in individual cases.

Perhaps the clearest expression concerning free speech appears in our Bill of Rights: "Congress shall make no law ... abridging the freedom of speech or of the press"; and the finest explication of the free-speech doctrine is to be found in John Stuart Mill's essay <u>On Liberty</u>. Little that has been written since adds much to his cogent argument. His primary object in writing his essay was to establish the principle that "the sole end for which mankind are warranted ... in interfering with the liberty of action of any of their number, is self-protection. That the only purpose for which power can be rightfully exercised over any member of a civilised community, against his will, is to prevent harm to others."[3] Included in the sphere of liberty of action is "the liberty of expressing and publishing opinions," even though such expression goes beyond strictly individual concern and extends to other persons. However, says Mill, since expression of thought is so closely allied to freedom of thought itself, it is practically inseparable from it.[4]

The champions of free speech, from Milton through Mill to Justice Holmes in our own day, have all been much more concerned with the preservation of the right of free speech for the individual--even though he be the only person in the nation who believes what he believes. Indeed, this is no more than the recognition of the fact that all progress in human affairs is possible only in an atmosphere which permits the unusual person, who is frequently the unpopular person, to get himself heard. The harm in silencing such a person is only incidentally the harm to him; the greater harm is to society, which may be thus deprived of the opportunity to learn a possible truth of which only he may be the master. The truth or wisdom of any issue, like the nature of the good and the beautiful, is never discerned by taking a vote; majorities as such have force on their side but little else. To silence a dissident is to solidify a position and thus to make less likely the possibility of change. Listen to Mill on this point:

> The peculiar evil of silencing the expression of an opinion is, that it is robbing the human race; posterity as well as the existing generation; those who dissent from the opinion still more than those who hold it. If the opinion is right, they are deprived of the opportunity of exchanging error for truth; if wrong, they lose, what is almost as great a benefit, the clearer perception and livelier impression of truth, produced by its collision with error.[5]

And again, with even greater force:

> I insist thus emphatically on the importance of ge-
> nius, and the necessity of allowing it to unfold it-
> self freely both in thought and in practice, being
> well aware that no one will deny the position in
> theory, but knowing also that almost everyone, in
> reality, is totally indifferent to it.   People think
> genius a fine thing if it enables a man to write an
> exciting poem, or paint a picture.   But in its true
> sense, that of originality in thought and action,
> though no one says that it is not a thing to be ad-
> mired, nearly all, at heart, think that they can do
> very well without it.... Originality is the one
> thing which unoriginal minds cannot feel the use
> of. [6]

This, however, is only one argument for free speech;
others are equally cogent.   Mill mentions three: first, a
suppressed opinion, though false on the whole, may yet contain certain elements of truth.   Accepted or "prevailing opinion on any subject is rarely or never the whole truth; it is
only by collision of adverse opinions that the remainder of
the truth has any chance of being supplied."   Again, even in
the unlikely event that on any given issue the opinion we hold
is the complete truth, our confidence in it becomes more
strongly intrenched as we see it in the light of lesser truths
or even of false doctrines.   And finally, says Mill, the meaning of the doctrine itself, if it is never challenged, may be
lost and become a mere formal profession accepted from
habit and not from conviction. [7]

Since the case for free speech is so solid in our historic tradition, in our constitutional guaranties, and in its
logical persuasiveness, it seems odd that the principle is
continually being challenged and has been fought several times
all the way up to the Supreme Court.   And yet it is not so
odd, for, as we have said, the concept of free speech is not
an absolute, and it is continually necessary for the courts
to determine where free speech may become a menace to
society or even to the achievement of short-term goals which
society, through its legislatures, may envisage.   The single
most important case involving free speech is the famous
Schenck case, heard before the Supreme Court.   Here the
decision of the Supreme Court was written by Justice Holmes
--not a dissent but presenting the unanimous opinion of the
Court.

In June, 1917, and May, 1918, Congress enacted legislation aimed at controlling speech which might be construed
as disloyal or seditious. The defendants, Schenck and his
associates, had been found guilty in the lower courts of mailing circulars calculated to cause insubordination in the mili-
tary forces; the circulars declared conscription to be des-
potism and urged the conscriptees to obstruct its operation.
The defense invoked the free-speech clause of the Constitution, and it is this aspect that makes the case important for
us. The statement of Justice Holmes in ruling on this point
has been often quoted, because it laid down a rule that comes
close to furnishing a yardstick, to drawing the line where the
constitutional protection of free speech no longer applies.
Said Holmes:

> We admit that in many places and in ordinary times
> the defendants in saying all that was said in the
> circular would have been within their constitutional
> rights. But the character of every act depends
> upon the circumstances in which it is done....
> The most stringent protection of free speech would
> not protect a man in falsely shouting fire in a the-
> ater and causing a panic.... The question in every
> case is whether the words used are used in such
> circumstances and are of such a nature as to cre-
> ate a clear and present danger that they will bring
> about the substantive evils that Congress has a
> right to prevent. It is a question of proximity and
> degree. When a nation is at war many things that
> might be said in time of peace are such a hindrance
> to its effort that their utterance will not be endured
> so long as men fight and that no court could regard
> them as protected by any constitutional right. 8

The key phrase in this decision is "clear and present
danger." The problem still remains to determine when a
publication or an act constitutes a danger to the state or to
society, but at least we have the right question, even if we
cannot always provide the right answer. Indeed, even the
Supreme Court was unable, in applying the test, to come out
with a consistent answer. This is most clearly shown in the
Abrams case, also decided in 1919, the year of the Schenck
decision. Abrams and his associates had strewed some leaflets from the roof of a building in New York. These leaflets were not aimed at interfering with the war against Germany but protested against American intervention in the Rus-
sian Revolution. Included in the protest was a call for a

general strike; this could be construed as interfering with the
war against Germany, therefore the group was indicted. No
strike was actually called, and there was no evidence that a
single person had been moved to stop any kind of war work as
a result of the leaflets. Nevertheless, the defendants were
found guilty in the District Court, and the sentence imposed
was upheld by a 7-2 vote of the Supreme Court. The great
importance of this case for us lies in the dissenting opinion
of Justice Holmes,[9] concurred in by Justice Brandeis; in this
opinion Holmes further develops the "clear and present danger" principle. He strikingly shows how strongly he has
been influenced by both Milton and Mill; his statement has
been said to be the greatest utterance on intellectual freedom
by an American and ranking with The Areopagitica and the
essay On Liberty.[10]

> Persecution for the expression of opinions seems to
> me perfectly logical. If you have no doubt of your
> premises or your power and want a certain result
> with all your heart you naturally express your wishes
> in law and sweep away all opposition. To allow op-
> position by speech seems to indicate that you think
> the speech impotent, as when a man says that he
> has squared the circle, or that you do not care
> wholeheartedly for the result, or that you doubt
> either your power or your premises. But when
> men have realized that time has upset many fighting
> faiths, they may come to believe even more than
> they believe the very foundations of their own con-
> duct that the ultimate good desired is better reached
> by free trade in ideas--that the best test of truth
> is the power of the thought to get itself accepted
> in the competition of the market, and that truth is
> the only ground upon which their wishes safely can
> be carried out. That, at any rate, is the theory of
> our Constitution. It is an experiment, as all life
> is an experiment. Every year if not every day we
> have to wager our salvation upon some prophecy
> based upon imperfect knowledge. While that experi-
> ment is part of our system I think that we should
> be eternally vigilant against attempts to check the
> expression of opinions that we loathe and believe
> to be fraught with death, unless they so imminently
> threaten immediate interference with the lawful and
> pressing purposes of the law that an immediate
> check is required to save the country... Only the
> emergency that makes it immediately dangerous to

leave the correction of evil counsels to time warrants making any exception to the sweeping command, 'Congress shall make no law ... abridging
the freedom of speech. '

I hope the implications for libraries of what I have
said have not been lost. If there is one agency above all
which has the power to put teeth into the principle of free
speech, it is the public library. I know of no nobler function
which it has to perform than this: the presenting of all points
of view, however unpopular, even loathsome, some of them
may seem; by the same token, I know of no greater evil, no
surer betrayal of that function, than the denial of the expression of certain viewpoints through a deliberate or contrived
censorship. This, you may say, is all very well in theory;
does it really have any application today? Today the great
competing political doctrines are, of course, democracy and
communism. Within the framework of democracy itself there
is room for dissension: the social welfare state versus an
uncontrolled laissez faire, to name but one conflict. No library is likely to quibble over the presentation of these two
points of view, or variations of them. The serious problem
does arise over the presentation of the literature of communism. Here is material the publication of which is clearly
sanctioned by the First Amendment; it is altogether legal by
any test we may apply. The understanding of communism is
as important as the understanding of democracy, capitalism,
or the divine right of kings. No court, as far as I know,
has rules that the distribution of the literature of communism
represents a "clear and present danger" to the security of
our civilization. 11 It is clearly up to us to give the widest
possible latitude to free speech within the political realm.

It is sometimes convenient to forget this principle in
the face of certain pressures against a given position. An
over-zealous American Legion post, a D. A. R. chapter, a
religious or national group, or even an individual may feel
so antagonistic toward another country or toward another faith
or philosophy that it would deprive everyone else of the opportunity to read about them. They do not apply the "clear and
present danger" principle; in fact, they apply no rational principle at all but act from a deeply felt emotion. Disagree
with them, and you are labeled "un-American"--a strange
transvaluation of values when a position espoused by the greatest American of our generation is called "un-American. "

Numerous presentations in support of free speech might

readily be cited; they are brilliantly summarized in a great
dissenting opinion by Justice Brandeis, concurred in by
Holmes. The case was that of Pierce v. United States and
consisted of the prosecution of three Socialists for distributing a pamphlet denouncing war. Said Brandeis:

> The fundamental right of free men to strive for bet-
> ter conditions through new legislation and new in-
> stitutions will not be preserved if efforts to secure
> it by argument to fellow citizens may be construed
> as criminal incitement to disobey the existing law--
> merely, because the argument presented seems to
> those exercising judicial power to be unfair in its
> portrayal of existing evils, mistaken in its assump-
> tions, unsound in reasoning or intemperate in lan-
> guage. 12

We do well to remember with Chafee, the author of
Free Speech in the United States, that the First Amendment
was designed to protect two kinds of interest in free speech:
the freedom of the individual to express himself and the freedom of society to listen, to weigh arguments, to balance
claims. The boundary to free speech "is fixed close to the
point where words will give rise to unlawful acts," and "the
great interest in free speech should be sacrificed only when
the interest in public safety is really imperiled, and not ...
when it is barely conceivable that it may be slightly affected."13 This is especially true in peacetime.

We next turn to free speech as it applies to religion,
a subject on which we tend to be more sensitive than on any
other. Criticism of one's most personal spiritual beliefs is
bad manners at the least. It may become a serious nuisance,
as it was when Jehovah's Witnesses hired loudspeakers to
condemn publicly the members or tenets of other faiths. As
a result many communities passed ordinances requiring li-
censes for the use of sound trucks. Jehovah's Witnesses,
however, ignored this legislation and continued berating other
creeds; they were arrested, prosecuted, and eventually ap-
pealed their case to the Supreme Court on the grounds that
such licensing requirement constituted an abridgment of free
speech. The Court, by a 5-4 vote, sustained the Witnesses,
and the ordinance designed to curb the overexuberant preach-
ings of this sect was declared unconstitutional. 14 An even
clearer case is that of Lovell (a Jehovah's Witness) v. Griffin (Ga.), where it was held by Justice Hughes, speaking for
a unanimous Court, that an ordinance requiring written per-

mission from the city manager for the distribution of literature of any kind was unconstitutional. "Whatever the motive
which induced its adoption," said Hughes, "its character is
such that it strikes at the very foundation of the freedom of
the press by subjecting it to license and censorship."[15] It
should be noted that free speech was the issue in both these
cases, not criticism of religion. This issue was not even
raised. Just as it is legally proper to criticize agnosticism,
paganism, atheism, or any other negative form of religion,
so it is proper to criticize its positive forms--Judaism,
Catholicism, or any of the branches of Protestantism.

Interference with the right to criticize religions has
been a serious library problem only sporadically in a few
localities. Christian Scientists objected to Edward Dakin's
biography of Mary Baker Eddy, published by Scribner's in
the 1920's; and you are undoubtedly familiar with the strenuous objection raised in New York and a few other places to
the Nation's series of articles by Paul Blanshard in which he
criticized certain aspects of the Catholic church. In neither
case did the issue reach the courts, for the right of publication guaranteed in the Constitution was too patent. Yet in
both cases pressures were brought against libraries, and
some censorship resulted. Censorship of the Blanshard articles in the Nation took a particularly serious form in New
York, for not only were the issues containing the offensive
articles removed from school-library shelves but subscriptions to the periodical were canceled at the direction of the
superintendent of schools. We find here an implied threat
against any periodical that may contemplate the publication
of any article to which some powerful and numerous group
might take exception.

It seems unnecessary to stress the library's responsibilities in this delicate area. The right to criticize religion
must not be abrogated any more than the parallel right to
criticize social or political beliefs. We plainly have the right
to look critically at any religion, and members of a religious
group lay themselves open to suspicion if they attempt to deny
to anyone this right. The answer to free speech is more
free speech, not its obliteration. Serious discussion of the
beliefs or operations of any established church is surely
proper material for a public library.

In spite of the dangers of censorship of political and
social ideas, it is in the area of morals that librarians have
experienced the greatest difficulty, both from external inter-

ference and from the nature of the decision concerning the
line between morality and immorality. Strictly speaking, it
is not morality that introduces the problem but such concepts
as obscenity, pornography, filth, or whatever other synonyms
one prefers. Here too, as in political censorship, the First
Amendment is invariably invoked by the publisher or author
whose book is objected to. He may claim that the book is
not obscene, or, less frequently, he may argue that the free-
speech principle confers an unlimited right and that considerations of obscenity are irrelevant. However, we clearly
have the right to legislate against the distribution of filth,
and in one notable case, United States v. Limehouse, the
Supreme Court upheld such a right. One Limehouse had
written letters which the Court characterized as coarse, vul-
gar, disgusting, indecent, and unquestionably filthy within
the popular meaning of that term.[16] Does this type of thing
create "a clear and present danger"? It would be difficult
to prove this, yet Justice Brandeis took the position that
Congress had the right to punish the distribution of filth.

It will be recognized that this was not the sort of
"free speech" the Founding Fathers had in mind when drawing up the First Amendment. It has nothing to do with ar-
riving at truth or rational decisions on the basis of conflicting ideas, of presenting evidence for a point of view, or even
of propagandizing for or against action construed in the public interest. The suppression of such speech harms no one
but the individual suppressed. His right to be obscene is
curbed in the interest of a larger right--that of the rest of
us to be saved from his obscenities. Chafee has likened this
to the curb we place on an individual to prevent his smoking
in streetcars. The injury in both cases is immediate, in the
discomfort caused the nonsmokers and in the shock to the
sensitive listener and reader. Free speech does not include
license or licentiousness; the "clear and present danger" test
cannot here be invoked to draw the line between the permissible and the proscribed.[17]

This, however, is only the beginning and the simplest
part of the problem. The major question remains that of an
operational rather than of a dictionary definition of obscenity.
This has turned out to be a matter of extraordinary difficulty,
and it has been treated with little consistency from one court
to another; frequently the decision seems to have been based
on hunch or intuition--at any rate, without the spelling-out of
a definition acceptable to other judges, to publishers, or to
librarians. We speak glibly about ours being a nation governed

by laws; but laws are not only made by men, they are also
interpreted by men, and one man's interpretation is different
from another's.   Hence the vast number of dissenting opinions, in obscenity cases as well as in others.

    Historically, American and British law has tended to
rely on the definition provided by Lord Chief Justice Cockburn, in 1868, in ruling against a pamphlet entitled The Con-
fessional Unmasked: "I think the test of obscenity is this,
whether the tendency of the matter charged as obscenity is
to deprave and corrupt those whose minds are open to such
immoral influences, and into whose hands a publication of
this sort may fall."18   By this definition we must determine
for any one publication whether its effect is likely to be that
envisaged by Judge Cockburn, and such decision is reserved
to the courts.   Usually, objection to certain books is raised
by local police, perhaps at the instigation of private individuals or groups, and is disposed of by local courts.   Federal
courts have been involved far less frequently.

    Lord Cockburn's formulation, continually cited as a
guide, has recently been considered quite unsatisfactory because it goes much too far.   It tacitly accepts as the boundary line the lowest common denominator of human intelligence.
Any book might conceivably fall into the hands of a child or
of a pathological adult who might thereby be corrupted.   As
Justice Qua, in the Massachusetts Strange Fruit case, observed: "A book placed in general circulation is not to be
condemned merely because it might have an unfortunate effect upon some few members of the community who might be
peculiarly susceptible."19   (Even so, Justice Qua joined the
majority of the Massachusetts Supreme Court in upholding the
right of the lower court to find the book obscene.)

    In general, the recent tendency has been--outside Bos-
ton--to permit considerable latitude to the author, though
most commentators agree that a line must be drawn somewhere.   Liberal and intelligent commentators--like Chafee
and Huntington Cairns, who as former assistant general counsel to the Treasury Department was charged with ruling on
literary importations--believe the line should be drawn at
pornography, and on this point Cairns has written as follows:

        Art ... has its own morality, its own integrity,
        which those who would limit its treatment of sexual
        detail would do well to recognize....   We have to
        recognize, however, that this principle of justifica-

> tion covers only half, or less than half, the case.
> Not all writing is literature, not all information is
> science.   There is ... that class of material which
> is put forward with no other purpose in view than
> the stimulation of the sexual impulse.... In their
> bulk, these photographs and drawings, these miser-
> ably printed pamphlets and books, are as far re-
> moved from art as they could well be.... The
> principle which accords complete freedom to the
> artist and scientist in the treatment of sexual detail
> plainly does not justify pornography. [20]

He then goes on to say: "There is no difficulty in distinguishing between those books the impulse behind which is
literary and those whose impulse is pornographic.   Any man
with a modicum of literary knowledge can do so without hesitation. " I wonder if Mr. Cairns would be quite so confident
today.   Consider the interesting case of Edmund Wilson's
Memoirs of Hecate County.   The book raised a storm of protest throughout the country, and the publisher, Doubleday,
was brought before the New York Court of Special Sessions
on the grounds of the book's alleged obscenity.   Here it was
judged obscene, with one justice dissenting.   He held that the
prosecution's interpretation of the law was "grossly inadequate," and he stated:

> The writer of the story is evidently and honestly
> concerned with the complex influences of sex and
> of class consciousness and man's relentless search
> for happiness.   That is a problem which also is of
> deep concern to the matured reading public.   That
> public is entitled to the benefit of the writer's in-
> sight and that right may not lightly be disregarded
> by excluding from consideration all interests but
> those of the young and immature. [21]

Nevertheless the book was held obscene, the judgment ap-
pealed successively to the Appellate Court, the Appeals Court,
and the United States Supreme Court, and all upheld the ruling of the lower court.   In the Supreme Court the vote was
a 4-4 tie.   Clearly the line between honest writing and obscenity is not easy to draw, even by persons with considerably more than Mr. Cairns's suggested "modicum of literary
knowledge. "

Perhaps the most widely publicized censorship case in
recent years is that of James Joyce's Ulysses.   This book,

published abroad, was held up in customs on the charge of
obscenity, and the case was heard before Judge Woolsey in
the United States District Court.   Judge Woolsey first raised
the question of author's intent and concluded that the book
was not written "for the purpose of exploiting obscenity."
"I do not detect anywhere," he wrote, "the leer of the sen-
sualist."   But a second question arises: in spite of the author's sincerity, in spite of the book's quality, is it likely to
harm the reader?   Or, in line with the somewhat lurid language of the statute, did the book tend "to stir the sex impulses or to lead to sexually impure and lustful thoughts?"
In short, what would be its effect upon the average man--
l'homme moyen sensuel?

To answer this question, Judge Woolsey depended not
only upon his own reading but also upon the opinions of two
friends.   Their conclusion was that the book did not tend to
excite sexual impulses but instead served as "a somewhat
tragic and very powerful commentary on the inner lives of
men and women."   Judge Woolsey said in his decision: "I
am quite aware that owing to some of its scenes Ulysses is
a rather strong draught to ask some sensitive, though normal,
persons to take.   But my considered opinion, after long reflection, is that, whilst in many places the effect of Ulysses
on the reader undoubtedly is somewhat emetic, nowhere does
it tend to be an aphrodisiac."22

Three elements in this case are worth noting.   The
first is the consideration of the author's intent; the second,
the possible effect on the reader; and the third, the method
used to arrive at a decision--that of inviting others to join
in judging the book.   In a sense this method is the same as
dependence on a jury but with this difference: that here the
friends of the judge were selected deliberately for their ability to make a mature judgment on a difficult work of literary
craftsmanship.

Thus far we have seen how the objection to obscene
literature revolves around a question of definition, a definition not contained in the statutes enacted against obscenity
but, rather, left to the courts.   First, we have seen that in
some instances pornography is readily identified and is beyond
the protection of the First Amendment.   Second, we have
seen that the "clear and present danger" test is difficult to
apply when the issue is obscenity.   Who can say where the
danger lies in being exposed to dirty language or unconventional situations?   If we were to apply this test to literature,

we might as well give up any attempt to bar filth. If a book is not obviously pornographic and if the "clear and present danger" test cannot be invoked, how shall the line be drawn? Here the answer has been the standards of the community, or, as Chafee suggests, how much frankness the community will stand. 23 This I frankly do not like; it seems to substitute one difficulty for another, without solving the basic problem. The "community" itself is difficult to define; is it a region, a city, or a neighborhood? Is it the majority of adults, and, if so, how do we know what they will accept? If we cannot depend on majorities, whose level shall be accepted as representing the community--that of a well-read minority or of a poorly read, superficial majority, or some thing in between? Under the circumstances, our best solution is probably the one Judge Woolsey hit upon: to rely upon the judgment of intelligent readers and to expect them to be as liberal as possible in making their decision. There is far less danger to the community, however defined, in permitting questionable literature to be published and read than there is in a strict definition of "obscenity" that would deny access to such literature. After all, what is the real objection? Are the censors afraid that we will be offended by books like Studs Lonigan? If there be any among us who would be offended, the solution is simple and readily at hand: we can close the book. Happily the freedom to read implies the freedom to desist from reading. But many of us will not desist, and that is what the censor truly fears: not that we will be offended but that we will be pleased. 24

Where does this leave the library? Shall the library provide books which some courts--notably in Massachusetts-- have ruled obscene? Shall it consider as unacceptable books that have actually been cleared by the courts? And what about the large mass of books that never come to the courts at all? In fact, it is this group that may cause the library the most heart-searching and even embarrassment. The library cannot wait for a test case to be brought to trial, yet it must make its decision shortly after publication. My answer would be that in the first case, where the courts have ruled a book obscene, it all depends on which court. If it is a state or municipal court, we need take its ruling seriously only when our library is within the jurisdiction of the ordinance on which the court acts. There is no reason for a library in Ohio to remove Strange Fruit from its collection merely because a Massachusetts court considered it obscene. In the second case, where a book has been cleared by the courts, that is a point in its favor, although there may be

other good and sufficient reasons why it may be rejected by
the library. A book should have more to commend it than
the mere absence of dirt before it is judged legitimate library
bookstock.

As for the third case, where we cannot look to the
courts for guidance, I believe we must depend on some such
test as that which Judge Woolsey applied. Here the librarian
himself must be the judge, and he should apply his best efforts toward determining whether the book in question, taken
as a whole, is to be considered obscene. In making his decision he should give the benefit of the doubt to the book.
Presumably, it is not "dirt for dirt's sake"; like most books,
it is not likely to lead the reader to sexual excesses or immorality; it is not likely to give offense to the normal reader
because of its language or frank descriptions. If the librarian,
like Judge Woolsey, wishes to check his judgment against that
of others, he may call on literate citizens at large, whose
judgment he trusts, for an opinion. They too should be very
slow to rule against a book, and in judging its possible effect
on the library's readers they should certainly not take as the
norm the adolescent or immature adult, nor should they give
undue weight to the probability that the book will offend some
people. Most important of all, they should never lose sight
of the fact of which Chafee reminds us, "that stamping on a
fire often spreads the sparks, that many past suppressions
are now considered ridiculous, that the communication of ideas
is just as important in this field as in any other, and that
healthy human minds have a strong natural resistance to emotional poisons."[25] Remember that Whitman's Leaves of Grass
was at one time considered unfit to be read; remember, too,
that books like The Naked and the Dead and The Young Lions
would probably not have found a publisher twenty years ago
but are today listed among the notable books of 1948.

Yet even with all these precautions some people will
protest. They may be a church group, a superpatriotic society, or even one or two individuals. The protest may be
lodged against books in the political or social realm or against
a novel. It may take the form of mere objection, or it may
become an ugly threat against the library or its librarian.
Even more important, perhaps, is the fear of such objection,
a fear that, oftener than we think, may lead a librarian or
library board to rule out certain books to avoid an embar-
rassing situation which may develop--in short, to deprive the
potential and interested reader rather than take a chance on
someone's objection. Such objection is thought to create bad

public relations, though we should remember that equally bad
public relations may develop by failing to provide certain
books.

Let us analyze this situation for a moment, taking the
matter of a potential objection first. We might as well recognize that this is an ever present possibility; we can never escape the chance that someone may feel unhappy about a particular book. Yet I think that in an overwhelming number of
cases, where a library has actually obtained the book, no
protest developed at all. Fear of protest usually turns out
to be a straw man. But suppose that a protest is lodged:
should it be taken seriously enough to withdraw the book?
We must consider the nature of the book and the nature of
the protestant. If the book was seriously weighed in the light
of its quality and of library policy and was acquired because
it met the standards imposed by the library, I see no reason
for its withdrawal. As for the protestant, does he represent
a sufficiently numerous citizenry, or is he speaking solely
for himself or for a special group? Even if the librarian
were to decide on the basis of numbers, why should he assume that more people would object to the book than would
welcome it or would at least be indifferent to its provision?

We hear a great deal these days about the need to protect minorities, particularly their right to free speech and
assembly. But in protecting minority rights we must be careful to distinguish between the right to express and the right
to dominate. Majorities also have their rights: no minority
should abuse its privilege so as to shackle the majority.
What "right" permits any minority--racial, national, or re-
ligious--tacitly to say to the rest of the community: "You
shall not read this book"? In assuring minorities their right
to self-expression, their right to object, let us not extend to
them the privilege of dictating to the rest of us what we may
or may not read. As the philosopher F. H. Bradley has
written: "What is not tolerable is that stunted natures should
set up their defects as a standard. It is an outrage, it is
sheer blasphemy, when they bring the divine creations of literature and art to the touchstone of their own impotence,
their own animalism, and their own immorality."[26]

Censorship is an evil thing. In accepting it, in com-
promising, in "playing it safe," the librarian is false to the
highest obligations of his profession. In resisting it, he retains his self-respect, he takes his stand with the great champions of free speech, and he reaffirms his fundamental faith in
the dignity of man.

NOTES

1. This paper was presented at the Fourth Annual Library Symposium, Kent State University, Kent, Ohio, on May 13, 1949.

2. Encyclopaedia of the Social Sciences, III (New York: Macmillan Co. , 1930), 290.

3. John Stuart Mill, On Liberty (Boston: Atlantic Monthly Press, 1921), pp. 12-13.

4. Ibid. , p. 16.

5. Ibid. , p. 23.

6. Ibid. , p. 90.

7. Ibid. , p. 72.

8. Schenck v. United States, 249 United States Reports 47 (1919).

9. Abrams v. United States, 250 United States Reports 616, 624 (1919).

10. Max Lerner (ed.), The Mind and Faith of Justice Holmes: His Speeches, Essays, Letters and Judicial Opinions (Boston: Little, Brown & Co. , 1943), p. 306.

11. It is worth noting that in the recent trial of the eleven Communists in the U. S. District Court in New York, Judge Harold R. Medina included the following statement in his charge to the jury: "Books are not on trial here, nor are you concerned with the philosophical validity of any mere theories" (New York Times, October 14, 1949).

12. Pierce v. United States, 252 United States Reports 239 (1929).

13. Zechariah Chafee, Jr. , Free Speech in the United States (Cambridge: Harvard University Press, 1948), p. 35.

14. Saia v. People of the State of New York, 344 United

States Reports 558 (1948).

15. Lovell v. Griffin, 303 United States Reports 444 (1938).

16. United States v. Limehouse, 285 United States Reports
        424 (1932).

17. Zechariah Chafee, Jr., Government and Mass Communi-
        cations (Chicago: University of Chicago Press,
        1947), I, 55-56.

18. Regina v. Hicklin, Law Reports, 3 Queen's Bench 360
        at 371 (1868).

19. Commonwealth v. Isenstadt, 318 Massachusetts Reports
        at 551-54 (1945).

20. Huntington Cairns, "Freedom of Expression in Litera-
        ture," Annals of the American Academy of Political
        and Social Science, CC (Philadelphia, 1938), 85.

21. Justice Perlman's dissent.

22. United States v. One Book Called "Ulysses," 5 Federal
        Supplement 182 (N.Y., 1933).

23. Chafee, Government and Mass Communications, I, 215.

24. "The objection which the Watch and Ward Society makes
        to many of the books it wishes to suppress is not
        that these books offend readers but that they de-
        light them.... The true fear of the censor is that
        the ideas set forth will in the long run undermine
        our present system of marriage and morality" (ibid.,
        p. 57).

25. Ibid., p. 215.

26. Quoted in Cairns, op. cit.

THE LIBRARY'S COLLECTION
IN A TIME OF CRISIS*

Margaret E. Monroe

It is almost too pat to speak of our era as a time of
crisis. What does this mean? A time of excitement? A
series of emergencies; problems that must be dealt with in
short order, demanding rapid analysis of difficulties and
swiftly chosen solutions? Or is it a time of quandary, when
the fundamental questions find no simple answers because
conflicting values are involved within each problem? Is it,
as Webster says, "a point at which hostile elements are most
tensely opposed"? Or is crisis a turning point--a point after
which things are never again the same, and thus an opportunity, perhaps, as well as a danger?

What is the role of the library at these turning points,
at these moments of decision? Is it a matter of too little
and too late? Must the library have made its contribution
long before or not at all? "Crisis" has the tone of heightened
emotion; surely the library's contribution is one of fact and
reason.

There is a litany of purposes which public librarians
have come to repeat: research, information, education,
recreation, and aesthetic experience. Army and hospital librarians join their voices in the familiar sequence. College
and university librarians adapt these, each to his own liking.

The Role of the Collection

In the first place, the library's collection contributes information. It must meet the informational demands which individuals and society make on it because of the crisis. The demands of the unemployed for books to retrain in vocational skills must be met, as well as the demands of the employer for materials to assist in the changeover within the industrial plant. The problems created for individuals by a public crisis must be assisted toward solution by the provision of information.

Second, the public crisis itself must be understood, and the library must contribute to a program of public education by supplying background information, the various analyses of the problem and their companion solutions. These must be available at the diverse levels of understanding required by the community to be served. Young, middle-aged and older citizens have different approaches to the problem of a rapidly aging population, and materials from varied points of view must be available.

Third, resources for research to alleviate the public crisis must be made available. Until the crisis is past there is hope for a useful solution, and information is the basic matter of the researcher. The solutions to the problems of school integration are still to be spelled out from the record in the literature of psychology, sociology, and education.

Beyond the passive supplying of information, the library's collection must direct attention to the public crisis in ways conducive to its happy solution. The availability of important titles, their promotion by display, the interpretation of their significance through reading lists, book talks, lectures and discussion are among the ways of ensuring use of the library's collection for the solution of the problem. For example, no public issue of the moment relies more heavily on the wide range of library techniques to stimulate attention than the present crisis in United States foreign policy.

Finally, the library's collection must be used with individual readers to sustain attention to important aspects of the problem. This is essential to informed public opinion and to readiness for decision and action. This is the educational function of the library's collection, which is marshalled to meet the needs of the inquisitive mind. This is Mr. Ul-

veling's "prescription service." The public crisis in the
field of science--the growing gulf between the scientist and
the layman, between the scientist and policy-maker--can be
bridged only by such sustained learning on a broad scale in
our society.

Principles of Selection

Librarianship has developed two principles on the relationship of its collection to a public crisis. These two principles guide librarians in selecting materials of opinion and
of fact.

The first principle makes clear that in areas of opin-
ion--such as most public issues present--the best statements
of the hostile elements and conflicting values must be available among the library's materials. A corollary has been
tentatively suggested: that the librarian should encourage the
reader to use materials representing more than one point of
view. A related assumption has been enunciated, but not
without contest: that--in the United States--we trust readers
to identify propaganda for what it is and to make sound judgments on the relative merits of varied positions on critical
problems. Some librarians see a fallacy in accepting the
public's discrimination as fact, rather than as an ideal essential to sound democratic function. These librarians propose rather that readers be given an opportunity to acquire
this kind of discrimination.

A second corollary is one not often acknowledged but
frequently the basis for judgment in building the library's collection. It is that in library collections serving educational
and informational needs, materials are to be judged not only
by their conformity with scientific fact and their sincerity of
purpose. They are to be judged also by their compatibility
with a few fundamental values upon which human society is
based, and which have been determined by a consensus of
responsible opinion distilled from all fields of knowledge over
the total period of man's culture. These values have not
been formulated exactly by librarians or by society; they are
discerned by the sense of outrage in the educated and civilized
mind when they are ignored.

The second principle which fortifies the library collection in meeting a public crisis is this: that in the areas of
science and documented knowledge, the collection for informa-

tion and educational uses be drawn from authoritative sources. Problems in application of this principle include, of course, the identification of "authority," and a decision in each separate field on what are truly validated facts and what really remains in the realm of opinion. Constant vigilance is needed in scanning new knowledge to redefine the legitimate areas of controversy, and in scrutinizing the library's collection for outdated materials which may deserve perpetuation as historical record but not acceptance as currently valid.

These two principles give appropriate weight to scientific fact and schemes of values in building the library's collection on any issue. In building and interpreting the collection, they obviously demand, if not a subject expert, at least a librarian conversant with the specialist's knowledge. They leave one question unanswered, however: since these two principles were developed in relation to collections to be used for information and educational purposes, how do they apply to materials for a research collection, or for recreational or aesthetic purposes?

Problems of Application

The research collection is one from which materials are not eliminated for reasons of doubtful or disproven validity, or because they embody values rejected by the consensus of civilized judgment. The relevance of the research collection to public issues and to meeting a public crisis lies in its long-term contribution of fact and opinion, of the record and its analysis and proposal, to the thinking of the specialist and of the research man. The dilemma of the research collection lies not in its materials but in their use by the layman and student for purposes of information and education.

A most important question has arisen over how far recreational materials and creative literature need conform to scientific validity and the consensus of civilized judgment in order to qualify as legitimate library materials. The only aspect of this broad question that concerns us here is the relationship of these materials to meeting a public crisis and illuminating a public issue. Librarians have often exempted such materials from conformity to the details of scientific fact (flying saucers are acceptable fictional adventure while unacceptable as fact) and have permitted great latitude in values to materials designed to create the aesthetic experience. The assumptions behind this practice are that the

reader has the ability to distinguish between fact and fiction
and that his personal scheme of values will enter into the
reading of creative literature and become an important in-
gredient in the aesthetic experience. These are highly de-
fensible positions for librarianship and are probably essential
to the discharge of its responsibility. The dilemma arises
as the library attempts to fulfill its information and education
functions with readers who, while literate, are in no sense
judges of scientific validity or participants in the consensus
of civilized judgment. This large body of illiterate literates
challenges the library's collection as it attempts to meet such
a public crisis as that of human relations.

So much for principles and corollaries.

Awareness of the relationship between the library's
collection and fulfillment of the library's basic purposes has
shown increasing sophistication. There was readiness three
generations ago to exclude literature "apologetic of vice or
confusing distinctions between plain right and wrong," as the
Boston Public Library report of 1875 put it. Librarians
recognized in time that too little is known about the effects
of reading to make such exclusions automatic. A later tendency was to take no responsibility for the effects of reading
on the public. This has been modified to view reader services (such as stimulation of worthy reading interests, individual guidance to suitable reading, development of critical
judgment in literature and ideas, etc.) as the intermediary
between the library's collection and the reader and what he
makes of what he reads.

The development of reader services as the intermediary between the library's collection and the reader in the
past generation has developed one guiding principle for meeting a public crisis: the library should make it impossible
for adults to miss the socially significant materials of their
time, and--as a corollary--the library takes no responsibility for telling people what to think but does take responsibility
for proposing what they shall think about. This serves well
in considering the library's responsibility to public education
about a public crisis.

THE SPECTRE AT RICHMOND*

Stanley Kunitz

To the librarians assembled, or preparing to assemble, at Richmond.

I bring you greetings and my best wishes for the success of your conference. The program that has been arranged for you is a varied one, from addresses on such broad and compelling themes as "Objectives of the Library Profession" to more particularized dissertations on "Microphotography" and "Methodology Used in Compiling a Bibliography in the Field of Agricultural Economics." There is even to be a paper with the teasing title, "So What?" One subject, however, I have failed to find in the program. It is not slated for official discussion. Yet I dare say that none of you will be able to shake your mind free from it for long. It will be a spectre haunting the halls.

I refer to your shockingly cruel and feudal policy with respect--or should I say, "with disrespect"--to Negro librarians at the conference. Let me quote from the "semi-official" letter sent to some of your professional colleagues--those whose skins are more highly pigmented than others':

> Because of the traditional position of the South in respect to mixed meetings it seems necessary to have the position of the American Library Association and its committees made known. It is also advisable to suggest to Negro librarians the conditions they should expect to find in Richmond during the conference.

*Reprinted by permission from the May 1936 issue of the Wilson Library Bulletin. Copyright 1936 by The H. W. Wilson Co.

These are the "conditions" at Richmond, corresponding,
it would seem from the language of the letter, with the "position" of the ALA (italics are my own):

> The American Library Association has obtained the
> promise from the John Marshall and Jefferson Ho-
> tels that Negro delegates to the conference may use
> the same entrance as the white delegates and will
> be received and housed in the same manner during
> the conference meetings. <u>This does not mean that
> Negro delegates may obtain rooms and meals at
> these hotels as this is forbidden by Virginia laws.
> All delegates will also use the main entrances</u> to the
> Mosque auditorium where the general sessions will
> be held. <u>Those meetings which are a part of break-
> fasts, luncheons or dinners are not open to Negroes,
> who may, however, attend sessions which are</u> fol-
> lowed by meals provided they do not participate in
> the meals.
>
> <u>Provisions will be made to seat Negroes in the
> front right hand section of the main floor of the
> auditorium during the general sessions.</u> This same
> section is reserved for them at the large group
> meetings and round tables at the hotels.

In brief, Negro librarians will be segregated throughout the conference; they will not be permitted to attend meetings where food is served.

Unless you believe that Negroes are incapable of being
insulted, you must agree with me that a minority group of
the ALA has been greatly offended. If you permit this organized insult to pass unchallenged, there is but one conclusion to be made: that American librarians do not, in their
hearts, care for democracy or for the foundation principles
of decent and enlightened institutions. No elegant platform
phrases of devotion to the idea of a free and equal society or
to the theory of liberty can be sufficient to obviate that conclusion.

You may say, as assuredly will be said, in defence
of the Negro policy at the conference, that it is merely con-
forming with the laws of Virginia. To this I reply that there
is a higher law ... and that we have forty-eight States in the
Union. Other organizations make a practice of convening only
in communities where their own standards of eligibility and

respectability are honored.   An association of American professional men and women cannot go into convention part white
and part black without doing violence to the best thought and
the highest hope of our national life.

For the culture of Virginia, mother of much that is
noblest in our American heritage, I have a profound respect.
Will a Virginian rise to tell me that his culture is not broad
enough or deep enough to tolerate the Christian spectacle of
black and white librarians meeting together in free fellowship
and dining at a common table?   Interracial student meetings,
I am informed, have been held before in the South, where
all delegates have eaten together.   Unless the clock turns
backward, the South will welcome more of these meetings,
will multiply them, where the bread of tolerance is broken
and shared.

Along with my greetings, then, I bring you the burden
of responsibility for action.   "The trusteeship of truth is a
serious responsibility," wrote the Vice-Chancellor of Birming-
ham University a few months ago in rejecting Heidelberg's
invitation to participate in the celebration of its five hundred
and fiftieth anniversary....   "Cooperation can be purchased
at too dear a price if one of the parties surrenders the first
principles of a free life....   Treachery to truth and betrayal
of the conditions in which alone truth can be saved and promoted are a breach of trusteeship, the consequences of which
may be irreparable."

You have your trusteeship.   What do you propose to
do with it?

SEGREGATED LIBRARIES*

Rice Estes

A recent issue of Library Journal (see LJ, Sept. 1,
'60) carried two news items whose juxtaposition should give
pause to all libraries. One of the items was headed "Danville plans private library after closing of public libraries."
The other bore the caption, "Books for Ghana." The first
told the melancholy story of how the citizens of Danville,
Virginia, had voted to close its public library because Negro citizens had won a desegregation order from a federal
court. The other told of a generous group of world-minded
library trustees in Massachusetts who decided to celebrate
their library's centenary by sending 1000 books and a check
to a Ghana library where books are needed to "help unite
peoples of different races, standards, religions, habits and
manners into one world of humanity."

The two stories could not have been more ironically
placed, showing up as they did one of the anomalies of our
time, namely, the American concern for the welfare of our
darker-skinned brothers in distant parts of the world on the
one hand, while on the other, failure to provide adequately
for the education of the Negroes of our own country. That
natives of Ghana may look to American libraries for help
while citizens of Danville, Virginia, bereft of access to books,
were left without a librarian's voice lifted in their behalf (to
the writer's knowledge), indicates the gulf that separates the
library profession as a whole from the social reality of our
times.

*Reprinted from Library Journal 85:4418-4421 (December
1960).   Published by the R. R. Bowker Co. (a Xerox Company). Copyright 1960 by R. R. Bowker Co.

The recent conference of the American Library Association at Montreal had as its theme "Breaking Barriers," a noble and uplifting slogan which undoubtedly brought inspiration to the 4000-odd delegates present. But, as was pointed out during the Conference, lofty terms unfortunately do not break barriers. When a barrier is set up, the only way to break it is to do something. So far no library association seems willing to do anything about the most pressing domestic issue the nation faces today, the integration and education of our Negro citizens. Instead librarians are piously declaring that they will not become involved in local problems. The term "local" is never defined.

But when did librarians become shy of local problems? Was not the Intellectual Freedom Committee of ALA set up primarily to deal with local interference with reading? When a book is banned in the smallest hamlet, there is a vigorous protest--as indeed there should be--that the Library Bill of Rights is defamed and that reading privileges are being denied. Such a protest is usually supported by a majority of librarians. But when a city takes away the right of citizens to read every book in the public library, we say nothing. The problem has suddenly become "local," a very good alternative for "untouchable."

The problem of segregated libraries in the South-- and the writer of these words is a southerner--is certainly a complex one and difficult for outsiders to understand. The curious difference in temper in various localities, the progress of some cities and the backsliding of others, are quite confusing. For instance, Danville and Petersburg, Virginia closed their public libraries rather than admit Negro readers on an integrated basis, while Norfolk and other Virginia cities, only a few miles away, voluntarily desegregated their libraries. The Norfolk Public Library, through the valiant efforts of one civic-minded woman, has developed a friends association with over 500 members to help improve library service for a completely integrated system. Chattanooga desegregated some years ago without incident, but in Memphis a near-riot broke out over the subject. This inconsistent pattern is perplexing but proves that progress can be made, for it has been made in many communities. And much more progress can be achieved if all educated people in the nation work toward a brighter future.

Many librarians are unaware of the fact that most public libraries below the Mason and Dixon Line are segre-

gated. In the majority of towns and cities Negro readers are
not only denied entrance to white branches, they are also denied entrance to the main central library where most of the
books are housed. They are thus not only confined to a
small branch or branches of their own but are deprived of
access to the principal book collection in the locality. Although some are permitted to borrow through inter-branch
loan, most Negro readers never are allowed to browse through
the primary collections and never know of the existence of
many books which their taxes help to buy and which are freely used by any white citizen. In some localities there is no
library service for Negro citizens at all. In one such place
where I was a recent visitor, I asked one of the librarians
how Negro readers were serviced. "Oh," she said, "they
are not interested in reading." I wondered if she had ever
read the poignant passage in Richard Wright's classic Black
Boy, which recounts his experience of illicitly withdrawing
books from the public library in Memphis. If only this passage could be reprinted and sent to every trustee of every
library in the South, surely fruit would be borne.

        The complacency with which so many librarians sit
back and accept the status quo is what is so disturbing today.
The urgent need for an educated, aware citizenry must be
apparent to each one of us if western civilization is to sur-
vive and yet we read negative editorials to the effect that we
"must not interfere." What kind of reasoning is this? Is
supporting the cause of public libraries for all "interference"?
Surely this cannot be the philosophy of a group of people so
aggressive as to lobby and see passed the excellent Library
Services Act which takes library service to areas where it
has never been before.

        The confusion seems to arise from our failure to under-
stand that Negro citizens in the South are looking to us for
support, not interference. It is natural that they should look
to us for we are the only librarians who are free to lend
support. Their own librarians, the majority of whom would
be overjoyed to see the present situation improve, cannot
easily speak out because of reprisals and political retaliation.
Many of the very people most willing and eager to help may
be unable singly to voice their opinion. It is these people
who must know that they can rely on us to bring light to an
utterly darkened situation where emotion has long since overwhelmed sound reason.

        To these whose fear of "interference" seems as emo-

tional as those southerners who fear "integration," would it
be too much to ask that northern associations, and especially the Intellectual Freedom Committee of ALA, write letters
to trustees of larger southern libraries urging an end to library segregation? Would a request be considered interference? Would it be too much to ask that we write officers of
state associations in the South and ask if a stand on the issue
might be taken? Would it be possible to find out where southern libraries have desegregated and where they have not,
lending support where we can?

These are measures that we would think any professional association would consider. An editorial in the Wilson Library Bulletin of September 1960 states, in discussing
this matter, that the American Library Association is as effective against segregation "as its structure permits." I
challenge this statement. The American Library Association
has been completely ineffective about the issue. It has never
even passed a resolution on the subject. It has never commended the efforts of Negro readers and organizations who
have tried to end library segregation by doing everything
from making a mild request to staging library sit-ins. It
has not attempted to bring a law suit or lent its name as
amicus curiae to any group bringing a suit.

Officers of the ALA have made countless speeches
across the land since the famous Supreme Court decision of
1954, but if any speech specifically called for improvement in
the library situation in the South, then that speech received
little circulation.

In Montreal we were told that ALA's attitude toward
segregation was defined in the Library Bill of Rights, but if
the principles of the bill are not implemented, of what value
is the Bill of Rights to Negro readers--or for that matter,
to anyone? Why can't ALA just come out and say it stands
four-square for integrated libraries? A mere statement is
better than nothing.

ALA has done many truly great things. It has a
splendid program of activities and publications. It has set
up an effective lobby in Washington; it has organized plans
for regional development; it has developed an international
program. But it has not done anything about segregation in
libraries. We haven't done anything because we haven't cared
enough. We have cared about the Victory Book Campaign and
the Books for Overseas Libraries but somehow it doesn't

seem to bother us that nearly ten million Negro citizens in
our land are totally or partially denied free access to publicly
owned books.   We would rather send books to Ghana than to
Danville because there is no one in Ghana to offend.   The
problem in Ghana is merely to educate Negroes.   But the
problem in the South is complicated, and therefore, easier
to ignore.

ALA already has the machinery with which to work
on this problem.   No new committee is needed.   The Intellectual Freedom Committee would do wonders if it would.
It could set up sub-committees of enlightened librarians and
library users in every state where needed.   These committees might then help in emergency situations.   Has it occurred to anyone that Petersburg might listen to the trustees
and librarians of Norfolk?   But who will ask Norfolk to speak
out and Petersburg to listen?   Someone must get these people together.   (The Petersburg Library has now opened on
an integrated basis--Ed.).   Groups of southern liberals can
surely be organized to work for the victory of reason but they
must represent someone more than themselves.   They cannot work alone.   They must have the backing of a strong organization, and the ALA, with its local chapters, has the
strength to support a program which could become an intellectual freedom campaign.

When we have public libraries and bookmobiles in all
parts of this nation open to all citizens who care to make
use of them, then we can pat ourselves on the back and say
we have done all that our structure permits, for this problem will then be solved.   As Harry Golden says: "When you
are worried about others, you are fearless.   When you fight
for others, you build an impregnable wall of security around
yourself. "

THE DISADVANTAGED MAJORITY:
Women Employed in Libraries*

Anita Schiller

In most professions women are the disadvantaged minority. In librarianship they are the disadvantaged majority.
Although librarianship traditionally has been open to women's
employment, and today about four out of every five librarians
are women, their salaries tend typically to be lower than
those of men librarians. The top positions in the largest institutions are held increasingly by men, and there appears
to be a growing trend toward greater inequality between the
sexes in the library profession. A national study of academic librarians in 1966-67 showed, for example, that the median salary for men ($8990), was about $1500 higher than that
for women ($7455), that men were about twice as likely as
women to be chief librarians, and that men who were not
chief librarians tended to earn more than women who were. [1]
The findings show further that as experience increases, median salary differentials between men and women grow progressively wider, even where educational levels of the two groups
are equal. These findings highlight the need to examine the
question of equality of opportunity for women in librarianship.

Although many previous studies of librarians reveal
similar kinds of inequalities, the status of women in the profession has not been singled out as a matter of special concern, and little serious attention has been devoted to the subject. A check of Library Literature from 1921 to date shows,
for example, that in the past fifty years only one published
monograph has appeared on women in librarianship, and this

---

*Reprinted by permission of the American Library Associa-
tion from American Libraries 1:345-349 (April 1970). Copyright 1970 by the American Library Association.

was done recently in Great Britain. [2]   Three master's theses
and occasional articles have attempted to assemble some basic
data, but even when taken together the picture they drew is
sketchy, at best.   The index to the 1969 <u>Bowker Annual</u> ...,
a basic source of current information about libraries and librarians, contains only one reference to women, and this is
for the address of the Women's National Book Association.
And despite the fact that library manpower has been considered as a top priority professional issue, there has been little, if any, attempt to examine the special kinds of personnel
problems which relate to women librarians, even though they
comprise the numerical majority of the profession.

Why then, when there are alarming signs of growing
inequality of opportunity for women in librarianship, does the
profession seem so basically unconcerned about uncovering
the facts and examining the issues?   Although other professions have begun to consider how women can be attracted to
their ranks in larger numbers, and several professional associations recently have passed specific resolutions aimed at
improving the status of women in their respective fields, the
library profession has remained remarkably aloof from this
matter.   Many librarians, it seems, would prefer it if the
subject never came up at all, or better still, if women had
never entered librarianship in the first place.   Just think
how this would have changed the librarian's image!

It is important to bring this view out into the open,
for because the majority of its practitioners are women, librarianship is different from most professions, and reluctance to discuss the status of women librarians may have
something to do with this important fact.   Librarians esteem
the contribution they make toward society, and they seek to
win the public recognition they believe the profession deserves.
By calling attention to the problems of women in librarianship,
public attention would continue to dwell on the fact that many
librarians are indeed women, and this is no mark of prestige
for any profession.   Furthermore, studies of librarians consistently show that men librarians, as a group, are typically
younger than the women, and the profession, by attracting
more men, would undoubtedly benefit from a lowering of
overall age levels as well.

It is not, then, in the best interest of the library profession simply to ignore the question of women as long as it
can, hoping that women eventually will cease to enter the field,
and join the other professions which claim to want them?

This, indeed, may be the implicitly desired goal of the present policy of the American Library Association. A do-nothing policy has an apparent appeal. But can the ALA continue to countenance basic social injustice within the profession which it represents? In its attempts to improve and upgrade librarianship, can the Association continue to ignore the status of the majority of its members? And can it remain impervious to the aspirations of this majority, while a movement for the rights of women is gaining worldwide momentum?

The United Nations Declaration of Women's Rights, adopted by the General Assembly on November 7, 1967, states that "discrimination against women, denying or limiting as it does their equality of rights with men is fundamentally unjust and constitutes an offense against human dignity." (Article I) This document goes on further to state that "all appropriate measures shall be taken to educate public opinion ... toward the eradication of prejudice and the abolition of customary and all other practices which are based on the idea of the inferiority of women." (Article III) While there are undoubtedly certain social conditions, in addition to open job discrimination, which contribute to the low status of women, and while these may operate much more subtly, if we genuinely believe in equality of opportunity, why don't we say so? In its reluctance to commit itself on this issue, the library profession has accommodated itself to social prejudice.

An interesting sidelight, which illustrates how out-of-touch with the times we are, is provided by the subject headings librarians have devised to categorize the attainments of women in the various professions: The Library of Congress Subject Headings.... for example, uses the term "Women as authors," not "Women authors"; "Women as physicians," not "Women physicians"; "Women as librarians," not "Women librarians," etc. [3] (Yet when we come to "Women as criminals," we are advised to refer to the heading "Delinquent women.") While it is delightful to note the cross reference "Women, see also Charm," and disturbing to find the heading "Women as colonists," it is clear that this terminology, which arose in a bygone age, is not in keeping with present conditions. The view that we should not seek equal opportunity between the sexes is similarly, but much more seriously, out-of-date.

Librarians today are in a unique position to challenge popular prejudice by actively seeking to promote genuine equality within the library profession itself. By seeking to

improve conditions of employment, and by raising educational
standards at all levels of the profession--the bottom as well
as the top--librarianship can strengthen its own position. Librarianship cannot upgrade itself without upgrading opportunities for women who constitute the majority of the profession.
Nor should it expect to gain the public esteem that it seeks
by tacitly endorsing inequality of opportunity, and furthering,
by its own inaction, the all-too-familiar image of librarianship
as a passive, unchallenging, and low-paid profession. If librarianship has sufficient self-respect for its own contribution,
it will not belittle itself by following other professions backward into the nineteenth century to exclude women from its
ranks or to keep them in less privileged positions, while
other professions begin now to lower the barriers to women's
advancement. On the contrary, since librarianship opened
its doors to women well before most other professions, it
can lead the way toward full social equality within the professions by seeking to become the first profession to establish
equal career opportunities between the sexes.

The library profession should be able to compete on
equal ground among all professions for the most talented and
capable recruits of both sexes. There is no good reason
why librarianship should lose competent women recruits to
other professions because it fails to offer women equal opportunities for advancement. Yet this may occur, if librarianship fails to improve the status of women while other professions offer them increasing opportunities for study and advancement. Similarly, there is no good reason why librarianship should lose competent men recruits to other fields because it fails to offer competitive rewards.

The best interest of the library profession cannot be
served by continuing to allow unequal opportunities for women.
By recognizing and facing this important social issue, and by
seeking consciously and deliberately to change, rather than
accept, popular prejudice, librarianship has everything to
gain.

What then should the ALA do to promote equality of
opportunity within the profession? First, the ALA should
openly state its willingness to deal with the issue, and express its conviction that equal opportunities for women should
be provided. A formal resolution recognizing this commitment should be drawn up and endorsed by the Association.

Second, the ALA should initiate and support a compre-

hensive research program, designed to examine the status of
women in librarianship and to determine how present conditions operate, overtly or subtly, to prevent women from
achieving and maintaining equal status with men. The findings of these research studies should be widely disseminated
among the profession, and used as a guide to official policy.

Third, the ALA should open up the channels of communication for discussion of equality of opportunity within the
library profession. This subject should receive a prominent
position on the agenda at the Association's next annual conference, and an open forum column should appear regularly
in American Libraries.

Together, these three proposals: acknowledging an
interest in improving opportunities for women, supporting research on the status of women and on the nature of discrimination, and encouraging expression of professional opinion
on this important subject, constitute some minimum and immediate steps for action by the ALA.

Fourth, the ALA should establish a special committee
on the status of women or some other suitable organizational
body to develop procedures to deal with specific instances of
reported discrimination. This committee might also be
charged with setting up some mechanism for publicizing top-
level job opportunities as they become available, so that qualified women candidates can be considered for these positions.

Fifth, the ALA should announce a stated minimum
salary for all librarians which is consistent with going minimum salary rates for comparable educational qualifications in
other professions where women do not necessarily predom-
inate. Institutions which fail to approach this basic minimum
should be censured by the Association.

Sixth, the ALA should support measures designed to
promote the rights of women, both in the librarian's professional work and through cooperation with other professions.

Seventh, using the findings provided research studies,
and recognizing that far-reaching programs may have to be
considered to bring about fully equal opportunity in the library
profession, the ALA should seek to develop a comprehensive
long-range action program, designed to restructure present
arrangements and effect significant change and improvement.

The following specific illustrations are offered as some possible examples of activities which might be undertaken within the overall framework suggested above:

> Statistical indicators which show the salaries and status of men and women librarians, and how the relative position of men and women in librarianship compares to that in other professions should be developed, both to reveal present conditions and to show trends over a period of time.

> A study on the status of women in contemporary life should be issued as part of the "Reading for an Age of Change" series.

> Subject headings which reflect customary prejudice toward women should be reconsidered and revised.

> A special fund to support advanced and continuing education for women of particular promise should be considered.

> Child care facilities should be instituted, perhaps in conjunction with other associations and institutions in local areas, to encourage the continuing employment of professionally trained women librarians.

> An interdisciplinary conference on improving career opportunities for women could be sponsored jointly by the ALA and other professional associations.

These proposals and suggestions are offered to launch a discussion on an important issue which has been seriously neglected. It is hoped that they will be refined, improved, or replaced by better ones which seek similarly to promote the interests and aspirations of the library profession and its members. [4]

NOTES

1. Schiller, Anita R.   Characteristics of Professional Personnel in College and University Libraries.   Illinois State Library Research Series, No. 16.   Springfield: Illinois State Library, 1969.

2. Ward, Patricia Layzell.   Women in Librarianship: An

Investigation into Certain Problems of Library Staffing.   Library Association Pamphlet, No. 25.   London: Library Association, 1966.

3.   Library Literature used the term "Women as librarians" until 1952, when the wording was changed to
read "Women librarians."

4.   On January 22, 1970 the American Library Association,
LAD/PAS Committee on Economic Status, Welfare,
and Fringe Benefits passed a motion instructing the
chairman to appoint a subcommittee to gather facts
relating to alleged sexual discrimination within the
library profession.   Such a subcommittee has now
been appointed.   As part of the fact finding program
librarians are requested to report alleged cases of
sexual discrimination in the profession to the subcommittee.   These reports will be analyzed to assist
the committee in assessing the need for remedial
programs.
       Report of alleged sexual discrimination should
be forwarded to: Pauline Iacono, chairman, Subcommittee Investigating Sexual Discrimination, c/o Coe
College, Cedar Rapids, IA 52402.

PART IV

LIBRARIES AND THE CONCEPT
OF LIBRARY SERVICE

Introduction to Part IV

LIBRARIES AND THE CONCEPT OF LIBRARY SERVICE

> Meantime the colleges, whilst they provide
> us with libraries, provide no professor of
> books; and, I think, no chair is so much
> wanted.
>   --Ralph Waldo Emerson

While the physical growth of library collections in the
United States over the past one hundred years has been impressive, as has been the development of library buildings,
if in any meaningful sense American libraries have made significant progress in this period it has been in the development of library services. The changes have been truly remarkable. From 1876, when most libraries were viewed
primarily as collections of book material, open on a restricted basis for a few hours a week, with little or no direct service to the user, we have come, in 1976, to a point
where most libraries have broad collections of books and other material, are open to almost all potential users for many
hours a week, and provide considerable assistance and service in the use of their collections.

Much of the impetus for these changes came, as our
selections show, in the period before and just after the turn
of the century, and developments since then have largely been
in the development and expansion of the basic concepts which
were set at that time. Thus our selections are heavily
weighted toward that earlier period; yet, in the inclusion of
articles by William H. Brett, John Cotton Dana, William
Fletcher, William F. Poole, Lewis Steiner, and other leaders, we are covering only a small portion of the numerous
writings on library service from that time.

In part, the selection of later articles was made more
difficult by the extent to which it has been the actual development of innovative library services (e.g., the establishment

of the Lamont Undergraduate Library at Harvard) that has
been the landmark event while the description of the service
has appeared in the literature almost as an historical footnote.   In more recent years, action, not words, has been
the key to improvements in library service.

On an overall basis we have sought to include in this
chapter a variety of articles dealing with the broader concepts
of library service as developed in various types of libraries.
While there may seem to be a disproportionate number of
articles included here as contrasted to other chapters of this
anthology, this reflects, in large measure, the remarkable
growth of library service that has already been commented
upon.

With the provision of wide-ranging library services an
accepted concept, libraries are now faced with the problems,
as the more recent articles included here indicate, of how
they can meet the increasing and new demands for service
that have been generated by the implementation in the past
one hundred years of the concepts so clearly enunciated by
Samuel Green at the start of this period.

THE FUTURE OF THE FREE PUBLIC LIBRARY*

Lewis H. Steiner

Large libraries, filled with collections of the written
and printed learning of the wise men of the world, have been
known for ages. They were for the few; for those who, retiring from the attractions of business and the allurements of
public life, lived among books, and ardently desired no greater occupation, no higher honor than to swell the number of
such monuments of man's intellectual power. No ambition
to extend the treasures of learning to the unlearned seemed
to animate the student of those days. To preserve and enlarge these wondrous mausoleums of laborious genius was
the chief object of their ambition. The great majority of the
race had no part in such treasures, was content to dig and
labor for a precarious existence, and to die, as it were,
glebæ adscriptus. Such was the relation of mankind to the
huge collections of books, known as libraries, in the early
days of learning.

But as years and centuries passed by, the people began to feel that they had a right to whatever was good and
ennobling in the lands where their lot was cast. There might
be a divine right inherent to kings, but there was also a divine right inherent to every human being to enter the halls of
learning, and, seizing everything that could intensify and enlarge the intellectual powers, aspire to the attainment of all
that tended to make him master of the world and its varied
secrets. The attainment of scientific knowledge, political
knowledge, --of all forms of knowledge, --must be made possible. Man had been made in the image of his Maker, and
therefore it was his right to aspire to mastery, and to use

*Reprinted from Library Journal 1:74-81 (1876).

everything within his reach as an adjuvant to such an end.
And so knowledge grew, and learning became widespread;
and libraries, instead of remaining the property of a chosen
few, became the most democratic institutions known to man.
And with this change, libraries ceased to be known as reserved for the few.   Their doors were flung wide open to any
one who could utter the magic "open sesame," which was
simply the articulate cry of the hungry soul for that which
would make it wiser, better, and more like that Image after
which it had been created.

      It would be a curious and not an unprofitable line of
study to trace the Genesis of the free public library, from
the nucleus which was hidden in the libraries that had first
been established solely for the learned, until it reached its
present stage of development--until, shorn of all exclusive-
ness, it became the freest instrument known to the 19th century for the elevation of the race from ignorance, and the
best and dearest friend of every one whose aspirations impelled him to acquire the secrets of the past and present,
as well as to battle for himself, his family, and fellow-citi-
zens in the future.   But such a study is denied me at present.   Let me, however, try to set forth, as clearly as practicable, some thoughts concerning the future of this mighty,
democratic agency of the 19th century.   It may be well to
pause for a while in the technical details of our professional
work--although these are so important, and must necessarily
claim much attention during our annual conferences--and, for
a few minutes, look at what may be the future development
of the public library, and at what it will require of those
who are honored with its charge.

      I take it for granted that the free public library has
secured such a hold upon the affections of the people, that it
can safely endure all possible antagonisms which may arise
from indifference or penurious considerations.   Communities
are already bearing cheerfully the necessary taxation for its
support, and millionaires have learned to regard it as a favorite object for the bestowment of the overflow of their bank
accounts.   A thirst for knowledge has seized the people, and
this can be satisfied in no way so well as by resorting to our
literary reservoirs for continuous supplies.   The public library is closely connected with the civilization of the age--
so closely that the two are becoming almost inseparable.   So
long as a free people possesses this thirst for knowledge, and
looks upon its gratification as a means of advancing its welfare, of freeing it from the curse of caste, and of making its

homes brighter and happier and better, the public library,
with its treasures of that which will amuse, interest, and instruct, must remain an institution very dear to their hearts.

1. Our schools do but fit their scholars for its use,
and it is no misnomer to speak of it as the people's university, where every aspiration for knowledge should receive,
not only kindly encouragement, but direct and invaluable assistance. And this brings me to my first proposition, that
"the public library must be kept in thorough sympathy with the
people," by furnishing not only the treasures of the past, but
whatever may belong to present discovery, both in arts and
sciences, or to topics that have come to the front as of burning value to mankind. It must always be a living fountain of
refreshment to the human soul. It cannot fossilize itself by
mere collections of the productions of the past. It is no
place for the mere hoarding of the severely classic. It must
also furnish the results of whatever the present brings forth,
and be ready to supply this on call of every age and condition.
It must disdain to furnish information on no subject, on account of its seeming triviality, nor shrink from the task of
supplying draughts from the most profound sources of human
wisdom, should these be solicited. It must become an ency-
clopaedic helper to the community, never at a loss for an
answer to a question, if the same can be found on the printed
page. On the lookout for the first rays of any light that penetrates the dark corners of the mind, it must gather up all
these, and preserve them for those who will be most in need
of their assistance. In this university there must not only
be knowledge, but that prescience which may predict and
recognize the faintest indication of the appearance of a new
discovery or a new application of a recognized principle, and
then generously put the same at the disposal of all its pupils.
It must, by loyalty to its sphere of duty, show its indispensa-
bility to its patrons, so that no public institution will become
more intrinsically valuable to them, and none be looked upon
with deeper affection and more ardent love. In this way it
will be true to its high mission, and demonstrate its right to
the confidence of the people; and these will learn, through
the recognition of such sympathy with their wants and needs,
to come to it always for aid and assistance in the various
problems that meet them in the daily struggles of life.

2. Who, then, is equal to the task of developing the
capabilities of this great university, and how can these be
made most useful to the crowds that will throng its halls?
There is much technique to be mastered. We meet and dis-

cuss this with earnestness.   Classification and mechanical
appliances to assist in the details of administration, the best
methods of doing this and that, the best forms of blanks
wherewith accounts can be kept and statistics made practically available, how time and labor can be saved by such an invention, --these and thousands of other subjects demand our
attention; and our time is so frequently occupied with them--
this tithing of "mint, anise, and cummin"--that we are in
great danger of forgetting "the weightier matters of the law"
--the great trusts confided to our hands, the immense responsibilities that have been voluntarily assumed, and which must
never be overlooked.   He who is to be the mentor of young
and old, who come with their unending questions on every
subject to the library, must not be content with a mere acquaintance, however exhaustive it may be, with the details
of library management.   He dare not despise these, since
they are essential to system and the successful performance
of his daily duties.   They must be familiar to him and his
assistants, but they belong only to the mechanical performance
of duties, while there are others of greater importance that
inhere to his professional position, which should never be
neglected, and without an attention to which he will fall far
short of the usefulness he should attain.   Constant study,
some familiarity with what has been done by the human mind
in all spheres of its activity, with the novelties of the age
as presented by specialists whose activity at present is truly
marvelous; in fine, with the learning of the world.   All this
would not more than meet the requirements of the situation
occupied by the librarian.   Who is sufficient for all this?
No one would arrogantly claim for himself such omniscience.
What then?   He can possess himself with an acquaintance
with the sources whence such varied information can be obtained, so as to be able to point the road that the inquirer
must take to secure correct answers to his queries.   And
this, I believe, must be the line of study to be taken by the
public librarian, so that he can help, advise, aid, and assist,
if he is unable to furnish the full information required.   He
may have his own special subjects of study, but he dare not
prosecute them to the detriment of this more important portion of his duties.

      The library, in the future, must not only be a collec-
tion of books to amuse and instruct, to aid and assist those
who are hungering and thirsting for knowledge, but it must
furnish guidance and direction for all who are unable to secure this from its stores.   It must furnish counsel for those
who would employ its treasures, and this function belongs

naturally to him who has been intrusted with its management
and conduct. He must not only cater to existing public tastes,
but assist in the creation of new ones on the highest possible
plane. He must become the superintendent of a class of assistants, who shall also be relieved of technical details, of
duties connected with the receiving of the fresh materials
that a growing library will be acquiring daily, of classifying
and making these readily obtainable from its shelves,--of all
duties connected with the economic administration of its daily
work, and, in fine, of everything that will interfere with the
most practical instructional work. These assistants will employ the keys that unlock the treasures of the library, and
make their contents available in the most intelligible way for
the hungry student. The Bureau of Information, that some
librarians have already felt themselves forced to establish in
their libraries, will increase in dimensions until it is so organized as to distribute its duties among those who are to become specialists in the different departments of human study.

The ideal public library of the future will thus not only
be a warehouse of books, where the most complete adaptation
of the best technical methods for their arrangement, classification, and management shall be employed, but a realization of a people's university, supplied with instructors--what-
ever names be given them--fully competent to guide and instruct its pupils, and to make its books of incalculable value;
over all of which will preside the one mind that is full of
sympathy with its students, and, at the same time, broad
enough and wise enough to comprehend all necessary practical details, while it commits these to subordinate officers--
some to manage those of a mere technical character, and
others to exercise those instructional duties that are demanded, in order to make the library most useful to the greatest
number.

It may be said that to accomplish all this will require
a large outlay of money, but the same can be said of all enterprises undertaken for the instruction and advancement of
the race. Still, we have found that, when the ideal of any
such enterprise approves itself to the judgment of the public,
the money for its full accomplishment comes sooner or later.
Our colleges have rarely sprung into existence fully equipped
for the tasks they have undertaken. They have generally
struggled under difficulties of the most disheartening character. But when their instructors have proven themselves equal
to their tasks, have made their pupils and the great public
see the beneficial results of their labors, we have found that

the money needed for their support, for the erection of suitable buildings, and the proper supply of books and instruments and the necessary appliances for illustration, has come at first in little rills, then in larger steams, and finally in quantity sufficient to supply these, as well as adequately to compensate the able and conscientious men who have devoted their energies to such noble work.   The collegiate institutions that have been ushered into existence through large and bountiful benefactions are simply evidences, in these latter days, of what the people have learned to admire and put confidence in, in the case of those that have fought the good fight in previous years, and thus secured confidence in the grand ideal.   Moreover, the age has begun to feel that money can be profitably employed in the establishment of vast institutions for the training of the young in industrial pursuits, in the practical applications of the fine arts, and, indeed, in a thousand lines of work, in which in former days unaided genius was content to struggle and labor without aid or assistance.   The tide of generous benefaction has been already directed towards the foundation and support of libraries, and it is manifesting itself in all directions in the form of gifts from the millionaire, who has begun to see how he may link his name inseparable with great good for his fellow-men by founding public libraries.   This movement will not be checked, but rather increased, when the management of the library shall show the practical results here set forth as possible. The fully equipped and intelligently managed people's university will continue to claim support from the hands of those who have great personal wealth, or directly from the people for whose benefit it is conducted.

A word now as to the quarter, whence may come, in the future, baneful influences, which will not only fetter the movement towards the attainment of the ideal here presented, but even seriously interfere with the work of the library in whatever shape this may be done.   Already signs of such influences have shown themselves, and have done some injury. I refer to the active agency of partisan politics in the selection of its officers and its general management, so that these shall be made to agree with the dominant majority, who, in accordance with the prevalent claims of machine partisan politicians, are entitled to the control of everything of a public nature in the body politic.   The public library is a non-partisan institution; the public librarian is a non-partisan citizen, however pronounced may be his political views, and however he may feel called upon to cast his ballot.   If he cannot keep his political views from controlling his conduct as librarian, he should not undertake such duties.   But when true to the functions of his high calling, he should be kept free from the perturbations of party, and guarded from fears that he may be made a victim either of its erratic likes or dislikes.

HEAR THE OTHER SIDE*

John Cotton Dana

> Failures confessed are guide-posts to suc-
> cess; weaknesses discovered are no longer
> weaknesses.

I sometimes fear my enthusiasm for the free public
library is born more of contagion than of conviction. Consider the thing in some of its more evident aspects.

Here is a building, perhaps erected to perpetuate a
good man's memory, a monument and of use only as a monument; or constructed in accordance with the views of an
architect whose ideas of beauty are crude and whose thought
of utility is naught; ill-adapted to the purpose for which it is
intended; poorly lighted, badly ventilated. In it are stored
a few thousand volumes, including, of course, the best books
of all times--which no one reads--and a generous percentage
of fiction of the cheaper sort. To this place come in good
proportion the idle and the lazy; also the people who cannot
endure the burden of a thought, and who fancy they are improving their minds, while in fact they are simply letting
cool waters from fountains of knowledge trickle through the
sieves of an idle curiosity. The more persistent visitors are
often men who either have failed in a career, or never had
a career, or do not wish a career. Libraries all have their
indolents, idlers and "boarders."

There is little that is inspiring, per se, in the sight
of the men who gather in the newspaper reading room of any

---

*This, the President's Address to the American Library As-
sociation, September 1896, is reprinted from Library Journal 21 (Conf. No.):1-5 (1896).

free public library.   There is not much that is encouraging
in a careful look at many of those who are the more constant visitors to the shelves of the reference department.
Who wear out our dictionaries, the students of language or
the competitors in a word building contest? Of those who
come to the delivery desk 60 to 80 per cent rarely concern
themselves, as far as the library knows them, with anything
but fiction, and in that field concern themselves generally
only with the latest novel, which they wish because it is the
latest.   And of this 60 to 80 per cent, a large proportion--
probably at least half--prefer to get, and generally do get,
a novel of the poorer kind.

        I am stating the case plainly.   I share the librarian's
enthusiasm; but that enthusiasm is sometimes to me, and I
believe to many others, a cause for surprise.   Has it not
often come sharply home to every librarian--the hopelessness
of the task we assume to set outselves?   The triviality of the
great mass of the free public library's educational work?
The discouraging nature of the field?   The pettiness, the aw-
ful pettiness, of results?

        Nor is this all.   That we strive for great things and
accomplish so little; that our output seems not commensurate
with the size of the plant and the cost of its maintenance,
this is by no means the only fact which may rightly sober
our enthusiasms.

        Fathers and mothers love their children and look after
their happiness.   The more they do this, the more they concern themselves that the human beings they have brought into
the world be self-reliant, self-supporting people, knowing how
to live in harmony with their fellows, and wishing so to live,
the more civilized are they.   Parental responsibility is something the sense of which has never been too acute.   That I
may rightly scorn and despise my neighbor if his children
be not decent, attractive, civilized; that my neighbor may
rightly consider himself disgraced if his offspring grow not
up in the fear and admonition of the good citizen; these things
are not yet commonly received.   The native manners and the
education of the American child are looked upon, not so much
as the result of parentage and home training, as the good
gift of God and the public school.

        A strong sense of parental responsibility, this is a
prime essential to the growth of knowledge and to the increase
of social efficiency.   And this feeling of obligation to train

properly the souls of one's own creation; this sense that the
parent can win public approval as a parent only when the result is an additional factor in the public's happiness and comfort; this rule of living would surely result, if rightly applied,
in careful consideration of the child's education. But what
have we done? We have turned the whole subject of education over to the community. We have made it depend very
largely on the result of an annual election. We have let it
slip gradually into the hands of those veritable and inevitable
children of government--the politicians. The American parent is indifferent to the character of the education of his children. The interposition of the community in what should be
his affairs, it has made others indifferent that he is so. He
pays his taxes. If the schools are poor, the fault is at the
school-board's door, not his.

   The free public library not only relieves the idle and
incompetent and indifferent from the necessity--would he have
books--of going to work to earn them; it not only checks the
growth of the tendency of the private individual to collect a
library of his own, adapted to his own needs, and suiting his
own tastes and those of his children; it also tends to lead
parents to become indifferent to the general reading of their
children, just as the free public school may lead them to be
indifferent to their formal education. Certainly, fathers and
mothers whose children use public libraries seem to care
very little what and how much their children read. They con-
ceal their solicitude from librarian and assistants, if it exists. Yet, if a collection of books in a community is a good
thing for the community--and we seem to think it is; and if
it is a good thing particularly for the children of the com-
munity--and we seem to think it is, then it is a good thing,
not in itself simply, not as an object of worship, not as an
adequate excuse for the erection of a pleasing mortuary monument on the public street, but for its effect on young folks'
manners and on young folks' brains. But to produce a maximum effect herein, to produce even a modest effect, the right
books must be put into the right hand at the right time. Can
public servants do this rightly unless the parents cooperate
with them? But the public library is not an institution which
the mother helps to support because she has come to believe
in it; because it is her pleasure; because she can and does
keep a watchful eye on its growth and its methods. It is
part of the machinery of the state. She confides her children
to its tender mercies in the same spirit with which her for-
bears confided in their king!

Furthermore, the essence of government is force. This essence remains whether the visible form be king or majority. It is open to question--I put it mildly--whether it is expedient to touch with the strong hand the impulse of a people to train with earnest thought their young, or the impulse of a people to give light to their fellows. People wish, in the main, that their children be well taught. Without this wish a school system, public or private, would be impossible. This wish is the fundamental fact; that the system is public and tax-supported is the secondary fact; the result, not the cause. People wish also, in the main, to give their fellows and themselves the opportunity for self improvement. This wish is the fundamental fact at the bottom of the free, compulsorily supported public library. It is on these fundamental facts we should keep our eyes and our thoughts, not on the feature of compulsion.

We should work, then, such is my conclusion, for the extension of the public library from the starting point of human sympathy; from the universal desire for an increase of human happiness by an increase of knowledge of the conditions of human happiness; not from the starting-point of law, of compulsion, of enforcing on others our views of their duty.

I have said enough in this line. To the observant eye our libraries are not altogether halls of learning; they are also the haunts of the lazy. They do not always interest parents in their children; perhaps they lead parents to be indifferent to their children.

But really, librarians will say, all this is not our concern. We find ourselves here, they say, loving the companionship of books: desirous of extending the joys they can give to our fellows; embarked in public service, and active--none are more so; zealous--none are more so; honest--none are more so, in our work of making good use of books. Your modern librarian in his daily life is no disputacious economist, idly wavering, like the fabled donkey, between the loose hay of a crass individualism and the chopped feed of a perfectionist socialism. He is a worker. If there are things to be said which may add to the efficiency of his attempts to help his fellows to grow happier and wiser, let us hear them; and for this we have come together.

I have said these things, not with the wish to lessen the zeal of one of us in our chosen work. A moment's look at the case against us cannot anger us--that were childish;

cannot discourage us--that were cowardly. It may lead us
to look to the joints in our armor; it should lead us to re-
new our efforts. If the free public library movement be not
absolutely and altogether a good thing, and he is a bold
economist who vows that it is, how urgent is the call to us
to make each our own library the corrective, as far as may
be, of the possible harm of its existence. A collection of
books gathered at public expense does not justify itself by the
simple fact that it is. If a library be not a live educational
institution it were better never established. It is ours to
justify to the world the literary warehouse. A library is good
only as the librarian makes it so.

Can we do more than we have done to justify our
calling? Can we make ourselves of more importance in the
world, of more positive value to the world? Our calling is
dignified in our own eyes, it is true; but we are not greatly
dignified in the eyes of our fellows. The public does not ask
our opinions. We are, like the teachers, students; and we
strive, like them, to keep abreast of the times, and to have
opinions on vital topics formed after much reading and some
thought. But save on more trivial questions, on questions
touching usually only the recreative side of life, like those
of literature commonly so called, our opinions are not asked
for. We are, to put it bluntly, of very little weight in the
community. We are teachers; and who cares much for what
the teacher says?

I am not pausing now to note exceptions. We all
know our masters and our exemplars; and I shall not pause
to praise the men and women who have brought us where we
are; who have lifted librarianship, in the estimation of the
wise and good, to a profession, and have made it comparatively an easy thing for you and me to develop our libraries,
if we can and will, into all that they should be, and to become ourselves, as librarians, men and women of weight and
value in the community.

I have said that your library is perhaps injuring your
community; that you are not of any importance among your
own people. And these, you tell me are hard sayings. In
truth they are. I am not here to pass you any compliments.
If for five minutes we can divest ourselves of every last
shred of our trappings of self-satisfaction, and arouse in
ourselves for a moment, a keen sense of our sins of omis-
sion, of things left undone or not well done, I shall be content,
and shall consider that we have wisely opened these Cleveland

sessions.   I would wish to leave you, here at the very beginning of our discussions, not, indeed in the Slough of Des-
pond, but climbing sturdily, and well aware that you are
climbing, the Hill Difficulty.   Others, I can assure you, will,
long before our conference ends, lead us again, and that joy-
fully, to our Delectable Mountains.

Pardon me, then, while I say over again a few of the
things that cannot be too often said.

Look first to your own personal growth.   Get into
touch with the world.   Let no one point to you as an instance
of the narrowing effects of too much of books.

Be social.   Impress yourself on your community; in
a small way if not in a large.   Be not superior and reserved.
Remember that he who to the popular eye wears much the air
of wisdom is never wise.

Speak out freely on matters of library management;
and especially, in these days, on matters of library construction.   In recent years millions of dollars have been spent on
library buildings in this country, and we have not yet a half
dozen in the land that do not disgrace us.   If we have stood
idly by and not made our opinions, our knowledge, our experience, felt by trustees and architects, then is ours the
blame, and we are chief among the sufferers.   Persuade
architects and their associations, local and national, who ignore us because in our inconsequence they know they can,
that they may wisely and without loss of dignity consult the
professional librarian about the building he is to occupy.   I
say persuade them; I might better say compel them.   To
compel them will be easy when you have become of importance in the world.   Even now it is not too soon to attempt
to confer with them.   You can at once make the beginning of
friendly and helpful relations with the American Institute of
Architects.   But you must ask, not demand.

Advertise the ALA and what it stands for.   Help to
broaden its field.   Support heartily measures which look to
a greater degree of publicity for it.   Interest your trustees
in it.   Interest your friends, and your patrons and constituents in it.   Be ready and willing to do your share of the
work, and there is no end of work that each year must be
done to keep it properly alive and well in the public eye.
Call the attention of your trustees to the difference between
the efficient library, such as the ALA advocates, and the

dead-and-alive collection of books, still altogether too common. Consider the contrast between the possible public library and the public library that is. If the causes for that contrast lie at your door, face them frankly and bravely and strive to remove them.

Do not forget the Library Department of the National Educational Association, recently established. It gives you excuse, and it gives you cause to take an interest, more active even than heretofore, in the introduction of books and library methods into school work, and to concern yourselves more than ever before with the general reading of teachers and their pupils. Impress upon teachers the value to them of your library. Persuade them, if you can, that to do their best work they must know well and use freely the good books.

See that your local book and news men are heartily with you in the work of spreading knowledge of the right use of books and in encouraging ownership of books in your community. If you come in contact with the bookseller and the publisher of the great cities, do what you can to persuade them that to join in the work of this association of librarians is not only to benefit the community at large, but to help their own particular business as well.

Be not slow in giving hearty recognition to those who have, in the beginnings of library science, taken the first place and borne the burdens and made an easy way for us who follow. If, perhaps against some odds, a librarian, man or woman, is making an eminent success of some great city library, may you not properly send him, once and again, a word which shall signify that you, at least, are alive to the fact of his good work and are yourself encouraged and inspired thereby? Like words of approval you may well extend to the good men, outside the profession proper, who have given their time and energy, a labor of love, to improve certain features of library work.

Interest in your work in your own community your local book-lovers and book-collectors and book-worms and private students and plodders and burners of the midnight oil. Get in touch with the teachers of literature in the colleges and schools of your neighborhood. Expound to such, and to the general reader as well, whenever you properly can, the difficulties and the possibilities of your calling, your conquests in classification and cataloging, and your advances in bibliography and indexing, and the progress in re-

cent years of general library economy. Remember that all
these things can be even better done in a small community,
in the village library of a few hundred volumes, than in the
large library of the great city.

Note the women's clubs, art associations, historical
societies, scientific societies. Do not forget the private
schools. In the small town you can gain without difficulty
the good-will of the local newspaper. You can often assist
the editor in his work, and lead him to help you in return.
The clergymen in your town certainly care somewhat for the
reading of their young people, and will cooperate with you in
any intelligent effort to increase it and improve it. The Sunday-school libraries of your neighborhood are open to your
suggestions, if you approach them properly. And the Y. M. C.
and the Y. W. C. associations will gladly take from you advice
and assistance in the management of their reading-rooms and
their libraries.

None are so poor that they cannot give to others; and
few libraries are so small that they cannot spare books and
magazines enough to make a little library which may be sent
out into a still smaller community and there do good service.

Do the business men and the business women, the active people, those who feed us and clothe us and transport
us, those who have brought about in the last few decades the
great increase in creature comforts for every one, do these
business people take an active interest in your library? Do
they care for you or for your opinion? If not, is it their
fault? Is it that they are gross and dull and material and
worldly; or is it that you, the wise librarian, know not yet
how to bring your educational forces to bear on the life that
now is? Our work is but begun so long as we are not in
close touch with the man of affairs.

Remember that as you in your town, or in your city,
widen the sphere of your influence, grow to be a person of
worth and dignity in the community, you thereby add so much
to the dignity and to the effectiveness of the whole profession.
If in a city or town near you there is a library which, in
its general arrangement is not what it should be, which is
but a dusty pile of printed pages or but a roosting-place for
a flock of cheap novels, yours is in part the fault, and you
are largely the loser. When a dweller in that town, one unacquainted with library affairs--and most are such--hears you
alluded to as a "librarian," he thinks of you as a person akin

to the bibliothecal pagan who fails to manage the library of
his own town, the only library he knows by which he can
measure your work.   He is a "librarian"; you are a "librarian. "   We wear the livery of our co-workers as well as our
own.

Keep these thoughts in mind and you will see how essential it is, would our profession reach the standing we wish
it to reach, would we make it everywhere an honor to wear
our name, that every smallest library be an effective educational machine, and that every humblest librarian be an active, enthusiastic, intelligent worker.

See that your library is interesting to the people of
the community, the people who own it, the people who maintain it.   Deny your people nothing which the book-shop grants
them.   Make your library at least as attractive as the most
attractive retail store in the community.   Open your eyes to
the cheapness of books at the present day, and to the unim-
portance, even to the small library, of the loss of an occasional volume; and open them also the necessity of getting
your constituency in actual contact with the books themselves.

Remember always that taxation is compulsion, that
taxation is government; that government, among present-day
human creatures, is politics; that the end of an institution
may not justify its means; that a free public library may be
other than a helpful thing.   See to it, therefore, the more
carefully that your own public library at least is rationally
administered, and promotes public helpfulness.

LIBRARY WORK FOR RURAL COMMUNITIES*

Liberty Hyde Bailey

There is a rural problem as there is also a city problem. Wherever persons come together there are problems
of adjustment, one to the other. The greater the number of
persons who come together, the greater and more difficult
are the problems. When the different interests with which
men have to do are organized, then the different organizations themselves tend to come together and the problems are
still further increased. The problems that confront city folk
are likely to be more apparent than those that confront country folk. They appeal to persons in the centers of activity.
They demand quick solution. It is not strange, therefore,
that city social problems have received more attention than
rural social problems. There are problems of the city and
problems of the country, but as those of the country have
received comparatively small attention and are just now being
discovered, we are likely to think that they are new. They
may be new to most persons. The country problem is in
fact no greater than the city problem, only it has been more
overlooked and neglected.

The country problems are to a large extent only rural
phases of fundamental human problems. That is to say,
there is a city side and a country side or phase to all questions of education, morals, social cleavage, and the like. In
some respects, however, the country problem is very unlikely
the city problem, and this is especially true as respects the
attitude of the individual toward his own work and his place
in the world.

The real countryman is likely to be a fatalist, al-

*Reprinted from Library Journal 33:381-385 (Oct. 1908).

though he may not know it, and he may resent it if told.
His work is largely in the presence of the elemental forces
of nature. These forces are beyond his power to make or
to unmake. He cannot change the rain or sunshine or storm
or drought. He is likely, therefore, to develop an attitude
of helplessness toward his condition, and to feel that there
is very little use to exert himself overmuch because he is
confronted by inexorable phenomena. The result of this is
that the man is either likely to develop a complacent and joyful resignation, taking things as they come and making the
best of them, or else to develop a species of rebellion which
leads to a hopeless and pessimistic outlook on life. I am
convinced that much of the inertia of country people is trace-
able to the essential fatalism of their outlook on the world.

This outlook of helplessness is to be overcome by
giving the man the power of science, whereby he may in
some degree overcome, control or mitigate the forces of nature, or at least effectively adjust himself to them. The
agricultural colleges and experimental stations are giving the
countryman no end of fact. We have not yet organized this
fact into such a philosophy of application, however, as to
give the countryman full confidence of his ability to contend
with his native conditions.

I now come to a point of application of my remarks to
the question of libraries. Libraries exist that persons may
read. To a large extent the effect of library work is to
cause persons to read for entertainment. The countryman,
however, needs to read for courage. Herein is where library
schemes are likely to be fundamentally weak, if in fact not
radically wrong for the countryman. I would not eliminate
the natural desire of anybody to read for entertainment; but
I would make a special effort to develop in the countryman a
habit of reading such things as will give him personal mastery over his conditions.

Much has been said of late as to what the country
problem really is. The country problem is not one thing
any more than the city problem is one thing. We always
need to direct and even to redirect our civilization. We
make progress by starts and leaps. Between these leaps are
periods of relative inaction or dormancy. We have been in
such a period in recent years in respect to country life. We
now feel the necessity of arousing ourselves to the situation.
In such cases the panacea-man always comes to the fore. He
sees one remedy for all ills. I have been informed recently

that the one remedy for the ills of the farmer is the resump-
tion of greenback currency; the controlling of trusts; the extension of good roads; and other specific and single acts.
The fact is that the panacea-man does not make very great
progress, because all human affairs are complex and touch
each other at many points.

Some of the things that need to be done for the general betterment of country life are:

1) The recognition of the countryman and of his problems.   The recent appointment by President Roosevelt of a
Commission on Country Life does just this.   This appointment recognizes that the countryman has problems which it
is the business of government to understand.   It places the
executive machinery of government behind the work.   The
appointment of this commission is in no sense a criticism of
the farmer, but rather a recognition on the part of the president of the United States that something definite and constructive should be done to enable the man on the land to
receive the best returns for his effort and so to remove
handicaps as to enable him to live the fullest life.

2) We need the enactment of laws and regulations
that have the farmer distinctly in mind.   I will illustrate
this by speaking of game law legislation.   I am convinced
that no type of legislation is in a more hopeless or chaotic
condition than that relating to the preservation of small game.
Laws are enacted that apply to particular localities and not
to localities adjacent to them, or which please a certain set
of sportsmen, or which have certain special interests in
mind.   Now, small game is to a large extent a natural product of farms.   All game, in fact, is a product of the earth.
So far as the earth is owned for productive purposes, it is
controlled by the farmer.   The natural result of game law
legislation and agitation is to antagonize the farmer against
the sportsman, whereas their interests ought to be harmon-
ized and unified.   Game law legislation, as all other legislation, should rest on fundamental principles, and these principles would necessarily recognize that the farmer has rights
as well as the sportsman.   Laws so made, I am convinced,
would put the farmer and the sportsman into sympathy and
cause them to work together to the betterment of each.

3) We need a consideration of the whole subject of
transportation with reference to the farmers' interests.

4) We need a similar discussion of all matters relating to rural social communication.

5) We should make a careful study of the control of products, with reference to the producer as well as to the market man.

6) We must consider whether the rural church is an effective organ and whether it also may not need a new study and redirection.

7) The rural schools need in some way to be so fertilized and redirected as to cause them to be a training place for boys and girls who are likely to live on the land.

8) We need to spread the reading habit; and here I come again into contact with the subject in which this audience is specially interested.

All these, and other agencies, working harmoniously together, will help to accelerate the development of a good country life. This development is already in progress. We need to recognize it and to direct it. As Sir Horace Plunkett has recently so well said, we need in the country to develop better farming, better business and better living.

What I mean to emphasize at this point is that the library and the reading-course have a distinct obligation to help on the whole work of rural progress. They must be inoculated with the missionary and the extension spirit and become real educational factors.

If the countryman is to be aided to the greatest advantage, it will not be enough merely to bring in things from the outside and present them to him. Farming is a local business. The farmer stands on the land. In a highly developed society, he does not sell his farm and move on as soon as fertility is in part exhausted. This being true, he must be reached in terms of his environment. He should be developed natively from his own standpoint and work; and all schools, and all libraries, and all organizations of whatever kind that would help the man on the land must begin with this point of view.

I may illustrate this by speaking of the current country movement to revive sports and games. I am much in sympathy with this desire. I am quite sure that more games

and recreation are needed in the country as much as in the
city.   In fact, there may be more need of them in the country.   The tendency seems to be just now, however, to introduce old folk games.   We must remember, however, that
folk games such as we are likely to introduce have been developed in other countries and in other times.   They represent the life of other people.   To a large extent they are
love making games.   They are not adapted in very many
cases to our climate.   To introduce them is merely to bring
in another exotic factor and to develop theatricals.

I would much rather revive the good old games that
have come directly out of the land.   Or if new games are
wanted I should like to try to invent them, having in mind
the real needs of a community; but it is doubtful whether
games invented out of hand can ever really be native.   I suspect that the germs of many good games and sports can be
found in the open country, and that they might be capable of
considerable extension and development.

Of course, not one of my hearers will feel that I
would limit the countryman's view to his own environment.
I have recently been accused of that very thing, but every
one of you knows that this is nonsense.   I would begin with
the things at home, the same as I would begin to teach the
child by means of the things that are within its range; and
then I would lead out to the world activities.   There is no
reason why a farmer should not have as broad a view of life
and of the things that lie beyond as any other man has, but
this comes as a natural extension of his proper education.

There is very little good literature that is specially
adapted to rural communities except the technical agricultural
books and bulletins.   It is often said that farm homes are
greatly lacking in books and in magazines.   This, no doubt,
is often true.   One reason is that there is so little literature
that is really adapted to the farmer's general demands and
also because his whole training leads him to think in terms
of experience rather than in terms of books.   There are
many farm homes that are well supplied with good literature,
and the number is rapidly increasing.   In the old days one
would be likely to find a copy of Pilgrim's Progress, the
novels of Scott and Dickens, a copy of Robinson Crusoe and
other books of the older order.   Pilgrim's Progress is excellent literature and a commanding allegory, but it is likely
to have a fatalistic influence on persons who accept books too
literally.   The Bible is found everywhere, but it is too often

read in the country, as in the city, from the point of view of "texts" and not interpreted in terms of present-day life. If I were making out a set of books for reading anywhere, I should want to include some of the modern expositions or adaptations of biblical literature in order that the scripture might be made applicable and vital to the lives of the people.

The novels have no special relation to the conditions under which the farmer lives and very many of them no relation to any present-day living. I would not advise that all reading have relation to the life of the present, but some of it certainly should be applicable in order that it may have meaning to the reader. We have practically no novels depicting the real farmer. We have a good many farmer characters in current fiction, but most of them are caricatures, whether so intended or not, and present a type of life and a vocabulary which, if they exist at all, are greatly the exception. Common novels are likely to be exotic. A good part of them are read because they are the best sellers of the time. Librarians know that the book that tops the market shortly after it is published may not have any real or abiding value.

The bulletins of the experimental stations and departments of agriculture are now widely distributed, but they are not used as much as they ought to be. This is in part because the mailing lists are not selective, and in part because the reader may have no real fundamental knowledge to enable him to use them effectively. In very many cases the bulletins themselves are unreadable and are only reference texts.

There are gilded publications that appeal to city persons who have an extrinsic interest in the country, or to those who have abundant money to spend; but they have very little, if any, influence on the development of a native country life.

We have practically no good poems of American farm life. A poem of the plowboy is very likely to be one that sees the plowboy from the highway rather than one that expresses the real poetry and sentiment of the labor on the land. I do not know where I can find a half dozen first-class poems of farm life. They are largely written from the study outward, and by persons who see farming at long range, or who come to it with the city man's point of view.

The nature books are largely forced and lack person-

ality. They do not have the true ring of truth. There are,
of course, distinct exceptions; but taking the books as a whole
my experience seems to justify this judgment. We need native and sensible books with country direction in them. We
need something like the Burrough's mode as applied to farm
operations and farm objects.

Of late the reportorial type of literature has developed
itself in country life directions. The reporter discovers a
high point here and there, does not understand relationships,
writes something that is effervescent and entertaining and
very likely misleading. The "wonders-of-science" idea has
also applied itself to agricultural writing, and we are beginning to develop a type of literature that is unsafe. Some
person who is doing good, quiet work in the breeding of
plants, or in other agricultural fields, is likely to be discovered by a facile reporter, and his work may be made to
appear as foolishness.

We have no history of farm life or farm people. I
have been much impressed with this lack within the last
month, when I have been trying to find biographical data respecting a great many persons who have had much influence
in developing good country life in North America. The careers of these persons do not appear in our standard biographies, although persons who may have accomplished much
less may be given full treatment. The result of all this is
that there is no ideal of leadership in agricultural or country
life affairs put before the boy or girl. The biographies that
the youth reads of are persons who have made their way in
other careers. Yet, as a matter of fact, hundreds of persons whose names are unknown to the standard books have
exerted an influence that is truly national in its character.
These persons should be listed amongst the heroes to whose
accomplishments the young generation may aspire.

We are much in need, therefore, of good native books
that will mean something to persons who live on the land.
We need a high class journal of a new type that will interest
men sympathetically and psychologically in farm life, devoting
only a secondary part of its space to questions of technical
farming.

There should be a library in every rural town. This
library should have relation to its community, as a school
or a church has. It should be an educational center.

The travelling libraries have provided a new way of developing the reading habit in the country and in remote towns. It undoubtedly has had great influence, although I think that the character of its literature needs to be reconsidered. It is gratifying to us, as New Yorkers, to know that the travelling library, as now understood, originated in New York with Melvil Dewey in 1892. He secured an appropriation to place books in rural communities that were too small to have libraries of their own. He purchased a small number of libraries of one hundred volumes each and distributed them. In 1895 Michigan and Ohio followed. In 1899 there were some twenty-five hundred travelling libraries in thirty states, distributing about one hundred and fifteen thousand volumes. In 1908 there were five thousand such libraries in nearly every state and territory, with the distribution not far under three-fourths of a million books. In 1907 Wisconsin circulated upwards of one hundred and twenty-two thousand volumes. There is a state library commission or organization at the capitol in the states of California, Colorado, Delaware, Indiana, Iowa, Kansas, Maryland, Michigan, Minnesota, Missouri, Nebraska, New Jersey, New York, North Dakota, Ohio, Oregon, Pennsylvania, Vermont, Washington, and Wisconsin. It is a great responsibility to distribute three-quarters of a million books, particularly when they go to persons who do not have many books and who are likely to place confidence in those that they receive.

Another mode of developing the reading habit is by means of reading-courses and reading-clubs, which are now beginning to be organized in the agricultural colleges. These are likely to have great influence in rural communities because 1) they are directly related to the life of the people, and 2) because they are dynamic or have an active follow-up system. The reading-course enterprise for farmers and farmers' wives has gained greater headway in New York State than elsewhere.

Every social or educational organization that exists in the open country should be a means of developing and spreading the reading habit. In New York State, for example, there are more than seventy thousand active members of the Grange. There are a good many hundred local or subordinate granges. Each of these granges should be a reading center. The Farmers' Institutes should leave behind them some kind of an organization that will continue the work of the institute and develop the reading habit. All country churches, and all country schools, should also be agents in the same cause.

All these organizations should be made distributive centers for good literature. They should all aid in distributing the bulletins of the Experiment station of that state. The local library should reach all homes and also be a dispersive center. The local library will often be able to distribute the Experiment station bulletins much more effectively than the Experiment station itself, because the library should know the local needs and the habits of life of its constituents.

We are very much in need of a co-ordination or association of all these various efforts. I have sometimes thought that there should be a state society, looking to the coordination of them all, but the tendency is to multiply societies overmuch. If there is no formal organization as between them all, I am sure that there should be a co-operative interest between them so that they will all work together harmoniously toward one end. All these agencies should be active. They should know what other agencies are doing. Each one of them should preserve its full autonomy, but it will do more concrete work if it knows its own field and will be stimulated to greater effort if it knows what other organizations are doing.

If libraries and librarians are only a means of distributing books, all that you need to do is to perfect the machinery or the mechanics of the work. If they are to energize the people and to redirect the currents of civilization, they must do very much more than this. They must inspire the reading habit, direct it, and then satisfy it. We need not so much to know just what kind of books to put in the hands of readers as to develop a new purpose in library effort. It is not enough to satisfy the demands of readers: we must do constructive work. I look on all library effort in rural communities as a part of the general educational and welfare work in which all persons are interested who are looking to the evolution of institutions and the betterment of their fellows.

THE NATIONAL LIBRARY CONCEPT

WHAT MAY BE DONE FOR LIBRARIES BY THE NATION*

Herbert Putnam

You have had suggestions as to what may be done for libraries by the city and what by the state. Whatever is left over--if there is anything left over--I am to treat as something that may be done by the nation--the nation not as an aggregate of its parts, but as a unit, acting through its central authority. There is a disposition to contend that everything which may be more effectively or more economical-ly done by a central authority for the larger area should be undertaken by that authority. I am not prepared to go so far. There may be a value in local effort that will repay its great-er cost. But in an educational work which involves the ac-cumulation of material some of which is exceedingly costly, only part of which is constantly in use, and little of which perishes by use; a work whose processes are capable of or-ganization on a large scale and the application of co-operative effort: there must be certain undertakings which, relatively speaking, are possible only if assumed by a central authority. It is such undertakings, for the largest area, that I am asked to discover and set forth.

To do so involves consequences which may be incon-venient. For a possible service means a correlative duty. And as I myself to a degree represent here the central au-thority in question, whatever I state as a service appropriate for that authority, I shall have to admit as a duty in which I must share. I shall try to be candid. But under the cir-cumstances I cannot be expected to be more than candid.

---

*Reprinted from Library Journal 26 (Conf. No.):9-15 (Aug. 1901).

In some respects the Federal Government of the United States has already influenced the constitution, resources and service of our public libraries. It has enacted laws which, having for their primary purpose the protection of authors and publishers, benefit libraries by encouraging the manufacture of books soundly, substantially and honestly made. It has favored public libraries by exempting from tariff duty books imported for their use. It has encouraged the study of the classics by laying a penalty upon the general importation of books less than twenty years old. In its executive capacity it is itself investigator, author, publisher, manufacturer, distributor, statistician, bibliographer, and librarian. It maintains at Washington, with a generosity not paralleled by any other government, bureaus for scientific research; it compiles, publishes, and freely distributes the results of this research. It is the greatest publisher in the world, and the largest manufacturer of books. In a single publication, repeated each year, it consumes over a million pounds of paper stock; and it maintains a bureau whose purpose is to replenish the forests which as publisher it thus depletes. It distributes gratuitously to the libraries of the United States each year over 300,000 volumes, embodying the results of its research, its legislative proceedings, and an account of its administrative activities. It maintains a bureau for the investigation of problems in education, for the accumulation and dissemination of information concerning the work of educational institutions; and it has included the public libraries of this country among such educational institutions. This bureau has issued three reports tabulating statistics concerning them, one also (in 1876) summarizing their history and two (in 1876 and in 1893) containing essays which embody the best contemporary opinion as to library equipment and methods. It has published as a document the ALA list of best books to form the basis of a public library.

Through its Bureau of Documents it is seeking to index and adequately to exhibit its own publications, to facilitate their distribution to libraries and to afford to libraries as to federal documents a clearing house for duplicates.

All such services are obviously appropriate for the national authority and may doubtless be continued and extended. If the interchange of books among libraries is to be facilitated by special postal regulations this can be accomplished by the national authority alone.

But in the case of a state a service has been described

which is to be rendered to local libraries by the library
which the state itself owns and maintains. Now the federal
government also owns and maintains libraries. What may
be demanded of these? Certain precedents have already
been established. The library of the Surgeon General's office
--the most comprehensive in the world within its special field
--sends its books to members of the medical profession
throughout the United States, relieving just so much the burden upon local libraries; and it has issued a catalog which is
not merely in form and method efficient, but is so nearly an
exhibit of the entire literature of the medical sciences that
it renders unnecessary duplication of cataloging and analytical
work within the field which it covers. This catalog has con-
ferred a general benefit not equalled by any bibliographic
work within any other department of literature. It is perhaps
the most eminent bibliographic work yet accomplished by any
government. The cost of its mere publication--which is the
cost chargeable to the general benefit--has already exceeded
$250,000.

     But this library is but one of several collections main-
tained by the Federal Government; the aggregate of which is
already nearly two million volumes. In each federal department and bureau there is a library. And there is a central
collection which in itself is already the largest on the western
hemisphere. It was created as a legislative library--for the
use of both Houses of Congress. It is still called the Library of Congress. But it is now being referred to as something more. The government has erected for it a building
which is the largest, most elaborate, and most costly yet
erected for library purposes. The seven million dollars
which it cost has been paid not by the District of Columbia,
but by the country at large. No such sum would have been
requisite for a building to serve Congress alone. It seems
to intend a library that shall serve the country at large, if
there is any such thing possible. In fact the library is already being referred to as the National Library of the United
States. What does this mean? or rather, what may this
mean? One naturally look abroad--to the foremost of national libraries.

     The British Museum is a huge repository of material.
In scope it is universal. Its purpose is accumulation, preservation, and the aid of research by accredited persons,
upon its own premises. Its service is purely responsive.
It has printed catalogs of its own collections, but does not
undertake bibliographic work general in nature, nor engage
in co-operative bibliographic undertakings. It lends no books.

But I fear you will hardly be satisfied with the analogy. The British Museum, you will say, is placed in a city which is not merely the capital of the British Empire, but the metropolis; the literary metropolis also of the Anglo-Saxon race. The Library of Congress is at the capital of the United States. But this capital is not itself a metropolis. No student in Great Britain has to travel over 500 miles to reach the British Museum. A student in the United States may have to travel as much as 3000 miles to reach the Library of Congress. The area which supports the national library of Great Britain is but 100,000 square miles; that which supports the National Library of the United States is over 3,000,000 square miles. The conditions differ, and therefore, you will say, the obligation. If there is any way in which our National Library may "reach out" from Washington it should reach out. Its first duty is no doubt as a legislative library--to Congress. Its next is as a federal library to aid the executive and judicial departments of the government and the scientific undertakings under governmental auspices. Its next is to that general research which may be carried on at Washington by resident and visiting students and scholars: which in American history, political and social science, public administration, jurisprudence and international law is likely to make Washington its center, and which, under the auspices of the Washington Memorial Institution--that new project for post graduate study involving the use of the scientific collections and scientific experts at Washington--is likely to be organized in various branches of the natural and physical sciences as well. But this should not be the limit. There should be possible also a service to the country at large: a service to be extended through the libraries which are the local centers of research involving the use of books. That claim may be made. Now what at Washington might be useful to these libraries?

(A lively imagination is not requisite.) Suppose there could be a collection of books universal in scope, as no local library with limited funds and limited space can hope to be: a collection that shall contain also particularly 1) original sources, 2) works of high importance for occasional reference, but whose cost to procure and maintain precludes their acquisition by a local library pressed to secure the material of ordinary and constant need, and 3) the "useless" books; books not costly to acquire, but of so little general concern as not to justify cataloging, space and care in each local library if only they are known to be preserved and accessible somewhere.

Such a collection must include also the general mass
of books sought and held by local libraries--the books for the
ordinary reader; the daily tools of research.   Its maintenance
will involve processes--of classification and cataloging--high-
ly costly.   Suppose the results of these processes could be
made generally available, so as to save duplication of such
expenditure upon identical material held by local libraries?

A collection universal in scope will afford opportunity
for bibliographic work not equalled elsewhere.   Such work
centered there might advance the general interest with the
least aggregate effort.   The adequate interpretation of such a
collection will involve the maintenance of a corps of specialists.   Suppose these specialists could be available to answer
inquiries from all parts of the country as to what material
exists on any particular subject, where it is, how it may be
had, how most effectively it may be used?

There are special collections already existent in various localities in the United States and likely to come into
being through special local advantage or incentive, or the interest of private collectors, or private endowment--which cannot be duplicated at Washington.   Suppose there could be at
Washington a bibliographic statement of that which is peculiar to each of these collections; in brief, a catalog of the
books in the United States--not of every library, not of every
copy of every book, but of every book available for an investigator?

There are various bibliographic undertakings which
may be co-operative.   Suppose there could be at Washington
a central bureau--with approved methods, standard forms,
adequate editorial capacity, and liberal facilities for publica-
tion--which could organize and co-ordinate this work among
the libraries of the United States and represent them in such
of it as--like the new Royal Society index--is to be international?

There is the exchange of material duplicated in one
library, needed by another.   Suppose there could be at Washington a bureau which would serve as a clearing house for
miscellaneous duplicates as the Bureau of Documents serves
for documents?   It might accomplish much without handling
a single article; it might, like a clearing house proper as it
were, set debit against credit, i. e. , compare the deficiencies
in one library with the surplus in another and communicate
the results to the institutions interested.   It might do this

upon slip lists sent in by each--of duplicates and of particular deficiencies--in sets, for instance. One of my associates
has been guilty of this very suggestion. It is likely to bring
something upon his head. He may have his choice between
live coals and the ashes of repentance.

Now those are some of the things which might be asserted as the duty of Washington to the country at large. I
have touched them as lightly as possible: but there they are.
And we may not be able to avoid them. Nay, we seem to be
drifting toward them. To some of them we are apparently
already committed.

There is the building: that in itself seems to commit
us. There is equipment. There are books. As regards
any national service the federal libraries should be one library. They contain nearly two million volumes. The Library of Congress contains net some 700,000 books and a
half million other items. It has for increase 1) deposits
under the copyright law, 2) documents acquired through distribution of the federal documents placed at its disposal for
exchange--formerly 50 copies of each, not 100, 3) books and
society publications acquired by the Smithsonian through its
exchanges, 4) miscellaneous gifts and exchanges, and 5) purchases from appropriations. These have increased from
$10,000 a year to 1897 to $70,000 for the year 1901-2.

Such resources are by no means omnipotent. No resources can make absolutely comprehensive a library starting
its deliberate accumulations at the end of the 19th century.
Too much material has already been absorbed into collections
from which it will never emerge.

But universality in scope does not mean absolute com-
prehensiveness in detail. With its purchasing funds and other
resources the Library of Congress bids fair to become the
strongest collection in the United States in bibliography, in
Americana (omitting the earliest), in political and social science, public administration, jurisprudence. If any American
library can secure the documents which will exhibit completely legislation proposed and legislation enacted it should be
able to. As depository of the library of the Smithsonian it
will have the most important collection--perhaps in the world
--of the transactions and proceedings of learned societies;
and, adding its own exchanges and subscriptions, of serials
in general. With theology it may not especially concern itself
nor with philology to the degree appropriate to a university

library.   Medicine it will leave as a specialty to the library
of the Surgeon-General's office, already pre-eminent, Geology
to the library of the Geological Survey.   Two extremes it may
have to abstain from--so far as deliberate purchase is concerned: 1) the books merely popular, 2) the books merely
curious.   Of the first many will come to it through copyright;
of the second many should come through gift.   (Perhaps in
time the public spirit of American collectors and donors may
turn to it as the public spirit of the British turns to the National Library of Great Britain.)   Original sources must come
to it, if at all, chiefly by gift.   Manuscript material relating
to American history it has, however, bought, and will buy.

Otherwise, chiefly printed books.   Of these, the useful books; of these again, the books useful rather for the establishment of the fact than for the mere presentation of it--
the books for the advancement of learning, rather than those
for the mere diffusion of knowledge.

Lastly there is an organization.   Instead of 42 persons, for all manner of service, there are now 261, irrespective of printers, binders, and the force attending to the
care of the building itself.

The copyright work is set off and interferes no longer
with the energies of the library proper.   There is a separate
division having to do with the acquisition of material, anoth-
er--of 67 persons--to classify and catalog it.   There are 42
persons attending to the ordinary service of the reading room
as supplied from the stacks, and there are eight special divisions handling severally the current newspapers and periodicals, the documents, manuscripts, maps, music, prints, the
scientific publications forming the Smithsonian deposit, and
the books for the blind.   There is a Division of Bibliography
whose function is to assist in research too elaborate for the
routine service of the reading room, to edit the library publications, and to represent the library in co-operative bibliographic undertakings.   There is now within the building, besides a bindery, with a force of 45 employees, a printing
office, with a force of 21.   The allotment for printing and
binding, in 1896 only $15,000, is for the coming year $90,-
000.

The immediate duty of this organization is near at
hand.   There is a huge arrear of work upon the existing col-
lection--necessary for its effective use, and its intelligent
growth.   It must be newly classified throughout; and shelf

listed.   The old author slip catalog must be revised and reduced to print.   There must be compiled a subject catalog,
of which none now exists.   Innumerable gaps--that which is
crooked can be made straight, but that which is wanting cannot be numbered--innumerable gaps are to be ascertained and
filled.   A collection of reference books must be placed back
at the Capitol, with suitable apparatus, to bring the library
once more into touch with Congress and enable it to render
the service to Congress which is its first duty.   The other
libraries of the District must be brought into association--
not by gathering their collections into the Library of Congress,
but by co-ordinating processes and service.   The Library of
Congress as the center of the system can aid in this.   It can
strengthen each departmental library by relieving it of material not necessary to its special work.   It can aid toward
specialization in these departmental libraries by exhibiting
present unnecessary duplication.   (It is just issuing a union
list of serials currently taken by the libraries of the District
which has this very purpose.)   It can very likely print the
catalog cards for all the government libraries--incidentally
securing uniformity, and a copy for its own use of each card
--which in time will result in a complete statement within its
own walls of the resources of every departmental library in
Washington.   It will supply to each such library a copy of
every card which it prints of a book in its own collections
relating to the work of the bureau which such library serves.

        To reduce to order the present collection, incorporat-
ing the current accessions, to fill the most inconvenient gaps,
to supply the most necessary apparatus in catalogs and to
bring about a relation among the libraries of Washington
which shall form them into an organic system: this work
will of itself be a huge one, I have spoken of the equipment
of the Library of Congress as elaborate, the force as large,
and the appropriations as generous.   All are so in contrast
to antecedent conditions.   In proportion to the work to be
done, however, they are not merely not excessive, but in
some respects far short of the need.   To proceed beyond
those immediate undertakings to projects of general service
will require certain equipment, service, and funds not yet
secured, and which can be secured only by a general effort.
But the question is not what can be done, but what may be
done--in due time, eventually.

        A general distribution of the printed cards: That has
been suggested.   It was suggested a half century ago by the
Federal Government through the Smithsonian Institution.   Pro-

fessor Jewett's proposal then was a central bureau to compile, print and distribute cards which might serve to local
libraries as a catalog of their own collections. Such a project is now before this Association. It may not be feasible:
that is, it might not result in the economy which it suggests.
It assumes a large number of books to be acquired, in the
same editions, by many libraries, at the same time. In
fact, the enthusiasm for the proposal at the Montreal meeting
last year has resulted in but sixty subscriptions to the actual
project.

It may not be feasible. But if such a scheme can be
operated at all it may perhaps be operated most effectively
through the library which for its own uses is cataloging and
printing a card for every book currently copyrighted in the
United States, and for a larger number of others than any
other single institution. Such must be confessed of the Library of Congress. It is printing a card for every book currently copyrighted, for every other book currently added--
for every book reached in re-classification--and thus in the
end for every book in its collection. It is now printing, at
the rate of over 200 titles a day--60,000 titles a year. The
entry is an author entry, in form and type accepted by the
committee on cataloging of the ALA. The cards are of the
standard size--3 x 5 inches--of the best linen ledger stock.
From 15 to 100 copies of each are now printed. It would be
uncandid to say that such a number is necessary for the use
of the library itself, or of the combined libraries at Washington. The usefulness of copies of them to any other library
for incorporation in its catalogs must depend upon local conditions: the style, form, and size of its own cards, the number of books which it adds yearly, the proportion of these
which are current, and other related matters. On these
points we have sought statistics from 254 libraries. We have
them from 202. With them we have samples of the cards in
use by each, with a complete author entry. Having them we
are in a position really to estimate the chances. I will not
enter into details. Summarily, it appears that our cards
might effect a great saving to certain libraries and some saving to others, and would entail a mere expense without benefit to the remainder--all of which is as might have been
guessed.

The distribution suggested by Professor Jewett and
proposed by the ALA had in view a saving to the recipient
library of cataloging and printing on its own account. It assumed a subscription by each recipient to cover the cost of

the extra stock and presswork.   There is conceivable a distribution more limited in range, having another purpose.
The national library wishes to get into touch with the local
libraries which are centers for important research.   It
wishes the fullest information as to their contents; it may
justifiably supply them with the fullest information as to its
own contents.   Suppose it should supply them with a copy of
every card which it prints, getting in return a copy of every
card which they print?   I am obliged to disclose this suggestion: for such an exchange has already been begun.   A copy
of every card printed by the Library of Congress goes out to
the New York Public Library: a copy of every card printed
by the New York Public Library comes to the Library of Congress.   In the new building of the New York Public Library
there will be a section of the public card catalog designated
The Catalog of the Library of Congress.   It will contain at
least every title in the Library of Congress not to be found
in any library of the metropolis.   In the Library of Congress
a section of the great card catalog of American libraries outside the District will be a catalog of the New York Public
Library.

I have here a letter from the librarian of Cornell University forwarding a resolution of the Library Council (composed in part of faculty members) which requests for the university library a set of these cards.   Mr. Harris states that
the purpose would be to fit up cases of drawers in the catalog room, which is freely accessible to any one desiring to
consult bibliographical aids, and arrange the cards in alphabetical order by authors, thus making an author catalog of
the set.   He adds "The whole question has been rather carefully considered and the unanimous sense of the council was
that the usefulness of the catalog to us would be well worth
the cost of the cases, the space they would occupy, and the
time it would take to arrange and keep in order the cards. "

There is a limit to such a distribution.   But I suspect
that it will not stop with New York and Ithaca.

There is some expense attendant on it.   There is the
extra stock, the presswork, the labor of sorting and des-
patching.   No postage, however, for the Library of Congress
has the franking privilege, in and out.   The results however:
one cannot deny them to be attractive.   At Washington a
statement of at least the distinctive contents of every great
local collection.   At each local center of research a statement of the distinctive contents of the national collection.

An inquirer in Wisconsin writes to Washington: is such a book to be had in the United States; must he come to Washington for it, or to New York?--No, he will find it in Chicago at the Newberry or the Crerar.

If there can be such a thing as a bibliographic bureau for the United States, the Library of Congress is in a way to become one; to a degree, in fact, a bureau of information for the United States. Besides routine workers efficient as a body, it has already some expert bibliographers and within certain lines specialists. It has not a complete corps of these. It cannot have until Congress can be made to understand the need of them. Besides its own employees, however, it has within reach by telephone a multitude of experts. They are maintained by the very government which maintains it. They are learned men, efficient men, specially trained, willing to give freely of their special knowledge. They enter the government employ and remain there, not for the pecuniary compensation, which is shamefully meagre, but for the love of the work itself and for the opportunity for public service which it affords. Of these men, in the scientific bureaus at Washington, the National Library can take counsel: it can secure their aid to develop its collections and to answer inquiries of moment. This will be within the field of the natural and physical sciences. Meantime within its walls it possesses already excellent capacity for miscellaneous research, and special capacity for meeting inquiries in history and topography, in general literature, and in the special literature of economics, mathematics and physics. It has still Ainsworth Spofford and the other men, who with him, under extraordinary disadvantages, for thirty-five years made the library useful at the Capitol.

The library is already issuing publications in book form. In part these are catalogs of its own contents; in part an exhibit of the more important material in existence on some subject of current interest, particularly, of course, in connection with national affairs. Even during the period of organization fifteen such lists have already been issued. They are distributed freely to libraries and even to individual inquirers.

But there may be something further. The distribution of cards which exhibit its own contents or save duplication of expense elsewhere, the publication of bibliographies which aid to research, expert service which in answer to inquiry points out the best sources and the most effective methods of research:

all these may have their use.   But how about the books themselves?   Must the use of this great collection be limited to
Washington?   How many of the students who need some book
in the Library of Congress--perhaps there alone--can come
to Washington to consult it at the moment of need?   A case
is conceivable: a university professor at Madison or Berkeley or San Antonio, in connection with research important to
scholarship, requires some volume in an unusual set.   The
set is not in the university library.   It is too costly for that
library to acquire for the infrequent need.   The volume is
in the National Library.   It is not at the moment in use at
Washington.   The university library requests the loan of it.
If the National Library is to be the national library---?

There might result some inconvenience.   There would
be also the peril of transit.   Some volumes might be lost to
posterity.   But after all we are ourselves a posterity.   Some
respect is due to the ancestors who have saved for our use.
And if one copy of a book possessed by the federal government and within reasonable limits subject to call by different
institutions, might suffice for the entire United States--what
does logic seem to require--and expediency--and the good of
the greater number?

The Library of Congress is now primarily a reference
library.   But if there be any citizen who thinks that it should
never lend a book--to another library--in aid of the higher
research--when the book can be spared from Washington and
is not a book within the proper duty of the local library to
supply--if there be any citizen who thinks that for the National Library to lend under these circumstances would be a
misuse of its resources and, therefore, an abuse of trust--
he had better speak quickly, or he may be too late.   Precedents may be created which it would be awkward to ignore.

Really I have been speaking of the Library of Congress
as if it were the only activity of the federal government of
interest to libraries.   That, however, is the fault of the
topic.   It was not what might be done for science, for literature, for the advance of learning, for the diffusion of knowledge.   It was merely what might be done for libraries; as
it were, not for the glory of God, but for the advancement
of the church.   We have confidence in the mission of libraries
and consider anything in aid of it as good in itself.

Their most stimulating, most fruitful service must be
the direct service.   The service of the national authority

must in large part be merely indirect. It can meet the reader at large only through the local authority. It can serve the great body of readers chiefly through the local libraries which meet them face to face, know their needs, supply their most ordinary needs. Its natural agent--we librarians at least must think this--is its own library--the library which if there is to be a national library not merely of, but <u>for</u> the United States--must be that library.

<u>Must become</u> such, I should have said. For we are not yet arrived. We cannot arrive until much preliminary work has been done, and much additional resource secured from Congress. We shall arrive the sooner in proportion as you who have in charge the municipal and collegiate libraries of the United States will urge upon Congress the advantage to the interests you represent, of undertakings such as I have described. To this point we have not asked your aid. In the equipment of the library, in the reconstruction of its service, in the addition of more expert service, in the improvement of immediate facilities, our appeal to Congress has been based on the work to be done near at hand. I have admitted to you the possibility of these other undertakings of more general concern. If they commend themselves to you as proper and useful--the appeal for them must be primarily your appeal.

LIBRARIES AND THE YOUNG

PUBLIC LIBRARIES AND THE YOUNG*

William I. Fletcher

What shall the public library do for the young, and
how? is a question of acknowledged importance. The remarkable development of "juvenile literature" testifies to the
growing importance of this portion of the community in the
eyes of book producers, while the character of much of this
literature, which is now almost thrust into the hands of youth,
is such as to excite grave doubts as to its being of any service, intellectual or moral. In this state of things the public
library is looked to by some with hope, and by others with
fear, according as its management is apparently such as to
draw young readers away from merely frivolous reading, or
to make such reading more accessible and encourage them in
the use of it; hence the importance of a judicious administration of the library in this regard.

One of the first questions to be met in arranging a
code of rules for the government of a public library relates
to the age at which young persons shall be admitted to its
privileges. There is no usage on this point which can be
called common, but most libraries fix a certain age, as
twelve or fourteen, below which candidates for admission
are ineligible. Only a few of the most recently established
libraries have adopted what seems to be the right solution of
this question, by making no restriction whatever as to age.
This course recommends itself as the wisest and the most
consistent with the idea of the public library on many grounds.

*Reprinted from Public Libraries in the United States of
America: Their History, Condition and Management, Vol. 1:
412-418. Washington, D.C.: US Commissioner of Education,
G.P.O., 1896.

In the first place, age is no criterion of mental condition and capacity. So varying is the date of the awakening of intellectual life, and the rapidity of its progress, that height of stature might almost as well be taken for its measure as length of years. In every community there are some young minds of peculiar gifts and precocious development, as fit to cope with the masterpieces of literature at ten years of age, as the average person at twenty, and more appreciative of them. From this class come the minds which rule the world of mind, and confer the greatest benefits on the race. How can the public library do more for the intellectual culture of the whole community than by setting forward in their careers those who will be the teachers and leaders of their generation? In how many of the lives of those who have been eminent in literature and science do we find a youth almost discouraged because deprived of the means of intellectual growth. The lack of appreciation of youthful demands for culture is one of the saddest chapters in the history of the world's comprehending not the light which comes into it. Our public libraries will fail in an important part of their mission if they shut out from their treasures minds craving the best, and for the best purposes, because, forsooth, the child is too young to read good books.

Some will be found to advocate the exclusion of such searchers for knowledge on the ground that precocious tastes should be repressed in the interests of physical health. But a careful investigation of the facts in such cases can hardly fail to convince one that in them repression is the last thing that will bring about bodily health and vigor. There should doubtless be regulation, but nothing will be so likely to conduce to the health and physical well being of a person with strong mental cravings as the reasonable satisfaction of those cravings. Cases can be cited where children, having what seemed to be a premature development of mental qualities coupled with weak or even diseased bodily constitutions, have rapidly improved in health when circumstances have allowed the free exercise of their intellectual powers, and have finally attained a maturity vigorous alike in body and mind. This is in the nature of a digression, but it can do no harm to call attention thus to the facts which contradict the common notion that intellectual precocity should be discouraged. Nature is the best guide, and it is in accordance with all her workings, that when she has in hand the production of a giant of intellect, the young Hercules should astonish observers by feats of strength even in his cradle. Let not the public library, then, be found working against nature by establishing, as far

as its influence goes, a dead level of intellectual attainments
for all persons below a certain age.

But there is a much larger class of young persons
who ought not to be excluded from the library, not because
they have decided intellectual cravings and are mentally mature, but because they have capacities for the cultivation of
good tastes, and because the cultivation of such tastes cannot be begun too early.   There is no greater mistake in
morals than that often covered by the saying, harmless enough
literally, "Boys will be boys." This saying is used perhaps
oftener than for any other purpose to justify boys in doing
things which are morally not fit for men to do, and is thus
the expression of that great error that immoralities early in
life are to be expected and should not be severely deprecated.
The same misconception of the relations of youth to maturity
and of nature's great laws of growth and development, is seen
in that common idea that children need not be expected to
have any literary tastes; that they may well be allowed to
confine their reading to the frivolous, the merely amusing.
That this view is an erroneous one thought and observation
agree in showing.   Much like the caution of the mother who
would not allow her son to bathe in the river till he had
learned to swim, is that of those who would have youth wait
till a certain age, when they ought to have good tastes formed,
before they can be admitted to companionship with the best
influences for the cultivation of them.   Who will presume to
set the age at which a child may first be stirred with the beginnings of a healthy intellectual appetite on getting a taste
of the strong meat of good literature? This point is one of
the first importance.   No after efforts can accomplish what
is done with ease early in life in the way of forming habits
either mental or moral, and if there is any truth in the idea
that the public library is not merely a storehouse for the supply of the wants of the reading public, but also and especially
an educational institution which shall create wants where they
do not exist, then the library ought to bring its influences to
bear on the young as early as possible.

And this is not a question of inducing young persons
to read, but of directing their reading into right channels.
For in these times there is little probability that exclusion
from the public library will prevent their reading.   Poor, indeed, in all manner of resources, must be the child who cannot now buy, beg, or borrow a fair supply of reading of some
kind; so that exclusion from the library is likely to be a shut-
ting up of the boy or girl to dime novels and story papers as

the staple of reading. Complaints are often made that public libraries foster a taste for light reading, especially among the young. Those who make this complaint too often fail to perceive that the tastes indulged by those who are admitted to the use of the public library at the age of twelve or fourteen, are the tastes formed in the previous years of exclusion. A slight examination of facts, such as can be furnished by any librarian of experience in a circulating public library, will show how little force there is in this objection.

Nor should it be forgotten, in considering this question, that to very many young people youth is the time when they have more leisure for reading than any other portion of life is likely to furnish. At the age of twelve or fourteen, or even earlier, they are set at work to earn their living, and thereafter their opportunities for culture are but slight, nor are their circumstances such as to encourage them then in such a work. We cannot begin too early to give them a bent towards culture which shall abide by them and raise them above the work-a-day world which will demand so large a share of their time and strength. The mechanic, the farmer, the man in any walk of life, who has early formed good habits of reading, is the one who will magnify his calling, and occupy the highest positions in it. And to the thousands of young people, in whose homes there is none of the atmosphere of culture or of the appliances for it, the public library ought to furnish the means of keeping pace intellectually with the more favored children of homes where good books abound and their subtle influence extends even to those who are too young to read and understand them. If it fails to do this it is hardly a fit adjunct to our school system, whose aim it is to give every man a chance to be the equal of every other man, if he can.

It is not claimed that the arguments used in support of an age limitation are of no force; but it is believed that they are founded on objections to the admission of the young to library privileges which are good only as against an indiscriminate and not properly regulated admission, and which are not applicable to the extension of the use of the library to the young under such conditions and restrictions as are required by their peculiar circumstances.

For example, the public library ought not to furnish young persons with a means of avoiding parental supervision of their reading. A regulation on making the written consent of the parent a prerequisite to the registration of the name of a minor, and the continuance of such consent a condition of the continuance of the privilege, will take from parents all cause for complaint in this regard.

Neither should the library be allowed to stand between pupils in school and their studies, as it is often complained that it does. To remove this difficulty, the relations of the library to the school system should be such that teachers should be able to regulate the use of the library by those pupils whose studies are evidently interfered with by their miscellaneous reading. The use of the library would thus be a stimulus to endeavor on the part of pupils who would regard its loss as the probable result of lack of diligence in their studies.

Again, it must be understood that to the young, as to all others, the library is open only during good behavior. The common idea that children and youth are more likely than older persons to commit offenses against library discipline is not borne out by experience; but were it true, a strict enforcement of rules as to fines and penalties would protect the library against loss and injury, the fear of suspension from the use of the library as the result of carelessness in its use, operating more strongly than any other motive to prevent such carelessness.

If there are other objections to the indiscriminate admission of the young to the library, they can also be met by such regulations as readily suggest themselves, and should not be allowed to count as arguments against a judicious and proper extension of the benefits of the library to the young.

Choice of Books

But when the doors of the public library are thrown open to the young, and they are recognized as an important class of its patrons, the question comes up, What shall the library furnish to this class in order to meet its wants? If the object of the library is understood to be simply the supplying of the wants of the reading public, and the young are considered as a portion of that public, the question is very easily answered by saying, Give them what they call for that is not positively injurious in its tendency. But if we regard the public library as an educational means rather than a mere clubbing arrangement for the economical supply of reading, just as the gas company is for the supply of artificial

light, it becomes of importance, especially with reference to
the young, who are the most susceptible to educating influences, that they should receive from the library that which
will do them good; and the managers of the library appear
not as caterers to a master whose will is the rule as to what
shall be furnished, but rather as the trainers of gymnasts
who seek to provide that which will be of the greatest service
to their men.   No doubt both these elements enter into a true
conception of the duty of library managers; but when we are
regarding especially the young, the latter view comes nearer
the truth than the other.

In the first place, among the special requirements of
the young is this, that the library shall interest and be attractive to them.   The attitude of some public libraries toward
the young and the uncultivated seems to say to them, "We
cannot encourage you in your low state of culture; you must
come up to the level of appreciating what is really high toned
in literature, or we cannot help you. "   The public library
being, however, largely if not mainly for the benefit of the
uncultivated, must, to a large extent, come down to the level
of this class and meet them on common ground.   Every library ought to have a large list of good juvenile books, a
statement which at once raises the question, What are good
juvenile books?   This is one of the vexed questions of the literary world, closely allied to the one which has so often been
mooted in the press and the pulpit, as to the utility and propriety of novel reading.   But while this question is one on
which there are great differences of opinion, there are a few
things which may be said on it without diffidence or the fear
of successful contradiction.   Of this kind is the remark that
good juvenile books must have something positively good about
them.   They should be not merely amusing or entertaining
and harmless, but instructive and stimulating to the better
nature.   Fortunately such books are not so rare as they have
been.   Some of the best minds are now being turned to the
work of providing them.   Within a few months such honored
names in the world of letters as those of Hamerton and Hig-
ginson have been added to the list which contains those of
"Peter Parley," Jacob Abbott, " Walter Aimwell," Elijah Kel-
logg, Thomas Hughes, and others who have devoted their talents, not to the amusement, but to the instruction and culture
of youth.   The names of some of the most popular writers
for young people in our day are not ranked with those mentioned above, not because their productions are positively injurious, but because they lack the positively good qualities
demanded by our definition.

There is a danger to youth in reading some books
which are not open to the charge of directly injurious tendencies. Many of the most popular juveniles, while running
over with excellent "morals," are unwholesome mental food
for the young, for the reason that they are essentially untrue.
That is, they give false views of life, making it consist, if
it be worth living, of a series of adventures, hair-breadth
escapes; encounters with tyrannical schoolmasters and unnatu-
ral parents; sea voyages in which the green hand commands
a ship and defeats a mutiny out of sheer smartness; rides on
runaway locomotives, strokes of good luck, and a persistent
turning up of things just when they are wanted,--all of which
is calculated in the long run to lead away the young imagination and impart discontent with the common lot of an unevent-
ful life.

Books of adventure seem to meet a real want in the
minds of the young, and should not be entirely ruled out; but
they cannot be included among the books the reading of which
should be encouraged or greatly extended. In the public library it will be found perhaps necessary not to exclude this
class of juvenile books entirely. Such an exclusion is not
here advocated, but it is rather urged that they should not
form the staple of juvenile reading furnished by the library.
The better books should be duplicated so as to be on hand
when called for; these should be provided in such numbers
merely that they can occasionally be had as the "seasoning"
to a course of good reading.

But the young patrons of the library ought not to be
encouraged in confining their reading to juveniles, of no matter how good quality. It is the one great evil of this era of
juvenile books, good and bad, that by supplying mental food
in the form fit for mere children, they postpone the attainment of a taste for the strong meat of real literature; and
the public library ought to be influential in exalting this real
literature and keeping it before the people, stemming with it
the current of trash which is so eagerly welcomed because
it is new or because it is interesting. When children were
driven to read the same books as their elders or not to read
at all, there were doubtless thousands, probably the majority
of all, who chose the latter alternative, and read but very
little in their younger years. This class is better off now
than then by the greater inducements offered them to mental
culture in the increased facilities provided for it. But there
seems to be danger that the ease and smoothness of the royal
road to knowledge now provided in the great array of easy

books in all departments will not conduce to the formation of
such mental growths as resulted from the pursuit of knowledge
under difficulties.   There is doubtless more knowledge; but
is there as much power and muscle of mind?

However this may be, none can fail to recognize the
importance of setting young people in the way of reading the
best books early in life.   And as the public library is likely
to be the one place where the masters of literature can be
found, it is essential that here they should be put by every
available means in communication with and under the influence
of these masters.

It only remains now to say that, as we have before
intimated, the public library should be viewed as an adjunct
of the public school system, and to suggest that in one or
two ways the school may work together with the library in
directing the reading of the young.   There is the matter of
themes for the writing of compositions; by selecting subjects
on which information can be had at the library, the teacher
can send the pupil to the library as a student, and readily
put him in communication with, and excite his interest in,
classes of books to which he has been a stranger and indifferent.   Again, in the study of the history of English literature, a study which, to the credit of our teachers be it said,
is being rapidly extended, the pupils may be induced to take
new interest, and gain greatly in point of real culture by
being referred for illustrative matter to the public library.

REPORT ON READING FOR THE YOUNG*

Lutie E. Stearns

For the purposes of this report fifteen questions, indicated by the headings below, were sent to one hundred and ninety-five libraries in the United States and Canada. Full and complete replies were received from one hundred and forty-five librarians to whom grateful acknowledgment is now made.

1. At what age may children draw books? Why do you have an age limit?

Thirty per cent of the libraries reporting, have no age limit, the seventy per cent varying from eight to sixteen years of age--the average age requirement being thirteen years.

Various reasons are given for an age restriction. "We must preserve our books" is oft repeated.

Milwaukee has never had an age limit, and the first case of malicious destruction or injury is yet to be reported. No better recommendation can possibly be given for a good book than to have it literally wear out.

"We must draw the line somewhere," say other librarians.

At the London Conference of 1877, Sir Redmond Barry, Librarian at Melbourne, said that if it were necessary to deprive people of seven years' reading, it would be better to strike off the seven years at the other end, and disqualify

*Reprinted from Library Journal 19(Conf. No.):81-87 (1894).

people at sixty-three; adding, that that view of his was a very unprejudiced one, as such a one would exclude himself.

"Our books are not suited to young people."

Nothing is of more importance in education than furnishing young people with the best literature. Mr. Horace E. Scudder has said:

"There can be no manner of question that between the ages of six and sixteen, a large part of the best literature of the world may be read, and that the man or woman who has failed to become acquainted with great literature in some form during that time, is little likely to have a taste formed later."

There has never been a time when a little money, judiciously expended, would go so far in the purchase of the best literature for children. Stories, fables, myths, and simple poems, which have been read with delight by countless generations, may be purchased in most durable cloth bindings, at an average of thirty-two cents.

Children will read; if wholesome reading-matter is not furnished them, they will read what they can get of their own accord.

Many libraries report that there is practically no limit, as children under fourteen use the parent's card; but through this method the parent suffers from the restriction, as it is obvious that the parent and his son cannot use the card at the same time. The greatest complaint among the librarians is the lack of supervision of the children's reading, on the part of the parents; and yet these same neglectful parents are entrusted with the task of taking out cards so that their children may receive books at the library!

The tendency among progressive libraries is toward the abolishment of the age restriction. J. C. Dana, of Denver, Col., writes:

"We give a child a card as soon as he can read. Children too young to read, get cards for books to be read to them."

Miss Perkins, Ilion (N.Y.) Free Public Library, writes:

"We have no age limit, because we wish children trained to love books from their earliest recollection. Our library contains linen and pasteboard nursery books which are drawn on card in name of child, with parent for guarantor. " (And this in a library of 6,000 volumes, in a city of 4,000 inhabitants.)

Miss Hasse, Asst. Librarian of Los Angeles, writes:

"We have an age limit of twelve years, for no other reason than because we are the victims of an absurd library custom, adopted before we knew better. "

Mr. Crunden, St. Louis, Mo. , says:

"No age limit. Don't believe in it. Let children take books as soon as they can read. "

Mrs. Wrigley, Richmond, Ind. , says:

"A child may take a book when he can carry it home safely. "

Mrs. Sanders, Pawtucket, R. I.:

"We have no age limit. Every pupil of the schools, either public or private, is expected to have a card. "

The librarian at Greeley, Col. , writes:

"Children take books when they are old enough to know pictures--usually at five years. "

The librarian of a Vermont library, who shall be nameless, for obvious reasons, writes:

"Our trustees are not progressive, and not willing to change. "

Miss Hewins, Hartford, Conn. , says:

"We have no age limit. A child may draw a book as soon as he can write his name. I wish that the age limit might be abolished in all libraries. "

The librarian who studies school statistics cannot help being impressed with the grave necessity for the extension of

library privileges unto the smallest child. In Milwaukee, out
of 5,766 children who entered the schools in 1885, we find
but 687 graduating eight years later. If we had an age limit
in Milwaukee, we would reach but twelve per cent of the number in school, to say nothing of the thousands out of school.

In Jersey City (school census of 1891), we find more
than half of those attending school in the first four grades,
from six to ten years of age. San Francisco (census of
1892) has 87,000 children between five and seventeen years
of age. Of this number, 40,000 attend school (less than
half), and sixty-four per cent of the number attending are
found in the first five grades. Of Boston's school population,
ninety-three per cent are found in the primary and grammar
departments. Minneapolis has 25,000 school children--
22,000 under fifteen years of age. St. Louis has 56,000
children under fourteen, each one of whom may have a card
as soon as he can write his name.

One library with an age limit of fourteen years, reports that not more than half a dozen children under twelve,
use the library--and this in the face of the fact that there are
41,000 children under fourteen in that city.

Protect the library's interests by a proper form of
guarantee, remove the age restriction, and bid every child
welcome. In this age of trash and printed wickedness, when
a professor in one of our western universities feels tempted
to say that the youth of this country would grow up to better
citizenship and stauncher virtue, were they not taught to
read, and when Frederic Harrison sees on every side the
poisonous inhalations of literary garbage, and bad men's
worse thoughts, which drive him to exclaim that he could almost reckon the printing press as amongst the scourges of
mankind--when we hear all this, and see for ourselves, bad
literature on every hand, is it not a pitiful spectacle to see
this sign conspicuously displayed in one of the circulating libraries in this country--"CHILDREN NOT ALLOWED IN THIS
LIBRARY. "

In opposition to such cruelty as this, let us quote the
words of the late Dr. Poole of Chicago:

"I could never see the propriety of excluding young
persons from a library, any more than from a church. From
ten to fourteen is the formative period of their lives. If they
ever become readers, and acquire a love of books, it is be-

fore the age of fourteen years. No persons return their
books so promptly, give so little trouble, or seem to appreciate more highly the benefits of a library, as these youth
of both sexes.

"The young people are our best friends, and they serve
the interests of the library by enlisting for it the sympathies
of their parents, who are often too busy to read."

No assistant should be employed in the circulating,
reference, or reading-room departments of a library, who
will not give a child as courteous and considerate attention
as she would a member of the Board of Trustees.

2.   Do the children use the library to an appreciable
extent?

This is answered in the affirmative in nearly every
case; variously stated as one-fifth, one-fourth, one-third, and
one-half of membership under sixteen years of age.

3.   Is the number of books a child may take per week,
restricted?

One hundred and fifteen libraries report no restriction.
Oswego, N.Y., Portsmouth, N.H., Terre Haute, Ind., allow but one book per week. Hartford, Conn., and Cleveland
Ohio, issue but one story-book to children under fourteen,
while schools are in session. Newburgh, N.Y., allows those
under ten years, but one book per week.

Two books per week--Germantown, Penn., Memphis,
Tenn., Grand Rapids, Mich., La Crosse, Wis., Richmond,
Ind., Kalamazoo, Mich., Nashua, N.H., Hamilton, Ont.,
Evanston, Ind., Watertown, Mass.

Three books--Fond du Lac, Wis., Evanston, Ill.,
Fitchburg, Mass., Springfield, Mass., San Francisco, Cal.,
Barry, Ill.

Twelve per week--Elgin, Ill.

4.   What per cent of your circulation is children's
fiction?

The average is about twenty per cent of the entire circulation.

5. Do you circulate Alger, Optic, Castlemon, Trowbridge, and kindred authors?

Nine libraries report that they do not circulate any of
the above-named. Eighteen libraries are allowing the first
three to wear out without replacing. Twenty-five libraries
circulate Trowbridge only. There seems to be a great difference of opinion in regard to the relative value and worth
of these authors. One librarian writes:

"Our set of Alger and Trowbridge are worn out and
not replaced. Poor, thin, much-abused Optic helps boys to
read, and leads up to stronger books;" while another librarian says: "I consider that Alger and Castlemon have done
irreparable injury to our boys, in their taste for more solid
reading. Since their purchase, solid reading for children
has fallen off ten per cent."

Buffalo, N. Y. , (partly subscription) reports:

"One set of Alger, some of Optic and Castlemon's issued on demand to holders of membership tickets, but their
use is discouraged, and none given to holders of school
tickets."

Pawtucket, R. I. , removed Castlemon from the shelves,
two years ago, but circulates Trowbridge. Milwaukee, Wis.,
has Trowbridge, only, for which there is but little demand.
Trowbridge is not sent to schools, and we find, at the main
library, that our boys prefer something better.

6. Do you have special lists or catalogues for children? State price, if not free.

The majority of libraries merely designate children's
books by some sign in the main catalogue. Twenty-five libraries report special printed catalogues, varying in price
from one cent to fifteen cents. Many are issued free.
Many libraries use Sargent's and Hardy's lists, with numbers
inserted. Four have special card-catalogues for children's
use. Some designate a child's book by a colored card, while
one librarian enters books for children under twelve, on yel-
low cards, and from twelve to eighteen years of age, on blue.
Poughkeepsie, N. Y. , has a set of nine small lists adapted to
various ages. Miss Hewins' (Hartford, Conn.) catalogue is
worthy of special commendation. The "List of books for
Township Libraries," prepared by Mr. Frank A. Hutchins,

State Superintendent's Office, Madison, Wis., is a model
list, in every particular, and may be obtained for the asking.

Milwaukee, Wis., has a children's catalogue, and also
prints little lists of "150 good books for girls," and "150
good books for boys," which are issued free, and used as
call-slips by the children.   The list is kept in the pocket of
the book with the card.   These lists are used by ninety-nine
per cent of the children.   We thus direct the reading of the
young by calling attention to the best books.   (We shall be
glad to send these lists to all who desire them.)

7.   Do you have Teachers' cards?   How many books
may be drawn at a time?   Are these books issued by teachers to pupils, or used solely for reference?

One-third of those reporting make no distinction between teachers and other borrowers.   Others issue a card
upon which teachers may take from two to twenty books--the
average being six.   Some libraries restrict the use of these
books to reference in the school-room, while others leave it
optional with the teacher.

If the object of this privilege is for purposes of reference, it is a wise one to follow; but if its aim is to supply
additional reading-matter to pupils, it is meagre in the ex-
treme--the tendency being to get books dealing with studies
taught, rather than good literature for children.   To "Let
teachers have as many as they can use" is the rule in an
increasing number of libraries.

8.   Do you send books to schools in proportion to
size of classes, i.e., fifty pupils--fifty books, to be issued
by teachers to pupils for home use?

Some one has truly said, "In the work of popular education through libraries, it is, after all, not the few great
libraries, but the thousand smaller ones that may do most for
the people."   Greatness of cities hampers individual work.
The librarian knows, from the school census, that there are
34,000 children, between six and fourteen years of age, in
his city.   By abolishing the age requirement, he may reach
those in the vicinity of the library; but what of the thousands
in the home districts--many of whom have never heard of the
existence of the library?

It seems to us that the teacher, the one who guides

and educates, the one who knows best the individual preferences and capacities of her pupils--it is the teacher who
should direct the reading.   The process is most simple.
The teacher comes to the library and selects from the shelves
a number of books, in proportion to the size of her class,
i.e., fifty pupils--fifty books.   These are sent to the schools,
and issued by the teachers for home use.   The selection is
made from all branches of literature--mythology, science,
useful arts, fine arts, poetry, history, travel, biography,
fairy stories, stories of adventure, &c., &c.   The books are
not intended, primarily, to supplement the school work.
They should be "books of inspiration" rather than those of
information; for "knowledge alone cannot make character. "
Another great object should be to create a love for books;
for "What we make children love and desire is more important than what we make them learn. "

     Each pupil should be provided with a library card--
with parent as guarantor--thus relieving the teacher's responsibility.

     Cleveland, Ohio, Los Angeles, Cal., Hartford, Conn.,
Grand Rapids, Mich., Bridgeport, Conn., Lancaster, Mass.,
Chicago, Ill., Burlington, Vt., Dover, N.H., and Milwaukee,
Wis., carry on this work to a greater or less extent.   Los
Angeles, Cal., sent 14,075 books to the schools from September 1893 to May 30, 1894, a remarkable showing.   Grand
Rapids, Mich., issued 3,415 books, which were circulated
15,905 times.   Cleveland, Ohio, sent 4,708 volumes, the
number of issues being 38,031, the books being kept at the
school during the school year.   (See The Open Shelf for June
1894, published by Cleveland Pub. Lib.--for description of
school circulation.)

     A few statistics may demonstrate the growth of this
plan in Milwaukee.   In 1888--the year of its inauguration,
1,650 books were issued by teachers, 4,702 times.   During
the school year 1893-94, 14,990 books were issued 42,863
times--the number of books sent being limited only by the
supply at our command.   The books were returned to the library at the expiration of eight weeks, when a new selection
was made by the teacher.   It must be understood that this
represents the number of books read at home by the children.
Much of the eighty per cent increase in the circulation at the
library, during the past winter, was due, not alone to the
hard times, but to the advertising which the library received
in the homes, through the schools.

Many teachers select books for the parents and older brothers and sisters of their pupils. The system of school circulation is being gradually extended, until it will eventually embrace every grade of every school--public, private, parochial and Sunday-school, which can be induced to avail themselves of the privilege.

There are many methods of awakening the teachers' interest in the matter of school distribution. We visit the class-rooms of the public schools and tell the children stories, thereby arousing a desire for books; we urge upon the teachers the necessity of furnishing the young with the best literature. Our superintendent of schools gives our system the heartiest encouragement and support. That he deems the plan of the greatest importance, will be shown in an article by him on "The Public Library and Public Schools," in the Educational Review (Nov. 1894).

9.   Do you send a number of copies of the same work to schools for supplemental reading?

Detroit, Jersey City, and St. Louis carry on this work extensively. St. Louis, Mo., has six sets of fifty copies each of Scudder's Folk Tales, Franklin's autobiography, &c, which are sent from one school to another. Jersey City, N.J., issued 11,844 volumes (twenty sets), in this manner, during the past year. The books are carefully graded and meet with much favor. Detroit sent 17,290 books to the schools, for supplemental reading matter. The superintendent of schools of Detroit, in his annual report (1891) says:

"The benefits to the higher grades, from the circulating library, furnished by the Public Library, are very decided, and there is a perceptible change for the better in the choice of selections made by the pupils; and it is the universal testimony, that there is a growing taste for good reading, among our school children."

This plan of school distribution has much to commend it. Educators are coming to realize that the modern school readers--the "five inanities"--are directly responsible for the habit of desultory reading. But we maintain that the furnishing of supplemental reading-matter--to be read in school-- lies wholly within the province of the school authorities of our cities. As Mr. Cowell, of Liverpool, says: "We leave the school-board to provide their own books, as they have more funds at their disposal than we have." But few libraries can afford to furnish such books, the demands of the individual tastes of the child being more than can be ordinarily supplied.

10. Do you circulate pictures in schools and homes?
In what form issued?

Newton, Mass., Ilion, N.Y., Wilkes-Barre, Penn., and Milwaukee, Wis., circulate linen and pasteboard picture-books among the smallest children. Gloversville, N.Y., sends portfolios of photographs to teachers who wish to illustrate certain lessons.

Los Angeles, Cal., Denver, Col., and Milwaukee, Wis., select suitable pictures from Harper's Weekly and Bazar, Leslie's, Scientific American, &c., &c., which are mounted on manilla, gray bristol, or tag-board, and sent to the schools. In selecting pictures, it should be the aim to choose those of aesthetic value--training the child's sense of beauty and imagination. Many, of course, may be used for language, geography, and history work. Teachers of Milwaukee organize "pasting and cutting bees," thus relieving the library of much of the work.

As an evidence of the popularity of the pictures, in Milwaukee, we have but to cite the fact that thirteen hundred pictures were circulated in the schools, during May and June. Los Angeles has fifteen hundred pictures at the disposal of teachers. (For "Pictures in Elementary Schools" see Health Exhibition Literature, vol. 13, pp. 54-77, and Prang Educational Papers, Nos. 1 and 4.)

11. Do classes visit the library?

Forty-four libraries report visits of classes for the purpose of viewing art works, illustrated books of travels, &c., &c. Lack of room, prevents many libraries from extending this privilege.

Gloversville, N.Y., organizes children's reading circles, and prepares a list of books to be used in connection with the courses of reading. The topics selected are generally supplementary to the school work. At the weekly meetings of the circles in the class-room at the library, the current events of the week are also discussed--in this way guiding the children in proper newspaper reading.

12. (a) Have you a children's reading-room? (b) <u>Is</u>
there a special window in circulating department, for chil-
<u>dren?</u>

(a) Minneapolis devotes the lower corridor to children.
They are admitted to cases and tables containing their books
--books being charged by an attendant at the gate.

Watertown, Mass., gives up one reading-room to children, placing therein periodicals, bound and current, and
other books suited to the young. Cambridge, Mass., are
adding a children's room, in which they intend to charge
books. Cleveland, Ohio, has a special alcove for children.
Omaha, Neb., has a special department, in its new building,
for book and picture displays, special study rooms, and one
"sample" room, in which will be placed the best books for
children, and where children, parents and teachers may make
selections.

Some libraries set aside a certain part of their reference and reading-rooms for children's use.

(b) Special window for children:

Los Angeles, Cal., "Disapproves decidedly of all such
segregation. "

Dayton, Ohio, has special window for display of children's literature.

Aguilar Library (New York City) does not permit children to change books after six p. m. (How about boys and
girls who work from seven a. m. to six p. m. ?)

Dover, N. H., "Have no such pernicious things as windows in our circulating department. We have an open counter
across which human intercourse is easy. "

13. Have you a special supervisor of children's reading?

Many librarians report that they overlook the matter
in a general way, some making it their specialty. St. Louis,
Mo., has just engaged an experienced teacher for that purpose.

Any one taking this work could find an exhaustless

mine of opportunities--some of which have been hinted at under the question of school circulation.

14. What other important work are you doing for children, not included in these questions?

Indianapolis, Ind., Cambridge, Mass., and San Diego, Cal., publish, each week, in one of the daily papers, a list of books for younger readers, on electricity, travel, stories, &c., or on some special topic of the times. These lists are very popular.

Many libraries place books pertaining to school studies, on special shelves, to which children have free access.

Bridgeport, Conn., and Fitchburg, Mass., have art departments with well-qualified assistants to show pictures to children, and adults.

Medford, Mass., has had talks given to the children, upon various subjects, by friends of the librarian.

Omaha, Neb., is planning delivery stations for the children.

San Diego, Cal., "Turns children loose among the shelves on Sundays. "

Dover, N.H., issues student's cards, on which any student, old or young, may take out a number of books on any special topic.

Peoria, Ill., gives two cards to each child or adult --one for fiction and another for purposes of study.

Portland, Ore., Beaver Dam, Wis., Greeley, Col., and others allow children free access to the shelves.

Free Circulating Libraries, of New York City, have "Children's Shelves" containing the best books, from which parents and the young may make selections.

Many libraries report special assistance rendered to Youths' Debating societies, essay writing, &c.

Gloversville, N.Y., organizes reading circles (to which reference has already been made).

The library classes at Pratt Institute, Brooklyn, and Armour Institute, Chicago, are starting home libraries in slum neighborhoods.

Miss James, of Wilkes-Barre, has organized a boy's and young men's reading-room in a similar locality.

Brookline, Mass., places college and school catalogues in reference-room at the end of each school year.

15. What ideas would you like to see developed in connection with the broad subject of Reading for the Young?

Miss James, of Wilkes-Barre, voices the sentiments of many, when she says: "I would like to educate the grandparents for three generations back--ditto, the teachers." Twenty-five per cent of the librarians deplore lack of interest and supervision of the child's reading, on the part of the parents. "Over-reading" on the part of many children is another cause for complaint. The idea may have its objections, but we think that a kindly, tactful letter to the parent, might have its influence.

Great care should be exercised in the selection of books for the young. Purity of English is a primary consideration. Books "written down" to children should be avoided, also those books which do not, at once, fix the attention of the child. What the boy world needs, are books of incident, of lively action, of absorbing interest, wholesome, interesting, attractive, in good English, and yet free from the ghastliness and vulgarity of the alluring dime novel.

Many librarians advocate courses of reading in connection with the school work; certain books to be read at home, by the children, and then discussed in the school room. Much latitude should be given children in the choice of books to read--thus not making it a task but encouraging a love of reading.

By addressing Teachers' Institutes and meetings, the librarian or supervisor of children's reading can do much in the way of enlisting the aid and support of teachers. We think the work done by the State Normal School, and Public Library, of Milwaukee, is unique in this particular. A course of library reading of the best authors is required of the Normal students, thus cultivating the tastes of the future teachers and bringing them in contact with the resources of

the library. Hundreds of copies of the best books for children are sent to the Normal school, and there read and crit-
icised by the students. Lists of the best books are printed
for future reference. Children in neighboring schools send
in lists of books they prefer, thus giving the students knowledge of what children really like to read. By talks to the
students at the Normal school, we emphasize the importance
of the work from the librarian's, teacher's and child's point
of view.

    We believe there are many fields still unexplored in
the provinces of children's reading. Some means, for example, should be devised, in the large cities, to send books
to factories where children are employed.

    Reading rooms should be opened, evenings, in school
buildings. They should be supplied with the best periodicals
for old and young, and if possible, interesting books adapted
to all ages.

    Besides study and class rooms, the modern library
should contain a hall, to which children may come for instructive and entertaining lectures. That this plan is feasible is shown by the course of free lectures given in the reading room of the library at Alameda, Cal., during the past
winter, to which extended reference is made in the August
(1894) Library Journal.

    The circulation of lanterns and lantern slides, tennis
and croquet sets and the best indoor games--a plan advocated
by Miss Kelso (Los Angeles, Cal.)--meets with the warmest
approbation from all lovers of children; for if "Books of Refreshment," why not "Games of Refreshment"?

    That the child is a volume to be studied, applies as
well to library as pedagogical science. We deprecate the
spirit which prompts a librarian to say, "We prefer to trans-
act business with older persons, as we lose time in making
infants understand." As opposed to this are the words of
another who writes, "Each assistant has instruction by no
means to neglect the children for the adults." The modern
library spirit may be expressed in the words of Miss Perkins
of Ilion, N.Y., who says:

    "We always treat children with the same consideration
and courtesy as grown people. We make them love to come
and stay here, and keep in touch with them in every way possible."

In closing our report, we desire to submit five questions for consideration:

How may we induce parents to oversee their children's reading?

How may we make the guiding of her pupils' reading a part of the teacher's work?

What can be done to help a boy to like good books after he has fallen into the dime novel habit?

What methods have been used with success in developing the taste of children?

What form of catalogue, if any, is of interest and value to children?

A full discussion of these questions will be helpful to many librarians who have the best interests of their child patrons close at heart.

ACADEMIC LIBRARIES

THE UNIVERSITY LIBRARY AND
THE UNIVERSITY CURRICULUM*

W. F. Poole

The leading purpose in the preparation of this address was to consider the relations of the university library to university education. I wished to show that the study of bibliography and of the scientific methods of using books should have an assured place in the university curriculum; that a wise and professional bibliographer should be a member of the faculty and have a part in training all the students; that the library should be his class-room; and that all who go forth into the world as graduates should have such an intelligent and practical knowledge of books as will aid them in their studies through life, and the use of books be to them a perpetual delight and refreshment. Books are wiser than any professor and all the faculty; and they can be made to give up much of their wisdom to the student who knows where to go for it, and how to extract it.

I do not mean that the university student should know the contents of all the most useful books; but I do mean that he should know of their existence, what they treat of, and what they do for him. He should know what are the most important general reference-books which will answer not only his own questions, but the multitude of inquiries put to him by less-favored associates who regard him as an educated man. If the question arises as to the existence, authorship, or title of a book, an educated man should know the catalogs or bibliographies by which he can clear up the doubt immedi-

---

*These extracts from the Phi Beta Kappa Address at Northwestern University, June 14, 1893, are reprinted from <u>Library Journal</u> 18:470-471 (Nov. 1893).

ately. The words Watt, Larousse, Graesse, Quérard, Hoefer,
Kayser, Hinrichs, Meyer, Hain, and Vapereau, should not be
unmeaning sounds to him. He should know the standard writers on a large variety of subjects. He should be familiar
with the best method by which the original investigation of any
topic may be carried on. When he has found it, he appre-
ciates for the first time what books are for, and how to use
them. He finds himself a literary or scientific worker, and
that books are the tools of his profession. It is one of the
most delightful and inspiring incidents in a student's experience when he has discovered a key to the treasury of knowledge, a method by which he can do useful and practical work,
and that he has a function in life. No person has any claim
to be a scholar until he can conduct such as original investigation with ease and pleasure. This facile proficiency does
not come by intuition, nor from the clouds. Where else is
it to be taught, if not in the college or university? With it,
a graduate is prepared to grapple with his professional studies,
to succeed in editorial work, or in any literary or scientific
pursuit for which he may have the taste and qualification.

It is a well-known fact, and one regretted by the
wisest educators, that the great majority of the students of
the colleges and universities of the country graduate with
very little knowledge of books or of their use. How the evil
can be remedied is a question easier to ask than to answer.
Any scheme which may be proposed meets with this objection:
the curriculum is so full it is not possible to increase it.
This objection furnishes me with the opportunity and a justification, if one be needed, for a discussion of the modern
university curriculum.

The attentive observer of higher education has seen
within the past two decades a marked improvement in college
and university instruction, and in the direction I have already
indicated. More thought is now given to the subject by ripe
scholars and experienced educators than ever before; and yet
there is abroad a feeling of unrest, and an impression that
our educational system is passing through a transition period
from one which was exceedingly faulty to some ideal method
as yet undeveloped, and still in the future....

To those of us who graduated 30, 40, or 50 years
ago, books outside of the text-books used, had no part in
our education. They were never quoted, recommended, or
mentioned by the instructors in the class-room. As I remember it, Yale College Library might as well have been in

Wethersfield or Bridgeport as in New Haven, so far as the
students in those days were concerned. The college societies,
however, supported and managed wholly by the undergraduates,
had good libraries, and here was where the students, and the
professors besides, found their general reading. I was for-
tunate in being connected with one of these libraries, and
there I began the study of bibliography, but never had the
slightest assistance from any member of the faculty. There
were no elementary books on the subject, and hence by groping alone through the book-shelves I picked up some knowledge
of books and acquired a taste which I have not been able to
throw off to this day. How much easier could I have made
the journey if I had found blazed trees along the way and a
guide who had travelled the path before me!

During the past 20 years there has been a great advance in the study of bibliography in the leading universities.
Among these may be especially mentioned Johns Hopkins,
Yale, Harvard, Cornell, and Michigan. Good work is also
being done in other institutions. None of the universities
named have as yet quite come up to the high standard of
having a professor of bibliography, but they are moving in
that direction. In several universities the librarians give
lectures on bibliography and instruction to classes in the use
of books. The development already reached is seen in the
rapid increase of these libraries in the accession of the latest and best works on all the subjects taught in the university; by the professors citing these books, calling attention
to them, taking them into the class-room, and by this method
instructing the students to make for themselves an independent
and original investigation of any subject. As the work has
been going on money has been liberally contributed by the
friends of the institutions for erecting suitable library buildings, and procuring the necessary books.

The question is sometimes asked: "Why do not the
public, and more especially men of wealth, take more interest in higher education?" Nothing more readily appeals to
the popular sympathy than work of this kind, or forms a
firmer bond of fraternity between the university and the community at large. The great universities which keep their
hands on the popular pulse are those which receive great en-
dowments from private munificence. On some special subjects of universal interest no libraries in the land have such
complete collections of recent books as some of the university
libraries. Writers who would have access to the most abundant materials must visit these libraries. By what method

can a great university exert a more beneficent influence and
retain the affection and sympathy of its own graduates?

The popularity of a university once depended wholly
upon the professional reputation of its instructors.   Now the
leading questions relate to the size, character, and value of
its library.   The presence of a large body of post-graduate
students is an inspiring feature of university life, and to the
public a guaranty of the high scholarship and superior educational advantages of the institution.   These students cannot
be secured and retained unless they have access to a large
and well-furnished library.

One of the most interesting features of modern benefi-
cence is, that so much of it has been devoted to the endowment and support of libraries; and yet the university libraries
of the West have not had their due share.   The Northwestern
University Library, through the generosity of the venerable
vice-president of the board of overseers, has received a library fund, which in the near future, it is hoped, will yield
considerable income; and he has also given $50,000 towards
the construction of the Orrington Lunt Library Building, to
cost double that sum; but still the library wants are not supplied.   There should be a further and large endowment for
the purchase of books of history, literature, natural science,
political and social science, the arts, and other departments,
which will enable the professors and students of the university to keep abreast of the latest development of literary and
scientific progress.   The larger the endowment the better.
If I should name the sum I thought was necessary it would
probably be thought extravagant; but it would not be larger
than the friends of the university can easily bestow.   Let us
hope that the completion of the new building will be the beginning of a larger development of the resources and usefulness of the Northwestern University Library.

UNIVERSITY LIBRARIES FACE THE FUTURE*

Keyes D. Metcalf

We are here today to dedicate a building which is a noteworthy forward step in library co-operation. I am proud and honored to have been selected to represent the outside library world. I take it that I was chosen because, some ten years ago, it was my good fortune to supervise a study, made by John Fall, of the New York Public Library, of the need for a regional library in the Middle West. [1] At that time I spent a day with the men who were then presidents of thirteen midwestern universities, a group that was struggling with the problem of inter-university cooperation. I must confess with some chagrin that many of the librarians of those universities were then opposed to a regional library, while the university presidents were, on the whole, favorable inclined toward the proposal. Funds were not available, and the project was held in abeyance for a happier time. In the last decade, most of those presidents have retired, as have most of the head librarians who were then in office. The change in presidents did not result in a different attitude toward the proposal. Happily, the change in librarians did.

Some of us are inclined to think that the world moves slowly as far as cooperation is concerned, but the fact that we are here today to dedicate this Center is the best of evidence that librarians, at least, have taken long strides during the last ten years.

---

*This paper presented at the dedication ceremony of the Midwest Inter-Library Center on Oct. 5, 1951, is reprinted by permission of the University of Chicago Press from Library Quarterly 22:5-12 (Jan. 1952). Copyright 1952 by the University of Chicago Press.

I want to take this opportunity to congratulate those
concerned with the planning and construction of this building,
particularly on two counts. First, on its appearance: it is
a noteworthy addition to library architecture at its best. You
can all be pleased by it and proud of it. Second, on its economical construction: it was built at no greater cost per
thousand volumes housed than was estimated by the University
of Chicago's architect ten years ago, when building costs
were about half what they are today, and that, I assure you,
is no mean feat.

I was asked to speak on the subject "University Libraries Face the Future," and I suppose that the title was
assigned because I ventured to speak at the dedication of the
Lamont Library at Harvard two years ago on "The Harvard
Library Faces the Future." That was a difficult task, but
to speak adequately for university libraries in general is much
more difficult. The program calls my talk "Inter-Library
Co-operation and the Future." What I have to say will, I
think, fit either title.

The first and most obvious thing to say about the university libraries of the future is that they will continue to
grow. Some of us have spent a good share of our lives trying to increase the size of libraries and have perhaps failed
to realize that one of the easiest things we could do was to
make our libraries grow rapidly. Library growth reminds
me of the Sorcerer's Apprentice, who turned on the water
but didn't know the combination with which to turn it off and
so was swamped by the results. That is now happening to
many of us, and, while we still enjoy the swimming, we are
beginning to be worried about the future. I often say that one
of my duties at Harvard--perhaps the most important of them
--is to keep its library from growing as fast as it has grown
in the past. So far I must confess that I have failed miser-
ably.

One way to describe the growth of libraries is to observe that we have as many university libraries today in this
country with over 1,000,000 volumes as we had in 1920 with
over 250,000--fourteen in each case. During the same period, the annual expenditures for books for these libraries have
more than tripled, rising from an average of less than $75,-
000 for each to about $245,000, and the money spent for staff
salaries has gone up from a little over $100,000 for each li-
brary to something approaching $500,000. While I hope that
we shall not grow so rapidly, percentagewise, in volumes and

in money used for staff and books in the next thirty years as
we did in the last thirty, I think it not unreasonable to expect
that in 1980 we shall have more libraries with 2,000,000 volumes than we had in 1920 with 250,000.

Libraries will grow in size, and, as one result of
that growth, they will require more and more money. This
cannot help meaning that, as we face the future, we are going
to have financial problems. Perhaps we had better speak
plainly and say that we shall be in financial difficulty. No
library, even in the boom days of the late twenties or the
somewhat similar period immediately after World War II,
ever seemed to have all the funds that its librarian would
have liked to have at his disposal. We always want more
money for more books, and then more space to take care of
those books. We want to spend more money for cataloging
not only because there are more books to catalog but because
the cost of cataloging increases as the library grows larger
and also because there is a tendency on our part to want to
do more and better cataloging. You may call this a beneficent or a perversive tendency, as you like, but it costs
money for staff and, incidentally, for space for the staff.
Then, for some reason or other, the better the librarian,
the better service to the students and faculty he wants to
give, and the students and faculty apparently do not object to
better service if it is made available.

So it seems to me obvious that, as we face the future,
there will be a constant demand for larger budgets. But
there must be a limit to the funds that we can, or for that
matter should, put into our libraries. For a large part of
the last thirty years we have been living in an age of economic expansion--of great university building programs and
of rapidly growing student enrolments--and, as a result, we
have not realized so fully as we should that in our libraries
we have a section of our universities that tends, year in and
year out, in good times and bad, to increase in size and
cost geometrically, while the rest of the institution grows
arithmetically. It is obvious that this cannot go on without
the library's taking an ever increasing percentage of our total
resources. That, expressed in other terms, means that, if
we have a fairly stable economic situation--that is, if we
have a return to "normalcy" and if our libraries are permitted
to continue to grow as they have in the past--each year (and
I put it as dramatically as possible) professors will have to
be dropped so that the money from their salaries can be spent
for library purposes. This, I submit, may very well turn

out to be an untenable situation from the over-all educational
point of view, one not desirable for the university or, for
that matter, for the library itself. Sooner or later we shall
find that there is a limit to the percentage of the funds in
each university that can be properly spent for the library.
As far as I know, there has never been an adequate study
made of this problem. The figures should, of course, vary
in different institutions. One that is interested primarily in
the scientific and technological fields and spends a large share
of its funds for its laboratories should, other things being
equal, use a smaller percentage for its libraries than an institution that specializes in the humanities and the social sciences. An institution that emphasizes its graduate work and
has a large research faculty will require larger library expenditures than an institution that is primarily undergraduate
in character. Even if a formula were found on which to base
library expenditures, it would have to be interpreted with
great discretion and changed from time to time. The percentage should undoubtedly be increased when a new library
building is constructed and then should decrease (very gradually, of course), as the years go on. In times such as we
have been going through during the last five years, when,
rightly or wrongly, clerical and professional library salaries
--because of the market rate of pay--increase more rapidly
than the salaries of professors, library expenditures inevitably increase more rapidly than those of the institution as a
whole, if service standards are to be kept up.

     We have recently had a study known as "The Public
Library Inquiry," sponsored by the Carnegie Corporation and
the American Library Association. I suggest that it would
be desirable to have the library situation in colleges and universities studied in a similar manner, and one of the important points to be considered should be the proper relationship
of library expenditures to those of other parts of an institution.

     If such an inquiry is made, I do not know what the
results will be. Undoubtedly, some institutions will find
that they are not spending enough for their libraries and
should be urged to appropriate more. Others will find that
they are already spending as much as can properly be devoted to the library without interfering unduly with the rest
of the university's educational program, and a few may discover that their libraries have overexpanded. But I am sure
that, in the years ahead, we are going to have to consider
more seriously than in the past the rate of library growth

which we encourage or permit, the total size of the accumulation of books that we gather together, and, finally, the whole question of the weeding-out of our collections. We may well set an outside figure on the number of books that we can afford to keep on our campuses. We should study the cost of weeding and the methods to be used in determining the books that may be discarded. We should plan our catalogs and records in such a way that we can "de-catalog" a book less expensively than is now the case. In brief, when we have found the proper level of library expenditures in relation to the rest of the institution, we must manage to stick to it; and, to do this, I am sure that we must have more inter-library co-operation than we have ever had in the past.

I have talked for a long time in order to provide a background for the main points that I want to make. As we face the future, with larger libraries, greater costs, and more financial troubles, we must have more inter-library co-operation along many lines. We must, for instance, go forward with co-operative storage in libraries such as this one, particularly when by so doing we can eliminate little-used, unnecessary duplicates; but we must not stop there and think of the Midwest Inter-Library Center as solely or even primarily a storage library for little-used books, because that is only a part of the picture.

I think that, ultimately, there should be, in addition to the Midwest Inter-Library Center, a number of other regional libraries, one in the Northeast, one near Washington in which the federal libraries should join, one somewhere in the South, and one in the far West. I hope that all these will be available not just to a limited number of libraries that take the initiative in starting them but to any library that is ready to co-operate and pay its fair share of the costs. In this connection let me add that, when institutions use collections brought together and financed by others, they must expect to pay their way directly or indirectly.

In addition to these regional libraries, I believe that we should have less pretentious and more local institutions, such as the New England Deposit Library, to house material that does not require on-campus storage but should not be too far away. These deposit libraries have their place. They have many important features, but their scope is limited, and they cannot take the place of the regional libraries. There might well be one of them in every large metropolitan center. I hope that the whole group of regional and deposit libraries will work closely together. I am sure that their collections should be recorded in the Union Catalog of the Library of Congress and that they should co-operate closely with the national library.

As I have already indicated, we should not stop with co-operative storage, and I am very glad to learn that the Midwest Inter-Library Center considers storage less important than joint acquisition programs. We must have such programs, both in connection with and separate from the regional libraries, programs through which fewer copies of books that will obviously be little used are purchased in the beginning, thereby saving cataloging, storage, and purchase costs and freeing funds for other, much needed books not now available. The Farmington Plan, even if it develops much farther than it has as yet, should be considered as only one step in this program. Some of these programs should be connected with the regional libraries, but others may be the result of unilateral agreements between libraries within a region, as there are some collections that are more suitably stored in a university library than in a regional library. In this connection, however, I think it will often be easier to persuade libraries to join in a regional plan than to agree on co-operative acquisition arrangements with another library that may have been a rival in the past. A neutral center, such as a regional library, should be helpful.

We must forget as far as possible about inter-library rivalry. We have gone a long way in this direction already by realizing that no one library can have everything and that unnecessary duplication of little-used books among libraries reduces the total research resources of the country and just does not make sense. On the other hand, we must realize that we cannot cure undesirable rivalry any more than race prejudice by going too fast or by being arbitrary in dealing with it and thereby arousing passions. It may well be that it would be better, theoretically, for Harvard to send its Gutenberg Bible and its Bay Psalm Book to Chicago, because Yale has a copy of each, but I doubt that we would promote inter-library co-operation at Harvard by proposing it.

We must not forget about microfilming, when that will help, or about microcards or microprints. I believe that there is a place for all three of these methods of photographic reproduction. Microfilming should be considered primarily when a single copy, or a very limited number of copies, is required. I might interpolate at this point my belief that

microfilm would have come into wider use in the last decade
if we had been wise enough to make it, particularly for reproductions other than newspapers, in sheet form somewhat
similar to "microprints" or microcards instead of in reels.
Microcards and microprints are edition methods. They are
not economical for a very few copies because of the cost of
making the original master negative, but they are suitable if
a large edition can be printed at once and advance orders
can be arranged.

     This brings me to another interpolation which seems
appropriate. It has been suggested for many years that
microreproductions of one kind or another should, in the
long run, replace a large part of our library collections and
that these copies could be made available for less than it
would cost to store the original volumes in co-operative storage warehouses. Expressed in a different way, the theory
is that it costs as little for each of a group of libraries to
own a microreproduction as it does for the group to share
the cost of housing the original. I have yet to be convinced,
with the high labor costs of today, that microreproductions
are cheaper than the storage of an original already in hand
and stored under inexpensive conditions, unless fifty copies
or more of the reproduction can be sold without great sales
expense. I suggest that further study be made of this problem.

     Neither am I ready to propose that all originals of
materials that have been reproduced photographically should
be discarded, but replacement of the originals in many libraries should be considered, if it can be proved that the
savings are great. If the library already owns a bound volume, the saving made by buying a photographic reproduction
may be negligible, and, as I have always said, we shall
rarely, if ever, find it possible for any library to replace a
large part of its collection by microfilm. But if not one of
a group of libraries owns a volume, the cataloging, binding,
and storage costs, as well as its purchase price, should be
considered. We may well find, then, that if microreproduction is kept in mind from the beginning and the material is
copied for a number of libraries at once, microreproductions
will prove to be even more useful and economical than we
have already found them.

     We must, incidentally, consider the acquisition of ma-
terial that is used heavily for a short time and infrequently
thereafter. This may deserve only temporary cataloging and

storage; and, when the proper time has come, we may dispose of it and rely on microfilm copies, with perhaps one copy of the original for the whole group of libraries.

This logically brings us to a kind of co-operation that has been neglected up to this time, namely, the co-operative acquisition of master-microfilm copies of bulky sets of little-used material, such as some foroign and state public documents. Those of us who have had our own microfilm programs have been inclined to try to sell as many copies of the film as possible, so as to reduce the cost for each copy, and have failed to realize that the net cost to the library would be less if a group of libraries split among them the cost of making master-negatives and then made it possible for each of them to acquire or borrow a positive of any part of the microfilmed material when it was needed. This may be a field of great importance for a library such as this one.

Some of us will object, of course, to this, as well as to all kinds of co-operative storage, on the basis that most material is of little use unless it is actually under our roofs at the time it is called for. Here I think we shall have to realize that we can no longer afford to store in our own buildings all the material that we may want. This is a fact that must be emphasized if the Midwest Inter-Library Center is to be a success. Our scholars will have to be content in many cases to wait twenty-four or even forty-eight hours for books or reproductions of books. It may be inconvenient, it may require a change in work habits, but it is practicable for most of us; and our methods of research will have to be adapted to current conditions just as they were in the past, when many of our scholars had to wait for years until they could make a trip abroad to see the books and manuscripts they needed. The choice may be between having several million additional volumes available on one or two days' notice and having a small fraction of that number under our own roofs.

I am sure we must continue the struggle to find better ways and means to carry on co-operative cataloging so as to hold down expenses in that field. This is another problem that we have by no means solved as yet. The Library of Congress cataloging takes care, to a very considerable extent, of the needs of our smaller university and college and public libraries. This, unfortunately, is not true for our great research libraries, and many of us have found that joining in co-operative cataloging as well as adapting Library

of Congress cards resulted in additional expense rather than
saving. I think that the time has come for a new study of
the co-operative cataloging situation and for a report on it to
the research libraries of the country.

Indeed, a full-scale study of the whole cataloging situation in research libraries is in order. While it is not
difficult to argue that the larger the library, the more detailed the cataloging should be and the higher the standards
used, it is also not difficult to prove that spending as much
for cataloging as many of us now do prevents us from acquiring additional books and pamphlets that might be even more
valuable to research workers than higher cataloging standards.

A third cataloging problem which must be faced within
a generation is whether the card catalog which we have come
to take for granted has not reached a state where it will begin to break down of its own weight in our larger libraries.
I believe that we shall always have card catalogs for our recently published material, but I am not at all sure that we
shall not find it more economical and convenient and more
useful for research, in the long run, if a number of our
largest institutions, in addition to the Library of Congress,
print catalogs in book form for older material, either independently or, better still, jointly.

Another problem on which I feel that special study is
required is the question of fees for library use by those who
have no official connection with the institution owning the volume required. Such use might include requests for inter-
library loan as well as use in person. I think that most of
us have felt in the past that there should be completely free
use of material by any research worker, but I am not so
sure that we are going to be able to promote inter-library
co-operation of the kind that I have outlined if a few libraries
carry most of the burden of the cost of acquisition, cataloging,
storage, and service of material and then find that the use of
the books is largely by others. We may well find that a reasonable system of charges for use by outsiders would, in the
long run, encourage library co-operation and joint acquisition
programs. This problem may prove to be one of the most
important and difficult ones to be faced by the Midwest Inter-
Library Center.

All these points which I have discussed seem to me to
be of importance, but there is another matter which I cannot
refrain from mentioning and for which I have no solution. I

am inclined to think that it may be more serious and more
important than all the other matters which I have taken up
put together, but it is one that we are prone to forget. Every year that goes by brings closer the time when a large
percentage of the printed material in our great research libraries will have reached a stage so near to disintegration
that further use may destroy it. Our public and college libraries, on the whole, will not have to worry about this
problem, for the books that they must have are mostly modern and replaceable, and it is easy to arrange to replace
books needed by a good many libraries; but there are millions
of different titles on poor paper in our larger libraries of
which few copies are available, and, though these are not
worth reprinting, we ought not to let them disappear off the
face of the earth. Microfilming, of course, will help. It
has largely solved this problem with newspapers, but it and
other ameliorating plans have not even scratched the surface
of the main problem. Are we ready to join Louis XV and
simply say, "After us the deluge! Let our successors face
the problem of paper disintegration"?

        Finally, we must make a special effort to eliminate
as far as possible the further building-up, and in many cases
the continuance, of large duplicate collections of very specialized, little-used material. Why should a single section
of the country have three large collections of Friesian literature, old textbooks, or material on Egyptology, for instance?

        This question, alas, cannot be answered by librarians
working alone or with one another. It will have to be answered on an inter-university level by the top university administrative officers. A library is primarily a service institution. If a university insists on giving advanced work in
Egyptology, it is up to its librarian to furnish the material
required, in spite of the fact that there may be two or three
other universities in the region, each trying to specialize in
Egyptology, each with only one or two students in the field,
and each with a large and expensive library collection on the
subject. But the decision is in the hands of the university,
and it would seem to me that the heads of the universities
must get together and make firm commitments for specialization in such fields as those just mentioned. Division of fields
on the university level, not just that of the library, is one of
the best possible ways to relieve financial pressure for the
libraries and for universities as a group, and it should release library funds and funds for instruction that can be put
to better use in fields not now covered in the same part of the
country, if at all.

Let me now attempt to summarize what I have said. As university libraries face the future, they must take into consideration the fact that libraries will continue to grow, that they will require larger and larger budgets, and that money will be short. Libraries cannot continue to grow as in the past without taking a larger and larger share of the resources of their institutions, unless we can bring about more inter-library and inter-university co-operation. That co-operation should include:

1. A careful inquiry into the library costs and their proper relationship to the total expenses of the institution

2. Regional and deposit libraries for the storage of little-used collections

3. Joint acquisition programs, going on from the Farmington Plan, in which regional libraries should take a leading part

4. Promotion of library co-operation in the field of microreproduction

5. A study of co-operative cataloging methods, including the question of printing catalogs in book form

6. An investigation of the desirability of fees for inter-library use

7. An attack on the paper disintegration problem

8. Consideration of the division of fields among universities, not just by libraries but by the top-level university officers as a group

I propose that foundation aid be solicited to finance a study of these problems by a competent outside group and that it be sponsored by the American Association of Universities and the Association of Research Libraries. I further suggest that the Midwest Inter-Library Center would provide a first-class background for much of the work and that one of the results of the study might well be the development of the next regional library.

NOTE

1. John Fall, "A Proposal for a Middle West Deposit Library" (MS in the New York Public Library, New York, N. Y.).

SPECIAL LIBRARIES

THE SPECIAL LIBRARY AND
SOME OF ITS PROBLEMS*

Ethel M. Johnson

Ten years ago the special library of the type to be discussed in this paper was almost non-existent. Indeed, we might go farther and say, that prior to 1909 the special library was a negligible factor in both the library and the business world. Today there are more than four hundred libraries of this kind in the country and their number is steadily increasing. Their interests are represented by an enterprising organization, the Special Libraries Association, which is affiliated with the American library association and by a very live sort of publication known as Special Libraries. The field, though still small, is rapidly developing. To librarians in the making, it should be an attractive one as offering a very possible opportunity for the use of their abilities and training.

What is the special library, and how has it come about? What particular needs does it meet? What are the distinctive features that make it "special"? How does it differ from the general library? What are the methods employed, the kind of service rendered? What are some of the principal varieties of special libraries, and what have they to offer in the way of professional opportunities to the ambitious? These are some of the questions to be considered in discussing the special library and its problems.

First as to terminology: what kind of libraries may

*Reprinted with permission from Special Libraries 6(10):157-161 (Dec. 1915). Copyright 1915 by the Special Libraries Association.

legitimately be called special? There is some difference in usage here. From one point of view any library that limits its scope to a particular subject or group of related subjects is specialized. So each department of a large general library is a small special library. So, too, is every private collection that follows a definite line of interests. Libraries of this type are not new. Almost from the start public libraries in the great cities have commenced to build up special collections; works about Dante, Shapespeare, Americana, incunabula, and so on. Then there are the departmental libraries of large colleges and universities. Again there are separate, independent libraries, devoted to a particular field.

From the subject side these are special libraries. For the most part, however, they differ from the general library only in scope. Their methods and service are similar; and the type of material they handle is apt to be pretty much the same, although far more detailed along one particular line. Subject matter alone does not make a library special in the sense in which we are using the term. What then does constitute a special library?

Let us turn to some of the definitions which the leaders in the special library movement have coined. These collected opinions of experts may serve to give us an insight into the nature, scope and functions of this new type of library institution.

Some Definitions of the Special Library

Dr. C. C. Williamson of the New York Public Library:

"A special library is an efficient, up-to-date, reasonable, complete collection of the literature on a particular subject, including not only books, but clippings, pamphlets, articles, reports, etc., all so completely indexed and classified that the latest and best data are available without the difficulties and delays that are more or less inevitable in a large general library."

Mr. Arthur D. Little, Boston Chemist:

"The special library should have for its business to collect completely and classify in a way to make instantly available every scrap of information bearing upon the materials, methods, products and requirements of the industry concerned."

Mr. A. G. S. Josephson, The Index Office, Chicago:

   Discussing "What is a special library?" at the meeting of the Special Libraries Association held at Ottawa, Canada, June 27, 1912, says:--

   "The special library covers a single definite subject
or related group of subjects. Special methods are used in
its administration. Documentation will be largely employed.
The methods of cataloging and classifying will also be somewhat different from those in use in a general library. The
classification must be much closer and in cataloging less attention need be given to the bibliographical description than
to the contents. Not only in methods does the special library
differ from the general, but its material is to a very large
extent different. It must have books, it is true, and pamphlets and periodicals, though right here does the difference
begin, because, while the general library must keep the whole
pamphlet, the special library will keep only what it needs.
Furthermore, the special library is to a much larger extent
than the general dependent upon material that has not yet
reached printed form, manuscripts, letters, notes of all
kinds, photographs, drawings, tabulated material, all this and
many other different means of information will be collected
and arranged for future use in special libraries. "

Mr. W. P. Cutter, Librarian of the Engineering Societies:

   Gives the following epigrammatical definition: "The
special library is one that serves the people who are doing
things, while a reference library is one which serves people
who are thinking things. "

M. S. Dudgeon, Secretary Wisconsin Free Library Commission:

   "The special library is a utilitarian establishment calculated to serve the worker too busy to take time for scholarly investigation. The special librarian becomes, in fact,
a bureau of investigation. In a special library the material
of most vital importance is not in books, often it is not even
in print. The special library is a clearing-house of live
ideas, of live problems. The general reference library depends largely upon the past, the special library deals primarily with the present and future, it deals only incidentally
with the past. The function of the special library is to deliver to the busy worker, ready for his use, the records of

other men's thoughts and work and experience, in order that
there may be no duplication of experimental effort and no
repetition of errors. In order to accomplish this function,
the material in the library or qualifications of the librarian
and the nature of the work done must be different from those
of a general reference library. "

Mr. John Cotton Dana, Librarian, Newark Public Library:

  In discussing the valuation of the special library asks
"What is the special library?" and answers: "Special libraries are the first and as yet the only print-administering institutions which professedly recognize the change in library
methods that the vast and swiftly mounting bulk of print is
demanding; realize how ephemeral and at the same time how
exceedingly useful for the day and hour is much of the present output of things-intended-to-be-read; and frankly adopt
the new library creed as to print management, of careful selection, immediate use, and ready rejection when usefulness
is past. "

Mr. Edward A. Fitzpatrick, Secretary of the Commission of
Practical Training for Public Service of the American Political Science Association:

  In a paper on "The special library and public efficiency" discusses the special library as "a collection of reliable,
important and adequate records, being interpreted as anything
which contains information; a book, a clipping, a tabulation,
a model. "

  From the foregoing discussion it is evident that the
most distinctive feature of the special library is not so much
its subject matter as its service. Before everything else,
it is an information bureau. The main function of the general library is to make books available. The function of the
special library is to make information available. The stock-
in-trade of the general library is represented by bound volumes of print. That of the special library is much oftener
represented by pamphlets, manuscripts, clippings, and filing
case material; while the most important part of its equipment
may not be printed matter at all, but human brains. The librarian of an engineering society, when asked what he considered the most valuable reference book replied at once,
"The telephone directory. " The response aptly illustrates
the kind of information service which it is the business of the

special library to supply, as an essential duty of the special library is to know the individuals and organizations that are experts on subjects related to its own interests, and keep in touch with them.

Of libraries that are special, not simply because of their subject matter, but because of the service they render, we may mention three divisions: the municipal reference library, the legislative reference library, and the business or corporation library. There is much similarity between the municipal and legislative reference library. Both have to do with public affairs information, and their subject matter is in many respects the same. The municipal reference library is, as its name implies, chiefly concerned with collecting information about cities and civic interests, particularly those of the municipality in which it is located. City charters, ordinances, reports of city departments, commissions and committees and of special investigations make up the principal subject matter of such a library.

An important function of the municipal reference library is to assist in drafting ordinances. For this purpose the charters and ordinances of other cities and reports as to their effectiveness are secured. Digests and compilations of such information as this are made for the use of city councilmen and other city officials. How does the commission form of city administration work in different states of the country? is an illustration of the kind of information such a library should be prepared to furnish.

There are today a dozen libraries of this kind in several of the larger cities. In some instances they are branches of the public library, in others they have been established independently. A growing interest in this sort of work is attested by the municipal reference course offered by the Library school of the New York public library. This is a graduate course open to candidates who have completed the work in recognized library schools.

The legislative reference library has a broader field. Laws of the different states, both proposed and enacted, federal legislation and the laws of other countries, as well as the reports of state and federal commissions, federal decisions, vetoes, test cases, represent the matter with which this kind of library works. As it is intended primarily as an aid to legislators, it is frequently associated with the state library. The first library of this sort was established in

New York in 1890.   Thirty-four states now have such institutions, and it probably will not be long before every state
is so equipped.

Expert service in interpreting material, and making
briefs and abstracts is provided.   An important feature is the
bill drafting department which is engaged in drawing up proposed legislation in concise, legal form.   A course of training for this kind of library work is offered by the Wisconsin
free library commission and the University of Wisconsin Library school.   The field is an excellent one for men and
women of special ability.   But in the nature of things it is
definitely limited.

It is the business library, however, the information
service department of the large corporation, the manufacturing, or mercantile establishment, that is our subject for chief
consideration.   This is the most recent library development
and represents an innovation in both the business world and
the library field.   Just when and how the first library of this
kind started, it would be difficult to say.   Miss Loomis in
an interesting paper on "Libraries that pay," in the Independent for June 26, 1913, tells how one special library came
to be organized by a business firm.   The firm in question
lost a valuable contract because they did not have available
information which would have enabled them to make a bed
rock bid.   As a result of this rather costly lesson, they established a service bureau to keep them in touch with matters pertaining to the industry.

I fancy, however, that the greater number of such libraries have developed gradually.   Heads of departments collected material of interest, then came to feel the advantage
of having it brought together in one place available for all.
Then the question of caring for it arose, and someone from
the clerical force was put in charge.   Finally, with the accumulation of material the need for expert service made itself felt, and a genuine library was evolved.   Mr. George
Lee, Librarian of Stone and Webster's, has an interesting
outline in Special Libraries for April, 1914, showing the development of the special library in the commercial firm.   It
is suggestive also in indicating the changing attitude of the
special library to the methods of the general library.

How do libraries of this type differ most conspicuously from the general library?   Mention has already been made
of the difference in scope and material.   Whereas the latter

attempts to cover the broad field of human knowledge, the
special library for the most part limits its subject matter to
one quite definite line of interest:--Engineering work; electric
wiring and lighting, traction service; factory architecture; or
retail selling. At first sight there seems in the make-up of
the business library a disproportionate amount of manuscript
and pamphlet material. In some instances the entire collection may be represented by this sort of equipment. The
rows of vertical files and transfer cases in which such a collection is kept, give the appearance of a business office rather than the conventional kind of a library. The atmosphere,
too, smacks largely of the business office. The telephone
occupies a prominent place as one of the most valuable reference tools. One of the definitions previously given sums up
points of difference in a nutshell: "The general library is
for the men that are thinking things, the special library is
for the men that are doing things. "

Popular conception pictures the library as a quiet,
spacious, book-lined apartment, where the scholar may pour
over weighty volumes, or the leisurely reader may while
away a pleasant hour or so. The business library trans-
forms this picture into a crowded office on the tenth floor of
a large commercial building, with every inch of space utilized,
and an alert attendant answering calls over the wire.

Particularly striking is the difference in type of service rendered. The public library is apt to be passive in its
attitude. The business library is active, aggressive even.
The public library brings together large collections of books,
and devotes its time to caring for them with much elaborate-
ness of detail while waiting with open doors for patrons to
come and avail themselves of its treasures. The business
library gets its material in shape for use in the quickest
possible time and sallies forth for its patrons, button-holes
them with the news: "I have information that is worth dollars and cents to you, come and see, " and if its patrons
prove obdurate, the library is no whit discouraged, but follows the time-honored example of Mahomet and the mountain.
And as in nine cases out of every ten the business man believes he is too busy to go to the library, the library simpli-
fies matters by going to him. This is done by keeping in
touch with the interests of the managerial force, directors
and heads of departments, and sending them information and
material that is known will be of use to them.

Press notices mention plans for establishing a similar

industry in a near-by city. News of this competitor is at
once sent to the manager. A consular report explains how
in a European country waste products from such factories
are utilized. The publication or an abstract of it is forwarded to the department chiefly concerned with this question.
How the current magazines are routed through the departments
is illustrated in an article in Syotem for July, 1914. In some
libraries the following method is employed: A list of the periodicals taken by the library is sent to the various department heads with the request that they indicate the ones they
would like to occ ao issued. An attendant then carries the
magazines around and the following day collects and redis-
tributes them. A director wishing to occ a magazine for a
longer time checks the tag attached to it with his name and
it is returned to him after it has gone the rounds.

The fact that the special library is a business proposition and must make good or show cause for its existence
explains many of the characteristic methods. It may not
boast a credit entry on the cash books, but it must prove itself an asset through the value of its service. To do this it
must be alert to anticipate the needs of its patrons.

As speed is an essential factor in business, the library must equip itself for prompt service. No time can
be given to unnecessary details; cataloging and other technical processes must be reduced to their simplest form. Full
names of authors and various possible spellings go disregarded. The yawning gap after the middle initial is allowed
to yawn, and dates of birth and death are left unverified.
Much of the imprint matter is omitted, as exact size, various paginations, and series entry. Time is money, and the
business man frowns on all such time-consuming trifles.

By the use of the vertical file much of the cataloguing
itself is done away with. For with guide cards arranged
alphabetically by subject and numerous cross references, the
file becomes its own catalogue, and by the addition of dummy
cards, uniform in size with the guides, it may include the
charging system also. This method is employed in the Youth's
Companion library which is represented almost entirely by
filing case material.

Space is another matter that conditions both methods
and material in the business library. Rent and overhead
costs are charged against the library, and in the business
sections rents are extremely high. The library must contract

itself into the smallest possible quarters and utilize every
inch to the best advantage.   A common complaint from public libraries is lack of adequate stack room.   Could they see
the meagre floor space allotted the majority of business libraries they might well regard their own domiciles as pala-
tial.

    This physical restriction plays a large part in deter-
mining the attitude of the business library toward its possessions.   Only material of vital importance and timely interest may be given house room.   Much discriminating must
be used in selection and rejection of printed matter.   If a
certain article in a magazine is of value, that is kept, and
the rest of the periodical discarded.   As soon as any part
of the collection has passed its usefulness it must be weeded
out.   The business library cannot afford to harbor dead material.

    A feature of the business library that makes effective
service possible with a very limited amount of material is
its dependence upon communication with other organizations
and individuals for much of its most valuable data.   What
are the United States regulations regarding the use of a certain substance in the manufacture of food products?   The
business librarian at once gets into telephone connection with
the local representative of the federal health department and
secures the desired information at first hand.   The public
library is much more apt to depend upon its own resources.
And if it has not the desired information available it is very
sorry, but that is all there is about it.   The business library
regards it as a part of its job to keep in touch with information sources of probable interest to the business, and make
the best possible use of them.   So important is this acquaintance with information sources that to a large extent it
may be said the business library is the librarian himself.

    What special demands does the business library make?
What opportunities does it offer?   What are its advantages
and disadvantages?   And how does it compare professionally
with the general library?   These are questions that to the
prospective librarian are of chief concern.

    First as to requirements.   Business ability, initiative,
adaptability, willingness to assume responsibility, count for
much more than technical training.   A college man or woman with the qualifications just enumerated would generally
be preferred to the library school graduate, although the ad-

vantage of library training is coming to be recognized. The
field is a fairly good one.   A special library organizer reports that ordinarily there are more calls from business
firms than applicants to fill them.   Also that there is a
greater demand for women than for men.   The reason, however, is hardly flattering.   It is the sorry, but well known
one, that women will accept a lower salary than mon.   The
same authority feels that the financial rewards and chances
for advancement in this field are much better for men than
for women.   The man librarian can make business acquain-
tances for the firm, he can do work that a woman would not
be asked to, and can meet other men on a business footing.

In general the rewards in the business world are higher than in professional or semi-professional circles, and the
same applies to the business librarian who makes good.
Personally I am inclined to think that business executives
consider service rather than sex, and that in so far as the
woman librarian proves herself of financial value to the firm,
her work will receive recognition.

Those whose ties or interest bind them to the East
should give particular attention to the special library.   For
while the best field for the general library work is in the
West or Middle West, the opposite holds true of the business
library for the very practical reason that nearly all of the
business libraries are confined to the Atlantic seaboard.

So far the business library field seems particularly
attractive.   It offers opportunity and recognition to the person with ability, initiative, and original ideas.   It gives freedom and chance for individuality in place of the often mechanical routine of the public library.   The large library has
come to be systematized much as the modern factory.   The
work for each individual is definitely planned.   There is, as
in the factory, the division of labor that disassociates the
worker from the work as a whole.   Except for the librarian
in chief, there is little chance for constructive, original
work.   And even the librarian himself may oftentimes be
hampered by a non-progressive board of trustees.

Are there no drawbacks in connection with the business library? A very serious, indeed to many, a prohibitive disadvantage of this work arises from the very nature
of business itself.   And that is its sensitive response to general financial conditions.   Business library positions are unstable because business itself is unstable, and is subject to

periodic depressions and panics. The general library in the
time of industrial stagnation goes on as a matter of course.
Lucky is the business library that suffers nothing more than
a sharp retrenchment. In many instances, however, it is
lopped off remorselessly as the readiest way of cutting down
expenses. This goes to show that the business library is
still in an experimental stage. A large number of firms
still regard it as a pleasing luxury to be cherished during
prosperous times and promptly dispensed with in adverse
ones.

Even here, however, there is compensation, for while
the library may be discarded, the librarian who has proved
himself of value is likely to be retained in another position
as assistant secretary, advertising manager or publicity agent
according as his talents show a bent. This might be cited
as another advantage of work in a business library, that it
opens the way for advancement in other lines of business,
while the routine of the resular library tends to rigidity and
makes difficult vocational shifting.

After all, the important thing in choosing one's work,
and the thing that really makes for success in it, is not the
stability or instability of the position, venturous spirits challenge change, nor financial reward nor advancement, but opportunity for growth and happiness. It is a very great truth
that Stevenson presents in that wonderful story of the Lan-
tern Bearers, that it is our joy in doing a thing that makes
that thing worth while and that "to miss the joy is to miss
all." In a very real sense the criterion of our success is
in our happiness in our work, irrespective of its tangible
rewards.

PROBLEMS IN LIBRARY SERVICE:
Librarians and Readers

PERSONAL RELATIONS BETWEEN
LIBRARIANS AND READERS*

Samuel S. Green

When scholars and persons of high social position
come to a library, they have confidence enough, in regard
to the cordiality of their reception, to make known their
wishes without timidity or reserve.

Modest men in the humbler walks of life, and well-
trained boys and girls, need encouragement before they become ready to say freely what they want.

A hearty reception by a sympathizing friend, and the
recognition of some one at hand who will listen to inquiries,
even although he may consider them unimportant, make it
easy for such persons to ask questions, and put them at
once on a home footing.

Persons who use a popular library for purposes of
investigation generally need a great deal of assistance. A
few illustrations will produce a vivid realization of the correctness of this statement. Here, for instance, is a wall-
painter who has a room to ornament. He wishes to assist
his imagination, and comes to the library to look at specimens of decorative painting. It does not serve the purpose
of such a man to send him to the catalogues of the library
and bid him select the books he desires. You must make
the selection yourself, get the works he needs, and hand
them to him. You have several to select from. Shall you
give him Jones's Grammar of Ornament or Racinet's L'Orne-

*Reprinted from Library Journal 1:74-81 (1876).

ment Polychrome? Certainly, if he wishes merely suggestion and inspiration, and to look only at details of ornamentation. These works contain examples of the best ornamentation in vogue in different ages and countries, and show the workman who aims at perfection what he has to attain to. Generally speaking, however, the work represented in these books is to elaborate for common use, is hard to execute, and would cost more than a householder is willing to spend in ornamenting a room.

The painter wishes also to see details in combination, and to judge of colors and figures in juxtaposition by looking upon the representation of a whole wall or room. His want is met best by giving him volumes of some such approved works as Architektonisches Skizzenbuch or the Journal-Manuel de Peintures.

An artisan has the legs of a table to carve. His imagination is momentarily barren, and he desires assistance. You do not ask him what book he would like to see, but get him Liénard's Spécimens de la Décoration et de l'Ornementatation, Talbert's Gothic Forms, Ungewitter's Gothische Möbel, or pictorial representations of such specimens of the work of Eastlake and Morris as you can lay your hands on.

A marble-worker calls for an engraving of a lion in some specified posture; a wood-carver wishes to see a representation of an eagle. You take the time that is necessary to hunt up whatever these men desire to see.

A member of a society of Englishmen wishes to find a particular representation of the contest between St. George and the Dragon. You request an assistant to look through the tables of contents of the London Art Journal, and by this means very likely find what is wanted.

A school-girl has heard that the number of feet in a yard-measure was determined by the length of some king's arm. She asks for the name of the king. Catalogues fail to show where the information is to be found. It at once occurs to the librarian, however, that answers to such questions can usually be had by reference to Notes and Queries. He sends for the indexes of this periodical, and finds the information desired. In handing the needed volume to the inquirer, he takes a minute to caution her that there are many stories and traditions which it will not do to accept as facts without careful examination of the evidence adduced in their

corroboration. The librarian utters a similar timely word
of caution when asked about other historical stories of doubtful credibility--when called upon, for instance, to give an
account of Captain Smith and Pocahontas, or of the Blue Laws
of Connecticut.

A school-boy calls for a history of the Suez Canal.
You see at once, probably, that what he needs is a brief
account, and refer him to some recently-issued encyclopaedia.
At the same time you show him how to use dictionaries and
encyclopaedias, and tell him he can often find answers to
questions himself by using works of this kind, but invite him
to come to you whenever he encounters snags or fails to get
the information sought after.

Another school-girl wishes to see a description of the
ceremony of the Marriage of the Adriatic. If the librarian
remembers in what book such a description may be found,
he has the book brought. Otherwise he sends for a dozen
volumes about Venice, and teaches the inquirer how to find
the desired account by the use of indexes and tables of contents. Very likely she will give up the search without finding
it. Then you take hold to aid her, and show her how to use
books and obtain information when wanted.

A citizen is building a house which he wishes to protect against injury from lightning. He is subject to the customary visits of the vendors of lightning-rods, and becomes
somewhat confused by the conflicting statements of these practical men, or is impressed by the conviction that some of
these worthies display great ignorance of the scientific grounds
upon which their opinions rest. He is crowded by business,
but still glad to spend a single hour in a library, if in that
length of time he can become acquainted with the views of
some of the best writers on the applications of electricity,
and so enable himself to proceed understandingly to the work
in hand. In such a case, of course, the librarian must get
the books which contain the desired information, and hand
them to the reader open at the proper pages.

Another business man wishes for certain statistics
of trade, manufactures, and inventions. He has no time to
spare in collecting the books he desires. He does not know
how to get hold of them so well as a librarian does. He
states his wants, and the librarian sends to the secretaries
of organizations having the interests of different manufactures
in keeping, to get the latest published statistics relating to

silk or wool manufactures, or the production of iron and
steel and other commodities. The inquirer is also furnished
with the volumes containing the record of the census, and
with other publications of the bureaus of our government,
and is supplied with such compendiums as the Statesman's
Year Book, Timbs' Wonderful Inventions, and the volume containing the papers recently printed in Harper's Magazine
which treat of the progress of the United States during the
last one hundred years in mechanics, commerce, and manufactures.

Men who consult the reports of the Commissioner of
Patents in order to see the specifications and drawings of
different patented articles, may frequently be greatly aided
by a word from the librarian. Almost all investigators are
glad to have their labors shortened by availing themselves of
assistance. The librarian knows, for instance, just what indexes of patents have been published, when the reports ceased
coming in the old form, what drawings have been issued by
the Office at Washington, and wherein the incompleteness of
a set of reports lies, and how its deficiencies may be supplied.

A young man has just become a member of a debating society, and is called upon to discuss such questions as
the advisableness of taxing church property; the comparative
value of the systems of prohibition and license in the treatment of the vice of intemperance; and the wisdom of placing
the management of railroads in the hands of the State, or of
continuing the use of the Bible in the opening exercises of
the public schools. Such a person is kept from discourage-
ment in his early attempts to get at information, if he can
avail himself of the aid of some one who stands by to show
him where to find the legislative reports, pamphlets, and
editorials which contain discussions of these questions. The
assistance he receives gives him confidence to pursue further
investigations. The librarian, too, in his intercourse with
him reminds him that in order to become a successful de-
bater he must always consider both sides of a question, and
weigh the arguments of opponents.

A small boy wishes to see a description of the eggs
of different New England birds. The librarian knows of some
good work with colored illustrations to give him.

A somewhat older boy wants to know how to build a
boat, and is furnished with book, magazine article, or papers
which contain the necessary directions.

Some inquirer has heard that there was a day in the last century during a large portion of which the obscuration of the sun was so great that it is known in tradition as the Dark Day. He wishes to know the date of this day, and to find a description of it. Perhaps it puzzles the librarian to tell where to look for the desired description. He begins a search, however, and in half an hour or so unearths the account from some town history--say that of Newbury, Newburyport, and West Newbury, by Coffin.

A curious woman asked me a few months since to give her a book which would show what the "scollop" is. This, you will remember, is an article of food which appears in considerable quantities in our markets. It was only after an hour's search that I found out from Verrill and Smith's Invertebrate Animals of Vineyard Sound and Adjacent Waters, etc., that it is the "central muscle which closes the valves" of a certain shell.

A reservoir dam gives way. Citizens become suspicious that too little care is taking in making the repairs. You drop a line to the chairman of the proper committee of the city government to say that you have just received Humber's Water Supply of Towns from London. He calls for the work, and takes it home to study.

An unlearned student wishes to know something about the families of languages or the recent explanations of the origin of mythology. You pick out for him some simple hand-book on the subject.

"Is it true," inquires a young lady, "that the little bust we see so often, and which is generally called 'Clyte,' should be called 'Clytie'?" The librarian answers "Yes."

"Isn't the sentence, 'God tempers the wind to the shorn lamb,' in the Bible?" asks another. The librarian answers "No," and refers for further information to Bartlett's Familiar Quotations.

One inquirer has to be told which is the best atlas to use in looking for places in Servia; another, which will give most accurately, and with greatest minuteness, the situation of the rivers and battlefields mentioned in current accounts of Indian hostilities.

A citizen is about to emigrate, and desires a late description of the State and town to which he intends to move.

A board of trade is discussing the question of the advisableness of introducing the metric system of weights and measures into common use. Members call upon librarians to furnish the best treatises on the subject.

A young man about to make the voyage to India for his health, asks you to give him a list of books to read while on ship-board. Another person wishes a similar list for use in a summer vacation.

The librarian is often consulted about courses of reading, and his judgment in regard to what are the best epitomes of the histories of different countries, and of different branches of knowledge, is frequently sought for.

When an inquirer has satisfied himself that a book recommended will suit him, he often wishes to buy it, and the librarian tells him its cost and where it can be procured.

A student in a technical school wishes aid in selecting the subject of a thesis, and in gathering materials to use in preparing it. A school-boy asks for hints and information to use in writing a composition.

A librarian is frequently asked to give information in regard to things and processes which he knows nothing about. Perhaps he is called upon to produce a description of an object the name of which is unknown to him. I remember slyly consulting a dictionary to find out what a "cam" is, and again for the definition of "link-valve motion."

But having acquired a definite notion of the object concerning which information is desired, the habit of mental classification, which a librarian acquires so readily, comes to his aid. He sees at once in what department of knowledge the description sought for may be found, and brings to the inquirer authoritative treatises in this department.

Enough illustrations have been given to show that readers in popular libraries need a great deal of assistance. Care has been taken to select principally such as show that this is particularly needed by persons unused to handling books or conducting investigations. In the case of such persons, as well as with scholars, it is practicable to refer applicants for information which you cannot supply, to libraries in larger cities in the neighborhood of your own library, or to other institutions in your own town. Business men go to

commercial centres so often that they can occasionally consult larger libraries than those accessible at home.

It would be easy to show that scholars, as well as
unlearned persons, receive much aid in pursuing their studies
from an accomplished librarian, although he has not the
knowledge of a specialist. It would make this paper too long,
however, to illustrate this part of the subject.

There are obvious limits to the assistance which a
librarian can undertake to render. Common-sense will dictate them. Thus no librarian would take the responsibility
of recommending books to give directions for the treatment
of disease. Now would he give legal advice nor undertake
to instruct applicants in regard to the practical manipulations
of the workshop or laboratory.

I have not been unmindful, in what has been said, of
the great value of the assistance rendered readers by certain
catalogues which have been issued lately. There is little
danger of appreciating too highly such work as that for which
we are indebted to Mr. Noyes, Mr. Cutter, and Mr. Winsor
and his able assistants. I need not remind you, however,
that many persons who use a library have to be instructed
in regard to the use of catalogues, and need practice before
they can use them to the best advantage. Entries are overlooked. Discrimination is lacking for separating good books
from those of little merit, and books adapted to the capacity
and particular needs of the user from those which are unsuited to his requirements. It frequently happens, also, that
readers do not know under what general subject to look for
a minute piece of information. Lately constructed catalogues
are so made as to facilitate immensely the researches not
only of scholars, but of the general unlearned reader. When
the admirable notes found in some of the catalogues of the
Boston Public Library, and in the catalogue of the library at
Quincy, Massachusetts, shall have been increased in numbers
and made to include information in regard to the literature of
all branches of knowledge, they will, particularly if kept up
to date, be found of inestimable service by the general reader and inexperienced student. But the time is distant when
the whole field of knowledge can be covered by these notes;
and even when it shall be occupied, much personal assistance
will still be needed by readers in popular libraries.

Of course, too, it will always be necessary for a librarian to extend to readers the hospitalities of his institution.

Among the good results which attend personal intercourse on the part of the librarian with users of popular libraries, the following may be mentioned.

First. If you gain the respect and confidence of readers, and they find you easy to get at and pleasant to talk
with, great opportunities are afforded of stimulating the love
of study and of directing investigators to the best sources of
information.

Second. You find out what books the actual users of
the library need, and your judgment improves in regard to
the kind of books it is best to add to it. You see what subjects the constituency of the institution are interested in, and
what is the degree of simplicity they require in the presentation of knowledge.

Third. One of the best means of making a library
popular is to mingle freely with its users, and help them in
every way. When this policy is pursued for a series of
years in any town, a very large portion of the citizens receive answers to questions, and the conviction spreads
through the community that the library is an institution of
such beneficent influences that it can not be dispensed with.

Fourth, and last. The collections of books which
make up the contents of the circulating departments of our
libraries have been provided for the use of persons of differing degrees of refinement and moral susceptibility, and
for those who occupy mental planes of various altitudes.

Now, the policy advocated of freedom of intercourse
between librarian and readers, when adopted in the conduct
of these departments, does much to give efficiency to the
efforts of the officers to get readers to take out wholesome
books and such works as are adapted to their capacity and
the grade of enlightenment to which they belong. It is a
common practice, as we all know, for users of a library to
ask the librarian or his assistants to select stories for them.
I would have great use made of this disposition. Place in
the circulating department one of the most accomplished persons in the corps of your assistants--some cultivated woman, for instance, who heartily enjoys works of the imagination, but whose taste is educated. She must be a person of
pleasant manners, and while of proper dignity, ready to un-
bend, and of social disposition. It is well if there is a vein
of philanthropy in her composition. Instruct this assistant

to consult with every person who asks for help in selecting books. This should not be her whole work; for work of this kind is best done when it has the appearance of being performed incidentally. Let the assistant, then, have some regular work, but such employment as she can at once lay aside when her aid is asked for in picking out books to read. I am confident that in some such way as this a great influence can be exerted in the direction of causing good books to be used. The person placed in charge of this work must have tact, and be careful not to attempt too much. If an applicant would cease to consult her unless she gives him a sensational novel, I would have her give him such a book. Only let her aim at providing every person who applies for aid with the best book he is willing to read.

Personal intercourse and relations between librarian and readers are useful in all libraries. It seems to me that in popular libraries they are indispensable. Six years ago I was a member of the Board of Directors of the Free Public Library of the city of Worcester, Massachusetts. At that time I noticed that its reference department was hardly used at all, and was fast becoming an unpopular institution. During the last five or six years, by the adoption of the means recommended in this paper, a large use of this department has grown up, and it has come to be highly appreciated in the community.

It is because an interesting experience in the Worcester Library has led me to place a high value upon personal intercourse between librarian and readers, that I have ventured to call your attention to the subject in the paper I am now reading.

Certain mental qualities are requisite or desirable in library officers who mingle with readers. Prominent among these is a courteous disposition which will disclose itself in agreeable manners. Sympathy, cheerfulness, and patience are needful. Enthusiasm is as productive of good results here as elsewhere.

A librarian should be as unwilling to allow an inquirer to leave the library with his question unanswered as a shop-keeper is to have a customer go out of his store without making a purchase.

Receive investigators with something of the cordiality displayed by an old-time inn-keeper. Hold on to them until

they have obtained the information they are seeking, and show
a persistency in supplying their wants similar to that manifested by a successful clerk in effecting a sale.

It is important to have a democratic spirit in dealing
with readers in popular libraries. The librarian is not, of
course, to overlook the neglect of deference which is due him,
or to countenance in any way the error which prevails to a
considerable extent in this country, that because artificial
distinctions of rank have been abolished here, there need be
no recognition of the real differences among men in respect
to taste, intellect, and character. But he runs little risk in
placing readers on a footing of equality with himself. The
superiority of his culture will always enable him to secure
the respectful treatment which belongs to him when confronted
by impudence or conceit.

What is needed in the librarian is a ready sympathy
with rational curiosity, by whomsoever manifested, and a
feeling of pleasure in brightening any glimmerings of desire
that manifest themselves in lowly people to grow in culture
or become better informed in regard to the scientific principles which underlie the processes of their daily occupations.

In personal intercourse with readers, there are certain mental tendencies which should be restrained. Idle curiosity is one of them. Many scholars prefer to pursue their
studies privately, and are annoyed if they think they are observed.

Respect reticence. If you approach a reader with the
purpose of aiding him, and find him unwilling to admit you
to his confidence, regard his wishes and allow him to make
investigations by himself.

Be careful not to make inquirers dependent. Give
them as much assistance as they need, but try at the same
time to teach them to rely upon themselves and become independent.

Avoid scrupulously the propagation of any particular
set of views in politics, art, history, philosophy, or theology. "Tros Tyriusque mihi nullo discrimine agetur" are
words which Virgil puts into the mouth of Queen Dido. The
North American Review has adopted them as its motto. The
promise they contain is one that should be kept by the librarian also.

The librarian who uses his position to make prose-
lytes prostitutes his calling. State the mental tendencies and
the characteristics of disputants, but do not become their advocates.

If a reader asks you for your own views regarding
some matter about which there is controversy, give them to
him if you choose. Decline to give them if you choose. Remind him, however, in either case, that if he wishes to have
an opinion of his own, he must study the subject in its different aspects and form one for himself. Say gently to immature persons that they can not expect to have opinions
upon profound controverted questions, and that they must wait
until they grow in knowledge, and until their reasoning powers develop, before their views on such matters will be of
value.

Avoid religiously the practice of cramming the minds
of young inquirers with one-sided views in regard to questions in dispute.

In the largest libraries it will be found impossible for
the superintendent to deal personally with many of the readers. If, however, of such a temperament that he takes
pleasure in associating with the users of the library, he can,
by only giving a few minutes in a day to the work, do a
great deal to make visitors and students feel that an air of
hospitality pervades the institution. Most of the intercourse
in such libraries must be between readers and accomplished
or specially informed assistants.

In many of the smaller libraries the officers can not
find time to mingle freely with readers. Perhaps, in some
such cases, it may be practicable for librarians to avail
themselves of gratuitous assistance by public-spirited and
educated residents. I should think there are, for instance,
many cultivated and philanthropic women in the country whose
services can be availed of to do work of the kind recommended. The boards of trustees and directors which manage public libraries may be relied on to appreciate this kind of
work, and are always inclined to further its performance by
allowing time to the librarian in which to do it.

The more freely a librarian mingles with readers,
and the greater the amount of assistance he renders them,
the more intense does the conviction of citizens, also, become, that the library is a useful institution, and the more

willing do they grow to grant money in larger and larger
sums to be used in buying books and employing additional
assistants.

In conclusion, I wish to say that there are few pleasures comparable to that of associating continually with curious and vigorous young minds, and of aiding them in realizing their ideals.

REFERENCE SERVICE: THE NEW
DIMENSION IN LIBRARIANSHIP*

Samuel Rothstein

I could begin where almost everyone else begins and
define reference work, but I won't. Instead, I prefer to begin with the more logical beginning--the absence of reference
service.

Reference service is so much a commonplace of present-day American library practice that many of us have tended to regard it as an inherent element of librarianship,
something that was always done, something whose place in
the library order of things is more or less settled. Yet a
consideration of foreign library practices would show that
reference work is still by no means universally regarded as
a fundamental part of library service. I can recall, for instance, that right here in Canada, where I assure you we
consider ourselves reasonably advanced in our methods, as
recently as ten years ago only one Canadian university library had a reference department formally labeled as such.
I have no personal experience of libraries on other continents,
but from my reading I would consider it a fair assumption
that the term and the service would both still be something
of a novelty outside the United Kingdom.

Even in the United States the reference librarian is
relatively a Johnny-come-lately on the library scene. May
I remind you that in the United States of less than a century
ago the library still took no responsibility whatsoever for the
provision of personal assistance to its users. Of course,

*Reprinted by permission of the American Library Associa-
tion from College and Research Libraries 22:11-18 (January
1961).

there were instances aplenty of personal helpfulness by librarians, but these were made as a matter of simple courtesy
rather than of responsibility.

Consider, if you will, how diffidently the case for such
service was first put. When a pioneer of American reference
work such as Samuel Swett Green of the Worcester Public Library first began to realize that the traditional policy of
laissez faire was inadequate to meet the needs of readers,
he ventured no more than to champion what he called--and
it is still my favorite title for a library paper--"the desire-
ableness of ... personal intercourse between librarians and
readers. "[1]

That was in 1876, and Green had good reason to be
modest in his claims; he was backing a pretty dark horse
in the endless race for funds and attention. For a generation
thereafter American librarians debated the value of the new
service. While they were supporters enough for what they
termed "access to librarians," many libraries were still inclined to doubt the practicability and value of personal assistance. For example, when the Examining Committee of
the Boston Public Library suggested in 1887 that there should
be in Bates Hall a "person whose sole duty it would be to
answer questions of all sorts, and to direct inquirers in
their search for information," the recommendation received
the stiff reply from the Trustees that it was hardly practicable in that it would require the transfer of personnel from
other work![2]

Well, I can't make a good suspense story out of this
conflict, because you already know who won; the name of
your division and your numbers here today are the best evidence of the magnitude of that victory. The point of this
story is that reference service has not been and is not now
an inevitable part of the library order. If libraries simply
were limited to "doing what comes naturally," they would
acquire, preserve and organize materials, and perhaps make
them available. Traditionally, and by the nature of the beast,
the librarian's role has everywhere been that of custodian,
collector, and cataloger. If in the United States and a few
other parts of the world he has also undertaken to furnish
personal assistance on an organized basis, it didn't just happen. We have reference service because it was once a
"cause"--a cause to be propagandized for, an idea to be
formulated, developed and brought to fruition!

I say then that both the historical development of reference work in American libraries and its comparative absence in present-day libraries elsewhere strongly suggest that reference service represents a new dimension in librarianship and that its establishment is the product of a more or less deliberate decision. I submit further that the future development of our reference services calls for an equally deliberate decision, and that our chief problem now is to decide on the proper dimensions of that service.

At this point in my argument it seems desirable to make sure that we are all on the same ground by agreeing on a definition of reference service--that is to say, I want you to accept mine. I represent reference work to be the personal assistance given by the librarian to individual readers in pursuit of information; reference service I hold to imply further the definite recognition on the part of the library of its responsibility for such work and a specific organization for that purpose. In short, we are willing to give help, and what is more, consider such help an important enough part of our obligations to justify training and assigning staff especially for this work.

Now, "help" is a great big tent of a word that embraces an enormous range and variety of activities, and the only way to distinguish the main features of these activities is to categorize or classify them. Putting out of consideration the many behind-the-scenes tasks in a reference department and concentrating only on the actual work with readers, we may first distinguish the groups of assignments that finds us, say, clearing up the mysteries of the filing system in the public catalog; making sure that the reader knows about using the index in the Encyclopaedia Britannica; directing him to the appropriate division of the library for a given inquiry; in some cases lecturing to a class on the bibliography of a field. In sum, instruction in the use of books and libraries.

We must reserve a second and separate pigeon-hole for the work that we do in response to requests such as; "What are some interesting books on dogs for children?"; "I want to do some systematic reading on psychology, where do I begin?"; "I've finished all the Zane Grey novels; what do I do now?" We used to call this sort of consultation "readers' advisory work", and at one time it bade fair to set up shop on its own, right outside the reference department. I think that is now back in the fold more often than not, and I shall include it in our roster under the heading guidance in the choice of books.

The last and by far the biggest pigeon-hole I allocate
for <u>information</u> service. The distinction here is that the librarian supplies the information itself and not just the books
where it may be found. We may call this most variegated
and most debatable aspect of reference service: <u>getting</u> <u>in</u>-
<u>formation</u> <u>out</u> <u>of</u> <u>books.</u>

Instruction in the use of books, guidance in the choice
of books, supplying information out of books--these then are
the three primary colors in the reference work picture. Almost every respectable library in the United States and Canada does some of each; almost no two libraries mix the colors in quite the same way.

Let us extend this color analogy somewhat further and
trace the reference spectrum. At one end we may have Library A, say, a smallish public library. It has two public
service librarians (they don't call themselves reference librarians) who are kept pretty busy by an eager clientele of
high schoolers and housewives. They do their best to help
the students with their assignments, but are very careful to
avoid what they call "spoonfeeding" them. They will show
them where to look for an answer but would no more hand
them a fact than they would the key to the vault. With the
adults they are more likely to "dig up the answer," but only
if it is narrowly factual enough for them to be able to find
it in a reference book. Anyway, few people really think of
referring to this library for specific information. They get
that by asking each other, or writing away for it, or most
likely just do without it. The men in the community regard
this library as a kind of cultural monument which fulfills its
function by just existing. Their wives know that the library
offers a good deal of light reading too, and the librarians
exert devious but determined efforts to inculcate in them a
taste for better books. Sometimes they are successful; mostly they are not and are regarded simply as the "library
ladies" who look after the collection.

Our next spectroscopic reading shows us Library B,
a university library of some size and consequence. The reference librarians here are very self-consciously such, and
they take deserved pride in their professional skill. They
dextrously and sympathetically steer the bewildered newcomer
into the easy familiarity with indexes, subject-headings, and
bibliographies that constitutes "library know-how." Occasionally, mind you, they find it easier to supply the date or the
population figure outright than to show the inquirer how to get

it, but they keep a wary eye out for the cunning student
whose pretended ignorance would lure them into doing his
assignment for him.

For graduate students and faculty the reference librarians are willing to do much more: verify a footnote,
trace a quotation, identify an obscure name, sometimes even
compile a bibliography. They rather enjoy a "difficult question," and delight in the challenge it offers to their ingenuity
and knowledge. They shy away, however, from summarizing
data or interpreting it; they take no responsibility for the
validity of the information they furnish.

The last spectrograph depicts a special library in action. Mr. X, is in charge of the library that serves the
research staff of a chemical firm. He calls himself a special librarian or an "information officer" or perhaps even a
documentalist. He doesn't worry a bit about doing anyone
else's work for him; in fact, he believes that that is what he
is there for. He compiles bibliographies, does literature
searches, submits reports on the "state of the art." He
tries to anticipate questions by distributing abstracts of articles pertinent to the current research projects. At times he
may prepare translations or even take a hand in editing material for publication. In short, he holds himself almost
completely responsible for the "literature side" of his firm's
research, and thereby frees his patron's time for concentration on the "laboratory side" of their projects.

You all recognize these libraries, but you may never
have stopped to realize that each bases its service on a different theory of reference work, or to examine the reasoning
these rest upon. James Ingersoll Wyer identified these
theories as "conservative," "moderate" and "liberal,"[3] but
I prefer the more mnemonic and alliterative sequence of
"minimum," "middling" and "maximum."

The minimum theory bases its case on education and
fear. The library admittedly has an obligation to assist the
inexperienced reader, but it serves him, best, so this argument goes, when it limits its help to showing him how. To
which the minimal theory would add by way of corollary the
supposition that the experienced reader or scholar does not
want or requires more than occasional personal assistance.
Ainsworth Rand Spofford wrapped all this up neatly in his
dictum of sixty years ago: "It is enough for the librarian to
act as an intelligent guide-post, to point the way; to travel
the road is the business of the reader himself."[4]

Of course even the minimum reference department
does offer something of an information service, but diffidently.
And here is where the fear comes in. Fear, first of all,
that the library can never hope to have the manpower to render more than severely limited assistance. Fear, again,
that the patrons will take undue advantage and make exorbi-
tant demands. And finally, errorophobia, my new word for
that old malady: the librarian's fear of making a mistake.
You know the feeling--the world of knowledge is so large and
much of it so hopelessly specialized; let's play safe by stick-
ing to our friendly reference books and ready reference questions. No mistakes, no worries--also not much service.

In sharp contrast, the maximum theory of reference
work takes its stand on the twin tenets of faith and efficiency.
Information, it contends, is of crucial concern to many people. For businessmen, legislators, researchers and scholars, it is more important that they have it than that they
learn how to acquire it, and extensive library assistance is
therefore economical and worthwhile in any case where the
time saved by the client is more valuable than the time spent
by the librarian. The chemist no longer blows his own glass-
ware and the doctor no longer takes temperatures; why should
they not have the librarian conduct literature searches for
them? And where efficiency suggests the librarians should,
faith says the librarian can do these things, and perhaps even
better than the client himself. Given the requisite subject
knowledge and sound bibliographical training, the librarian
can, in this view, become the specialist in "finding out, "
even to the point of validating the data he secures.

Between the "conservatives" and the "liberals" stand
the "moderates" ... in the middle and, I fear, in a muddle.
They affirm the pedagogical superiority of instruction over
direct provision of information, but wonder whether this is
an appropriate reason to limit assistance to their non-student
clientele. They want to promote demand for the library's
service, but are unwilling to extend the scope of the service
most in demand. They range wide but seldom deep. Ex-
pediency vies with principle.

The result is a pattern of wonderful inconsistency. I
have the impression that the patron who comes to a public
library looking for, say, Babe Ruth's home run record, is
likely to be directed to Menke's Encyclopedia of Sports; if he
were lazy enough to telephone instead, he would find that the
same reference department ran a very efficient information

service. I know from personal experience that an ingenious
student can, by writing a plausible letter to a neighboring
university, have compiled for him the bibliography that his
own library would never produce. A request from the City
Hall or the President's Office produces wonders of reference
work.

Do I seem to you to have presented an inaccurate picture of the three theories? I have no doubt that my slips
and prejudices have been showing, and I now abandon the
attempts at impartiality and give you my own opinions.

I say first of all that we should give up our reserva-
tions about the direct provision of information and recognize
information service as a principal and worthy obligation of
the library, something we should try to push forward as far
as we can. Let us admit frankly that our <u>instructional</u> ef-
forst are logically applicable only to students, and that our
other customers have no more reason to be guided in the
techniques of finding out than they have in being shown how
to fix a defective carburetor. Again to quote Wyer: "It is
service, not suggestion, that is at a premium."[5]

Wyer made this statement three decades ago, and I
believe that the value and need of such service have mounted
with the years. For the general public there is now greater
need than ever for the public library to serve, in W. S.
Learned's famous phrase, as "the community intelligence
service."[6] In an age when the media of mass communication assault us every day with a barrage of distortions and
half-truths, the public library can make an almost unique
contribution by serving the community's center for reliable,
detailed information. The public library may sometimes find
it hard to compete with television, picture magazines and the
like when it comes to furnishing entertainment and escape.
But why compete? I hold with Dr. Robert Leigh and the Public Library Inquiry that the natural and appropriate role of
the public library in our time is to emphasize and develop
the kinds and qualities of service that the mass media are
not equipped to give.[7]

In the libraries that serve scholars and research scientists, the case for an amplified reference service is even
stronger. In the first place, it may be conceded that the
social importance of their work warrants these people special consideration. More important is the fact that research
workers stand in growing <u>need</u> of a full-scale reference ser-

vice. A recent textbook on the theory and practice of industrial research puts it this way: "It is inefficient to expect a
research worker to obtain all this information on his own.
In any case, it is barely possible for him today to keep up
with current information in his own particular specialty,
much less maintain his contracts with other fields. The library ... staff ... in any efficient research group must
maintain or have access to all the sources of information
which would be of utility to a worker in a given project. For
best results, they should be able to prepare bibliographies
and abstracts of pertinent material rapidly and to furnish
specific literature which the researchers feel would be of
additional interest. "8

    This statement brings out the chief reason for the in-
creasing dependence of research workers upon librarians. I
refer, of course, to the astounding proliferation of scientific
literature since the Second World War. All of us have seen
the fearsome statistics that prove this point, and it is now
quite evident that the volume of pertinent literature in any
single field, except possibly in the most narrow specializa-
tions, has outstripped the capacity of the individual research
man to cope with it unaided.

    The scientist's bibliographical difficulties are com-
pounded by a number of other factors: the acknowledged deficiencies of the abstracting and indexing journals in covering the literature; the present-day tendency to publish results
in the relatively inaccessible "technical reports" rather than
in the standard journals; the fact that scientific research has
increasingly emphasized the interdisciplinary approach and
hence has forced the researcher to gain cognizance of work
done outside the realm of his own bibliographic competence.
Without going into details on these much-discussed matters,
I think I am quite safe in concluding that the task of tracing
and using scientific literature has become considerably more
difficult in the last decade. The effect, it seems to me, is
to justify a place for an intermediary between the research
man and his literature, and to suggest that the location of
information almost necessarily becomes a specialized function
devolving upon specially assigned personnel.

    You will have already noticed that, in the foregoing
analysis, I have leaned rather heavily on the reference librarian's potential contribution to scientific research. It is
certainly true that the subdivision of labor implied in this relationship is more readily applicable to the physical sciences

and technology than it is to research in the humanities and
social sciences. It is, I concede, equally true, that by far
the greater number of people actually functioning in this capacity of "research librarian" (or call him what you will)
work in libraries attached to industrial research laboratories
or in scientific institutes.

Yet I refuse to admit that the reasoning that makes
an amplified reference service feasible and desirable for scientific research does not extend to other fields of investigation.   The humanities and social sciences suffer from a like
proliferation of publication.   Team research and interdisciplinary research are certainly no novelties here, either.
And most convincing of all is the fact that a research service, catering especially to the humanities and social sciences,
has actually worked very well in such institutions as municipal and legislative reference libraries, special libraries, and,
not infrequently, in university libraries.   May I recall to you
the "research librarianships" established with Carnegie Corporation funds a generation ago?   At Cornell and Pennsylvania, these "research librarians" engaged in such projects
as: a report on methods used in handling strikes in Austra-
lia; biographical sketches of sixty-four early British writers
on economics; a study of King Charles I's theory of government as indicated in his speeches. [9]

And this was the confidential judgment rendered on
this service by one of the most eminent humanists at the
University of Pennsylvania: "It was of the utmost value.   I
have never habituated myself to obtaining help in such research as I have done, and it was a surprise and satisfaction
to find the immense advantage of such trained and intelligent
help ... I have not the least doubt of the value of such assistance.   I was not so sure of it at first.   The only difficulty, it seems to me, is on our part, that is, to formulate
our problems in such a way as to make his contribution to
their solution available. "[10]

This is glowing testimony, and I wish the situation
were quite as this famous scholar pictured it.   I wish indeed
that the "only difficulty" about an amplified reference service
were on the part of the recipients.   You and I know that "it
just ain't so. "   We know that the Carnegie Corporation's
scheme of "research librarianships" never spread beyond the
two universities of the original demonstration.   We remember that the Detroit Public Library's plan for an Industrial
Research Service died aborning.

It is all too easy to see the large practical difficulties
that attend any grand-scale information service: the need for
highly-trained staff that can combine high bibliographical skill
with special subject knowledge; the problem of discriminating
between the trivial and the important request; above all, the
problem of numbers. I recall being told some years ago on
a visit to the New York Public Library that, in the Information Division there, each reference librarian was expected to
deal with fifty to sixty inquiries an hour! I could only shake
my head.

I do not have ready-made, overall answers to these
genuine problems, and indeed it would be presumptuous of
me to present such solutions, for these can only be worked
out in the individual library, with due regard for the circumstances attending each situation. Every case is special. I
do suggest the following possibilities as food for thought:

1. Library budgets can be increased--perhaps several
times over--without putting the slightest strain on the economy of either the United States or Canada. As a British librarian recently stated, when the cost of a single missile
may exceed the combined expenditure on the country's libraries, it is absurd to speak of library costs. The scale
of our present services would have seemed utopian a generation ago; why should we see the future as static?

2. The reference services--and especially the information service--can get a large share of the existing library
budget. I have no wish to start one more civil war in the
ALA, but it may well be that we spend too much money on
our technical processes and not enough on our public services.
(By the way, I happen to be in charge of technical processes
at my library.)

3. There seems to be sound reason for hope that
advances in library technology can produce savings which
could be applied to the expansion of information services.
Much of our cataloging, circulation, and acquisitions work
can be mechanized, and for that matter, we are promised
machines for "information retrieval" too. In any case the
point is the same; the library is freed to concentrate on the
really intellectual tasks in librarianship, and prominent among
them the information service.

4. A foundation--and of course the Council on Library
Resources springs promptly to mind--might be persuaded to

sponsor adequate demonstrations of amplified reference service, say adding a dozen subject specialists to each of a
number of public and university libraries. In the special library setting the workability and value of such service is already an established fact; what we need to work out now is
just how the goal can be realized in the far more complicated
context of the general library. The Carnegie Corporation
"research librarianships" constituted a test of sorts, but
were hardly conclusive. A full-scale experiment is now in
order.

And now may I permit myself a few last words of
summary and peroration. Historically and indeed in most
of their present-day functions librarians have been technicians,
handmaidens of both sexes, who work with books rather than
in them. When reference service and particularly an information service became established as a regular part of American library practice, it really constituted a new dimension
in librarianship; we began to deal in knowledge and not just
volumes.

It was a radical idea, a big idea, but sometimes I
fear that we have been guilty of considering it too big for us.
Though the concept and techniques of an information service
began in the general library, we general librarians have been
diffident about exploiting it. Other people have done so, and
very effectively; now they threaten to establish themselves
as a wholly separate profession. History gainsays them,
but our claims must rest on more than history. Both the
needs of our clients and our own self-interest say that we
should look for ways to work at greater range and depth,
to do always more not less. If first-class reference service
is valuable enough for the businessman to buy, then it is
also important enough for the community and the university
to support.

This is a large objective, and to reach it we must
somehow surmount great practical difficulties. But I would
remind you that practical solutions are always a secondary
matter; what comes first is conviction. If we can achieve
a clear-cut decision on direction and policy, if we can settle
on ends, I have no doubt that we can find some of the means.

NOTES

1. Samuel Swett Green, "Personal Relations Between Li-

brarians and Readers. " Library Journal, I (1876),
74-81. The longer title was used for the original
reading of the paper at the 1876 conference.

2. Boston Public Library, Thirty-fifth [Annual] Report ...
    1887, p. 18.

3. James Ingersoll Wyer, Reference Work: a Textbook
    for Students of Library Work and Librarians.
    (Chicago: American Library Association, 1930),
    pp. 6-7.

4. Ainsworth Rand Spofford, A Book for All Readers (New
    York: G. P. Putnam's Sons, 1900), pp. 204, 213.

5. Wyer, op. cit., p. 9.

6. Williams S. Learned, The American Public Library
    and the Diffusion of Knowledge (New York: Har-
    court, Brace, 1925), p. 14.

7. Robert Leigh, The Public Library in the United States
    (New York: Columbia University Press, 1950),
    p. 46.

8. David Bendel Hertz, The Theory and Practice of Indus-
    trial Research (New York: McGraw-Hill Book Com-
    pany, 1950), p. 303.

9. Cf. Samuel Rothstein, The Development of Reference
    Services ... (ACRL Monographs, Number 14. Chi-
    cago: Association of College and Reference Li-
    braries, 1955), p. 94.

10. Quoted in Rothstein, op. cit. , p. 95.

THE OPEN LIBRARY*

W. H. Brett

The question of permitting at least partial access to
the shelves does not appear to be a difficult or doubtful one,
excepting in the larger libraries, and particularly in the
larger free libraries.

By partial access I mean access to the practical working library, that portion of the library which is used mainly
by readers in the rooms, and from which the circulation for
home use is almost entirely drawn. Because the users of
the library are admitted to the shelves containing these volumes it by no means follows that they must be admitted without restriction to whatever the library may have of specially
rare and valuable books, such as early printed books, rare
editions, or fine illustrated volumes.

Every public library which has been growing for years
probably has also an accumulation of books, the demand for
which is past or which are very rarely used.

Such books might be shelved where they would take
least room, and need not occupy valuable space in the cases
to which readers are admitted.

Cutting off thus in one direction the most valuable and
in another the least used books in the library, there remains
what is practically the library to almost the whole number of
its users. Public librarians generally recognize the fact
that access to these books is something which their readers
desire, something which they would undoubtedly enjoy, and
something which would probably be beneficial to them. The

*Reprinted from Library Journal 17:445-447 (1892).

opinion has however prevailed that this was a privilege that could not safely be granted. In some libraries it has been customary to admit certain classes of readers, notably professional and literary men and women, to especial privileges, but it has not been deemed feasible to admit a young man from the workshop who comes into the library with his dinner-pail on his arm, wanting a text-book of electricity or a volume of Herbert Spencer, to the same privileges as the professional man who may want possibly only the last good novel for his hours of relaxation.

The question, however, of permitting all users of the library free use of the books with the exceptions first noted, while not a difficult one in college and society libraries, in most subscription libraries, and in the smaller public libraries where the librarian may know personally those using the library, appears more difficult in the larger ones from the fact that those in charge can know personally, or even know anything about only a fraction of those using the library. The objections are mainly economic ones. It is feared that books will be so disarranged upon the shelves as to cause serious trouble, and that the loss of books will be too great.

These are practical questions upon which theories or preconceived ideas are of little account. From the experience of some libraries it would appear that these are real difficulties, on the other hand the experience of others which are successfully operated, goes far to show that these difficulties may be so diminished by moderately careful management, as to cease to be serious obstacles.

It is also urged that the temperature of the room comfortable for readers is too warm for the health of leather bindings, hence the advisability of storing the books in an adjacent room which can be kept cooler. The causes of the deterioration of leather bindings in libraries seems hardly to have been absolutely settled. It is quite possible that impure coal gas and its predecessor, the coal-oil lamp, have been the greatest enemies, and that the introduction of electric light may improve the conditions. Another objection which has weight is the greater space required. It is undoubtedly true that it requires more room to shelve books on the open alcove plan, or any other which will permit free access of the readers and careful oversight by those in charge, still this is in part compensated for by the fact that less space is required in the public room, if those using the library are scattered through the alcoves. Room can also be

saved by withdrawing from the alcoves and shelving closely
those books which are little used, as before noted. There
are some compensating economic advantages. The labor of
bringing the book from the shelf to the inquirer is entirely
saved; the reader goes where the book is instead of having it
brought to him, and is usually glad to do so. Each assistant,
too, can be placed in charge of certain classes of books, for
which she is held definitely responsible and in whose good
order she takes pride. She becomes continually more familiar with them and more enthusiastic about them, and can be
vastly more helpful than an assistant who has no especial responsibility for any part of the library, but is asked at one
moment for a novel, and at the next possibly for a volume in
philosophy.

While wider experience only can tell what may be the
balance of economic advantage between the open and closed
library, there can be no doubt that the moral and educational
advantages of the open library are incomparably greater.
The railing or counter in the library forbidding closer approach to the books says as plainly as words, "We think we
cannot trust you to handle our books; you will probably be
careless; you may be dishonest; stay out." The open library
says, "Come in, we have confidence in you."

The difference in the moral effect of the two methods
is incalculable. It is exactly the difference which exists between that school discipline which enforces rigid rules by
monitorial oversight and that which places the older boys and
girls upon their honor, and expects them to behave like ladies
and gentlemen. A teacher in a high school having more than
a thousand pupils told me recently of the great improvement
effected in this school in a few years by the abandonment of
the old rigid way and the adoption of a more liberal and trust-
ing attitude toward the pupils. The confidence shown in the
very fact that it is thrown open is unlikely to be abused, and
can hardly fail to have a good effect upon those who need
such influence most. The closest library, that is the library
in which books can only be selected from a catalogue, absolutely repels two classes of readers. At one extreme are the
children, and that great number of older ones whose mental
growth has not kept pace with their increasing stature, in
short those who need most its influence. These can hardly
use a catalogue easily and have no trained judgment of books
to help them. They need suggestions and assistance, which
it is not easily to give in a closed library at any time, and
is an impossibility during busy hours. They are repelled by

the difficulty of procuring books which interest them, and use the library less than they should.

At the other extreme is the worker, to whom the use of many books at the same time for study, the chance to sit down among them, is essential to his work. To him the open library can be of great service.

That great number of readers who are to be found between these two extremes may use a library by means of a catalogue, and without the privilege of selecting from the shelves, with profit and with no great discomfort except at extremely busy times.

However, for all these the educating power of the library may be greatly increased by throwing it open.

One asking for Josephus, from the catalogue, will probably succeed in getting it. Possibly it is the only book he knows of on the subject; but if he could visit the cases he would find on the same shelf several modern and attractive books, more interesting and useful to him than the voluminous record of the old Jewish historian. He may inquire for "Gibbon's Rome," and find after he has it at home that it does not cover the period about which he wished to read. He would have been less likely to have made the mistake had he selected from the shelves.

The inquirer for some popular book levelled against Catholicism will generally be surprised to find how great is the volume of literature upon the subject.

He finds that the book he asks for is only one of many advocating similar views; that there are as many others defending the claims of that church and Catholic doctrine, discussing the infallibility of the Pope, and many histories of the church from various standpoints. He can hardly fail to carry away the idea that it is a great subject, one upon which there is room for wide and honest divergence of opinion, and one not to be settled absolutely by one writer, nor all that is worth knowing about it to be included within the covers of one book. To that extent at least his education is progressing.

Take again a practical subject, as electricity. A printed catalogue two years old is behind time; one five years old entirely out of date. This may in a measure be replaced by bulletins, special publishers' lists, and such aids, but as in most public libraries, the demand far exceeds the supply. An inquirer may ask for book after book and find them not in, and finally must ask the attendant to choose for him. If he visits the shelves he can at least choose for himself; and in so far as he compares books and exercises his judgment in reaching a choice, he is educating himself.

I think the educational value of this examination and comparison of books cannot be too highly estimated. It broadens the field of choice and affords the freest scope for the development of individuality in reading and thought.

The tendency of the closed library is to deal with its readers in the aggregate. So many thousand books to so many thousand people. The open library recognizes the tastes, needs, and rights of each individual.

It matters less on what subject, in what book a man reads, than in what spirit, with what purpose, he reads. The open alcoves of the free library are broad highways. Offer they the flowers of history, the facts and theories of science, the beauties of art, the richness of literature, or the delights of philosophy, they may all lead if rightly travelled to that same goal-culture.

That man who can enter a great library, and know it is all free, all his own, can say as can no other mortal:

> For me your tributary stores combine;
> Creation's heir, the world, the world is mine.

PART V

THE TECHNICAL ASPECTS
OF LIBRARIANSHIP

Introduction to Part V

THE TECHNICAL ASPECTS OF LIBRARIANSHIP

> A library is not worth anything without a
> catalogue--it is a Polyphemus without any
> eye in his head.
>
> --Thomas Carlyle

Articles and books on the technical services and management functions of libraries occupy a prominent part of the
literature of librarianship. Here writing has had a considerable influence on practice. The selection, therefore, of
articles to stand as landmarks in this area becomes a difficult task of deciding how best to identify and reflect the literature and its impact on our development. It is impossible
to include more than a sprinkling of the many outstanding
contributions that have been made.

This is especially true in the area of cataloging and
classification. Schemes for the organization of knowledge
and the classification of books are many and ancient in origin. This period has, of course, seen the fullest development of classification theory and practice. During the same
period cataloging techniques have similarly been developed
and refined. In Milestones in Cataloging Donald Lehnus has
sought to identify through citation analysis those articles in
the field of cataloging and classification which have had the
most influence on other writers and he lists many significant
contributions to the field. We have attempted here, as explained by the general introduction to this book, to do much
the same. Forced to make choices we have, in this area,
elected to select primarily articles which have been influential in challenging the existing concepts of cataloging and
classification. Thus iconoclastic voices such as Andrew Osborn, Fremont Rider, Ralph Shaw, and Joseph Wheeler have
been included rather than what are now the more traditional,
but certainly significant, voices of Charles Ammi Cutter and
Melvil Dewey. They question existing methods and present

new ones; they urge us not to accept the status quo but to
make more effective use of all of the technological advances
that are open to us in order to provide better service to library users.

It is less true in the area of library administration
and management which, while an important function, is somehow rather poorly reflected in the literature to this time.
F. M. Crunden's early plea for the use of business methods
has found reflection in more recent years, again beginning
at the Graduate Library School of the University of Chicago
in the 1930s, in an abundance of writings, much of it adapted
from work done in other fields, on the administration and
management of libraries. That, in particular, the pioneering
work of Ralph Shaw in the application of the techniques of
scientific management to library operations is not included
here is only because of his representation in other chapters
of this anthology. Richard Meier's article is included as
being representative of how far we have come in this period
in the administration and management of libraries.

Cooperation in the development and sharing of library
resources is the theme that has most consistently been expressed in the literature as being the most significant aspect
of library resources and is in actual fact the most significant
aspect. For that reason we have included here four articles
emphasizing that theme to the exclusion of articles dealing
with other aspects of resource development. While, in many
respects, libraries have developed a more effective means of
cooperation and sharing of resources at all levels than other
American social organizations, the discrepancy between theory
and reality is still great. Our desire for cooperation and the
real need for cooperation, as expressed in articles such as
those included here, has not been matched as yet by what we
have been able to accomplish.

All of these technical aspects of our work may often
not seem important to our users but they form the fundamental basis of our work which enables us to provide service to
our users in a coordinated and more systematic basis. They
are, thus, ultimately as important to our users as they are
to us.

CATALOGING & CLASSIFICATION

THE CLASSIFICATION OF BOOKS*

Lloyd P. Smith

However they may differ on the subject of cataloguing, librarians are agreed that books should be arranged on the shelves according to subjects. Experience teaches that it is impossible to attach too much importance to the advantages flowing from a wise and methodical order in the arrangement of a library. It is when it comes to systems of classification that experts--a limited number--begin to differ; and the reason is not far to seek. It is mainly because of the hardness of the task, which is so great that Aristotle, who executed it for the King of Egypt, was said by Strabo to be the only man who was ever able to arrange the books of a large library in an orderly and systematic manner. From that time to the present, the classification of human knowledge has occupied, more or less, the attention of some of the wisest of mankind, including such men as Bacon, Leibnitz, D'Alembert, and Coleridge. I refrain from wearying you with an account of the various systems which have been put forward from age to age. Those who wish to examine the history of the subject, will find it set down in detail in Woodward's System of Universal Science (Philadelphia, 1816). Suffice it to say that the genius of orderly arrangement seems, in modern times, to have taken up its special abode with the French, who have succeeded as well in classifying books as they have in ordering some other things usually considered more important.

The system of dividing a library into five classes--Theology, Jurisprudence, Sciences and Arts, Belles-Lettres, and History, the whole followed or preceded by Bibliography--is commonly ascribed to the great French bibliographer,

*Reprinted from Library Journal 7:172-174 (July 1882).

G. F. De Bure, a bookseller of Paris (1731-1782); but he
appears to have merely adopted the plan of his predecessor
in the same business, Gabriel Martin (1679-1761), who himself borrowed from Jean Garnier's Systema Bibliothecae Col-
legi Parisiensis Societatis Jesu (1678). The plan, being
found to work well in practice, has since been commonly followed in the catalogues and libraries of France, and, indeed,
of the Continent generally; and, in the arrangement of its
books on the shelves, a system not very different is now
practised at the British Museum. This plan was also deliberately adopted, but not without valuable improvements in
detail, in the preparation of his catalogue of the Philadelphia
Library (1835) by my learned and painstaking predecessor,
the late George Campbell. That classified catalogue was a
thorough and scholarly piece of work, to which was added a
copious alphabetical Index; but in the meantime the Philadelphia Library had no classification on the shelves, it being
probably the only large collection of books in the world where
the volumes were arranged by sizes only, and in the order
of accession. The defects of that system--or want of sys-
tem--were so serious that, on the occasion of removing the
Loganian Library and the greater part of the books of the
Library Company, in 1878, to the Ridgeway Branch, the opportunity was embraced to make a more logical disposition
of them on the shelves, and one based, as to its main features, on the system of the printed catalogue of 1835. It
was in the actual execution of this work--res sane magni
momenti multique sudoris--that the accompanying classification was wrought out; and as a bibliographical system, to be
of value, must be the fruit of experience rather than an effort of genius, it has occurred to me that my fellow-mem-
bers of the American Library Association might possibly find
in it some useful suggestions.

The classification is intended to be permanent only so
far as the six main classes A, E, I, O, U, and Y, and their
sub-classes a, b, c, d, e, etc., are concerned. In its details it is open to modification to suit the needs of libraries
devoted mainly to the collection of one or a few classes of
books. As the volumes multiply on the shelves, it is obvious
that the divisions 1, 2, 3, 4, etc., can be added to indefi-
nitely--by each librarian for himself--without deranging the
system. Moreover, the divisions can themselves be subdi-
vided by supplying arbitrary marks. For example, under
Zoology (I I 6), I have made but one subdivision, that of
Birds (I I 6+), whereas an Academy of Natural Sciences
might well find it expedient to distribute their works on the

animal kingdom in accordance with the elaborate plan set
forth in Agassiz's Essay on Classification. On the other
hand, a small library may content itself with the classes and
sub-classes marked by letters only, or even with the classes
A, E, I, O, U, Y, alone. It is to be remarked, in passing,
that, by this arrangement, whatever improvements may be
made from time to time in the details of the system, the
books have always a relative, and not a fixed location on the
shelves, so that they may be moved from shelf to shelf,
from case to case, and from building to building, without
altering the shelf-marks.

The system is available, not only for the arrangement
of books on the shelves, but also for their classification in
a subject catalogue. Indeed, the shelf-lists themselves form--
when properly made--a subject catalogue, which may be sent
off to the printer as soon as there is money enough to pay
for setting them up in type. It is true that most of the ends
of a subject catalogue may be gained by the modern dictionary catalogue,--combining authors and subjects in one alphabet,--which it is to the credit of Mr. Poole to have invented,
and of Messrs. Cutter, Noyes, and others to have developed;
but, nevertheless, to my mind, the ideal printed catalogue
is a classified one, with a copious alphabetical index. Suppose that the British Museum had such a printed catalogue
to-day, how much would the usefulness of that great institution be enhanced.

It is only too obvious that the librarian who adopts
this, or indeed any plan for the classification of books, must
sometimes be at a loss to decide exactly under what subdivision to place a particular book, the problem, in difficult
cases, being quite the highest proposed to a bibliographer.
The rule is to place each book under its most specific class,
but, nevertheless, two successive librarians--or, indeed, the
same one at different times--might, without impropriety,
classify the same book under different heads. To secure
uniformity, therefore, and to make the work of cataloguing
and classifying books arranged on this plan more easy, the
accompanying Synopsis and Classification are followed by an
alphabetical Index. In its preparation, I have made use of
the subject Index of my ingenious friend, Mr. Melvil Dui, in
his excellent Classification of a Library (Amherst, 1876).
By his kind permission, it is here reproduced, with the addition of about nine hundred new catchwords which were found
desirable in practice; for some of the latter I am indebted
to Mr. F. B. Perkins' Rational Classification of Literature

(San Francisco, 1881), which reached me as these sheets
were passing through the press. The alphabetical class-
signs in my system are placed alongside of the numerical
class-signs in Mr. Dui's system. The reason for adopting
an alphabetical instead of a numerical designation of the several classes and sub-classes, was simply to prevent confusion in calling for a book by its number, it being thought
that the number of the class might be mistaken for the number of the book. This, of course, is a matter of detail
which may be changed without affecting the system.

      Whether the classification itself is more or less log-
ical than that of others who have attempted this hard and
thankless, but needful, task, it is not for me to say. It
has at least the merit of not being made out of nothing, but
rather of having been evolved from a preexisting system which
has the approval of the best bibliographers of Europe, and
which has been tried for centuries, and not found wanting.
Nolumus leges Angliae mutare. I believe the groundwork of
the system to be good, but I know very well that the building
I have raised upon it can be improved; and, therefore, any
one who thinks of making use of either, would do well to
study--among others--the Table Méthodique of Brunet, and
the classification--which, however, is rather crude--of the
British Museum. The latter can be consulted in Henry
Stevens' Catalogue of the American Books in the Library of
the British Museum (London, 1866). Mr. Dui's and Mr.
Perkins' highly original systems are also full of valuable suggestions, though the former is, to my thinking, not sufficiently worked out in detail, while the latter, with its six thousand classes--ten times as many as are used in the British
Museum--is, if anything, too much so. The reference alpha-
bet--first used by Mr. Dui--gives their systems of classification, in point of practical utility, a decided advantage over
others; and Mr. Dui's decimal division brings in an element
of simplicity which has, in theory at least, some obvious advantages. It is also steadily making its way into practice,
and I understand there are more American libraries now using
that plan than any other. Mr. Perkins "believes that his system accomplishes some good things which Mr. Dui's does not,
and cures some defects in it;" and I agree with him. If I
did not think that mine was on the whole better than either,
I should not publish it. Nevertheless, I am free to say, that
in working out the details, I consider Mr. Perkins' arrangement, in some respects, better than my own, and If I had
seen it in time I could have improved mine in several ways.
Mr. Schwartz's Mnemonic System, and that of Mr. Cutter--

described in Vol. IV. of the Library Journal--are also worthy
of the highest consideration. Doubtless the true Classification of Books, at once rational and convenient in practice,
is a thing yet to be established, but at any rate the materials for it exist; and if the present System with its Index--
on which I have been working more or less for the past four
years--contributes in any degree to make the labors of those
who follow me more easy, it is all that I expect.

I have only to add my thanks to our excellent Secretary for his kindness in undertaking the publication of the
work, and to say that its profits, if any, are to go to the
American Library Association.

SYNOPSIS.

Class A.   Religion.
      E.   Jurisprudence.
      I.   Sciences and Arts.
      O.   Belles-Lettres.
      U.   History.
      Y.   Bibliography and the history of literature.
Sub-classes.   a, b, c, d, e, etc.
Divisions.   1, 2, 3, 4, etc.
Subdivisions.   +, △ , □ , IV, V, VI, etc.

CLASSIFICATION SYSTEMS*

Ralph R. Shaw

I must admit to a considerable degree of diffidence in
dealing with the subject of classification systems. I am not
sure whether this diffidence stems from wisdom about classification systems or ignorance about them or, simply, just
plain prejudice. In my travels around the world, I have
evolved a law of librarianship that says that the degree of
interest in classification systems is inversely proportional
to the state of development of librarianship and bibliography
in the area. It is not surprising, under this "law," that in
the newly-evolving field of documentation, where ontogeny is
recapitulating phylogeny, there is great interest in this field.

Having provided this caveat, I should now suggest that
there are several ways of looking at classification systems.
They can be divided first into universal as against specialized
schemes. It is obviously much more difficult to provide a
classification system that will cover all subjects for all times
and places and will provide hospitality for all time for inclusion of new subdivisions of subjects as well as for deletion
of entries we thought were subjects but turn out not to be.
It is not very difficult to provide a good classification or coding scheme for the parts in a particular storeroom as is done
by Mr. Brisch, or for the research projects currently in
hand in a particular location as is commonly done by Calvin
Mooers. In this latter case, the universe is finite and we
need only satisfy the need for handling the recognized parts
of a system of knowledge that is our concern for a given
time. It is understood that if conditions change, a new clas-

*Reprinted by permission of the American Library Associa-
tion from Library Resources and Technical Services 7:113-
118 (Winter 1963).

sification scheme may be necessary. It is understood that
if the field broadens, it may be necessary to recast the classification scheme. This discreet and useful job can be done
and can satisfy requirements with a relatively low level of
sophistication on the part of the classifier. It is, therefore,
rarely treated in the "scholarly" disquisitions in the documentation literature. Nevertheless it serves a useful purpose.

A second approach to the recognition of types of classification systems is to divide them into hierarchical as
against synthetic schemes. The hierarchical scheme as
represented by the Dewey Decimal Classification or the Library of Congress Classification catalogs knowledge in advance and arranges it in some sort of alleged order which
is frequently alleged to be logical by its proponents and has
problems of hospitality in provision for new classes and sub-
classes. The synthetic scheme attempts to avoid this problem by providing some simples which can be combined in
various forms to create concepts of varying degrees of complexity. This latter is exemplified by the Ranganathan Colon
Classification and by Mortimer Taube's original version of
coordinate indexing.

Unfortunately, this is an oversimplification because
it is almost impossible to find a system that is either completely hierarchical or completely synthetic and almost any
of the hierarchical schemes, including even the simple Dewey
Decimal Classification, have synthetic numbers such as form
numbers which can be applied to any point in the hierarchical
structure. Similarly, systems of simples which can be added,
subtracted, multiplied and divided, in theory, to create ideas
of any degree of complexity do have structured orders and
must have structured orders of arrangement of these simple
concepts and therefore do become hierarchical in a sense at
least. So, for example, we find the Universal Decimal Classification System which is an offshoot of Dewey can by means
of colons, dashes, quotation marks, etc., combine any number of the collections of symbols that normally represent
hierarchical arrangement into patterns of more and more
complex and detailed description of a document. And simi-
larily, we have systems such as Perry's Abstraction Ladders
which, while intended to permit machine searching on any one
of the levels of complexity, really turn into just as rigid a
hierarchical scheme as does Dewey, Universal Decimal Classification, or the Library of Congress Classification.

It would appear therefore that instead of just slicing

this in two pairs of ways as indicated above, each of these may be resliced in a number of additional ways so that inevitably there are many pieces of this slippery banana peel lying around to trip up the unwary.

This is all complicated still further by the common confusion that exists between what is called classification and what might more properly be called notation schemes. The literature on the "newer" classification approaches is full of castigation of the alphabetic index as something that is good for small popular libraries but is not good for scientists and just "ain't" scholarly. There are many people who are convinced that because we express a concept in decimal notation it becomes logical and scholarly, whereas if we express it in words that any laymen can understand, it is popular and unscholarly. It is doubtful that there is anything that can be written in any one notation scheme that cannot equally effectively be written in another notation scheme. One of the exercises to which I subject my students, is that of writing the letters "A, B, C, D, E," on the board and asking them what the arrangement of the letters is on the board. We get, invariably, quick and easy agreement that this is alphabetic arrangement. I then put next to each letter an equal sign and next to "A" I write "1.1," and next to "B" I write "1.2," and next to "C" I write "1.3," and next to "D" I write "1.4," and next to "E" I write "1.5." I then ask the class what the arrangement of these decimal notation units is and invariably we get into an argument about whether this is alphabetical arrangement or whether it is classified arrangement with a good many in the class believing that this is classified arrangement because it has a decimal notation instead of the letters for which they stand. Certainly, if this arranges material in alphabetical order, it is alphabetical arrangement whether we use the letter "A" or the notation "1.1" for the letter "A." This confusion is not confined to beginners in library schools.

Another exercise is asking the class to find a purely alphabetically-arranged bibliography other than a brief popular library list. To date, except for the short one or two page library reading lists which are not properly termed bibliographies in this sense, no one has yet found for me a subject bibliography which does not have some form of hierarchical subdivision among its entries.

This, as I have suggested above, might be a slightly jaundiced view of our exercises in classification.

If synthetic classifications have any basis, it rests in
the fact that different people need to have the same materials, or some of the same materials plus some other materials, regrouped for their own purposes in a different manner
than they find it grouped in its original state, whether that
be the state of lying in a heap or in the state of classified
arrangement in an abstracting journal, a bibliography, or
other source.   This is the most common of needs in utilization of materials.   Everyone of us who has ever used literature to write a book or an article or even to get a comprehensive understanding of the literature has had to make notes
and then recast the notes into the order in which he needs
them for the purposes for which he is going to use them.
This is a classifying or grouping process.   Our needs differ
from situation to situation and from task to task as well as
from person to person and from place to place.   We thus
need to be able to recast classifications or arrangements of
materials into new forms for our particular needs.   A good
example of this is the Bibliography of Agriculture.   Because
of the size of the Bibliography it has not been feasible to list
each entry under each of the topics to which it may properly
apply.   In this case, taking the subject of silviculture for
example, we have to decide whether to put it under Plant
Science or under Forestry.   Whichever we choose, the people
in the other discipline who need silviculture as a part of their
normal day-to-day information requirement must remember to
look in a second or third or fourth or fifth place.   They
would like it better if they didn't have to.   Each one of us
needs knowledge grouped into a particular pattern for a particular purpose at a particular time and may need the same
information regrouped into a different pattern for a different
purpose at another time.   Our point of view determines the
level in the hierarchy at which each one of these things
should be placed for our particular purpose.   Thus it is reasonable, from the point of view of the Forest Service to consider Autogyros as a topic that forms a subdivision of the
topic Forest Fire Fighting which in turn is a subdivision of
Forest Maintenance, which in turn is a subdivision of a broader field of Forestry.   It would not be reasonable to expect
the autogyro manufacturer to be happy with that classification
scheme.   To him, the apex of the pyramid is the autogyro
and the use of the autogyro for forest fire fighting, logically
and naturally, becomes a subdivision of the heading Uses,
under the main heading Autogyros.   Now it would be very
nice and really quite useful, if we could automatically recast
each of these hierarchical pyramids to bring it into conformity
with the needs of the person who is using the material, from

the point of view from which he needs to use it. To do that by a normal hierarchical classification scheme would require that the classification scheme be made bulkier and that all these interrelationships be shown. I do not believe that anybody has actually done careful flow process charting and costing of this operation to determine whether or not it is feasible. We have a good many statements in the literature that say that it would not be feasible, but they do not say under what conditions it would not be feasible or under what conditions it might possibly be feasible. We are thus encouraged to substitute manual or machine manipulation of simple concepts, recasting them or casting them up into the hierarchical pyramid needed for each individual situation as an alternative to what, by allegation, has been proven to be impossible or uneconomical if done in the usual pre-printed fixed arrays of the same materials in all the same relationships. Whichever of these points of view is right, it is certainly right that in order for information to be of maximum use to any individual person for his particular need of the moment, he must be able to get it recast into the form that appears most suitable at that instant, whether he does it by repetitious printing in a book or by manipulation to create the arrangements anew.

This subject brings to mind my old chemistry professor, Dr. Tower. One of the most interesting things he ever said to us, in our elementary chemistry class, was that since time began people have been looking for a universal solvent but no one ever stops to think of what he would keep it in if he found it. I think there is a little of this in the desire to find quick and easy and automatic approaches to recasting of materials into new forms so that you would have it easily and conveniently without having to do any work. I'm not sure how much would be lost in this process since we don't know how serendipity works or to what extent feedback from what would appear to someone else to be unrelated material may help in creating not only the arrangement of knowledge but the arrangement of ideas that results in the creation of new knowledge in the mind of the creative researcher.

On the other hand, it must be pointed out that any hierarchical system that attempts to anticipate all the possible rearrangements and subordinations and relationships of subjects really is attempting to determine the answers to all questions of science before we can ask the questions. After all, the creative part of research appears to be, in large measure, the ability of a research man to take a miscellane-

ous group of data and to recast it, i. e. reclassify it in his
own mind so as to give it new meaning.   This is something
that only a small percentage of the people who dabble in science or in research in the field of literature ever succeed
in doing, and it is really pretty close to the essence of creative work and research.   If we can assume that it is possible to prepare a hierarchical scheme that has all the possible relationships of all the possible things that have not yet
been thought of built into it, then it would seem that this
would be a very cheap and simple substitute for research
and, of course, we would not only not need research but we
wouldn't need literature and we certainly wouldn't need classification schemes for it because we wouldn't need libraries
because we would know everything.

The only way that I have felt that I, for one, have
been able to get out of this never-never world with enough
sanity to attempt creative work is by putting all this into
perspective.   In the first place, there is no evidence that
the best single classification system, whatever that may mean,
is any better than the worst single classification system,
whatever that may mean, for all sizes of Universe and all
types of materials.   The only reasonably good studies that
we have had on comparison of classification schemes, including the so-called alphabetical arrangement of subjects (with
classificatory subarrangement within the alphabet) as well as
Colon Classification, Universal Decimal Classification, etc. ,
have not indicated any great difference in the amount of material retrievable or the speed or ease or cost or time of
retrieval between one system and another.   There is also
considerable evidence that can be obtained from any of us
who have actually supervised classification programs that a
much greater difference may be caused by the quality of
supervision and the training of the group doing the classification than there is in the classification system itself.   By
this I mean, it may be more important to provide training
and supervision so that we get reasonably uniform application
of the system and that a high degree of uniformity of application of the scheme may be more important in ability to re-
trieve material than is the nature of the scheme itself.   Certainly the most ideal scheme we could postulate that was applied by whim would be the same as the most intricate scheme
applied by whim because each application would duplicate the
theoretical work that went into designing the scheme.

Also, when we are thinking in terms of machining,
the machine is not concerned with the meaning of the symbols

that it handles. The primary requirement for machineability
of a scheme is compatibility of the scheme with the machine's
system and its suitability for machining. By this definition
any scheme that achieves the same purpose with brief notations is much better for computer or punched card application
than is one that uses longer symbols or words. This is
simply a function of the limited capacity of punched cards or
the limited internal storage capacity of the computer. Since
any allegedly lovely logic of arrangement of the symbols
means nothing to the computer or to the punched card machine or to the notches on a notched card--for obviously all
that the machine does is match notches or no notches, holes
or no holes, bits or no bits, regardless of which scheme or
machine we use--the important thing in talking to the machine is to make our words, short enough so that the machine can cope with them without unnecessary overloading of
the mechanism.

       To bring this into perspective I should like to recite
two experiences in the application of classification or coding
schemes. One cannot be documented in detail because of the
nature of the organization but the other will soon be published. In the former case I took more than 100 documents
that had been classified by analysts of subject competence and
experience and returned the same documents in clean copy to
the analysts who had classified them before for classification.
In not a single case did we get identical classification for the
same document. The same type of experiment was repeated
by Dr. Isaac Welt in the preparation of his cardiovascular
bibliography, and with the same results. It does seem a little absurd to worry about carrying out a theoretical classification scheme to the ultimate in subdivision when we cannot
be sure that well-trained people who are competent in the
subject field and who know the classification scheme and who
have been applying it for some time will apply even the major subdivisions uniformly.

       On the retrieval side a similar experiment submitted
a large number of questions to the reference librarians who
had encoded the questions for machine search, and again we
found that they did not come up with identical coding for
search each time they prepared a search for the same question using the same classification scheme.

       This indicates to me that a more pragmatic approach
to classification is required than that proposed by its enthusiasts and by the sophisticated developers of schemes that
are supposed to do our thinking for us.

In this respect I would point out that while library book classification is supposed to be the application of a number to locate a physical object rather than ideas, and bibliographic classification is supposed to be a system for bringing out the ideas in publications, in both cases they simply locate a specific bit of text in a specific location and that their major function is primarily that of letting us return to something we have recorded as allegedly saying something about the subject we are looking for. When we blow them up beyond this level I don't think we are fooling the machines and I don't think we are fooling the systems. I think we are fooling ourselves.

For many reasons people want fancy classification schemes. If these are defined carefully and applied uniformly they don't do much harm. I have yet to see any case in which per se they do much good. However, since the enthusiasm of users of systems in this field demands "superclassification" schemes, I suspect that we may as well learn to live with them without letting them interfere too much with our basic function which is the storage, processing, retrieval, and delivery, of information in recorded form.

THE CRISIS IN CATALOGING*

Andrew D. Osborn

A wise German librarian has linked the library administrator and the cataloger as working for the common
aim of economy in work and cost coupled with better utilization of a library's resources. This aim, he thinks, is expressed in various kinds of co-operative work, of pooling interests, and of setting standards. It is to be developed pru-
dently, he says, with the objectives setting limitations in
such a way that more values will not be destroyed than are
created. 1

This ideal he set out in a chapter entitled "Tasks for
the future. " There was a time, and not so very far back,
when the library administrator and the cataloger worked side
by side. In the more immediate past, however, the two have
become separated, so that their closer collaboration does
need to be set down as a task for the future, the immediate
future at that. Many new problems of administration have
served to busy the administrator, and most catalogers have
had more work than enough, with the result that administrators have come to know less and less of cataloging, and catalogers have come to know less and less about general library
administration. The situation now is that the administrator
will be forced to pay more attention to cataloging because it
has become a major problem field. Neither the administrator alone nor the cataloger alone can solve the many problems. Collaboration is essential, and to this end administrators must know more of cataloging and catalogers must
know more of administration.

---

*Reprinted by permission of the University of Chicago Press
from Library Quarterly 11:393-411 (October 1941). Copyright 1941 by the University of Chicago Press.

This is not to say that administrators must be catalogers, although it is true that there is a great need for catalogers who are administrators. The administrator does need
to know enough of cataloging from the inside to be able to
control the destiny of his catalog department wisely. Thus
it would appear that, if the internship is to be looked on as
a possible element in the training of a library administrator,
then one excellent way of exploiting the internship would be
to have the prospective administrator spend a year in a good
catalog department. Another way for prospective administrators to study the problems to be found in a catalog department is to take the second-year course in cataloging in library schools where that course is treated as a seminar devoted to problems of catalog department administration and
not merely as an advanced course in cataloging techniques,
as, for example, the cataloging of rare books. Library
schools should be encouraged to plan such a course with administration uppermost in mind, and administrators should
be urged to take it.

It seems a little odd to be saying such things when as
far back as 1915 Dr. Bishop put the matter in classic form
in his address to the Albany Library School entitled Cataloging as an Asset. "The cataloger," he said, "must be an administrator if he is to meet the needs of the future: and the
administrator can not afford to be ignorant of these problems
of cataloging, which must be solved."[2] And again: "If you
are to administer libraries, you must know libraries, you
must be able to work your machine, you must have practical
knowledge of its parts. Nothing in the craft should be foreign to you, least of all the art of cataloging."[3]

Cataloging is an art, and as an art it is technical.
Its basic rules are actually rather few and simple, and, in
so far as the rules are kept few and simple, it is a delightful art to practice. That is admittedly the romanticist point
of view. A period of romanticism tends to be followed by a
period of classicism with its subservience to rules, and this
is what has been happening to cataloging. More and more
rules and definitions are being worked out constantly, until
at the present time it begins to appear that classicism is
taking full control. Thus it is that cataloging has become
elaborate, highly technical, a skill too often existing in and
for itself. This is the kind of cataloging that the administrator finds himself out of touch with, at a loss to comprehend, and without sufficient depth of understanding to guide it
to safer and surer paths. Cataloging does not need to call

for so much sheer craftsmanship. In point of fact, the less the cataloger is a craftsman pure and simple, the more room there is for him to be just an excellent librarian.

Much of library science and library administration is not at all scientific. Over a period of years good administrators have developed a body of sound practice, and this it is that can be called library science. Perhaps there has been a minimum of theory and a maximum of common sense in developing this body of sound practice, and it may be that there are certain losses in minimizing the role of theory.

The Legalist Theory of Cataloging

Actually there are a number of theories of cataloging more or less vaguely in application today. The principal ones might be characterized as the legalistic, the perfectionistic, the bibliographic, and the pragmatic.

The dominant one is probably the legalistic. According to it, there must be rules and definitions to govern every point that arises; there must be an authority to settle questions at issue. So the reviser sits in judgment on the cataloger, and the head cataloger is the supreme court for his particular library. Many of the decisions handed down are purely arbitrary, partly because many of the points at issue are simply a matter of taste or judgment.

On the face of it, this seems too arbitrary to be true, but it is precisely the way things are done. Here are a few examples from everyday practice. The cataloger says in the collation that the book contains a portrait. The reviser changes the collation because she says it is not a portrait, the reason being that it is not the picture of anyone named or determinable; or it is the picture of the author's wife standing in front of the great pyramid, and so the reviser rules that it is to be taken as a picture of the pyramid instead of as a portrait; or it is the picture of a native in a book on ethnology, the native being taken as an object of study rather than as an individual, apparently; or a hundred and one other nice distinctions. Here is another case in point. Thomas Thompson writes a book of short stories entitled Lancashire Lather. The setting is a barber's shop, and the frontispiece depicts a barber. The cataloger enters in the collation front. (port.). There is no question but that it is the portrait of a real person attired as a barber; but it

might be an actor dressed up to represent a barber; at any
rate, it does not say "Tom Smith," who could be verified as
this particular Lancashire barber.   Accordingly the reviser,
with much justification, changes the collation from <u>front.</u>
(port.) to mere <u>front.</u>

It requires definite skill to determine when a portrait
is not a portrait.   The cataloger must pass on caricatures,
likenesses on coins and medals, effigies from tombs, pictures of mummies, spirit photographs, and a host of other
difficult situations.   And then, of course, there is the group
portrait to add to the problem.   How many people are needed
to make a group?   Here is the autobiography of a distinguished English lawyer.   The frontispiece shows him in his
wig and gown attended by various flunkies in front and behind.   Since it is a picture of three or four people, the cataloger enters in the collation <u>front.</u> (group <u>port.</u>).   The reviser changes the collation to <u>front.</u> (port.) on the ground
that the flunkies do not count and that the intention is to provide merely a portrait of the author in an appropriate setting.

This kind of procedure is part and parcel of the daily
conduct of catalog departments.   Examples could be multiplied to show that there is the greatest of confusion in catalogers' minds as to what a facsimile, a map, or many another seemingly innocent thing might be when they begin to
take on some of their varied forms.   The cataloger takes
time debating the question; the reviser takes still more time;
and the head cataloger may be called on for a final decision.
Debate, discussion, and decision eat up a surprising amount
of time.   Hence the demand in some quarters for a cataloging code that will define or rule on all debatable points.

Some catalogers are so impressed by this legalistic
theory of cataloging that they are ready to maintain that a
fully developed body of definitions, rules, decisions, and
precedents will result in decreasing the cost of cataloging.
The argument is that if everything has been covered in the
code of laws then there will be no more debates, no more
wasted time.   If there are "57 varieties" of facsimile, they
must all be differentiated.   Some kinds would be called fac-
similes on the catalog card and others would not.   It would
not matter if the word <u>facsim.</u> in the collation stood ambigu-
ously for any of the valid kinds of facsimile.   The decisions
are not concerned with that kind of knowledge.   The decision
is simply to determine whether in this particular instance the
general term <u>facsim.</u> has been used legitimately or not in the
collation.

Thus the classical tendency in cataloging tends to push on to the final phase of classicism--the phase that leads to decline, the valuing of rules and definitions for their own sake. In this way cataloging can become an end in itself, and the cataloger can become a craftsman instead of a librarian. Such cataloging does not ask whether the close definition of a facsimile results in economy of work and cost coupled with better utilization of a library's resources. The systematic determination of out-of-the-way, unusual, or exceptional points, the attempts to rationalize vague, ambiguous, and highly diverse concepts--these result in a theory and practice of cataloging neither economical nor particularly effective.

The weakest point in the legalistic theory is its treatment of matters that must be left indefinite. The proposed revision of the ALA cataloging code has been worked out from a legalistic point of view. Where it has failed most signally, in the light of its own theory, is in the rules that result in a choice of entry. In the old code such rules (e.g., in the treatment of collections under editor or under title and in the treatment of government and other publications under personal or corporate name) led to great difficulty. They were probably the hardest rules in the whole code to apply. The proposed revision has not improved the situation in the slightest, simply because matters of taste and judgment are too intangible to operate well in cataloging or other codes.

A second serious defect in a legalistic approach to cataloging is that, once it is decided to formulate rules and decisions for all points, the process must go on indefinitely. When in the future a point arises not covered in the past, the cataloger cannot use judgment to settle the matter but must set a complicated decision-giving apparatus in motion. Time and attention must be given to settling an infinite variety of small details such as the scholastics of the Middle Ages might have delighted in debating.

A final weakness worth emphasizing is that codification tends to obscure reasons and principles. Much of the original meaning and intention has been lost from the 1908 code. As a result the approach to cataloging becomes less and less a matter of comprehending principles and more and more a matter of the mere learning of arbitrary rules and definitions. Thus elements of cataloging practice that were introduced for historical reasons come to be accepted and perpetuated without any understanding of why the rule was made. For example, there was sound reason for introducing the cataloging form known as hanging indention. That reason no longer exists, yet the form carries on and receives new emphasis in the proposed new code. Survivals of this kind tend to make the teaching and the practice of cataloging mere techniques.

Since the proposed revision of the ALA cataloging code has the weaknesses of the legalistic point of view, it is accordingly to be deprecated strongly. The dignity of cataloging as an art calling for the display of intelligence and sound judgment is something that stands in sharp contrast to a tendency that would so define and regulate that catalogers would need little more enterprise than good clerks.

Perfectionism

Since the legalistic approach to cataloging is the principal danger to be watched at present, there is little need to discuss the perfectionistic and bibliographic approaches in detail.

The perfectionist cataloger is guided by the compelling desire to catalog a book in all respects so well that the job will be done once and for all. In 1935 the Library of Congress promulgated a definition of cataloging along such lines. Every detail on the catalog card is verified according to some authority, nothing has been omitted, and all users of the library now and in the future must be satisfied with the product.

The error behind the perfectionist theory is that so far no cataloger has succeeded in doing work that would last indefinitely. Invariably one generation of catalogers does over the work of its predecessors. This fact is clear from the history of older libraries. The library of Harvard University has had a dozen or more catalogs since 1764.

Obviously there is much to be said for a theory of cataloging which will not be rapidly outmoded. Ways and means must be found to make cataloging products endure. Yet recataloging proceeds apace in many a library, while classification, subject headings, and other details are constantly subject to change with the lapse of time. Tastes and needs change continually, and with them go the elements in cataloging that are based on taste or the needs of the time.

The perfectionist cataloger has been overwhelmed by
the enormous masses of material constantly flowing into
twentieth-century libraries. As a result many libraries have
accumulated considerable arrearages of cataloging, material
has sometimes been temporarily processed, records may be
made inadequately or temporarily with the expectation that
the work will be done over more fully at a later date, and
all the time the cost of cataloging increases. Perhaps even
more disconcerting is the fact that if there were time and
opportunity, owing to less pressure from the current work,
much good work could be done polishing up what has been
accomplished in the past and planning for the future.

So the judgment on perfectionism must be that, although efficient technical work is to be desired in cataloging,
perfectionism is not necessary to such work. The time element is the great foe of perfectionism. Catalogs cannot be
created at one stroke; they contain many inconsistencies and
imperfections. Many of these inconsistencies and imperfections hurt no one but the perfectionist.

Bibliographical Cataloging

The relationship between cataloging and bibliography
has been a difficult one to define. The two have many points
of contact and many elements in common. Their history has
been intertwined in many respects.

The bibliographical theory of cataloging attempts to
make cataloging into a branch of descriptive bibliography.
The collation and the bibliographical notes are much affected.
They become detailed to a degree. This detail is right and
proper in its own place; it does harm when it is applied to
everyday cataloging. For example, much processed material
is being produced and cataloged today. How much of it needs
to be collated in the detailed way that the printed book is?
It is not at all uncommon, when bibliographical details are
overemphasized, for the collation to become a meaningless
conglomeration of terms which puzzle even the most experienced cataloger.

Descriptive notes, such as "Head and tail pieces,"
"Title vignette," "Illustrated lining-papers," tend to fill up
the catalog card without serving any real library or bibliographic function. Some of these formal descriptive notes are
fortunately passing into disuse, and more could do so without

loss. Examples of notes that are drifting from use are
"Plates printed on both sides," "Title in red and black," and
"Reprinted in part from various periodicals," the latter being
for a volume of poems.

Kaiser's criterion of cataloging reads: the minimum
of cost and effort in conformity with the best use of the li
brary. It is from the practical point of view that the problem of bibliographic cataloging must be approached. The
card catalog is at best a barrier between the reader and the
book. "To the books themselves!" must be the motto for as
much as possible.

The ordinary book and the rare book commonly need
little bibliographic description; the one because it is ordinary,
the other because there are printed bibliographies to provide
much of the description. It is an intermediate type of book,
the one that belongs in a local collection or a highly developed
special collection, that may call for more detailed work from
time to time. Such books are not treated as ordinary holdings
and are not so likely to be listed in readily available and
well-known bibliographies.

The Pragmatic Theory

Many libraries have for long been conducting their cataloging along purely practical lines. Rules hold and decisions
are made only to the extent that seems desirable from a practical point of view. As a consequence nothing is pushed to an
extreme, and hence the rules and definitions have no opportunity to become ends in themselves.

The quality of cataloging in such libraries is satisfactory, because it has been developed with the practical needs
of the library constantly in mind. The legalistic cataloger
would not approve of its standards because they have not been
defined to any very great extent; the perfectionist cataloger
would dislike the omissions and the failure to check enough
authorities; while the bibliographical cataloger would think the
job only half-done.

It is difficult to systematize cataloging according to
the pragmatic theory. In the first place, standards and
practices need to be set for a number of types of library.
Where the legalistic code is likely to set one standard, ignoring the needs of certain types of libraries, or leading to a

degree of standardization whether wisely or not, the pragmatic emphasizes the differing needs of various types of library. The school library, the special library, the popular
public library, the reference library, the college library,
and the university library--all these have differing requirements, and to standardize their cataloging would result in
much harm. There have been standardizing tendencies: the
ALA cataloging code, the use of Library of Congress cards,
the development of union catalogs, and the teaching of cataloging in library schools. Some but not all of this standardization has been good. For example, all types of libraries
can and should use Library of Congress cards--not necessarily all available Library of Congress cards, but still some;
yet this does not mean that such libraries should adopt any
more Library of Congress standards than are right and
proper for their particular type of institution.

        The forgotten man of cataloging is the college library.
The last annual report of the Library of Congress showed
that the principal user of Library of Congress cards is the
college library. One-half the cards sold by the Card Division
go to college libraries. But the ALA cataloging code of 1908
was made without regard to college libraries. It was made
for "larger libraries of a scholarly character,"4 and there
was not a single representative of the college library on the
editorial committee. The college library has found it expedient to use Library of Congress cards and to follow the
ALA cataloging code. There are many college libraries but
relatively few large, scholarly libraries. More attention
should be paid to the needs of these many libraries, and they
should more frequently express their requirements.

        The ALA List of Subject Headings presents an inter-
esting study from this point of view. It was one of the very
few tools worked out for the medium-sized library. The effectiveness of that list and the satisfaction which everyone
who used it had for it seem to indicate that the medium-
sized library may have an important stabilizing role in cataloging practice. The ALA List of Subject Headings is dead
and should never be brought back to life, but its significance
should not be forgotten. Perhaps more tools should be
worked out with the interests of the medium-sized library at
heart; perhaps this type of library should be willing to take
on more responsibility and leadership in cataloging councils.

        Rules specially worked out for large scholarly librar-
ies did not result in plain sailing for those libraries. The

biggest of them--the Library of Congress--steadily lost
ground, acquiring annually some thirty thousand more books
than could be cataloged on this basis.   When the cumulative
effect began to be felt, the Library of Congress had amassed
several million uncataloged books.   The cataloging system
had plainly broken down.   At present the old rules need simplification, not amplification, if the Library of Congress is
to carry on.   In other words, a practical set of cataloging
rules must be drawn up for such a library.   The day of the
legalistic, perfectionist, or bibliographic cataloger is over;
the day of the pragmatic cataloger has begun.

If this is true for the Library of Congress, it must
apply likewise to the other large scholarly libraries of the
country.   No regular library need calls for more detailed
cataloging than that done at the Library of Congress.   Other
libraries, then, should simplify their cataloging and should
adopt the practical point of view.   Consequently, the new cataloging code ought to be drawn up from that standpoint.

Generalizing, and passing over many minor matters,
a pragmatic approach to cataloging and to the catalog code
would result in the following developments:

1.   All cataloging practices would be meaningful, so
that libraries where certain factors were present or absent
would know whether they needed to adopt a given practice.
For example, hanging indention would not be prescribed unless it was clearly understood for what use hanging indention
is intended.   It would be the function of the catalog code to
make known such reasons or lack of reasons, so that libraries could determine whether to follow the particular rule or
not.

2.   Three distinct and approved grades of cataloging
would be followed in the code and in many libraries.   These
would be standard, simplified, and detailed cataloging.   The
classes of books which would be treated according to these
methods should be specified.   Standard cataloging would be
less detailed in many respects than the 1908 code or the Library of Congress formerly required.

3.   In addition, self-cataloging methods must be put
in good standing and exploited.   This would apply in some
measure to city directories, college catalogs, documents,
large duplicate sets on open shelves, pamphlets and other
ephemeral material arranged by subject, special collections

of recreational reading, telephone books, and items in vertical files. Some or all of these practices are being used in one way or another; their use should increase.

4. Rules for cataloging would be relatively few and simple, partly because they would not attempt to cover exceptional and unusual cases. Revisions of the catalog code would thereafter result in slight change, so that whole classes of material would not have to be recatalogued.

5. The quality of the work would be high for anything regarded as essential. Nonessentials would be given little attention or passed over.

6. Catalogers would be trained to use their judgment, not to expect a rule or a precedent to guide them at all turns. It is hard to do intelligent work if that work has to be all by rule of thumb. If catalogers are called on to use judgment, the work will again become more interesting.

7. Unwritten rules and practices would be subject to the same pragmatic scrutiny. Some catalogers, for example, think that the sequence of subject headings in the tracing should follow certain requirements. Attention to such a detail is completely valueless except where printed or mimeographed cards are concerned, and even there its value is doubtful.

8. The interpretation of any point will follow practical lines. If certain illustrations were intentionally included in a book as portraits, whether they are caricatures, representations on coins, or effigies on tombs, they can be recorded in the collation as portraits. This is the natural thing to do. Much artificiality has resulted from ignoring natural and obvious methods of procedure.

9. The cataloging of serial documents and nondocuments should be reviewed to see what extent this class of material needs cataloging. Should superior indexes be provided instead for government publications? Should the Union List of Serials serve as the catalog for such serials as it covers?

Organization of the Catalog Department

Catalogers and library administrators are thus faced

with many and difficult cataloging problems of a technical nature. Organizational questions are equally pressing however.
Far too little attention has been given in library literature to
the organization of catalog departments, while in actual practice physical conditions have controlled matters to an undesirable extent.

Large or small divisions and sections are followed in
some libraries. In others small groups of catalogers are
under the control of revisers. Again the work may be done
by units consisting of an experienced and a junior cataloger.
Some catalogers do their own typing, ordering Library of
Congress cards, or filing, while in other libraries special
people are set aside to do such work. Some libraries are
organized to catalog for others, as is the case with school
libraries in Chicago and Los Angeles or with departmental
and branch libraries. These are some of the many organizational patterns in use today.

Many catalog departments pay too little attention to the
flow of material and hence tend to be organized less advan-
tageously. The catalog department of any size will have to
be streamlined in the future. Material that can move rapidly
should be segregated from other books that move at an average or at a slow rate. Fiction, second copies, other editions,
books to be stored directly in deposit libraries--these and
others can be treated with considerable rapidity. Rare books
and difficult cataloging of one kind or another may move very
slowly. If the various types go along together, there are two
dangers. One is that the slower books will obstruct the general flow, and the other is that if a cataloger pays special
attention to getting the faster books along the others may be
slighted either through setting them aside to be done when
time permits or through treating them in the same way that
an easy book might be treated.

Many popular libraries have for years streamlined
their cataloging departments. It is not difficult to do if the
types of cataloging are easily determinable, as, for instance,
if second copies in considerable number keep coming into the
catalog department as intentionally purchased duplicates. It
is in the larger catalog departments where there may be many
gifts and exchanges as well as purchased books that stream-
lining has been slow in developing. This may be partly due
to the fact that such a department would need more central
administration to take care of the decisions involved and to
direct the flow of work.

It has commonly been stated that the three essential departments of a library are reference, circulation, and cataloging. In some school, branch, and departmental libraries the catalog department has been eliminated. More catalog departments ought to disappear in the near future. Cataloging can and should be supplied as a service in many libraries. It is possible that the development of regional deposit libraries will provide the means and the accommodation for regional cataloging centers. Neighboring libraries of a common type can at least share the work or concentrate it in one particular place.

This question is related to the further one regarding the future of official catalogs. Large libraries are finding official catalogs an increasing burden. It may cost the very large library ten thousand dollars a year to maintain such a catalog. If the building were designed so that all users of the library were conveniently brought together, then an official catalog would be unnecessary, provided the pressure on the public catalog were not too great. Money is better expended on service than on duplicating records. If library buildings can be designed so that an official catalog becomes unnecessary, the organization of a catalog department will be a simpler thing to control. As official catalogs have grown it has become increasingly hard to operate catalog departments efficiently. A layout that was close to ideal in the beginning may in the course of time result in situations far from ideal, owing to the growth of the official catalog as well as of the staff and its duties.

Mention of service, which is a basic factor in library work, brings up the need for considering the concentration of trained librarians who are working behind the scenes in catalog departments, while at the same time student assistants, untrained help, or insufficient professional help may be working with the readers. This is a major problem of organization, namely, how to make that concentration of trained people more generally useful throughout the library.

The Situation as Regards Classification

The many problems confronting catalogers and library administrators are not confined to cataloging proper; they are both significant and numerous in the field of classification. The complicating factor in classification is that the theoretical literature on the subject is in a state of confusion. This is in no small measure due to the emphasis that certain writers place on the classification of knowledge and on bibliographic classification. German philosophers and scientists delighted in drawing up schemes for the classification of knowledge all through the nineteenth century. Such schemes had some slight value but were too much on the order of intellectual pastimes. As a practical matter library classification is far removed from any such schemes.

Bibliographic classification has been worked out and successfully applied in such an undertaking as the enormous card bibliography developed by the Brussels Institute for Documentation. Miss Mann successfully applied bibliographic classification in the classified catalog at the Engineering Societies Library in New York. On the books, however, she used relatively simple Dewey numbers. This example of the Engineering Societies Library shows clearly the difference between the two types of classification. Bibliographic classification is unsuited to the classification of books in workaday libraries; that classification must be governed by practical requirements.

In its application classification calls for a high degree of good judgment. Classification can be a game. It is good fun to build up long numbers, to put books in precise but out-of-the-way classes, to debate academic niceties. Such classification hurts a library. The classifier with good judgment will not waste time arguing which alternative is the better; the case will be decided pragmatically, according to the wording of the title, for example. There must be in the realization that some books have one precise class, while fully as many again could go equally well in one of a number of places.

Reclassification raises problems of two kinds. The daily question of reclassifying an odd book or two is one, while the reclassification of a whole library is another. As regards the former, it requires constant administrative pressure to prevent much reclassification. Relocation is, of course, a separate matter, as the relocation of a book from the reference room to the stacks. Much reclassification is purely academic in nature. A cataloger or a professor thinks that a book would be better in some other class. This kind of reclassification must be resisted as much as possible, and all the more so if the book concerned shows every evidence of not having been used in many a year.

Decisions to reclassify a whole library should be arrived at only after clearly realizing that the old classification scheme was ineffective to a high degree. Many libraries are using poor classification schemes, usually homemade ones. As long as those schemes work there is no real reason why they should be given up. Classification schemes age very rapidly. Both Dewey and the Library of Congress scheme have suffered the ravages of time. That situation will be aggravated with the further passage of time. Total reclassification of a library is terribly expensive. Partial reclassification may be a desirable compromise. Less used books may be left according to the old scheme, so that the new classification will represent a live collection of books; or some main classes which are unsatisfactory can be changed, leaving unchanged those that were satisfactory.

Suitability of a particular scheme to the type of library is a matter of importance. Modification of a standard scheme may be a solution. At the least, great caution is necessary before reclassifying a whole library. Some libraries have made serious mistakes by adopting the Library of Congress classification; it is not true that it is necessarily the best scheme for a college library. Perhaps the situation as regards classification and reclassification can be summarized by saying that the golden age of classification is over.

The Situation as Regards Subject Heading

If it is necessary to say that the literature on classification is in a state of confusion, it is equally necessary to say that the literature on subject heading is almost nonexistent. At most, it would be only a slight exaggeration to say that Cutter's Rules for a Dictionary Catalog, the fourth and final edition of which appeared in 1904, provides the latest word on the theory and practice of subject heading. Cutter's work was that of the pioneer. He saw a new day dawning with the printing of Library of Congress cards, but neither he nor anyone else has been a guide through this era of printed cards.

Even the best of cataloging instructors admit they do not know how to teach subject heading properly. The theory, practice, and needs are all ill defined. For such reasons it is better to say less rather than more about subject headings here.

In part the trouble springs from the use of words,

since words can be local, obsolescent, or technical, or they
can stand for vague, ambiguous, or emergent concepts, or
they can even be lacking for some ideas or relations of ideas.
In part the trouble comes from trying to make a science of
subject heading when it is necessarily an art. Some subject
heading has no other dignity than the mere expression of opinion; much of it has to be based on judgment, in which experience counts greatly; some has to be precise. In part the
trouble comes from differentiating insufficiently between the
needs of different types of libraries. Here the compelling
dictionary-catalog idea has been a handicap.

The principle of the dictionary catalog is to provide a
record that will make for a maximum of self-help on the
part of readers. This means that the catalog must be adapted to the needs of varying institutions. It also means that
the maximum of self-help can be obtained only as long as the
catalog does not become too complex. Many dictionary catalogs are becoming too complex and are accordingly defeating
the ends for which they were created. That is why there are
signs of the decline of the dictionary catalog, as would be indicated by the possibly unfortunate trend toward a divided
author and subject catalog and by the search for substitutes
for the dictionary catalog.

What the Library Administrator Needs to Know

These, then, are the things the library administrator
needs to know about cataloging and these are the pressing
problems which confront cataloger and administrator alike.
It is not that the library administrator needs to be a technician, though some knowledge of cataloging technique is desirable. It is rather that he must know the nature of present-day cataloging problems if he would be in a position to
help in their solution and to supply a certain amount of leadership and direction.

A crisis has been reached in cataloging history. The
system that shaped up about the year 1900 showed ominous
signs of falling apart in 1940. In the Library of Congress
the system actually broke down, and what happens in that library as far as cataloging is concerned affects libraries
throughout the country while the Library of Congress holds
the key position that is does.

Excellent work was done between 1900 and 1940.

Praise and appreciation can properly be expressed for the accomplishments of those four decades. Perhaps at the same
time there is a certain satisfaction in realizing that the giants
of those days did not solve all the problems, leaving little if
anything for their successors to accomplish. This problem
field known as cataloging is still a challenge to clear thinking
and sound judgment.

The foremost problem confronting library administrators has been set down as the cost of cataloging. Elements
contributing to that problem are questions as to what theory
of cataloging to follow, how to work out a satisfactory cataloging code, how best to organize a catalog department, what
classification scheme should be used, and how it should be
applied. These and many other questions of greater or less
significance are what the library administrator must know
about the be prepared to tackle in collaboration with catalogers.

Cataloging policies and practices are about to be set
for another generation. Whether the people of the 1980's
will say librarians and catalogers of today had as much understanding and ability as can now be attested for the people
of the early 1900's depends on the success of the delibera-
tions of the 1940's.

It is important to say that the awareness of these
problems is not to be taken as one generation criticizing another. I have cataloged through twenty of the forty years
that made up the era which I believe has now come to an end.
In 1920 there was enough remaining of the original inspiration to make itself felt and appreciated. Nevertheless, there
were clear signs that the picture was rapidly changing. Pressure of work was in no small measure responsible, resulting
as it inevitably did in systematization and standardization to
an unwelcome degree.

Those of us who see ourselves bridging the two eras
have an added responsibility. We know and respect what was
good in the past. We honor the traditions in which to greater or less extent we participated. And for such reasons our
leadership in charting new courses should and can be so much
the wiser.

NOTES

1. Rudolf Kaiser, in Fritz Milkau, Handbuch der Biblio-
   thekswissenschaft, II (Leipzig, 1933), 318.

2. W. W. Bishop, Cataloging as an Asset: an Address to
   the New York State Library School, May 1, 1915
   (Baltimore, 1916), p. 8.

3. Ibid., p. 22.

4. Catalog Rules (Chicago: American Library Association,
   1908), p. viii.

THE POSSIBILITY OF DISCARDING
THE CARD CATALOG*

Fremont Rider

Two years ago one of our national library bodies appointed a committee to consider the practicability of printing
in book form the Library of Congress depository catalog. At
a recent meeting a group of college librarians discussed the
alternate possibility of printing in book form the complete LC
union catalog. Obviously such a project, running not into
mere thousands but hundreds of thousands of dollars, is not
one to be undertaken nonchalantly. Under these circumstances
the fact that the proposal was deemed worthy of serious discussion is, of itself, significant.

At first glance, nothing would seem to be more soundly entrenched in library practice than the card catalog. The
very fact however that it seems so soundly entrenched should
put us on our guard. For it is a truism of mechanical, as
it is of biological evolution that it is exactly when an organism seems to have reached perfection that the seeds of its
decay begin to germinate. Differentiation, development, gi-
gantism, disappearance--these seem to constitute the inevitable sequentiae of all progress. That the card catalog has
today reached the gigantic stage, few librarians would probably deny; that it has also reached the "gigantistic" age is
probable.

It is not, however, the purpose of this paper to prophesy the early doom of the card catalog, still less to propa-
gandize for any specific successor device. Rather this is an

*Reprinted by permission of the University of Chicago Press
from the Library Quarterly 8:329-345 (July 1938). Copyright
1938 by the University of Chicago Press.

attempt to summarize and correlate briefly a study of the
whole problem of the handling of indefinitely cumulating records, based on some experience, over a number of years,
in the printing and distributing, as well as the editing, of
them.

In defense of the card catalog it must be said flatly
and unequivocally at the outset that, whatever its defects, no
other device at present exists which will do what it does;
none, that is, which permits of that immediate and indefinite
intercalation which is its distinguishing characteristic.   In
other words, no matter what devices we may consider for
the reproduction of the card catalog, we never escape the
card catalog itself.   In every case it, in some form, is basic.
One would be brash indeed to assert that some device which
will entirely supersede the card catalog will never be invented;
but the fact remains that none has yet been even intelligently
forecast.   We have, then, to deal with an almost impossibly
awkward, bulky, costly, inefficient tool, for which, nevertheless, we have been completely balked in our efforts to find
a substitute.   There are substitutes; but always they are substitutes for copies of card catalogs.   None of them will do
what, at the beginning, only the card catalog can do.   It is
therefore with copies of the card catalog, and our need for
them, that this paper will really deal.

The gravest single defect of the card catalog is that
it is unitary.   A card catalog might be described as a bibliography in an edition of one copy.   If we want a second copy
of it (for official use, let us say), or several copies of it
(for public branch library use, or college departmental use),
and we want that second copy to be also in card catalog form,
the only way to get it is to make a second card catalog.   And
to do this we must duplicate most of the work of making the
first copy.   We do not, of course, have to do the cataloging
again; but this paper concerns, not cataloging, but the material embodiment of cataloging.   True, we may dexigraph or
otherwise copy our cards mechanically, at some saving.   But
copy the cards individually we must, and file them individually in card drawers we must.   So long as our catalog remains
in card form there is no way to escape the essential separate-
ness that is inherent in cards, no way of multiplying copies
cheaply and easily, as we may multiply copies of the lines in
a printed book.

Although this primary defect of the card catalog is apparently irremediable, its other drawbacks do not, at first

blush, seem quite so hopeless of correction. They are (1)
continuous cost of filing, (2) physical bulk, and (3) awkward-
ness in use.

That the maintenance of a growing card catalog involves astonishingly heavy, and constantly increasing filing
cost is well understood by any library possessing a depository catalog, or having a catalog of its own approaching depository size. And the words "constantly increasing" need
particular emphasis because in the early days of card catalogs
it apparently was not realized that the cost of filing a card
was not constant but would actually increase per card filed,
as the catalog itself increased in size. Card filing has now
become a serious item of library expense. According to our
cost-accounting records at Wesleyan, the filing of our depository catalog alone runs to over $1,200 a year; in large li-
braries such costs, of course, amount to many thousands of
dollars annually. This cost is particularly exasperating because much of the work, depository filing, for example, is
constantly duplicated in scores of other libraries the country
over.

But, although filing is an obvious problem, it is not
an easily solved one. Some twelve years ago the possibility
of using the Hollerith machine in certain library techniques
was suggested. One such ingenious adaptation was described
in an issue of the Library Journal two years ago. However,
the literature contains no discussion of one revolutionary pos-
sibility--that of alphabeting catalog cards mechanically by
means of a mechanism of the Hollerith type. It may not be
generally realized that the automatic alphabeting of catalog
cards is even now theoretically possible. That means filing
cards at the rate of three hundred a minute--so fast that
they would fall into their proper alphabetic sequence in a continuous blur, instead of at the present hand rate of two or
three a minute! But, to say that the alphabeting of catalog
cards mechanically by some adaptation of the Hollerith technique is possible is by no means to say that it is immediately practicable. [1]

So far as relief from filing expense goes, we are as
yet offered little practical aid. Shall we do any better when
it comes to the alleviation of the physical bulk of the card
catalog? It is clearly a fanciful overstatement to say that
catalogs "will grow until there is no room for books," but
those who have installations running into millions of cards
know that their sheer bulk is a real problem. When this

problem of bulk is resolved into its component parts, however, it is evident that the space occupied by card catalogs is a matter not so much of their own cubic contents as of their surface area in a crucial plane. In case of the card catalog this crucial plane is, of course, the vertical surface of the card drawers, for the principal space taken up by any card catalog is not that occupied by the catalog itself but that taken up by the aisles that give access to it. [2]

Our standard 7 1/2 x 12 1/2 cm. card was, undoubtedly, originally selected because it would hold sufficient single-spaced type-written material to accommodate most catalog entries. "Typewritten," you will note, not "printed"; for printed cards, with their much greater compactness of matter, were not then envisaged. Today the situation has changed, for, thanks chiefly to the splendid work of the Library of Congress, a large proportion of all catalog cards are now printed. Not only that, but in the last twenty years typewriter type faces have been designed which permit a legible compactness of entry on cards almost equal to that afforded by printers' type. In other words, the reasons that were controlling when the 7 1/2 x 12 1/2 cm. catalog card was established as a standard no longer obtain.

If Mr. Dewey and his confrères had ever dreamed of the Brobdignagian dimensions to which their embryonic card catalogs would attain in half a century, there is little doubt that they would have selected as standard some card smaller than 7 1/2 x 12 1/2 cm. Careful measurement of the actual type area of a number of LC catalog entries, or of the type superficies of average entries in the catalogs of the Library of the British Museum and the Bibliothèque Nationale reveal that a card 6 x 9 cm., for example, provides all the space necessary for the average catalog entry. Such a small card is also almost as easily read and handled. [3]

The advantages of such a smaller card ramify in various directions. The cost of card stock would, per entry, be cut in half; and, in manufacturing large editions of cards, stock is by far the greatest single item of expense. Where cards are being printed, the smaller card cuts presswork costs in half because more cards can be printed at a time. Even in typewriting, card costs can be somewhat reduced by typing them gang-wise.

But we are now speaking particularly of storage costs. Here smaller cards effect tremendous savings; obviously from

70 per cent to 80 per cent more drawers may be put in a given aisle space.   But that is not all.   It is also possible to increase the length of the drawers.   For drawer length is, of course, governed primarily by the weight of the cards in the drawer; and, if the size (and consequently the weight) of a given number of cards is cut in half, it becomes possible to double drawer lengths.   Altogether, a half-size card would effect almost a fourfold reduction in storage space.

At this date even to suggest the possibility of a change in the accepted standard size of catalog cards sounds fantastic, and I am in no sense recommending it.   But it certainly is one of the possibilities.   Probably to the librarians of the seventies, with their catalogs full of the "blanket cards" which they had inherited from the incunabula days of card cataloging, [4] the proposal to substitute for them a new, reduced, size 7 1/2 x 12 1/2 cm. card sounded just as fantastic. And we have today something they did not have in the seventies, namely, a photographic process by means of which all existing 7 1/2 x 12 1/2 cm. cards could be reduced, very quickly and at relatively slight cost, to any new proportionate size that seems desirable--if a new size seemed desirable.

Finally we come to the user's objection to the card catalog--and by "user" we mean the nonprofessional user, the general public.   Few of us would deny, probably, that the public prefers book catalogs to card catalogs: that it is impatient, or even a bit afraid, of the latter.   But suppose the public does prefer book catalogs.   Can anything be done about it?   Is there any possible way of arranging catalog cards that will permit of their easier use?   In essence, we mean: is there any possible way to arrange a consecutive series of cards so that the faces of a considerable number can be seen at a glance?   For what the public using the card catalog really wants is to see entries, many at once, as it sees similar entries on the page of a book; and to "turn" them, many at once, as it turns the pages of a book.   It is this desire for "many at once" that makes most of the great European libraries cling tenaciously to some variant of the scrapbook, pasted-entry catalog.

To this problem the various index visibles seemed at first to hold some hope of solution.   But it became all too quickly apparent that the cost of equipping any large card catalog with "visible indexes," and the cost of filing into them afterward, would be prohibitive.   The same objection applied to the so-called "Wheeldex" file, in which cards are ingeni-

ously mounted and automatically "fanned out" on the periphery
of a large revolvable wheel, and to a half dozen other less
well-known devices which have been brought out in the last
twenty years. Some of them are astonishingly ingenious; but
none yet is really practical when it comes to large library
card installations.

It may seem that all we are doing is raising straw
men possibilities for the sake of knocking them down. But
may not even this process give us a clearer understanding
of our difficulties? This whole problem of making cumulative
entries of any sort indefinitely and easily intercalatable, and
at the same time easily viewable, is one of the most intrigu-
ing ones ever presented to the inventor; at first it looks so
simple of solution; in the end it turns out to be so completely
baffling.

In the last few years we have been hearing much, and
rightly, regarding the applicability of microphotography to bibliography. It is quite unnecessary to repeat that for their
admirable pioneer work in this field we in the library profession are deeply indebted to Mr. Raney, Mr. Metcalf, Dr.
Draeger, Dr. Tate, Dr. Bendikson, Mr. Rush, Professor
Binkley, and a score of others. Their attitude toward this
new method of textual reproduction has been throughout such
a commendable blend of cautious restraint and contagious enthusiasm that it has gone far to convince the rest of us that
it is quite within the bounds of possibility that in some as
yet unforeseen microphotographic development may lie the
happy solution for our whole problem of catalog recording.

Nevertheless, the greatest enthusiasts for microphotography will probably be the first to admit that it is not yet
able to offer a complete solution and this for the same basic
reason that the printed book cannot. Like the book, the record made by the photofilm is static--it does not easily admit
further intercalation. Of course, intercalations may be made
in a film by cutting and splicing it, just as, by analogy, intercalations may be made in a printed book by pasting in additional entries, or by tipping in additional interleaves. But
both processes are plainly in the nature of subterfuges; for
both are prohibitively expensive; and both, in practice, soon
break down of their own physical complexity. The only really practicable way to intercalate new entries in a printed
book is to reprint the book. And the only really practicable
way to intercalate new entries in a series of catalog entries
in film form is to make a new film.

On the other hand, no librarian needs to be told that the chief characteristic of microphotography today is the rapidity of its development, that any statement made about it on page 10 of an article will probably have to be corrected, or qualified, on page 20. So, immediately, it becomes necessary to counter to the objection just made (despite the fact that we termed it "basic") by admitting that intercalation in a microfilm catalog may be made entirely unnecessary by re-filming the catalog anew. It is as though we said: "Burn that card catalog; it's cheaper to make a new one than to file a few additional cards into it!"

This fantastically revolutionary suggestion is not yet justified, although it may be soon. The cost crux of this particular phase of the microphotographic problem has not yet been explored, so far as I know. This crux isn't film cost, or processing cost--at least it isn't these if a film is used to its full capacity. For, technically, it is quite possible to put fifty thousand cards on one reel of film occupying only six cubic inches of space and costing only six dollars. The real difficulty is that there exists at present no mechanical device which will arrange fifty thousand cards into position for such a compact filming as that here suggested, and will then re-sort them back automatically into drawer order. For, if these two card-sorting operations must be done by hand--and I have experimented with a number of auxiliary devices to help in the work--their costs are many times film cost.

It may be replied in turn that raw film is so cheap that such compact filming is unnecessary: that such semi-automatic card-feeding as the Recordak offers is enough. And this may indeed be true if but a single film copy is wanted. But at some "edition" stage, film cost "crosses" handling cost. Again we face that most crucial factor of our whole catalog-copying problem: exactly how many copies of our catalog do we want? For, if we want an edition of one copy, a noncompact microfilm is almost surely our answer. But a ten-copy edition of our catalog may demand an entirely different technique; a hundred-copy edition probably quite another; a thousand-copy edition surely still another. This particular point--the correlation of reproductive process to edition size--is nowhere so clearly analyzed as by Professor Binkley in his recent Manual. 5

But microfilm catalogs have to surmount another hurdle, their fragility. The splendid experimental work done by the

New York Public Library assures us, they say, that the public can be trusted not to abuse film. Perhaps. But handling
films of occasionally used books, or even of newspapers, is
quite different from handling the films of a catalog. Few
not familiar at firsthand with the terrific punishment of constant use suffered by one of our great public library catalogs
are able to realize how it literally wears out the toughest of
cards.

To this objection we are, in turn, given two answers:
first--the answer already discussed--that filming costs so
little that a film catalog can be refilmed anew if it wears
out; second, the ingenious answer offered by the Filmbook
Corporation, viz. , the film container. For any public catalog in film form, some form of a container, obviating any
need of constant rethreading, would seem to be essential.
Although this latter may be questioned, as a completely satisfactory solution, it is probably fair to say at least that to
put a container in and out of a projector is no more of an
obstructional technique than to pull a catalog drawer in and
out and to admit, further, that the Filmbook people's fascinating stroboscopic indexing device is an actual improvement over guide cards. No one is more enthusiastic than I
am over the ultimate possibilities of microphotography. If
present difficulties are here mentioned, it is only to get them
the sooner removed!

Granted then that, for a few-copy edition of a catalog,
microphotography is, as the doctors would say, "indicated,"
the same is in no sense true for a multicopy edition. Here,
it seems to me, we would do well, as librarians, at least,
to consider again, but from an entirely fresh point of view,
that embodiment in which all library catalogs started--namely,
the book. Personally, I am inclined to feel--however much
this may today sound like a sort of iconoclastic atavism--
that the supposedly long outmoded book catalog offers very
practical present possibilities. For one thing, it encounters,
as has already been mentioned, less "sales resistance" from
our catalog users. And, although the preferences of these
"customers" of ours do not necessarily speak the final word,
they should properly be given weight.

The rise and fall of the American printed library catalog is one of the most interesting of the unwritten chapters
of the history of bibliography. Card catalogs received their
first great impetus in the eighties. The linotype came into
use in the same decade. All our great American library book

catalogs, with their thousands of pages of fine print, came out before that and were set entirely by hand. None of these early printed catalogs cumulated; and the reason they did not cumulate was twofold: it was financially quite impracticable to buy and hold foundry type in such quantities as cumulation would have required; and it is tedious, and so almost impossibly expensive, to "cumulate" hand-set type matter. It is perhaps an idle speculation to consider "might have beens," but it is quite possible that, if Mergenthaler had succeeded ten years earlier in his efforts to perfect the linotype, the public card catalog, as we now know it, might never have come into being!

But, why, since linotype metal costs much less than foundry type, and linotype slugs can be cumulated alphabetically almost as fast as cards, do we have, nevertheless, not book, but card catalogs? One reason is that implied above-- inertia--the fact that in the eighties and nineties the card catalog, as we colloquially put it, "got a head start." But there are other reasons. Why does the H. W. Wilson Company print the whole range of its invaluable indexes in 6-point type, instead of in an 8-point type which would be easier on the eyes? Not to save paper and binding, for these costs are relatively inconsequential in editions of the sizes in which bibliographies are issued. The controlling reason is that, because the superficial area of 8-point type matter is to the area of 6-point type matter as their squares, 8-point type matter requires almost twice as much linotype metal per word as 6-point. And, when we are dealing with type composition which has to be held, stored, and cumulated indefinitely, one of the largest items of cost is one seldom thought of, namely, the interest on the investment in, and the insurance, depreciation, and storage costs on the enormous tonnages of idle metal which all cumulative processing requires.

Also linotype metal is, and to cast properly must be, a relatively soft metal, so soft that, if it is printed from again and again, and particularly if it is "proved up" repeatedly, its face wears down rapidly to the point of worthlessness. So, though it is true that linotype slugs may be intercalated indefinitely, and intercalated almost as easily as cards may be, they cannot be printed from indefinitely. With the exception, therefore, of one special form--what we might call the "continuously cumulative" catalog[6]--all printed catalogs force us to choose between the two horns of the same old, bad dilemma. We must either reset our entire catalog with

each reprinting, at an almost prohibitive composition cost,
or we must hold great tonnages of composition metal permanently idle, at an almost equally prohibitive holding cost.

Of recent years there has arisen a new printing technique which, if certain objections can be overcome, may
prove the happy way out of these two hitherto unescapable
alternatives.   I refer, of course, to the photo-offset process,
another application of photography to catalog making, in this
case one used to make a book instead of a film.   Photo-offset printing involves the printing of matter on paper by the
photographing of an original.   This original may be printed,
handwritten, or typewritten, and it may be rephotographed
repeatedly without depreciation.   It is in this latter, and not
sufficiently considered fact that the peculiar applicability of
photo-offset printing to cumulative bibliography lies.   For we
may type (or, if we prefer, we may typeset) an original copy
(in our case, catalog entries); we may photograph that copy
(or, in the case of typeset copy, a proof of it) on a sensitized plate; we may, by the interposition of a rubber blanket,
print our book from that plate, and then discard the plate.
And then later, when we desire to intercalate additions into
our original copy, we may do it by means of tools no more
complex than scissors and rubber cement; we may photograph
the integrated result on a new sensitized plate and print a
new book from that plate.

The extremely significant point, from our standpoint
as catalogers, is that with this new reproductive medium we
hold from one revision of our catalog to another (for the purpose of "cumulating" our catalog entries), not a cumbersome,
space-consuming, money-eating tonnage of linotype metal, but
simply a few thousand sheets of paper; and we "cumulate"
our new entries into a new whole, not by handling metal
slugs--an expensive technological process--but by handling
paper slips--an inexpensive clerical process.   It is true that
the offset printing process is somewhat more expensive than
the typographic printing process; but, when our other, and
much more important, costs are taken into account, this difference in printing expense ceases to be material.   All things
considered, this new method, although it has never yet been
tried, as far as I know, in cumulated catalog work, seems
to offer extremely interesting possibilities.

Why, then, hasn't it been used for library catalogs?
Offset printing itself is no novelty.   Every librarian is daily
receiving booksellers' catalogs so produced.   The Publishers

Weekly tried it for a period last year for their "Books wanted" supplement, and then gave it up. The difficulty is that offset printing does not yet give really satisfactory results. Most booksellers' offset catalogs are sad looking affairs. They convey a certain amount of rather blurry, unattractive appearing information--that is about all that can be said for them. But is it really necessary that offset catalogs be blurred miniatures of sloppy typewriting? Is there any reason why they can't be made to look like real printed matter? The answer to this question is at once simple and complex: when one says that they can be, but haven't been, one says nothing new. It was pointed out at the microphotography symposium at Richmond that what offset printing urgently needs is a new copy-making machine, what might be called a "typographic typewriter." For, if we are dealing with hitherto unprinted materials, the original copy for our offset printing must be typewritten copy. 7 We object to typewritten copy for our books, not because it has been produced on a typewriter, but because it looks as though it had been --which really isn't the same thing at all. What we, as book readers, want is offset typography that looks like letterpress typography, that is, compactly set type matter, with justified margins, an adequate variation in type faces, and clean presswork.

Now, rather curiously, it would not be at all impossible to design and construct a typewriter that will produce "copy" that will have, to all practical intents and purposes, the appearance of typeset matter. Even from the mechanical standpoint, it would not be very difficult to do; although it would involve, of course, a number of material modifications of present typewriters of the type-bar family.

First, there would have to be provision for a much greater number of characters. For instance, for any given face of type, at least five additional alphabets beside our present Roman caps and lower case, would be necessary, viz., upper and lower-case italics, upper and lower-case bold face, and small caps. All seven faces are essential because all normally occur on the printed page; and, without them, offset typography from a typewritten original cannot imitate the appearance of, or do the work of the printed page.

Second, provision must be made for such extra characters as brackets, cedillas, and asterisks, and particularly for the ligatures, *fi, ffi, fl, ffl*, etc., which are one of the subtle distinguishing earmarks of the typeset page.

Third, there must be provision for removable "sorts" type bars, similar to the "sorts" matrices of the linotype, that will permit seldom used characters that cannot be given keyboard recognition to be typed into the copy.

Fourth, if our "typographic typewriter" is to be adequate, it must provide for line justification, i.e., the typewritten lines must line up evenly at their righthand margins, as typeset lines do. Several devices, ranging from a crinkly, stretchable copy paper to a "variant-spacing" device recently put on the market by the Royal typewriter people, have been invented to solve this problem of justification. Some of them are ingenious; all interesting; none completely satisfactory.

Fifth, there must be better (i.e., blacker and more uniform) inking facilities than those afforded by the conventional typewriter ribbon; for offset, being a photographic process, can print letters no blacker or more clean cut than the letters of its copy. This requirement has been recently tolerably well met by a new carbon-paper ribbon, specially devised for offset copy use. (This paper ribbon can be used but once, and requires special attachments.)

And finally, and by far the most important requirement of all, a proper typewriter for offset copy must provide variant widths for its letters, for it is the outstanding drawback of all present typewritten matter, from the standpoint of typographical appearance, that all of its letters, its m's and w's as well as its i's and l's, have the same "body" widths. The average font of foundry type is cast on some twenty different body widths. Twenty body widths aren't necessary. It is possible to design a typewriter face on three or four body widths, which so closely imitates the appearance of typeset matter as to deceive all but the expert. And three body widths of letter can be provided for on any typewriter without difficulty by means of an automatically variable space-escapement mechanism.

It will be asked at once, if such a typewriter as this is so badly needed--as unquestionably it is--and if it can be so easily constructed, why hasn't it been? That question is difficult to answer. Because this particular phase of the problem greatly interests me, I have in the last ten years repeatedly discussed it, by letter and in conference, with the sales or the patent departments, or both, of almost every large typewriter manufacturer in the country. Although, as has been said, the building of such a new "typographic type-

writer" presents no insuperable technical difficulties, the
typewriter manufacturers approached have uniformly pro-
fessed lack of interest in the matter.   Their attitude has been
that the possible market for such a machine did not seem to
them large enough to justify the experimental and tooling-up
expense which would be involved.   I have ventured to disagree with them.   Indeed I prophesy that before long such a
machine will be produced and will be placed on the market by
someone; that, when it is produced, and is made practical,
it will completely revolutionize many types of bookmaking and
book publishing.   A typographic type-typewriter of German
origin was announced a few months ago.   My efforts to procure one have so far been fruitless; but the samples of its
work which have been shown in this country are not at all
attractive.   There, at present, this phase of our problem
rests. [8]

It must not be inferred, however, that such a new
typographic typewriter as the one just forecast is essential
to the application of offset printing to cataloging.   It is quite
possible even now to produce a cumulatively printed book catalog by means of a combination of our present typewriter and
our present offset press.   Further study of this phase of the
subject, or, better yet, an actual trial of this type of cumulative catalog making by some venturesome library, should
prove of the greatest value to the whole library world.

In summary, our choice between a card catalog and
any other type of catalog is predicated on this: do we, in
the specific situation involved, desire one copy, several, or
many additional copies, of our catalog?   If we really need
only one copy, there is no question that, at present, one copy
must be a card catalog because, as already stated, every catalog, no matter what it may later become, must start as a
card catalog.   But, if we consider the underlying question
afresh, free from all prejudice of tradition or precedent, it
will, I venture, develop that there are very few cases indeed
in which a unitary catalog is completely satisfactory, and
very many cases in which a multiple copy catalog would be
greatly desirable.

It is true that at present the average public library
seems to get along with a single-copy catalog on cards.   But
how much broader and more efficient service it could give if
its complete catalog were multiplied in printed form, so that
copies could be located in each working department in the
main building and in each branch library?

The average university library likewise seems to manage at present with a single-copy card catalog. But how much broader and more efficient service it could give if its complete catalog were multiplied in printed form, so that copies could be kept in every separate college, departmental, and seminar library, and even in the private libraries of faculty members.

In the case of any large university, where the "library" is really a bewildering complex of libraries divided between scores of schools, departments, seminars, museums, and galleries, scattered perhaps not only over a city but over a state, the unifying and stimulating effect of a consolidated printed catalog, making all its library materials everywhere available, would, it seems to me, pay dividends, in inspiration and in scholarly service, far beyond its cost, heavy though that cost would necessarily be. (And this, to say nothing whatever of the inestimable value of the printed catalog of such a library to the rest of the world of scholarship.)

Finally this should be said: were our cataloging problem properly approached, the cost of printed catalogs would no longer be an insuperable obstacle. A genuine utilization of the advantages of regional co-operation would, in many cases, so much reduce total costs as to enable a common printed catalog to be produced for actually less than the independent card catalogs of the same libraries now cost. This would hold true for any fair-sized group of libraries, were that group one of type, of geographical propinquity, or both, if it should decide to make a thoroughgoing pooling of all its cataloging work.

But the qualifying word here is "thoroughgoing." Perhaps we are not yet ready for that.

NOTES

1. Because the situation here is typical of that encountered in almost every phase of this card catalog problem, it may be worth listing a few of the more serious difficulties. (1) Provision would need to be made for punching with tiny holes all the cards to be filed. The pattern of these holes (by compressed air intervention) would govern the alphabetic filing of the cards. This would be a negligible expense if many cards could be punched at the same time--as with

LC printed cards, for example--but a prohibitive expense if only a single card were punched at a time. (2) It would be necessary to change the size either of the Hollerith machines or of our present index cards. (3) Since the Hollerith machine provides only an 80-place distribution, such editing of our headings would be necessary as would insure that none were over eighty characters long. (4) Hollerith tolerances are, of necessity, exceedingly fine and would require a uniformity in the cutting of cards and in the thickness of card stock more exact than we are accustomed to in library practice. (5) It would be necessary to reserve a portion of every card for the punch holes, since, if sprinkled over the card, they interfere with the type matter. (6) Any form of mechanical filing necessitates the removing of all cards from their drawers at every filing, and running the entire card catalog through the machine, in itself no small labor, and one placing considerable wear upon the cards.

2. Mr. Metcalf comments that, in cases like the New York Public Library, where from one to two hundred persons may be consulting the card catalog at once, considerable floor space is needed to accommodate them, aside from that necessary to give access to the drawers.

3. There is also a literally "half-sized" card--7 1/2 x 6 cm.--which is in wide commercial use. I have been using it very satisfactorily for several years in the editorial work of the American Genealogical Index committee. This has the advantage of having standard equipment regularly sold for it by the Library Bureau and other file manufacturers, and our existing 7 1/2 x 12 1/2 cm. files can also be easily adapted to it. This half-size card files and handles easily, holds a surprising amount of matter, and saves one-half in drawer space and card stock.

4. It was not until 1935 that we finished the recataloging of the last of our old 5" x 8" cards at Wesleyan!

5. R. C. Binkley, Manual on Methods of Reproducing Research Materials; a Survey Made for the Joint Committee on Materials for Research of the Social Science Research Council and the American Council of Learned

Societies (Ann Arbor, Mich. :   Edward Bros. , 1936)
--a book, by the way, so comprehensive, so well
"documented" with samples, in fact so altogether excellent, as to seem to me to deserve Andrea del
Sarto's benison--"So such things should be !"

6.   This form of printed catalog seems to me to hold large
     possibilitioo, cspecially under certain special bibli-
     ographical conditions.   It has never yet been tried
     anywhere.   It should be.

7.   If we had to set new type copy, one of the main econo-
     mies of the process would be lost.

8.   Since writing the above, the International Business Ma-
     chines Corporation have announced that they will soon
     place on the market such a new typewriter.   In a
     letter received from them late in January they say:
     "The machine is now in process of development and
     is not yet in production.   No price has been estab-
     lished. "   A footnote to this letter states that it "is
     written on the International Photo Offset Composing
     Machine. "   The letter shows no attempt at justifica-
     tion: otherwise it is an unprecedently successful
     typewritten imitation of typographic composition.

TOP PRIORITY FOR
CATALOGING-IN-SOURCE*

Joseph L. Wheeler

     After a century of public library service and progress,
public libraries attract less than a third, perhaps only a quarter of the adult population, either to read and borrow books,
or to look up information. But nearly 60 per cent of the
population is over 21. Currently a few large city libraries
show slight decreases in annual circulation, the major measure of their usefulness.

     Yet, nationally, circulation and the informational use
of public libraries have in general steadily increased, especially in the last decade. Possibly because the number of
public, college, university, and special libraries doubled,
from 13,676 reported in 1960, to 27,746 in 1968 (Publishers'
Weekly, January 20, 1969). And there are more than that
many school libraries.

     Possibly also adult book reading is increasing outside
of public libraries, which are so slow on new and recent
book inflow that many adults have given up trying to use
them. A recent Gallup poll reports that 26 per cent of their
sampling had read a book within the month, compared with
21 per cent from 1958-1963, and 23 per cent in 1965 (PW,
June 2, 1969).

     Strangely, the U.S. Office of Education's latest esti-
mate (which we question) that "in 1966 ... circulation from
public libraries will approximate one billion books loaned to

---

*Reprinted by permission from Library Journal 94:3007-3013
(September 1969). Published by the R. R. Bowker Co. (a
Xerox company). Copyright © 1969 by R. R. Bowker Co.

some 50 million citizens" (Bowker Annual, 1968) has been
scarcely noticed or publicized by libraries or by ALA,
though "one billion books" is something to crow about, if
true.   Maybe that magic figure was reached in 1968.   It is
an impressive accomplishment; a big item to capitalize for
public relations; it makes a dent.   But what about only "50
million citizens" out of 200 million?

Two pertinent major developments increasingly evident in American society have hardly wiggled the cobwebs in
the ultraconservative minds of so many librarians and trustees, who have generally been, as Carleton Joeckel said, in-
tensely self-satisfied and conservative. [1] First is that a few
large city libraries are now doing impressive things to combat poverty, dropouts, and unemployment.   But what city libraries are campaigning and striving mightily and with determination to build their adult nonfiction circulation and information service among the crowds of normal intelligent
adults?   Experience and observation persuade me that most
city libraries could jump their circulations of adult nonfiction
50 per cent inside of two years by really trying.

The second noticeable trend is toward more democratic management and administration, to increase participation
among more employees and colleagues, not only in schools
and colleges but in business, industry, and government.
More sharing is needed by those not in the hierarchy or the
Establishment.   After nearly a century, Enoch Pratt Library
has just included a Negro among its trustees.   What, no woman?   A new ruling is needed: no federal aid to a library
which doesn't have the same proportion of women, and of
blacks and other minority group trustees, as has the city
population itself.   This participation includes what School &
Society calls "student hyperactivism," meaning rioting with
violence, now ominous.   Much of it is due to students' resentment of their neglect by faculty and officials, and of "administrative rigidity and obtuseness" as Columbia's Cox Commission report so well phrases it.

In a few libraries, staff participation flourished a half
century ago; very slowly it penetrates the thinking of other
directors and trustees.   Having discussed varied problems
with nearly 200 boards, I confess dismay that so many trustees and librarians fear and distrust the public: "The less
we say about this in the papers the less trouble we'll stir
up."   They echo Alex Hamilton's "The People, Sir, is a Great
Beast."   For a public librarian, what's wrong about the public?

Scores of news items and reports might be cited to show that as yet the libraries' clienteles have seldom been invited or permitted to share in the game. Even most Friends of the Library groups are kept at arms length, if permitted to exist. And just how much library policy and planning is centered on services to readers? ALA's Adult Services Division has just drawn up a draft version of "a bill of rights for the adult patron" (LJ, August, p. 2745-46), and I hope to be able to see it in its final form before I take off for cloudland. At the Kansas City ALA, Bart Lytton, Los Angeles financier and library trustee told the audience: "If the nation's libraries don't improve their service, they might end up like the village blacksmith." This included "greater participation and taking library products and personnel out into the community." In an Ivy League unreleased report in 1968, several college faculty committees called for "bringing a much broader range of opinion to bear on ... policy ... broader participation in decisions." We foresee a constructive revolt by users against the way in which some libraries are run. Libraries need to seek out rather than resist new ideas and attitudes, and to invite and follow through on any criticism of their services.

Unless librarians wish to see the public use its libraries less and less, libraries need a drastic revolution in their philosophy and methods:

a) to imbue every person in each library organization, at all levels, with the conviction that satisfactory service to each individual user, old and young, shall have first priority, and to find the ways to accomplish this;

b) to realize that books, reading, and information seeking, are of paramount and increasing value and importance to society, and that Reading will continue to be First of the Three R's;

c) to speed up the availability of reader materials: promptness and haste are not synonymous;

d) to pay more attention to readers' frustrations and to invite and follow up on their criticisms as to library operations and services;

e) to concertedly seek ways to improve present services so as to satisfy all categories of users, including the underprivileged;

f) to organize, finance, and pursue a continuing nation-
wide effort, backed by the head and staff of every local library, to attract 75 per cent, instead of 25 or 30 per cent,
of normal intelligent citizens above college age, to use their
libraries, to do more good reading, to look up more reference-informational questions of a significant sort, and to use
this information in their daily lives. Not many libraries are
even trying with any determination to do the foregoing, which
among other things means a constant flow of publicity and
good public relations.

As yet numerous state agencies neglect statistics as
to reference-informational questions looked up (minimum
standard is 3/4 reference question per capita;[2] several libraries now handle more than one per capita, e.g., Dallas,
1.3 in 1968). Most librarians agree that circulation is the
easiest obvious service measure, but many state agencies
fail to require libraries to report as three separate items
their adult fiction, nonfiction, and juvenile circulations. Yet
the proportions are of great significance if a librarian cares
whether his library is promoting its "educational and informational" function and its adult services and not just drifting
with the tide. (In libraries using charging systems which
produce no daily breakdown, six samplings a year can be
made for a fair estimate.)

Every hour of every day there's a long procession of
men and women, mostly busy persons, who have taken the
time and trouble to come to the library with high hopes.
They stand on one foot waiting at the service desks, or run
about, looking for help. What do they get? Numerous questions deserve real and immediate study, about users, and
also about intelligent non-users, including their motives and
attitudes, their difficulties as to library use, and just why
they don't use libraries more.

The Big Waster

One operation wastes more library money, absorbs
more time and attention from library staffs high and low, delays public service and frustrates every reader, more than
anything else that public, college, school, and special librarians undertake. We refer to the unsolved excessive costs in
ordering, receiving, cataloging, and other "processing" of
newly added books. But we refer no less to the inexcusable
delays which at this moment are found in centralized, or

regional, as well as in local libraries, in getting all this
preliminary work done before the reader can have his book;
before the college student, the faculty member, the high
school student or teacher, the busy man or woman, in any
occupation, or for his leisure activities, can get his hands on
his or her book. One regional cost study (which shall be un-
identified, to avoid embarrassment) reports that "with present help, there will still be a delay of 3 to 5 months before
books reach contracting libraries. It will be necessary to
add 140 hours per week to get their books out in 4 to 6 weeks
after book is received" (our italics). Are there any words
for such a situation (and it's a common one) more appropriate than terrible, deplorable, inexcusable? The public has a
right to library service which can find a way to end this continuing national logjam. One cataloger told me with a
straight face: "you have spoiled the people of Baltimore,"
because in the 1940's the library got so many of its new
books, especially important nonfiction, onto reader shelves
on publishers' release dates.

       In 1969, despite all the chatter about computers,
mechanizing, regionalizing, and centralizing, we have made
little progress as to this vital aspect of library service,
since 1900. Beguiled by "regional processing centers" as a
great cure-all, and hypnotized by the idea of transmitting
cataloging data "in less than a second" electronically, or other computer use, we are tempted to mistakenly think we are
getting somewhere. He who doubts is pictured as afraid of
machines, fearful of change, or just mulish. Not so; the
actual benefits and economies have not appeared. Until they
do, it is okay to doubt. Whole classes in library schools
are spending time on the methods and marvels of automation
(which obviously are applicable in circulation, fiscal, and
statistical and other repetitive operations in large libraries)
when the largest, busiest library in the world (LC) has not
found electronic retrieval of printed information practicable
in any of its public information-service departments, where
hundreds of the nation's busiest inquirers and researchers
come every day to get help. In the Legislative Reference
Service alone, "we are handling roughly 1000 Congressional
inquiries a day.... We certainly have not employed retrieval,
and we are only reaching for it now," according to LC's
Coordinator of Research.

       Costs of cataloging have bothered all librarians for
more than half a century. In Ohio in the 1920's, we worried
over our library's 22 cents per book after its receipt until

on the reader shelf, and gathered cost data from other public
libraries, with the high reported at 75 cents. That library's
rationalizing comment was: "We are not concerned at what
seems like a high cost because we are doing high quality
classifying and cataloging," whereas it was doing no better
quality than some of the others but paid no attention to sim-
plifying and workflow.

In 1968, Leonard prepared a 95-item bibliography[3] on
cataloging costs. And Hendricks made a 1964 study of centralized costs compared with those in local libraries;[4] it was
more than difficult to prove that centralized cataloging for
35 Northern Illinois libraries was appreciably cheaper, or as
prompt, as local cataloging (the promptness factor got little
attention except to report the complaints of participants on
the tardiness of their books).

Cataloging costs continue to be excessive, whether the
professional decisions are made locally or in regional centers. And the duplication of work and costs among regionals
is staggering. One efficient local library with a $35,000
book budget had a half-time trained cataloger who made the
decisions and directed an able typist and a paster and mark-
er, at 92 cents per book from typing the book order to getting the book ready for use and the cards filed within four
days of receipt. This library dragged its feet as to joining
a system which was trying to get costs down to $1.25. (How-
ever, I'm for systems, if they're housed with the largest
local library in the system, and freely use their resources
and materials together.)

Regionalizing should and in many cases does cut costs.
Logically there seems no sense in local cataloging. At the
end of World War I, this writer persisted in getting an ALA
committee appointed to set up a centralized processing routine
and headquarters, but it was a do-nothing committee. But
there is a great slowdown, time lag, in the paper work,
transmittal, reporting, and all the other steps involved when
a local has its processing done at a regional. And the typical costs at regionals run around $1.25 and $1.50, with college library costs still higher, sometimes $3. The fact that
some states subsidize regionals so they may charge locals
only 70 or 80 cents does not cut real costs to the taxpayer.
And it does not count the local library's paperwork all along
the line. The regional systems in New York State are de-
servedly praised and some of them are efficient, among them
Nassau where the cost per book in 1967, including overhead,

space, supplies, was $1.18, which nevertheless absorbed 35
per cent of the system's budget. [5] On the other hand Nioga
System, for 1967, was trying to find new methods to avoid
raising the price to member libraries, from $1.50 per book
to the newly analyzed cost of $2.60, which had risen from
$2.14 as analyzed in 1964 in Nelson Associates' Survey re-
port. [6]

    An advance copy of a new book on processing says of
the intensive study made of several seemingly excellent regional processing centers: "Average cost for the nine selected libraries to acquire and process a volume is $4.09,
disregarding institutional overhead." The comparable CAL-
BPC cost will be $3.10 or $2.96. Maybe so, but that is
still a pretty terrible cost, and nothing is said about promptness. "It is known that a certain amount of batch processing can be expected."[7] Every processor yearns to have a
group of libraries, even if variously located, make up all
their minds about the same book at the same time, so a
"batch" of copies can be run through together. Not so hard
to manage when a number of city or regional branch selec-
tors can meet, examine, discuss, and decide together, but
unrealistic for separate libraries and faculty members. And
batching, even for city branches, has an element of superficial decisions under pressure. But batching, if it means
holding up one library's order hoping for others, is just another type of frustration for the alert library.

    The presumably substantial economy of compelling four
state college libraries to have their processing centralized at
University of Vermont Library meant that one third of their
book budgets was transferred to the University's budget to
pay the "processing" costs. Any library cries "Ouch" when
it loses any of its book fund. But here went a third of it.
But in another two years it had become clear that one third
of book funds didn't really cover the costs. So now 40 percent is deducted, and the delays are excessive. Yet a project is being considered to centralize all processing for all
state college and university libraries in New England, totaling
about 30. Similar combined college library projects are in
operation in other states, e.g., currently a six-college co-
operative in Colorado. The deplorable time lag is completely ignored. The "22 library systems which blanket N.Y.
State" are preparing to centralize processing for all 22 systems and their individual libraries, and no doubt later for all
the school libraries of the state, and an application has been
filed for $250,000 of federal aid for 1969. Staggering is the

word, especially when it appears that an attempt will be made
to computerize, with its immense equipment investment.
Just how much good will the computers do?   New York State
has about one-twelfth of the U.S. population.   So how many
million dollars per year would that mean for the U.S. ?

Centralizing, computing, electronic transmittal of
cataloging data--these are not the answers or solutions to
the "processing" problem.   No one can take this problem
with equanimity, nor solve it with mere dollars and mechanizing.

The only solution, prompt and economical, for this
costly, delaying and belittling problem, which concerns every
library, and is giving all libraries a black eye, is to resume
Cataloging-in-Source on a permanent basis, at least for two-
thirds of the annual flow of 25,000 or 30,000 new titles; those
titles which may actually interest and be acquired by many
libraries.   It need not necessarily be done at LC, but it
should be done at one point for the whole country, and the
data printed in the book itself, probably with some modification in its technical details and its objectives, as compared
with the 1958-59 tryout.

Uncomprehending Turndown, 1960

In the whole history of American libraries one cannot
find another such body blow to all libraries and to all their
services to the American public as the Library of Congress'
negative report[8] on the one-year tryout, 1958-59, of Cataloging-in-Source: "It is concluded that neither a full nor a
partial Cataloging-in-Source is desirable.   [What a whopper!]
The Publishers' Weekly and the SACAP programs have suggested methods by which the potential promise of Cataloging-
in-Source might be realized in a much more economical way.
There should be no further experiments with Cataloging-in-
Source."   What a presumptuous final decision and order!
This was after a tryout on 1,203 books cataloged-in-source,
about 150 titles a month, from July 1958 to the conclusion in
February 1959.   Nothing could have been "wronger" than this
decision, as is evident from the three-page report of "ALA's
Cataloging Policy and Research Committee" of nationally
known catalogers, "Recommendations on the Consumer Reac-
tion Survey ...," which directly refutes some of the statements just quoted.   The "SACAP" (Selection, Acquisition,
Cataloging and Processing) involves the "cards with books

idea" and has to await the completion and availability of LC
or other printed cards and getting them to the jobber or to
the card source to distribute to the libraries.

With due respect, it does not appear that those connected with this tryout realized the limited viewpoint with
which this half-hearted project was approached and carried
through. The grant, for an estimated need of only $55,000,
was made by Council on Library Resources on recommendation of a cataloging specialist;9 the Council granted the
amount asked. Compared with the millions of dollars being
spent in 1969 on only automation and electronic transmission
of cataloging data, plus the additional millions of dollars
being spent now on local and regional cataloging, the $55,000
was only peanuts. The matter at issue is one involving increasing millions of dollars a year and affecting the use of
50,000 or 60,000 libraries by millions of Americans. It demands a fresh and affirmative attempt to solve it.

The reasons which LC gave for concluding that a
permanent full-scale program of C-in-S would not be justified were: a) the high costs to publishers and to the library
(but the cost to the grant was less than $50 per title; a tiny
amount compared with the costs of cataloging the same title
by traditional methods); b) its disruption of publishers' schedules (but the report noted the willingness of most of the publishers to continue; and on a permanent basis, the availability of much larger book funds by savings on processing would
be increasingly evident and substantial); c) the high degree of
unreliability of the resulting catalog entries and their consequent low utility (but in the Library's own showing no less
than 58 percent of the books were cataloged with complete
accuracy while nearly half of the errors were self-correcting
and completely dispensable statements about collation; furthermore, despite the "unreliability" and "low utility," American
librarians actually were avid for the service).

That we are not alone in deploring LC's turndown of
Cataloging-in-Source is evidenced by the almost unanimous
and enthusiastic testimony gathered by the late conscientious,
perceptive Esther J. Piercy's Committee's "Consumer Reaction Survey," as to the great need for Cataloging-in-Source.
There are twice as many school libraries now, and many
more college, junior college, public, and special libraries
than when that consumer survey was made. We quote Ralph
Ellsworth in the Fall 1968 issue of Library Resources & Technical Services: "opposition to the cataloging-in-source idea--

printing LC card copy in each book--has never been understood. It represented a setback for centralized cataloging. "
Without gathering gossip or cultivating the grapevine, two of
the then LC cataloging group have told me that the real reason for LC's turndown of C-in-S was the strong resentment
and opposition by the staff involved toward the whole idea of
speeding up the cataloging and classifying of new books, with
its unremitting pressure to meet deadlines, especially when
real deliberation was involved in making adequate decisions.
But such an attitude, such a consideration, ramifying into departmental philosophy, management, and morale, cannot be
permitted to prevail.

In ALA's 1965 Inventory of Library Needs, the 1964
gap between current bookstock and the expenditures needed
to buy the books required to reach a fair standard was estimated at $472 million for the public libraries, whereas to
buy "the books and pay the [processing] costs to put them on
the library shelves" would require an estimated $816 million.
The difference was about $344 million, or about 42 percent.
In the minds of the committee which made these estimates,
these costs were chargeable to the processes of ordering, acquisition, cataloging, classifying, subject heading, typing,
pasting, etc.

But the study and estimates gave a larger picture.
If school, public, and academic libraries are included, the
shortage of 390,000 books would cost an estimated $1,609,-
000,000 to buy at library discounts, but to buy and process
would cost an estimated $2,557,000,000. In other words
$948 million--nearly a billion dollars--for clerical and pro-
cessing costs. No breakdown for these costs is given in the
Inventory report, and they appear to be very high. But anyone acquainted with the operations in these types of libraries,
which, combined, must now equal about 60,000 libraries, may
safely estimate that even with printed cards from various
sources, or with data assembled by electronic transfer, at
least half of these enormous costs would be absorbed in assembling the data and in classifying, cataloging, subject heading, sending for, filing and filling in cards if they are purchased, and in the numerous steps already discussed, and
which could be cut down to 30 or 35 cents clerical cost per
book, if Cataloging-in-Source were in effect.

That is, C-in-S could save half of $948 million, at
least $450 million, if, as will never happen, all these indi-
vidual libraries could build up their collections to standard,

and if we were talking about books not yet published, instead
of books already published without C-in-S.

According to USOE's <u>Statistics of Public Libraries ...</u>
<u>at Least 25,000 Inhabitants, 1965</u>, only 1,114 reporting pub-
lic libraries added 16,178,000 books, including gift books,
and spent $52,400,000 for books. We have tried to present
figures to indicate the immense costs of processing under
existing conditions.

This major library problem cries for a far broader
viewpoint, far greater financing, staffing and salaries, than
it received in 1958, plus a determination to succeed. As
Walter Kaiser says "I have long believed that the fantastic
waste in cataloging and related processes has been a professional disgrace.... A goal such as 'Books in by 9, out by
5' should be set. Why not? It can be achieved."

A few basic principles deserve attention:

1. The crux of "processing" (a hateful term for a
highly intellectual procedure) is the knowledgeable decisions
as to class numbers, subject headings, questions of author
entry, and cross references, which are based on the professional's educational and cultural background, his awareness
of current developments in subject fields, his ability to perceive and to predict the various reader approaches to and use
of a book in numerous connections.

2. It is these decisions which determine how useful
a book will prove to the users of every library which gets a
copy of it. These decisions are what take time and valuable
costly judgment. For that reason, they should be made at
only one central point, if possible, and utilized by all the libraries in the least time-consuming way.

3. To date, overemphasis has been given the matter
of obtaining and using printed cards, disregarding the time
consumed in ordering, awaiting, filing and unfiling them,
plus in most cases looking up the LC or other card number,
which at best is usually another time-consumer.

4. It is the time consumed by both professional and
clerical workers, in getting the <u>cards and their book together,</u>
or in making out written or electrically transmitted requests
for cards, or data, and then assembling them, which is a
dead loss. But the cataloging, or "processing" cannot get

underway for a given book, until this information is laid out
with the book, for the cataloger or typist to use and carry
through.   Book and cards, or data, have to be together, or
else, by any procedure, additional time is wasted.

5.   This is the reason why the careful, thoughtful
cataloging and classifying of each individual book of nonfiction
by well-backgrounded trained catalogers cannot now, or ever,
be "an activity which at best is considered antiquated. "   No
other device or routine can be nearly as prompt or nearly
as inexpensive as Cataloging-in-Source, where all the essential information is in the book itself.   Then a competent typist, who in many cases such as school and small libraries,
may be a student or a part-time worker, can proceed at once,
with adequate instruction, to copy the items onto a key-copy
card, from which duplicates can be made either by typing,
or by duplicating device (depending on how many cards needed) without sending off for, awaiting, paying for, or filling
in any printed cards whatever, or assembling any data.

Present Substitutes for C-in-S

Printed Cards

LC itself, in fiscal 1968, was selling over 78 million
printed cards a year, to school, public, college, and other
libraries; its receipts for card sales were more than $6 mil-
lion.   Likewise the H. W. Wilson Co. sells millions of printed cards produced from its own catalogers, and due to their
greater simplicity Wilson cards are preferred by many libraries.   Without going into detail, printed cards can be obtained also from several other sources, including at least 50
book jobbers and dealers,[10] even electronic servicers, including film.   From the latter, of course, they have to be
translated back onto fileable cards.   We omit discussion of
LC's advance proof sheets and proof slips of card copy; to
use either sheets or slips involves heavy costs to file and
unfile, plus time diverted from trained personnel, in many
libraries, to scan the titles and discard items which obviously will never be used by those libraries.   All this handling
is a dead time-loss, and often is overlooked in cost recording.   There is also the unfortunate backup of card orders at
LC, partly due to lack of space "to store our stock of approximately 4 1/2 million titles, " so that they have "to back
order a high percentage of the 60,000 order slips received
daily" (letter to a customer from the Chief of the Card Division, June 13, 1969).

In several cases, this availability of cards is coupled
with the availability of labels, bookpockets and cards and all
items of stationery bearing the call number and short entry
for the book. One source for sets or kits of these materials
for juvenile titles is LJ Cards, at a reasonable 29 cents a
set. Bro-Dart, however, has the largest coverage (over
45,000 titles) of pre-school through young adult titles, with
kits, also at 29 cents per kit.

Cards with Books

The major jobber and major source for library purchases, carrying over 120,000 "live" titles in stock, has
given continuous and widespread publicity to its arrangements
for sending out the needed catalog cards with the books ordered. So have other major book suppliers, the idea having
been pioneered by Bro-Dart. The fact that books and cards
are together is a great asset as a major time-saver. But
everything has to await the availability of printed cards, and
LC could not produce the cards on time, so various jobbers
supply cards which often are created by such a concern as
Bro-Dart, which has its own staff of trained catalogers.
Nevertheless, cards are not available for a large number of
titles in current new-book flow and this raises the question
whether any such routine is, after all, an effective substitute
for Cataloging-in-Source, as was asserted in LC's 1960 report. There is still a considerable amount of "custom processing" at costs of $2 or more per title, even from some
of the largest jobbers. We would note that numerous jobbers, and several publishers, some of them giving the cards
free for their own publications, also distribute LC printed
cards or LJ Cards, with books ordered. Among "kit" suppliers without books, LJ Cards does a large scale business
in originally cataloged juvenile titles.

American Book Publishing Record

In the case of Publishers' Weekly, there is a further
development. This is the monthly issue and the annual cumulation into one consistent list, arranged by decimal class number, of all the Publishers' Weekly entries for new and recent
books, and provided with a title and an author index, so that
any book and its cataloging data, if its publication year can
be easily found, can be quickly located in the file of annual
American Book Publishing Record, since 1960, at $14-$25
per year. (The years 1960-1964 are cumulated into one set
of four volumes.) A bargain indeed, if one is compelled to

look up "LC cataloging data" so as to catalog a book in any
kind of local, or regional, or "cooperative" library, and if
one is not wishing to buy and catalog the book so it can be
ready for readers' shelves in less than a month or six weeks
after publishers' release date (sometimes two months or longer before the data gets into Publishers' Weekly, and another
two or three weeks into the issues of Book Publishing Record).
Carlos Baker's Ernest Hemingway; a Life Story began distribution in February 1969, but showed up in the PW of May 26.
The 1968 annual volume, announced for March 1969 but actually issued late in June 1969, for example, contains 28,762
titles, arranged by Decimal classed subjects, and indexed by
author, title, and detailed subject.

It may be argued that by using BPR, libraries spending $3000 a year on books could do most of their cataloging
themselves with mostly clerical or subprofessional help.
But there are several ifs beside the several weeks delay at
the best. We come up against such obstacles as: a) there
is always some delay, for the whole thing is based on LC's
cataloging and printed cards being available within six or
eight weeks of the first copies of the book coming from the
publisher's bindery to LC; b) whoever searches BPR for an
item has to be not only intelligent, but educated, for often
the title does not appear in BPR as it is written on a reader
or faculty request slip or in a current advertisement or review (what about "corporate authors"?), and the search comes
to a stop; c) frequently no one knows nor can find the year of
publication; consequently one annual volume, then another and
another, has to be searched. The result is a great time
loss, which cancels out some of the virtues of this processing routine, though we are frank in agreeing that in most libraries it is the least costly and the most prompt present
procedure for adult American books since 1960.

Shared Cataloging

In this brief, inadequate summary of what is now a-
vailable to help local and regional or other system libraries
do their cataloging and "processing" most economically and
promptly, it does not appear that the Shared Cataloging project and its ramification MARC are pertinent. Originally
created to serve the very large libraries, especially large
university libraries, and to include a large inflow of titles
from foreign countries, this project involves not only very
costly electronic hardware and expensive transmittal procedures, but high salaries for operators, and such high total

costs, including the duplication of these high initial and overhead costs at each center which joins the project, that many
librarians, who might favor the idea are concerned that even
as few as a hundred largest individual and system librarians
may not be able to make a go of it, even in a period of in-
flation and with a high proportion of federal aid, always subject to unexpected drastic cuts. So far as the thousands of
typical public libraries up to 300, 000 population, or all school
libraries, or any except the few largest college and university
libraries, and a few out of about 10, 000 special libraries are
concerned (there are at least 60, 000 such libraries), this
whole project appears visionary, even on a regional basis,
because of the great delays from selection and ordering to
availability on the reader shelves, and the much greater cost
per book (including the equipment investment per set-up)
than at present. Whereas if Cataloging-in-Source were in
effect, even with the simplifications suggested below, Shared
Cataloging and MARC would not be needed except for foreign
books, nor in more than half a hundred of the very largest
libraries. In advocating Cataloging-in-Source as essential,
we are fully aware of the vested interests, which multiply
each year, as well as the inertia and the opposition to change,
which have to be overcome. That's why "the will to win" is
a major necessity.

Get C-in-S on the Rails

        If all the money, attention and study, the enthusiasm,
and the determination now being expended on a wide variety
of costly procedures, including computerizing, were concentrated on an equally determined effort to have Cataloging-in-
Source, all libraries would be saving a substantial portion of
their annual budgets, equivalent to adding from a quarter to
a third to their book budgets; a great number of able, trained
librarians (though by no means all, in large libraries) could
be freed from cataloging for other professional services, especially for badly needed public reference-informational service which is, in general, in a badly undeveloped status; new
books would flow through to the public with less than a third
the present delay and time lag, i. e. , inside of four or five
days; and millions of library patrons would have a new respect
and appreciation for the library profession, and dedicated librarians would have a new respect for themselves, instead of
a deadening frustration.

        As noted above, the vital cataloging data which librar-

ies need, to turn "processing" from a costly, duplicated
professional job, into a brief prompt clerical job, include
a) author entry, preferably with author dates if easily found
(and the publisher should supply them), and accepting pseudo-
nyms, for good reasons which have been discussed for years
by catalogers; b) title entry; c) the carefully determined
realistic class number, both DC and LC; d) the appropriate
subject headings; and e) whatever cross references are needed (which most libraries have been minimizing in recent
years). Items c, d, and e demand from the cataloger a substantial cultural background plus training and experience in
cataloging.

Ideally and logically Cataloging-in-Source should be
done at Library of Congress, from quickly transmitted page
proofs. However, we have the interdict that "There should
be no further experiments with Cataloging-in-Source," and it
may be that some other organization or a completely new one
will be needed to handle this large-scale project.

We propose that an affirmative-minded committee, of
not over five members, composed equally of some dynamic
library administrators and of perceptive leaders of ALA's
Resources & Technical Services Division, work out with the
responding parties, appropriate details of the following summary:

a) persuade the Library of Congress, if possible, to
resume a modified Cataloging-in-Source;

b) if not LC, then arrange with an appropriate organization, or set up a national processing center in or close
to New York or Washington, to carry on C-in-S from a
single point;

c) decide and record the essential data enumerated
above, and return it within 12 or 24 hours to the publisher
for inclusion in the page proofs, to appear preferably, but
not necessarily, on the back of the title page preferably in
the style of LC cards, but not necessarily; note that publishers' schedules through the printing and binding procedures
are tighter now than in 1959; this is one reason for trying to
be satisfied with cataloging from galley proofs rather than
page proofs; obviously every effort should be made to catalog
from page proofs;

d) omit the collation or pagination, because this cannot

be determined until the book is locked up on the composing
tables and in the pressforms. (In LC's 1958-59 tryout, 47.5
percent of all the discrepancies between the pre-prepared
card copy and the final book "were in collation");

e) the catalog data entry should conclude with a caveat-
line, such as "this cataloging data is prepared from galley
proofs; for added details consult final Library of Congress
cards";

f) this operation calls for an adequate staff of well
educated, experienced, trained classifiers and catalogers,
with special subject backgrounds and preferably experienced
also in reference and other reader service; salaries should
be better than those paid elsewhere, plus adequate pay for
clerical workers. All personnel should be dedicated to producing expert, perceptive and knowledgeable decisions for
prompt transmittal to the publishers;

g) the paging or collation should be filled in by the
local library as a sub-professional or clerical step, when the
cards are typed or duplicated locally; several thousand smaller school and public libraries will omit pagination altogether.

h) finance this large scale national project by a 10¢
per book fee, paid quarterly by every library, and based on
each library's number of new titles added. On the other hand,
it seems logical to seek a foundation grant for a two- or
three-year initial stage, and then insure its continuance as a
national service by federal aid funds.

Some comment on the foregoing is pertinent. The at-
tention-emphasis is shifted from the overevaluation of printed
cards, or a printed card form, to the basic decisions which
are the heart of classifying and cataloging. It is these decisions which the local library needs, to do its own processing promptly and inexpensively. It is not exaggerating to say
that many libraries make a fetish of the printed card, as
though it had some mystic magic and authority which no other
card form can approach. Granted its authority and perfection
of form, are these so essential as compared with clear black
typewriting of equally authoritative data onto equally white
cards? We are trying to bypass the bottleneck which persists
due to lack of a really successful catalogers' camera giving
100 percent clear black and white output, and because we cannot believe that this photoreproduction of an elaborate special
card form is essential anywhere except in a few super-libraries.

It is the catalogers' decisions which are essential, and they
will be in the book for a typist to copy off accurately from
the C-in-S book, inserting the final pagination which appears
in the book itself.   This copying of the card copy from the
book will cost from 15 to 25 cents per book, depending on
length of entry, and assuming that larger libraries will use a
duplicating machine, of which three or four are on the market, e. g. Chiang Small Duplicator at $55, or the Mini-Graph
at $275, in both cases using stencils.

       We are aware that LC's cataloging has occasional err-
ors, and that many librarians disagree with some of the class
numbers and subject headings it assigns.   "Order Department
sources do not share LC's fondness for corporate entry, "
for example.   For these and similar reasons numerous librarians and catalogers would be satisfied if Cataloging-in-
Source were centered somewhere else than at LC, where the
decisions will more nearly meet the needs of the typical college, public, special, and large school library.   There are
more than 50,000 such libraries, all of which would no doubt
welcome C-in-S, assuming they understood its pros and cons.
Some months ago I had assurance from a well posted source
that the publishers would be glad to cooperate again in whole-
sale continuous Cataloging-in-Source.   No wonder, for it
would release millions of badly needed dollars for bookbuying.

Left-Over Topics

       We have avoided discussing book-form catalogs for
local use, though we have recommended them in other connections.   We do not consider the subject pertinent here.
Book-form or printed catalogs are highly expensive.   Every
item in a book-form catalog has first to be prepared in careful individual entry form, usually exactly or approximately
the detailed copy as it appears on a standard catalog card.
Many printed catalogs are prepared by overlapping columns
of catalog cards or entry slips and photo-reproducing them.
Here again, it is the cataloging decisions which form the
basis for this special format, and the real or imagined virtues of the format have little connection with the original
cataloging procedure.

       We have avoided further discussion of centralized pro-
cessing because appreciable savings are not as yet evident;
the temptations are constant to get into mechanized procedures
which have not as yet proved economical; the delays are uni-

versally deplorable and increasingly criticized by the local library participants and their users. Whereas if Cataloging-in-
Source were in effect, everything could be handled locally,
much more economically and within a few days after the books
arrive, and the librarians of America could have a feeling of
accomplishment.

Also, we have to pass over the increasing problems
of processing audio-visual materials (see articles in Library
Journal, November 15, 1968, p. 4345-53), which are common
now to most school libraries, where personnel is so short,
and so few school librarians have any time left to help the
students. We are aware also that "Indexing-in-Source" of
periodical articles is being advocated. But with printed analytic monthly indexes, such as the various Wilson indexes,
it is hard to see what would be gained even at great cost,
though similar indexes for numerous other subject fields are
not yet available but should be. We badly lack a series of
similarly prompt analytic indexes of the detailed contents of
most government documents, in a dozen major subject fields,
including economics and current political and social problems,
supplementing the invaluable Public Affairs Information Service. Electronic retrieval cannot produce this analysis and
distribute it into the hands of people who will use it nearly
as cheaply nor as promptly as in monthly or weekly printed
cumulated form. The Great Illusion of electronic retrieval
and information specialists ignores the fact that every item
of electronic input and storage has first to be put in careful
and intelligent typed form by a subject-competent analyst or
indexer. Most information science non-librarians also overlook the fact that printed indexing can be just as intensively
analytic and descriptive as anything fed into a computer, and
the user of printed analytic indexes has a chance to study the
entry in relation to other entries which can easily be seen on
the pages of printed indexes, but may not be delivered to any
computer, and quickly evaporate. Such entries can then be
put into print for inexpensive use everywhere within a few
days. The whole New York Times is carefully written, assembled, and printed inside of every 24 hours.

                                NOTES

1.   Wheeler, Joseph & Herbert Goldhor.   Practical Admin-
          istration of Public Libraries.   Harper, 1962, p. 42.

2.   Ibid., p. 332.

3. Leonard, Lawrence E. Cooperative and Centralized
   Cataloging and Processing: A Bibliography, 1850-
   1967. (Occasional Papers, No. 93). Univ. of
   Illinois Library School, 1968.

4. Hendricks, Donald J. Comparative Costs of Book Processing in a Processing Center and in Five Individual Libraries. Illinois State Library, 1968.

5. Letter from Andrew Geddes, November 4, 1968.

6. Letter from J. W. Hurkett, November 13, 1968.

7. Leonard, Lawrence E. & others. Centralized Book
   Processing. Scarecrow, 1969.

8. The Cataloging-in-Source Experiment: a Report to the
   Librarian of Congress by the Director of the Processing Department. Library of Congress, 1960.

9. Osborn, Andrew D. Cataloging-in-Source: an Opportunity for Cooperation Between the Four Major
   Book Arts. American Library Assn., 1958.

10. Westby, Barbara. "Commercial Processing Firms: a
    Directory," Library Resources & Technical Ser-
    vices, Spring 1969, p. 209-86.

THE MANAGEMENT OF LIBRARIES
AND THEIR RESOURCES

BUSINESS METHODS IN LIBRARY MANAGEMENT*

F. M. Crunden

It is not many years since the popular mind pictured
the librarian as an elderly man of severe and scholarly aspect, with scanty gray hair, bent form, and head thrust forward from the habit of peering through his spectacles along
rows of books in search of some coveted volume. He was
supposed always to have led a studious and ascetic life, to
have had his boyhood and youth in a previous state of existence, and, since becoming a librarian, to have lived wholly
in the world of books, without any knowledge, thought, or
care regarding the world of men and things. Nothing more
was expected of him than that he should be erudite and orderly, know where to find his books, and be ready to point
out sources of information wanted by his first cousin, the
professor, or by another class of individuals, who also stood
apart from the rest of mankind, and were regarded as gods
of Parnassus or as imps of Bohemia. Of late years authorship has become more common. Every one has a friend who
writes for publication in some form. Authors are, perhaps,
less exalted but more respectable than formerly. The professor has long since been recognized as sometimes young
and athletic and jovial; and for the last ten years the librarian also has been abroad, and is now becoming pretty well
known. He is found to be generally young in years and always young in spirit. When librarians first came together,
each, I believe, was surprised to see how young the others
were. In '79, when I attended my first convention at Boston,
I expected to find myself among a body of patriarchs. Dr.
Poole, I thought, must be a bent and decrepit old man; and

---

*Reprinted from Library Journal 12:335-338 (1887).

Mr. Dewey, though I had only lately heard of him, I had pictured as a little, withered, bespectacled old Dryasdust, who
had given his life to the development of his decimal system,
and was warning young men against the dangers of diffusive-
ness. Subsequent observation has shown me that librarians
not only have had a youth, but that they find in these conventions the means of continually renewing it. There were two
or three who impressed me in '79 as perhaps a little old,
who last year were completely rejuvenated.

     The librarian, then, of the present day is not like his
predecessor of a generation ago; and other and different duties
are imposed upon him, and other offices expected from him.
There still, however, remains considerable misconception ro-
garding his proper functions. When I entered the profession
I received numerous congratulations on the great opportunity
afforded me for gratifying my taste for reading. Most of my
friends, one after another, have learned that my duties are
numerous and varied, and that my reading for personal improvement or pleasure must be done in the hours common to
all for rest and recreation. Still in the popular conception
the librarian combines business and pleasure by spending a
great part, if not the greater part, of his time in reading
books. Very few laymen, even among the better-informed,
realize how closely the conduct of a library resembles the
management of a business; and even among professionals there
may be occasion for emphasizing the value of a more thorough
adoption of business methods by librarians and by library directors.

     The primary lessons of a library apprentice are the
same as those of a boy who enters a business house. He
must learn neatness, order, accuracy, punctuality, and despatch. And with all these, if he is to succeed in the issue
department, which to the public represents the library, he
must cultivate politeness and equability of temper. He must
treat every applicant as a salesman does a customer. He
must not let him go away without the article he wants if it
is in stock; and if it is not he should show his concern by promising to give notice of the deficiency, and supply it later if
possible. As the youth goes up the ladder of promotion,
all these talents and acquirements find a wider field for exercise; and, as subordinates look to him for direction, other
faculties are brought into play, and other qualities are required. One of these is a liking, an enthusiasm, for library
work and a thorough belief in the particular institution served.
A librarian or an assistant in a position of any authority who

does not "swear by" his library cannot do justice to his work;
and on business principles his services had better be dispensed with. The head of a St. Louis jobbing firm told me
not long since that he would keep no one in his employ who
did not think Blank, Dash & Co. the greatest hat and cap
house in the West. Any salesman known to hold different
views would be instantly discharged.

    The application of business principles also demands a
certain degree of loyalty on the part of subordinates towards
the chief officer, as well as to the institution. Disaffection
is contagious; a house divided against itself cannot stand; and
a board of directors is not acting in accordance with approved
business methods if it does not speedily secure harmony of
action by removing the disturbing element. In one of the
large manufacturing establishments of St. Louis the rule is
that any man who cannot get along with the foreman of the
shops is at once dismissed. There is no investigation, no
hearing of complaints. The company look to the foreman for
results, and recognize that responsibility must be accompanied
by corresponding authority; and, as long as their superintendent satisfies them, the men must suit him.

    A chief librarian is in a position analogous to that
occupied by the head of a commercial house. He must know
his wares, i.e., his books; he must know his customers, the
community; he must study their wants; and, like a merchant
of the highest type, he will endeavor to develop in them a
taste for better articles. Like a merchant also, he must
advertise his business. He must let the people know what
the library offers to them, whether gratis or for a subscription fee. All the more is this necessary in the latter case.

    To be more exact in my comparison, the duties of a
chief executive of a library differ in no essential from those
of a manager of a stock company carrying on a commercial
enterprise. In both cases there is a board of directors to
dictate the general policy, which the manager is to carry out.
In both cases the details are left to him; and, if he occupies
a proper position in the esteem and confidence of the directors, they rely on him largely for suggestions as to measures for furthering the objects in view. If he cannot be so
relied on, he is not fit for the place, and another man should
be appointed.

    It seems hardly necessary to call attention to the li-
brarian's function as purchasing agent, in which his judgment,

or the lack of it, is a direct gain or loss, greater or less
according to circumstances.

The librarian, like the business superintendent, is expected to organize his subordinates so as to secure the most
efficient service at the least outlay for salaries.   To this
end the largest powers should be given him in the appointment
and removal of assistants, especially those upon whom he
must most immediately depend.   Let him have assistants of
his own choosing, and then hold him to a strict accountability for results.   If from personal favoritism or bad judgment he selects lazy or incompetent people, let him suffer
the consequences.   If he possesses the requisite discernment
and powers of observation, the innate selfishness of human
nature may be relied on for the rest.   The success of the
library is his success; and he may be trusted not to jeop-
ardize it by surrounding himself with incompetent friends.
The business man who does this ends in bankruptcy; and so
must the librarian--bankruptcy of position, reputation, and
self respect.

In keeping his institution before the public, the librarian may profit by the methods of the business man.   In the
case of a public library, he will generally find the local press
willing to render very valuable assistance by publishing news
concerning the library: such as noteworthy gifts or purchases,
reports of directors' meetings, abstracts of annual reports,
and occasionally an appeal for aid or an explanation of some
feature of the library which may be of public interest.   Mercantile and other class libraries, though not on an equal footing with public libraries in this respect, are still in a measure public institutions, and may therefore expect a share of
the notice which a liberal press accords to all things that are
for the general good.

How much the press of St. Louis has contributed to
the building up of the Public Library there, it would be difficult to estimate.   Its willingness to assist in such work is
attested by four large scrapbooks filled with clippings relating
to the library, which furnish in outline a sketch of the institution from its organization to the present day.   It goes without saying that no public enterprise can succeed without the
help of the press; and I think the converse is true, that no
paper can achieve great success which ignores public interests.

Library affairs doubtless do not interest as many people as a base-ball match or a notable burglary or divorce suit;

but it can hardly be that, among the mass of readers of a
great daily, there are not a respectable number who would
rather hear something about the new books added to the libraries than to learn that a John Smith, of Wayback Corners,
Tex., was killed in a drunken brawl, or that a William Wilson, of Skrigglesville, Me., had his thumb cut off by a cir-
cular saw, or any of the thousand and one petty incidents
that make up the regular columns of Crimes and Casualties.

As an illustration of immediate results from a press
notice: Some years ago one of our papers published a communication from me asking citizens to give to the library old
directories and other books of no further use to them, especially anything relating to St. Louis. Within a week or
two sixty or seventy-five volumes and a number of pamphlets
were received. How many subsequent gifts this brought, I
cannot tell; but nearly two years afterwards sixty-eight volumes and twenty-four pamphlets, the greater part popular
novels and juveniles, in excellent condition, were received,
accompanied by a note stating that the donor had sent them in
response to my request, which she had happened to see in an
old paper.

But over and above all this, the librarian will find
his advantage in the business man's use of printer's ink.
Four or five years ago I distributed through the schools and
throughout the central portions of the city 75,000 circulars.
During the next six months more than three times as many
new members were added as in the previous year. To these
circulars the increase was largely due. Last December and
January the board adopted my suggestion to insert regular
advertisements in the daily papers. An expenditure of $100
brought an addition of at least $200 from new subscribers.
Some of these probably had lived in the city for years and
had never before heard of this library of 65,000 volumes;
and at this day I dare say there are thousands of old citizens
who are in a similar benighted condition, despite all our efforts for their enlightenment. Others had a vague idea that
there was such a place; but it would not have occurred to
them to become members if they had not seen the suggestion
in the newspaper.

An eminently legitimate and proper mode of advertising is the distribution of a large edition of the annual report;
but methods must vary with circumstances, and from time to
time new ones must be devised.

I have found a personal canvass in the schools productive of immediate results.   I take a book or two with me,
or sometimes send a package of ten or twelve books.   I di-
late upon the benefit and the pleasure of reading, explain at
how little cost these may be obtained through a membership
in the library, putting it at the price per week, exhibit the
books with appropriate comments, and end by reading an
entertaining extract from one of them.   In short, I play to
the best of my ability the role of a commercial drummer.

I have said the librarian is expected to do so and so.
Expected by whom? Well, to some extent and in some particulars by the public, whom he has in the last few years taught to
look for what previous generations never thought of.   But the
highest and heaviest demands are those of conscience and professional pride.   The public is vastly more exacting than it used
to be; but the true librarian keeps always in advance of his
community, and constantly educates it to make greater demands upon him.   The body of the profession fixes a high
and ever advancing standard, which each individual must
strive to reach, or allow himself to be shelved among specimens of the antique.

The modern librarian, then, must be, as of old, a
scholar and a gentleman; but, more than that, he must be a
good business man.   And with all this, unless he have the
industry and endurance of a Napoleon and the patience of a
Job, he shall sometimes fail to satisfy his constituents and
at all times fall short of his own ideal.

EFFICIENCY CRITERIA FOR THE
OPERATION OF LARGE LIBRARIES*

Richard L. Meier

It is rather surprising that behavioral scientists have
not discovered libraries much sooner in their search for institutional environments suited for the testing of theoretical
hypotheses. Librarians and their assistants respect research
and scholarship and are inclined to go far beyond the call of
duty in helping the investigator, even when they are skeptical
(rightfully, in most instances) of the usefulness of such research for the improvement of their own organizations. Data
and related information are necessarily treated with greater
precision and discipline in libraries than in factories and
most bureaucratic offices; therefore, significant results can
often be obtained with smaller samples and in shorter periods
of observation. People working in libraries do not feel they
should curtail disclosures about basic processes. Elsewhere
professional employees are obligated to preserve trade secrets from competitors or to suppress facts which might be
considered scandalous by legislative committees. At least as
important to an investigator is the fact that one or more libraries almost always lie close at hand--there could hardly
be any more convenient institution.

Perhaps the only reason libraries have been neglected
until now as the setting for social studies is that the dramatic
changes in society seldom take place there. Librarians do
not wield power, nor do they get involved in the long, vio-
lent controversies that can only be settled by research. However, book collections are readily admitted to have an im-

*Reprinted by permission of the University of Chicago Press
from Library Quarterly 31:215-234 (July 1961). Copyright
1961 by the University of Chicago Press.

portant influence on social, cultural, and political affairs,
even though that influence is exerted in an exceedingly indirect fashion. Thus the library cannot be dispensed with as a
trivial institution; most people would attribute greater influence to it than to county governments, garden clubs, lodges,
or consumer co-operatives, for example, all of which have
been subjected to study. Library staffs may expect to see
more sociologists, administrative scientists, economists, and
industrial engineers who, in attempting to understand the fundamental relationships in organized human activity, wish to
collect data on the operation of libraries as it is related to
various underlying influences for order and for change.

        This inquiry, for example, sought a contemporary in-
stitution that was representative in many respects of the patterns of communication in the metropolitan environment of
the future. It had already been recognized that the processes
of automation and ordinary instrumentation tended to save
time, energy, and scarce materials, but they require substantial increases in the transfer of messages, reports, statistics, etc. [1] Thus the investigation required an environment that was handling messages of varying degrees of complexity at a more rapid rate than presently exists in our cities and which was also subject to an increasing rate of communications. The latter requirement is invoked because urban centers are becoming increasingly communications-ori-
ented.

        The broad aims of the study can be described only in
a most abbreviated form. I was participating in a multi-
disciplinary attack on the identification and measurement of
the stresses induced by too much communication. We wished
to discover whether there were any special indicators of
stress within a social organization that were triggered off by
increasing rates of interaction with outside agencies and individuals. It was hypothesized that a limit existed to the
rate of incoming messages, or requests for action, that an
organization like a library could handle and that efficient
operating procedures change markedly when the capacity for
handling messages is approached. [2]

        A library for research and higher education cannot be
successfully understood if it is considered as an isolated unit.
On the one hand, it must be treated as one among many similar elements in a bibliographic system that serves a whole
society--perhaps we cannot stop short of including the whole
world--while, on the other hand, such a library must be re-

garded as part of the apparatus and paraphernalia that is required for the functioning of a university. The notion of
judging the whole performance of a library over time is only
tenable in terms of the specialized functions assigned to it
within these overarching institutional systems. Even then we
cannot get very far unless we are given, or have discovered
from explorations in the field, the legitimate demands which
may be generated by the clientele of a library.   Only then
is it possible to sketch out a "model"--a simplified, abstract-
ed prototype--of the library as a social institution.

Behavioral scientists have in the past been concerned
largely with interactions between members of a social organization.   March and Simon[3] have recently summed up much
of the thinking and analysis of the past two decades that has
been pioneered by Gouldner, Selznick, Merton, and Simon
himself.   Save for the arguments relating organizational history and long range planning, [4] their work, it appears, provides a useful background for assessing the normal behavior
of organizations.   In this article, however, I shall be concerned with the somewhat more restricted questions that are
concerned with the performance of a whole library over time
--as judged by its professional staff and regular employees,
by the users of its services, and by the superordinate social
institutions, in this case a university, a state, and society
as a whole.   The significance of the findings of the study for
the design of library facilities, the assembly of special collections, and the general policies for handling information at
high rates will be described elsewhere.

Optimizing for Libraries

The raison d'être for a library is clearly public ser-
vice--the capacity to supply a publication when it is requested
--although once the primary service has been established
many subsidiary information-gathering functions are accreted
by libraries.   A modern library operates as a free public
utility, presenting its users with only minor service charges
and excises.   A university is also a public utility whose operations are subsidized by the public to a somewhat lesser extent.   Quite a few other public utilities are provided on a
free or nearly free basis--fresh water supply, police and
fire protection, use of streets and roads, playgrounds, for
examples.

How much of the public's resources should be spent

upon the provision of such free goods? This is one of the
paramount problems of government. The simplest criterion
is that each good should be supplied up to a point where felt
wants are satisfied. If, as is almost always the case, the
resources at the disposal of government are inadequate, the
scarcities need to be distributed in an equitable manner.
Recognizing the inability to meet all wants, administrators
look for changes in procedures which promise to get more
services per unit of expenditure. Since the budgets are allocated in terms of money and usually also in terms of
permanent positions made available, it is now possible to
quantify costs. But what of performance? Any innovation
that permits more welfare (the term is used here in its economic sense) to be obtained from a given quantity of resources would be welcomed, but its detection requires measurement of the value of the service.

The need for measurement encounters many paradoxes
and inconsistencies, yet substantial progress has been made.
In a public water service, for instance, the measurement of
the volumes of water supply to various places during given
periods of time is elementary. Even the purity of the water
can be specified, but the degree to which it is free from pollution evades full quantification. There are now convenient,
standard units for measuring quantity and composition, so
that consumption in each city can be meaningfully compared
with consumption in other cities. However, the quality of
the water and, therefore, part of its value to consumers re-
sists such intercity comparisons. Nevertheless, a basis for
equity still exists. Marked differences in the value of water
service due to differences in quality can be detected by creating indexes for bacteria count and biological oxygen demand,
for example, which are presumptive evidence for water quality. It is even possible to set up a flavor-testing panel for
judging changes still undetected by chemical instrumentation.
Thus, by expending increasing amounts of effort upon techniques of measurement and the collection of operating statistics, it is possible to say that one state of affairs is consistently better or worse than another. Sometimes it will be
admitted that the tools for measurement are still not sharp
enough to discriminate adequately, so that for practical purposes the respective instances being compared are equal.
At other times the potentials for improvement of the quality
of the water supply are judged not worth the cost of collecting the necessary information.

Similar criteria have been offered for technical librar-

ies by R. E. Maizell, director of documentation research for
the American Institute of Physics. [5] He starts by emphasizing
that interlibrary comparisons serve as a means of highlight-
ing the normal functions and sizes of libraries.   Once the
profiles of these characteristics are collected for a representative sample of such libraries, each person can judge for
himself whether a given institution is leading, lagging, or
holding close to par.   In this profile the quality of the holdings, as measured by the fraction of contemporary citations
quoted by the peer group specialties (e. g. , engineers, scientists, academics) that can be made available upon request,
is an exceedingly important component.   Another is the adequacy of the reference service, as judged by a score on the
number of questions answered or problems solved successfully.
Overlapping these to some degree is a "performance index"
which registers the fraction of titles actually delivered in a
reasonable amount of time in response to requests (90 per
cent is a good record for a medium-sized modern technical
library, somewhat less for larger libraries).   Finally, a
series of rather qualitative features is included which de-
scribes the degree to which library personnel participates in
the larger organization it serves and the degree to which library materials and services have become an intrinsic part
of day-to-day operations of the larger organization.

Any single measure of library performance must be
influenced by all these factors.   Moreover, the respective
factors should be weighted according to their significance for
public welfare, as far as it can be agreed upon by responsible observers.   Once an index of performance has been obtained, we must still consider carefully whether it is better
to maximize performance by itself for a given period of time,
the performance obtained for a given share of the budget, the
performance of a given unit of physical equipment, or some
other factor.

Finding an Appropriate Unit

So far, we have commented upon the usefulness of an
index of library performance and the variety of functions it
would have to represent and summarize.   The act of measurement itself, the identification of small bits of performance in
such a way that they add up to a total, imposes a series of
requirements.   From experience we know that the best unit
is one that (1) is sharply and unambiguously defined, (2) permits comparison between all institutions that claim to provide

the same service, (3) can be counted by techniques that are easily learned and readily agreed upon, and (4) is no larger than the smallest typical transaction.

Now let us consider the normal state of affairs in a library. Several different kinds of routine counts--measurements of service provided--are undertaken. Circulation is the most important of these, mainly because it is most susceptible to audit. A careful standardization of the reporting of circulation has been worked out by the ALA, so that any outsider making an independent check would arrive at totals within a small per cent of the reported figures, and often even closer. The accuracy will be about the same as encountered in the census enumerations. The discrepancies are due to different interpretations of the marginal instances. Acquisitions are also subject to close corroboration because a discrete step is involved in the addition of a volume to the collection. The counting of holdings is less standardized. The inventory of a library, expressed as a number, is subject to sharp revaluations, just as is the assessment of capital worth in other organizations. The differences obtained when comparing library to library are as great as those obtained between firms in business and independent agencies in government. Many libraries also attempt to count reference questions answered, and a few estimate the table use of library materials by the public. These two kinds of statistics can be influenced heavily by the behavior of the librarians and the design of the interior of the library. Much more often than not, such statistics tend to be understatements, because librarians are apt to lose count at the busiest moments, and the figures collected are, therefore, less than helpful to the administrator. He sees the daily totals leveling off just at the time that the librarians seem to need help.

College and Research Libraries has faithfully reported each year the library budget, the number of employees (in full-time equivalents), the book stock, acquisitions, and circulation in a large number of academic libraries. These tables are not unlike the abstracts of annual reports of other public utilities, including those that appear in the business sections of newspapers. In business the speculators know that these figures hide some striking differences in meaning, and the stock quotations reflect this judgment. Experienced librarians know that statistics can mislead, so they tend to attribute high status to those institutions that work hard and systematically to maintain quality of service, regardless of what the statistics seem to say.

The recognized devices of accounting, as applied to
utilities, do not yield satisfactory measures of performance
for libraries. Home circulation and table use of library materials may be coproducts, but thus far no method has been
suggested for equating the two kinds of service. To make
the matter more complex, should reference service be labeled
a by-product or merely a "sales expenditure"? The inconsistencies in argument that appear are so severe that attempts
seem useless. The statistics are not measurements of the
output of service but serve mainly as indicators of relative
change in demand over time and between institutions. Deviations in trend may be traced to reorganizations within the
library as often as to changes in the patronage.

In search of a measure of output we are forced to follow the suggestion of Adler[6] and look somewhat deeper for
the appropriate unit. It should be the smallest meaningful
item that can be conveniently identified and counted. For
those who think in analogies, it should play the role of mor-
phemes in linguistics, molecules in chemistry, and cells in
microbiology.

A unit that fits all the criteria that have been introduced so far for measuring the performance of libraries is
the item-use day. An "item" refers to a book, newspaper,
pamphlet, map, recording, or other documentary artifact that
could be charged out to the user as an identifiable unit.
"Use" implies whatever a person being served would fairly
define as such upon being interviewed and asked such a question as "How many books did you use yesterday?" The "day"
is defined in a common-sense way as the interval between
rising and retiring. Thus, the unit is "operational" in the
sense that simple surveys of the same situation should yield
concrete figures that can be reproduced. The ambiguities encountered in deciding whether a behavior does or does not
constitute a given number of units have been purposely minimized.

There are some added advantages to this choice for a
unit. Both circulation and table-use aggregates can, with the
aid of periodic surveys, be reduced to item-use days. It
will be argued later that we may expect fairly constant ratios
between routine, but audited, internal counts and the number
of item-use days of service provided to the public. Under
these conditions we see the role of the reference librarian
as an expediter who visibly increases item-use days with little or no lag. Book selection and acquisition are indicators

of a category of investment aimed at maintaining the output
of item-use days of service over the long run. Most of the
unrecorded housekeeping efforts also result in the maintenance
or improvement of item-use days of output; even such labors
of love as filling gaps in collections have this result because
complete sets attract the peripatetic scholars whose library
use is rather extensive when they are at work.

It is possible to become still more detailed in judging
the value of the use of library materials by its public. For
example, an estimate can be made of the amount of time
spent on library materials as compared to other time spent
receiving "to whom it may concern" types of publications.
However, the amount of time spent reading turns out to be a
relatively difficult and expensive accounting problem, since
people do not remember to clock themselves when engaged
in a sequence of tasks. [7] Interestingly, there is considerable
discordance between one's own assessment of the manner in
which one's time is expended and descriptions obtained from
external, presumably impartial, observers. In a quite different direction we may estimate the potential information imparted, [8] but such a technique is still far too gross for measuring the performance of libraries. Measures of time expended and information imparted enable us to make only the
broadest comparisons with behavior in other aspects of life.
These comparisons are nevertheless valuable because they
make it possible to decide on relatively rational grounds
whether extra resources, should they become available to the
society, ought to be assigned to libraries or allocated to
some other activity. As we shall see, modern libraries offer
some very productive possibilities for public investment.

Methods and Procedures

The item-use day is a convenient unit in part because
days have very definite boundaries in human experience. In
addition, the number of items from a library used in the
course of a day seldom exceeds the "magic number of seven"
--the normal span of items that are identified as individuals
rather than as a group or class. Thus a diary employing
many of the little mnemonic devices of the kind employed in
consumer surveys for inducing complete recall should get
good results. If diaries are used, the public must be well
delimited and its internal structure understood, so that the
universe can be sampled. A university population fits this
category very nicely because it possesses its own library

system.   Some problems are raised, however, by the academic calendar, which creates abnormal seasonal peaks in library use.   Thus a proper survey needs to be undertaken at representative dates throughout the year.

To rule out seasonal differences and keep sampling error low, several thousand such diaries would represent a thorough survey.   At an average cost of several dollars apiece, plus an equivalent amount for analyzing the results, this kind of survey promises to be too expensive except when crucial decisions are anticipated.

A substitute procedure, considerably cheaper but also more risky, is to design questionnaires to be sent or distributed to a representative sample of the population.   In order to interpret the results, it is necessary to get a high rate of return and to establish the kinds of bias to be found in that part of the sample which did not return questionnaires.

The crucial question underlying the item-use day statistic can be framed as follows:

How many books, journals, pamphlets, newspapers, reference works, records, etc., from the library, did you use yesterday?

In order to interpret the numbers given by the respondents, some additional questions must be asked.   They might include:

1.   What facilities in the library were used yesterday? (This question should be accompanied by a check list.)

2.   Length of time spent in library.   (Check one of four or five ranges of time.)

3.   Number of books charged out of library yesterday.

4.   Your own status in the university community. (Accompanied by check list.)

5.   Suggestions for improving library service.

It might be thought that the third supplementary question, which deals explicitly with circulation, should yield aggregates for whole population which are equal to the recorded home circulation of the library.   This is not the case,

however, because neither students nor faculty are aware of
the specific meaning assigned by librarians to the term
"charged. " The existence of reserve collections either fully
or partly closed to home circulation introduces ambiguity,
because the procedures at the desk often closely resemble
those employed for charging books for home use. The faculty
often seems to be in doubt regarding the proper term to be
applied to the use that they make of the reference works kept
at the librarian's desk.

There is a strong tendency for new investigators of
social phenomena to formulate very explicit questions. They
do this without reference to the situation of the respondent
when he is making his reply. The result, particularly among
undergraduates, is that confusion ensues regarding what the
investigator really wants. The fraction of questionnaires not
answered then becomes alarmingly large. The questionnaire
may be cheap and convenient, but it is a blunt instrument at
best.

The call for suggestions for improving library service
(see last item above) may be built up somewhat by hinting between the lines in the introduction that a shake-up is being
planned and that suggestions at this time may do some good.
Then the students are more apt to be serious. This strategy
may easily boomerang, however, because the library staff,
who will no doubt see the questionnaire, are far more sensitive to its implications than are the students. The survey researcher who uses this device for improving his data, even
after explanations designed to alleviate the suspicions of the
staff, may still expect to incur some resentment because he
is undermining the public relations of the institution. These
reactions to investigations with potentials for triggering change
are quite generally applicable to all human organizations and
so do not reflect upon libraries in any way.

The techniques, whether they employ diaries, questionnaires, or interviews, are being developed and standardized
for the general public by market-research firms. The standard "exposure, " or reading day, of the Alfred Politz Media
Studies, for example, is an exact equivalent of the item-use
day. 9 It is possible to standardize the more economical techniques useful to libraries against the expensive thoroughgoing
analyses undertaken in the market-research field.

One of the advantages that a university library has over
the usual subjects of market research is that most of the item-

use days are consumed in public where individual reports can
be checked against observations and internal operating statistics. Also, the patterns of use of various categories of books
read outside the library are likely to be similar throughout
the country--it should be a general property of the culture.
Therefore, only one or two studies of use in home, office,
and laboratory may be sufficient, unless they reveal marked
deviations from the national norms. Within the library the
organization of the collection and the services that are provided could determine the number of item-use days per person entering its portals. The various checks available make
it likely that the number of item-use days can be measured
with a probable error of less than 10 per cent.

Discussion of Findings

        Two separate small-scale investigations were under-
taken in a large library for research and higher education in
the Middle West. The first was concerned with what was
felt to be the high-valued use by teaching and research faculty
and their assistants, while the second focused upon a new
facility designed for students.

Faculty Questionnaire

        A questionnaire (referred to hereinafter as "Q") was
sent to a sample obtained from the university directory for
1957-58. Of the estimated 7,500 entries (many of them institutional), about 4,000 qualify as "staff" for library services, and, of these, 3,420 qualified as being residents on
the campus but not members of the library staff itself. Of
these, 1,800 held academic appointments, the remainder serving as teaching fellows, research associates, research assistants, resident physicians in the hospital, administrators,
and the like.

        In the population of 3,420 qualified recipients, 800
were sent Q's and of these 52 were returned marked "not at
address" while three others were returned with apologies for
inability to co-operate. Thus the true sample became 745.
The total number of useful Q's obtained from the staff after
one reminder was 453 (61 per cent). By various tests the
returns seemed quite representative of the population, with
medicine at 49 per cent being the most under-represented
sector.

A major portion of the Q was devoted to the estimation of the quantity of library materials that the staff used
over the preceding week. Based upon the rate of return, we
judged that perhaps half of the respondents used the Q as a
diary, postponing its return for a week, while the others used
their memory. Altogether, 2,066 item-use days were reported, 44 per cent from books, 36 per cent journals, 10 per
cent from abstracts, indexes, and bibliographical references,
5 1/2 per cent encyclopedias, handbooks, etc., and 5 1/2
per cent from government publications. When the sample was
inflated so as to cover the whole population and compared
with one week's circulation from the library as a whole at the
time the Q was being answered, an estimated 13. 0 item-use
days were obtained for each circulation unit recorded by the
library. There is some reason for believing that faculty tend
to understate their use of library materials (they are likely
to forget uses associated with some hobby or sideline), but
at the same time some of the respondents may think of themselves as students, rather than as teaching assistants or instructors, and mark their charge slips accordingly. These
influences appear to be of the same magnitude and pull in opposite directions, so we may assume 13 item-use days are
associated with each unit of circulation to the staff. About
25-30 per cent of this use occurs at home, in the office, or
in the laboratory, and the remainder within the library facilities themselves. This means that each volume that circulated to a staff member, who may retain the book as long as
a full term, is only used on the average of three to four different days. [10]

Student Questionnaire

A subsequent study of the student use of library materials was designed to take advantage of the extensive operating statistics collected in a building expressly designed for
students. This facility was equipped with a set of turnstiles
so that a crucial new datum called attendance, meaning the
number of entries to the building by potential users, was
made available. The sampling of the student population could
be based upon these turnstile counts. Somewhat simpler questionnaires than those used for the faculty were prepared and
pretested. Altogether, 790 Q's were distributed and 570 (78
per cent) were returned.

Who did not return such a Q? Rather detailed observations upon student behavior in this library building had
been undertaken prior to the development of a questionnaire.

The significance of these studies for the design of student libraries will be reported on at a later date, but one fact illuminates a bias in the sample. Previous observation showed that 28 per cent of the students remained in the building for less than 15 minutes, while only 11 per cent of the Q's reported visits in this range. It is easy to understand that persons who had come in for no other reason than to return a book or look for a friend would regard the two or three minutes required to fill out a questionnaire as something of a nuisance. No other bias could be detected.

How honest were the students? Only about one per cent of the returned Q's showed any signs of non-seriousness. The reliability of student replies was based upon comparison of their statement on the Q regarding the number of personal books and notebooks brought into the building and used as against an objective count by an observer at the exit control station. Students reported 1.8 such items were used, while counts at exit control points revealed 2.0-2.2 were carried with them, depending upon what was defined as books and notebooks.

A comparison of the number of "volumes, bound journals, pamphlets, etc., charged out of the library" with the counts made by librarians showed some marked differences. It was quickly discovered that almost all students considered closed reserve books to be "charged out." When these misunderstandings were taken into account, the student reports were still 13 per cent too high. The difference may be due to sampling error, but the circumstances required for answering the questionnaire (it needed to be done before coming up to the charging desk) suggest that some students recorded intentions on this score rather than the actual number of items charged out.

A real surprise was obtained when trying to compare student claims for use of library materials while in the building as compared to the internal statistics. Over-all usage reported by students was 84 per cent more than could be obtained by the most complete objective counts that could be undertaken by the library. The reasons for the discrepancy were revealed through subsequent interviews and closer observation. It was discovered that whenever books were known to be scarce the student's best strategy was to look for another member of the class. The odds were rather good that this person would have the book or would be waiting for someone else to finish with the copy. Thus, as students became ac-

quainted with the book shortages, a series of private arrangements were created which permitted the book to pass through
the hands of as many as half a dozen persons before it was
reshelved by the student helpers on the library staff who were
assigned to that job and were responsible for counting the
number reshelved.   The books on closed reserve were even
more likely to receive such treatment.   In a few instances,
couples were seriously engaged in reading the same book
simultaneously.   Librarians sometimes discouraged the se-
quential unrecorded transfers, but they were not in a position
to bring about any important change in the behavior of the students.   Depending upon interpretation, the students reported
1.8-2.3 item-use days for each book reshelved in the library.

On the "typical day in April" that our Q's were distributed, there were, according to our best estimate, 0.98
item-use days per student entry into the building.   Of this,
0.04 item-use days were registered in the use of materials
at the reference tables, 0.04 in the use of musical recordings, 0.02 in the reading of newspapers, with remainder
devoted to reading books at the tables taken from open shelves
(or closed reserve) or occasional browsing at the shelves.
A marked cycle has been noted in student use of books:
early in the semester the reading is exploratory, is then nar-
rowed to "required reading" for the midterm examinations,
then begins to expand again to meet the needs of term papers,
the peak being reached in the third week of May or the second week in January.   Then students revert to textbooks and
lecture notes in studying for final examinations.   Therefore,
we may expect the number of item-use days per unit of attendance to start at a moderate level, rise to a plateau, then
to a peak around 1.3 item-use days, and then fall to as low
as 0.3-0.5.   Thus attendance does not provide a stable foundation for an index of student book use, while circulation
seems to be strongly accelerated when seating capacity is
approached.

A Composite Index

For this building (which is shared by the engineering,
education, and transportation collections) a composite index
should reasonably approximate total item-use days.   This index is made up of the sum of the following:

a)   circulation of books two weeks or longer has a weight
     of 3;
b)   circulation of one-week books has a weight of 2;

c)   circulation of overnight books has a weight of 1;
d)   changes of closed-reserve books have a weight of 3;
e)   reshelving has a weight of 2;
f)   all musical recordings used have a weight of 2;
g)   all reference use has a weight of 1; and
h)   all errors discovered upon shelf reading have a weight
     of 1 (attributed to misshelving by students).

Such an estimate, compiled month by month, is presented in Figure 1. It probably represents an understatement
of the total number of item-use days that would be revealed
by an exhaustive study, but the ratio between the index and
the actual use of the library over the academic year should
be quite constant. Any major change in the organization of
the library or in acquisitions policy is likely to modify these
weights, so that a partial resurvey would be called for after
the new patterns of use had become stabilized.

Librarians, like other professionals, are always faced
with judgments that are essentially economic in character but
rarely are provided with the kinds of data that enable a com-
putation of an optimum. For example, is it better to open
the library from 8:00 to 9:00 A. M. rather than 10:00-12:00
P. M. ? Or is it still better to spend this sum on extra copies

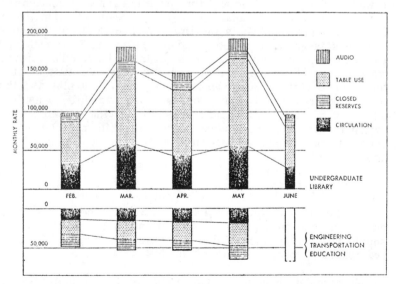

Fig. 1. --Index reflecting item-use days of library service
during a spring semester

of popular titles? An experienced librarian using internal
data, and perhaps instituting a private survey, can estimate
the probable outcomes from each change in policy. It could
be put in the form of extra attendance, extra circulation, or
extra table use, for example. The cost side could always be
converted into dollars (or man-hours in each general category,
if that were the important issue), but the extra service obtained from each alternative could not be compared satisfactorily. If an index similar to the above has been prepared,
however, it is possible to compute the expected outcomes of
seemingly extraneous issues in the same terms. A dollar
may yield 30 units of service in one direction, according to
the index, as against 10 in another. After a quick check has
confirmed that the bases for the original estimations were
reasonable and that questions regarding the status of the institution as a whole were not at stake, the issue could then
be settled rather quickly in the public interest.

University libraries also serve special publics that
have less interest in the contents of books. The rare-book
room more often than not functions as a museum, and other
collections may have an archival role. The telephone on the
reference desk may keep the secretaries in the whole institution from making the kind of errors in reports and correspondence that would diminish the institution's prestige and
respect in the eyes of those coming in contact with it. Such
services are hardly reflected in the index, because, if they
should be strongly expanded or reduced, insignificant changes
would be produced in the over-all figure. The extra services
are rarely large enough consumers of resources (although in-
active holdings retained for their historical value do threaten
to reach serious levels of expense) to warrant separate indexes. The appropriate procedure is to separate these services in the cost accounting so that the marginal cost, at
least, is identified. Then the subsidy that is rendered to the
antiquarians, the historians, and the classicists may be explicitly compared with that given to the natural scientists for
their laboratories and museums. When administrators become worried about balancing these special services with general library services, the comparisons between one major
library and another can be illuminating, but what is revealed
more often than not is a series of unique bequests, funds,
and commitments to other institutions that frustrates any
further generalization.

The findings as reported above fall short of establishing the item-use day as the fundamental unit of performance

because that can only be accomplished by demonstrating that
it will fit the primary services supplied by the full range of
institutions designated as libraries; but the findings illustrate
the process by which relevant information can be obtained,
tied to operating data, and used in making decisions regarding the provision of services. Obviously, many more measurements are necessary. Since surveys of library services
are not uncommon, it is suggested that they do not stop short
of obtaining item-use days and, particularly, of some indication of the way in which such a measure of use is related to
home circulation.

Analysis of Costs and Benefits

When their contributions to the public welfare are being
appraised, the various public services and utilities can be
treated as enterprises. They use scarce capital, expensive
time (much of it regarded as labor), energy, and various
kinds of products, while they produce one or more "goods"
in return. These enterprises should create a "profit" for the
public by choosing to engage in activities which yield greater
over-all benefits than the costs incurred. They should achieve
a profit over the long run, even if that does not seem immediately feasible.

Indeed, we may go further and require than an additional unit of service provided by a public utility should use
no more of the scarce resources available to society than
are required by the other opportunities for serving the public. If the returns are deferred--so that they accrue at some
expected future date--they should be discounted to the date
that the resources are irreversibly committed by applying the
going interest rate in the society. The knowledge that people
wish to extract from a library almost always yields deferred
returns. Often years go by before the information acquired
can be put to productive use. The lag between the acquisition of knowledge and its utilization may result in loss due
to forgetting, obsolescence, or destruction of records. Such
risks, too, must be taken into account.

If all such conditions are met and the opportunities
for benefit are equitably distributed through the population,
we should have squeezed the most public welfare from a
limited supply of resources. In practice, however, we often
find that estimates and judgments must replace the collection
and analysis of actual data because the effort required for

assembling and processing the data is too great. Smaller
enterprises, such as libraries, repeatedly encounter the problem of excessive costs for acquiring relevant data; informed
estimates must be combined with whatever measures of scale
of operations are available. A survey of the literature on
the operation and management of libraries revealed an active
concern regarding what happened inside library facilities but
provided very few clues concerning the indirect costs of gaining access to the collections. Thus, the estimates that
seemed to be of greatest significance, and which had never
been obtained before, were those concerned with over-all
costs to the public per item-use day of service. In particular, it was worthwhile discovering how much time was necessarily expended by users upon relatively non-rewarding activities.

Measuring Staff-Time Cost

       A survey was made of the time the university staff
lost getting to materials in the largest single collection in
the university library, comprising more than a million volumes. The typical staff member must leave his office or
laboratory, proceed by foot (or walk to his car, drive to the
parking garage nearest the general library, and walk from
there), obtain the call number from the catalog, request the
book or else find it himself, charge it out, and return to
either his office or his car. By pacing out the distance from
representative points, an estimate could be made of the time
required starting from various buildings. Since the Q for the
staff reported the number of trips taken to the general library
by the staff members, each trip could be weighted with a
time estimate. It was found that six trips and 1.5 hours of
time cost were associated with the circulation of each book
to the staff (not including library staff). We may deduce that
many trips involve failures to find what was desired, but the
majority were for reference purposes and the reading of periodicals. Most trips, no doubt, had multiple purposes. Estimates showed that obtaining a book from a collection not associated with one's own department was just as time-consuming as obtaining a book from the general library but that in
the departmental collection the time costs were much reduced.
This is a sufficient explanation for the strong faculty pressure
favoring a branch library for each department, but in subsequent reports we will describe others that appear to be at
least as important.

       A monetary equivalent can be very easily attached to

such time loss. The average value of time for faculty members, including overhead and fringe benefits, is about $6.00
per hour. Thus, the 13 item-use days associated with one
unit of circulation must cost the university somewhere between
$5 and $10 before the staff member even gets a chance to
read. Since about a third of the operating costs in the library are allocated to circulation, each book circulated is
estimated to cost the library an extra $0.60-$0.80. This is
a reasonable approximation of the marginal cost that is needed for economic analysis.

There is another method of assessing the value of
time lost by staff members that yields even more spectacular
figures. Since roughly half of the time of faculty is devoted
to teaching and the other half to research, we may assume
that time used for gaining access to library materials reduces
the opportunity for both instruction and research. It now appears that the return to society on an investment in higher
education (all forms lumped together, including engineering,
fine arts, humanities, etc.) has been in the range of 10-20
per cent per year--this is somewhat higher than was obtained
in risk enterprises during the same period. [11] The returns
from research and development when calculated on the same
basis appear to be running 100-200 per cent per year, or ten
times the profitability of other enterprises. [12] Time lost from
research would seem to represent very considerable losses to
the economy. These opportunity costs may justifiably be assessed at $30-$50 for the 13 item-use days associated with
the circulation of one book, given the current estimates of the
productivity of higher education and research.

It will be noted that there is a large disparity between
the marginal costs of a unit of circulation inside the library
and various assessments of the marginal cost outside. Some
improvements in library operations involving a small increase
in expenditures might be expected to enhance the convenience
for the faculty and generate more instruction and research as
a result. They might constitute, in many instances, overlapping and duplicating services at points only a few hundred
yards apart. It appears that library services would have to
be developed a long way before the costs of such improvements would approach the probable benefits. Each such improvement, then, would result in a considerable profit for the
society at large.

The demand for books by the faculty is quite elastic.
This million-volume library was enabled to remodel and im-

prove the access of books shortly after the survey was completed. The faculty responded by increasing circulation by
8-9 per cent per capita the next year. Various pieces of indirect evidence point strongly to the conclusion that, for each
minute of time saved in getting to library materials, the
faculty was induced to spend two or three minutes acquiring
and reading more literature.

Student Time-Costs

The marginal costs in the student library were obtained through experiment. A random sample of titles used
by students was placed upon cards. Students were then hired
to find and charge out (or leave on table, according to the
relative frequencies reported in the library) a set of these
titles, being clocked at each stage. The time required to
find a book under typical conditions experienced by students
in this library was found to be only 7-8 minutes (standard
deviation was about 4 minutes).

The alternative average value of student time, when
working away from the university, is about $200 per hour.
Therefore, the time cost inside the library for obtaining the
title he wants is only about $0.25. As the building approaches
seating capacity, more books are in use and a larger fraction
of students are disappointed, raising time losses to the students by about 20-30 per cent per title obtained. These
losses are balanced by even greater gains in efficiency on the
part of the library organization (because the same staff and
equipment, assisted perhaps by a few extra hourly paid students, is producing more book use).

The evidence concerning the elasticity of demand for
books on the part of students is even stronger than for the
faculty. This special facility for students reduced the access
cost, as measured by loss of time, by perhaps half, and the
student response was to double circulation (the only comparable statistic available) within two years. For students the
average item-use days seems to imply the spending of 20-30
minutes with the item. [13]

How Much Service Is Optimal?

Optimal library service is almost as hard to define as
an optimal health or park service. It is most explicitly determined by a long list of statements about what is obviously

not optimal. The best lies somewhere in the region that has
not been already excluded. When an organization, such as a
library for research and higher education, is still a long way
from optimality the general direction to take is easier to
specify. The library that we studied was compared to others
at leading universities across the continent and found to be
typical of the better installations with respect to the completeness of the collection and service. Therefore, it seems likely that the steps that have been taken to improve service are
similar to those that have already been undertaken elsewhere
or which could be instituted in the near future.

The item-use day is a statistical unit designed to measure simultaneously the services to research and education
made by a multipurpose library. It even incorporates some
of the special service functions of such an institution, such
as the provision of recordings for language teaching and
music appreciation. An innovation in organization that brings
about more item-use days of service is certainly desirable
if this is done with a disproportionately small increase in
budget. This unit has only peripheral value, however, when
appraising the degree of success of various systems of documentation that expedite the flow of information between scholars.

It appears that each channel of communication (news-
letters, journals, abstracts, books, meetings, conferences,
etc.) may require a different basis for measuring the service
that is rendered. Every approach, including the one used
here, is reducible in theory to two common indexes of value:
(a) the amount of personal time allocated by the scholar to
the respective opportunities for communication, and (b) the
non-redundant information actually transmitted. Because optimization in documentation requires the prediction of future
needs quite a bit further in advance on the average than in
libraries, the risks are greater and the criteria may be expected to be more imperfect. Optimization procedures by
both documentation specialists and librarians are based upon
the belief that there exists a large unsatisfied demand for library services which can be filled if more is known about the
needs and habits of the public using the facilities.

A larger share of the pent-up demand for library services would be tapped if systematic approaches to reducing
total access cost were explored and applied. Thus, a new
criterion is suggested--the sum of the marginal cost of providing a unit of service and the marginal cost for the user

should be a minimum. Improvements in library service
should continue as long as total costs per item-use day decline. This is the kind of criterion that appeals to a broad-
minded cost accountant or budgeting officer. But for libraries
it will probably fall short of the optimum because much of
the gain from the use of literature in libraries is a contribution to education or research, both of which have much
longer run consequences than reading for pleasure or for participation in current affairs. The evidence is now very strong
that both education and research must become more important
activities in the United States in the future. If such is the
case, library development must precede the enlarged public
and private investments in education and research. The library costs should be, therefore, somewhat higher than in
the joint minimum suggested by the above criterion, if the
new expenditures under consideration contribute to improving
the organization and the quality of the collection.

The revolution now beginning in teaching methods will
have considerable impact upon library use. Educators find
that for most courses attentive reading of carefully prepared
works is a more effective educational procedure than lectures.
The undergraduate honors courses have already divorced themselves from adherence to textbooks. The regular courses are
following in their footsteps. The results, as judged by achievement, are superior when the books are available to the students as they need them. Even the laboratory sessions are
becoming much less dependent upon exercises and "cookbooks"
and more concerned with the proper design of experiments,
which in turn demands a greater knowledge of the scientific
literature. The most productive mixtures for higher education
clearly requires more book use, more organized discussion,
more guided exploration with experiments and reading, or other forms of synthesis, and more writing. It needs fewer lectures and less time spent waiting or looking for things.

Research, too, seems likely to make heavier demands
upon the large library. If research is actually as profitable
as the latest analyses suggest,[14] it may be necessary to erect
many more "specialized information services" that concentrate
upon the literature problems of specific research groups.[15]
Many of the most technical new contribution in documentation
are directed to facets of these special services. In those instances the item-use day may be too gross a unit. New and
smaller units may possibly be devised that are better adapted
to the specific goals of the research group. On the whole,
however, we see such special services depending upon a com-

prehensive collection as a backstop.   They would operate as
a corporate entity or "middle man" that generates item-use
days for the main library.

      We have to assume in these arguments that the pro-
fessional investigator, teacher, and student is the best judge
of the value of the use of his own time.   We must also assume that his reading habits will not greatly change as his
range of choice improves.   There is no evidence as yet that
these assumptions are improper, except in infrequent individual cases.   The assumptions imply that a relatively constant proportionality will be maintained between item-use days
and the human time expended in the use of recorded material.
An occasional corroboration of the assumption in the course
of assembling indexes of library performance would be wise.

      At this point we can take up the many objections that
may be raised against the employment of a purely economic
calculus.   Certain conceptions commonly held in the library
fraternity seem to be directly in conflict with the prescriptions for efficiency suggested here.   For example, the experienced librarian is convinced that some titles are more
significant than others irrespective of their immediate popularity.   Such books appear to be authoritative and may be
consulted a decade or two thereafter with some assurance
that the contents are still valid.   Librarians pay a great deal
of attention to these permanent values when building their collections.   Similarly, reference librarians realize that it is
rather easy to find something relevant to the questions that
are put to them, but it takes real skill to dig up the crucial
citation or fact.   In effect, it is felt that some item-use
days are more important than others and that a good librarian can forecast some of these.

      A related argument is made for the preferential sup-
port of the humanities.   Every library is in part an archive
that makes available the records of the present generation to
future generations.   It is important that this record be as
complete as possible, if the historians and analysts of literature, the arts, and of popular culture are to interpret the era
correctly.   In this case the argument is made in inverse,
namely, that one cannot know what item will be crucial, so
that the collection should contain many "long shots" in order
to improve the likelihood of a conclusive finding at a later
date.

      Now, let us consider carefully what is involved.   Li-

brarians long ago gave up keeping complete collections of all
printed records but have restricted themselves to serious
matter. Thus the repetitive elements in advertising and the
highly redundant materials are rejected, and in most instances
the ephemera unlikely to be consulted at any time in the future are eliminated. Only those materials are now selected
that seem to be worth the $10. 00-$30. 00 per item expense
for ordering, cataloging, and storing. The critical choice
seems to be between obtaining an extra copy of a popular
item and an obscure title that stands a good chance of not
being looked at during its 50-100-year lifetime. An extra
copy of a popular title is almost sure to provide some extra
item-use days shortly after it is received, but later it is
worse than useless because extra effort is needed to retire
it from the collection. On the other hand, the availability of
many scarce titles should over the long run generate circulation among the more obscure works and the better-known
titles. All other things being equal, the expected yield of
item-use days should be about the same either way in an active research center.

Similarly, when a reference librarian does manage to
serve the user in an unusually perspicacious fashion, he generates appreciation of the library. Such a user gains confidence in his ability, with assistance or otherwise, to obtain
what is needed from the literature. The good will that is
generated also contributes to increasing use of the facility
over the middle to long run. Thus, the item-use day volume,
or any seasonally adjusted index based upon it, seems to be
a sensitive measure of service rendered by a library organization, but current volume is not necessarily a reflection of
current service. 16

It would appear that, for a modern university environment, increased service is produced by boosting the total
item-use days to a level as high as feasible. When scholars
and students are no longer willing to allocate more of their
time to the use of library materials as accessibility or range
of opportunity is improved, the practical limit will have been
reached. For example, if the typical chemist referred to in
the Case Institute operations research study (n. 7) was induced to spend 20 hours a week in scientific communication
instead of 16. 5 (the amount of reading runs about half, writing a quarter, and talking a quarter) and felt that allocating
more time would be unrewarding, the saturation level would
have been reached. The libraries would have achieved, with
the typical chemist at least, the maximum possible public service.

Thus, for both research and higher education, the optimum allocation of governmental resources would seem to call for investments in books, facilities, specialized personnel, and organization as long as these additions promise to yield increased over-all use. This means that the library should become relatively more important in the university than at present and should at the same time become a far more complex and decentralized operation. It seems quite probable that the larger library will have to set up its own research and development staff and even a development planning group if optimum arrangements are to be approximated.

Summary

It is possible to conceive of a library, for research and higher education particularly, as a public utility. It has thus far resisted the kinds of measurements of efficiency that have been applied to other public utilities because a variety of services were provided, most of them free of charge, and because no standard measure of value could be attached to the respective services. Inability to assess library outputs seems to have led to an under-allocation of resources to libraries, but even if these misjudgments were rectified, library staffs would find it impossible to determine what kinds of expansion would yield the greatest public welfare.

The item-use day is proposed as catch-all unit for measuring the service provided. It has a convenient size for statistical aggregation. The term is completely operational, since it is based upon distinctions made by professional librarians and library users. The "item," for example, is defined as an entry in the catalog or inventory, so situated that the effort in obtaining access to it is minimized. "Use" is defined by the population of users when interviewed about what they did with the item when it came into their hands. "Day" provides us with a time interval that is most free of ambiguity when asking questions. Item-use days of service obtained from a library may be estimated by means of interview, questionnaire, and in part by observation. Even the storage function of the library is encompassed by this unit, since material that is not likely to generate at least a few item-use days in the future is not worth preserving.

Exploratory surveys were undertaken at a large state university in the Middle West. A questionnaire directed to university staff (other than library staff) showed that on the

average 13. 0 item-use days of service were obtained for each
unit of circulation which the library recorded to faculty.   A-
bout 70-75 per cent of this use occurred in the library facilities themselves.   Books accounted for 44 per cent of the
use, journals, 36 per cent, abstracts, indexes, and bibliographical sources, 10 per cent, encyclopedias and handbooks,
5 1/2 per cent, and government publications, 5 1/2 per cent.
Faculty use is rather stable over the year, but student use
is highly variable.   In a library building designed for students
and with a collection assembled specifically for their needs
and interests, it was deduced that the average book used in
the library and left on the table for reshelving was used by
two different people and the restricted number of books in
the closed reserves were used by almost three people each
time they circulated.   In this library 4 per cent of the item-
use days were registered in use of materials at the reference
tables, 4 per cent in the use of recordings, and 2 per cent
in the reading of newspapers.   On the basis of such findings,
it is possible to construct an index based upon internal library statistics which approximates the quantity of service
supplied by the institution.   Whenever a major change is
made in the facilities and type of service provided, a new
survey would be needed to re-establish the appropriate size
of the parameters in the index.

It was shown that the faculty obtained on the average
about two item-use days per trip to the main collection in
the general library and that each trip cost fifteen minutes of
time on the average for traveling to and finding (or not finding) what was wanted.   The direct cost to the university in
lost time associated with obtaining service runs to about
$0. 80 per item-use day, in addition to $0. 05-$0. 06 in library
operating costs.   Improvements in library service which reduce time costs for gaining access to library materials seem
to stimulate the faculty to spend two to three minutes reading for every minute saved.   This indicates highly elastic
demand for library materials.

The time required for students to obtain a desired
title, once inside the library, was 7-8 minutes, including the
time lost in unsuccessful attempts.   The value of this time
spent at some alternative activity was set at $0. 25.   The
cost to the library, including building overheads, was estimated to be $0. 25.   As more books are put into use and the
capacity of the facility is approached, the costs to the student increase, while for the library they decrease until capacity is exceeded.   Thus, total costs remain relatively unchanged over quite a wide range of operations.

This method of analyzing cost per unit of service enables comparisons to be made between various proposals and various institutions. It is concluded that the best criterion for allocation of resources to libraries is that improvements should be made in the quality and scale of service until the combined costs to the library and the user reach the value of the alternative uses for the time of the faculty and students. Because the immediate prospect calls for rapid growth in the demand for library facilities and because the investment must be made one to three years prior to rendering a service, this rule of thumb is still likely to lead to underinvestment.

NOTES

1. R. L. Meier, "Communications and Social Change," Behavioral Science, I (1956), 43-58.

2. Some preliminary findings from various other directions of this investigation are reported in J. G. Miller, "Information Input Overload and Psychopathology," Journal of the American Psychiatric Association, CXVI (1960), 695-704.

3. J. G. March and H. A. Simon, Organizations (New York: John Wiley & Sons, 1958).

4. R. L. Meier, "Explorations in the Realm of Organization Theory III: Decision Making, Planning and the Steady State," Behavioral Science, IV (1959), 235-44.

5. R. E. Maizell, "Standards for Measuring the Effectiveness of Technical Library Performance," Institute of Radio Engineers Transactions on Engineering Management (EM-7 [1960]), pp. 69-72.

6. Franz Adler, "A Unit Concept for Sociology," American Journal of Sociology, LXV (1959-60), 356-64.

7. A rather thorough study has been undertaken of the uses of time by chemists (the largest category of scientists), where the time estimates obtained from diaries and observation were corroborated through the use of random settings of an alarm on a wrist watch (Case Institute of Technology, Operations Research Group, An Operations Research Study of the

Scientific Activity of Chemists [Cleveland, 1958]). These scientists spent 16. 5 hours in scientific communication and 6. 7 hours in business communication as against 10. 4 hours with equipment, 3. 0 hours in data treatment, and 2. 5 hours in thinking and planning. For spoken communication there was one scientist listening, while for written communications there were fourteen readers. It was shown that proper organization could double the effectiveness of this communication process.

8. R. L. Meier, "Measuring Social and Cultural Change in Urban Regions," Journal of the American Institute of Planners, XXV (1959), 180-90.

9. See esp. Alfred Politz Research, Inc. , How Reading Days Accumulate ("A Study of Seven Publications, " No. 6 [Pleasantville, N. Y. : Reader's Digest, 1958]). For a discussion of methodology, see Alfred Politz Research, Inc. , A Study of Four Media--Their Accumulative and Repeat Audiences (New York: Life, 1953), pp. 141-76.

10. A comprehensive library survey would have to investigate the effects of the annual academic cycles upon such a ratio, but this went beyond the scope of our own interests, since we were concerned primarily with peak load problems. Circulation to faculty, however, remained quite steady throughout the year except for a strong dip in August. Discussion with scores of faculty members in a wide variety of disciplines made it seem likely that the over-all bookuse pattern revealed by the Q's is maintained over most of the year.

11. T. W. Schultz, "Investment in Man: An Economist's View, " Social Service Review, XXX (1959), 109-17.

12. Z. Griliches, "Research Costs and Social Returns, " Journal of Political Economy, LXVI (1958), 419-31.

13. This estimate was arrived at by combining a series of observations. Very close to one hour of student time was spent in the building for each unit of attendance. Of that hour 10-13 per cent was spent socializing with other students, 9-11 per cent in movement, preparations, etc. , and 9-12 per cent

of the time in sleeping and "gazing off into space,"
so that 66 per cent was spent working with books
and library materials.   It was impossible for observers to determine from a distance whether students were using their own textbooks or library
books.   The overlapping use was quite considerable.
It seemed most likely that they were using library
materials one-half to three-quarters of the time,
except during the final examination period.   We have
less evidence concerning book use outside of the
library, but inferences drawn from reading lists
and term papers strongly point to a tendency to
read specific selections, or to skim the contents,
rather than read a whole book.   Thus, student book
use is quite different from normal book use in public libraries.

14.   A more balanced view that is coming to have currency
but has not yet been explicitly formalized is that
research and education are joint inputs into the nation's economy.   Innovation is of no real value unless it can be disseminated by education, and extra
education in turn is not likely to generate new income unless it introduces innovations to those persons being educated.   This makes most valuable
whatever demonstrated skill is in scarce supply.
University teaching will be as important as research
in the United States in the decades ahead.

15.   An evaluation research on the behavioral factors related
to documentation is incorporated in a report recent-
ly submitted to the National Science Foundation (H.
Menzel, L. Lieberman, and J. Dulchin, Review of
Studies in the Flow of Information among Scientists
[New York: Bureau of Applied Social Research,
Columbia University, 1960]).

16.   These indexes are not impervious to corruption.   It is
quite possible that an opportunistic organization will
study very carefully various methods for generating
"requests" for titles.   Some procedures that are
then adopted may force the user to be more superficial and routine.   For example, a "circulating list"
for new materials may be set up so that teachers
and researchers are forced to cross their name from
the list in order to give the next person a chance.
If each name crossed out rates as at least one item-

use day, the statistic is likely (but not always) to
represent less public utility than a self-initiated request for a title.   The indexes that provide short-
cut estimates of item-use days are even more susceptible to being degraded, but through the use of
periodic surveys they can be restandardized every
few years.

COOPERATION IN LENDING AMONG
COLLEGE AND REFERENCE LIBRARIES*

Ernest C. Richardson

It is a matter of common observation that with the
present limited facilities for our American libraries, students, whether dependent on college libraries or on general
reference libraries, are constantly in lack of the books which
they want for their work. This, on the one hand, discour-
ages work, and on the other results in the production of inadequate and imperfect books. The greatest handicap comes
from the fact that the majority of the books cannot even be
found in America, the next from the difficulty of finding
where in America such works as there are are located, and
a third from the great expense involved in travelling even to
American books.

There are four practical methods by which co-operation may come in to ameliorate this situation, and these may
be described under "Cataloging," "Purchase," "Specialization,"
and "Lending."

By co-operation in cataloging is meant the employment of some method by which it may be readily known
where books can be found. This method has been carried
out splendidly for scientific periodicals in the check list to
Bolton's catalog. By co-operation in purchase is meant some
arrangement by which libraries may supplement rather than
duplicate one another in the getting of that majority of books
not now owned by any American library. By co-operation in
specialization is meant that method of co-operation in purchase by which various libraries take and develop some specialty to the intent that there shall be, so to speak, a Sur-

*Reprinted from ALA Proceedings 15:32-36 (1890).

geon-General's Office library for every department of knowledge, and that the scholar may know at once the most probable supply for his need.   By co-operation in lending, finally, is meant the development of some practical scheme whereby, without hardship to the larger libraries, the great expense of travelling to books may be eliminated, so far as
American libraries are concerned, by sending books from one
library to another.

All these methods involve one another more or less,
but in this paper they will be touched on from the standpoint
of co-operation in lending, by which is meant here simply the
method already in use among American libraries, and still
further developed abroad, systematized, authorized, and extended.

The present system is an evolution.   At first books
as special favor were loaned to known individuals.   Then
gradually, and for obvious reasons, the rule now generally
in use grew up, that books might be loaned to a library but
not to an individual.   The system is extending more or less
all the time and is already a relief to the situation, but the
chief objection to it as now practised is that it throws too
great a share of the burden on Harvard, Columbia, and a
few others, and its use is limited by the fear of trespassing
on good nature.   The object of this paper is to find some
practical method by which the objection may be removed and
the method extended.

First of all, let us try to get at a realization of the
situation by the analysis of a definite list of books, and for
this we happily have the material at hand in the "Library
check list" of Bolton's Catalogue of Scientific Periodicals.

In Bolton's list there are 8600 periodicals mentioned.
Of 5440 of these there is no copy known in this country; of
the remaining 3160, 1153 have but one copy, 521 have two
copies, 307 three, and the remaining 1179 have more than
three copies.   Of the 3160 periodicals, Harvard has 919 and
Columbia 791.   That is to say: of existing scientific periodicals, nearly two-thirds are not to be found in this country at all; one-third of the remainder are represented in this
country by a single copy, and another third by not more than
three.   Only one-eighth, therefore, of the scientific periodicals mentioned in Bolton's catalog are to be found in more
than three out of our (say) 500 college and reference libraries,
and the very best equipped of our university libraries have

only one-tenth of these periodicals at most, and less than
one-third of those which some one has actually found important enough to buy for this country.

Now, making all allowances for the fact that many of
these not yet acquired by American libraries are of secondary
value, it is nevertheless true that there is hardly one which
should not at some time be wanted for consultation in this
country. The most impressive lesson of the analysis is,
therefore, the absolute lack of books in this country, but the
complementary and hardly less impressive lesson is that while
we already have more than 3000 sets in this country, even
the best equipped universities in the land can consult less
than 1000 of these on their own campuses.

What is to be done about it? Shall 500 colleges continue in an indiscriminate way to struggle towards an ideal
8600 periodicals, all of which some one will want some time,
but not one in 20 of which some of them will want once in
20 years, or shall we look forward to some sort of definite
co-operation, and the sooner the better?

Even if it were not a total impossibility for all college libraries to acquire all the scientific periodicals in the
near future, supposing, for the sake of reducing to absurdity,
that it were possible, it would involve a waste at the present
market value of periodicals, reckoning that there are 500 libraries, of not less than one-quarter of a billion of dollars
in the unnecessary duplication of 7000 sets, while two or three
copies of each, at a total cost of not more than two or three
million dollars, would fairly well supply the need--say, an
economic waste of $250,000,000 in a total investment of
$253,000,000. Absurd as this is, it is not unlike what we
are now doing on the present go-as-you-please every-one-for-
himself principle. We are duplicating, every year, a great
many sets of periodicals, as we would not need to do under
some system where all were free to borrow.

I am entirely aware that there are many periodicals
which must be in every institution; that there are many of
these even of which there should be several copies in each
great institution, but I am not speaking of these. I am speaking of those periodicals which are only used occasionally, and
which form the majority in every library.

A suggestive example of both classes is found in Liebig's Annalen. The latest series are necessary to every in-

stitution for constant use. The first series, while extremely valuable for historic purposes, is only a small fraction of the whole; is only needed occasionally even in the largest institutions; costs as much as all other series put together, and there are already 25 copies in the country. The competition of libraries 10 to 25 in getting their complete sets has advanced the price of the series from (say) $50 to $300, and the next five years will probably take it to $500. Suppose, now, that library 26 has reached the stage of affording Liebig. Shall the librarian pay $300 for all of Liebig that is often wanted and get also one or two other much-needed-all-the-time sets, or shall he pay also another $300 for this series which will be used once a year, and of which there are already 25 copies in the country, and go without the other? There is already $7500 worth of first series of Liebig in the country, and, with proper system of co-operation and lending, this plant will supply our need more than twice over. The next $7500 available for Liebig's first series might then get 50 more needed sets, and would have the incidental advantage of reducing the fancy prices which now prevail for full sets. That is to say, of $15,000 put into 40 Liebig's, $1000 should, economically speaking, have been put into 10 copies, and $14,000 used for other books.

Now, Liebig is even more than a fair example of the matter, because everything which can be said in favor of complete sets counts also in its favor. Whatever applies to Liebig in this connection, therefore, applies, with still greater force, to many of the 300 others.

Here, then, you have on the one hand a great waste of money through unnecessary duplication of copies, and on the other an immense number of sets inaccessible except through a journey to Europe. You have again, on the one hand, the fact that we have a large number of sets in this country, and on the other, the fact that two-thirds of these are inaccessible to even the very best equipped universities, except through expensive journeys or through borrowing.

Now, the ideal way of meeting this situation both for economy and for convenience is undoubtedly a central, national, lending library of the least frequently needed books-- a library having, perhaps, a central library in Washington with branches in New Orleans, San Francisco, Chicago, and New York. But the thing that we are after now is not an ideal, but a practical one. Even if such a library should be established at once, it would be many years before it could

be expected to be free of the need of the co-operation of existing libraries. What we have to consider now is how far
the same result of increase in apparatus and decrease in labor and cost of getting at it can be gained in some other way,
and that way is, of course, co-operation among the already
existing institutions. There are, as has been said, various
ways of practical co-operation to this end, but the foundation
of all is co-operation in lending. With this principle well
established, co-operation in specialization and co-operation in
cataloging will at least receive an immense new impetus,
while co-operation in purchasing will logically and inevitably
follow on the basis of the co-operative work in cataloging.
In a practical age, in a practical land, with the example of
great combinations for personal gain before us, it ought to
be possible to devise suitable machinery and secure extensive
adopting of this machinery. I do not ignore the fact that there
may be obstacles to universal co-operation. There may be
legal or political reasons why a municipal library or an endowed reference library could not enter in a combination.
There will be personal objection and suspicions of any definite and formal combination on the part of many, but in a
matter where the economy and the advantage are so great to
all the members, it ought not to be hard to persuade them to
go into the deal. If trusts are profitable for private gain,
why not for public welfare.

It is not at all necessary, however, to a practical
scheme that all libraries should enter it. Suppose that only
the eight university libraries, which have over 100,000 volumes, should enter--still an immense gain for them and for
America could be made. Suppose even that they only go in
a little ways, still every step that they go in is concrete
gain. I would, myself, like to see every American library
of any size, whose legal and political bonds would permit,
go into the matter. I would like to see some central bureaus,
preferably, perhaps, the Library of Congress or the Smithsonian Institution amply endowed to organize existing resources, guide their future development and supplement them
as far as possible. I would like to see enough altruism or
patriotism or far-sightedness, or whatever you choose to call
it, infused into the scheme to admit the smallest incorporated
library to its benefits.

But if this seems too ideal and remote, and you ask
for something more practical, I propose that at least the effort be made to have all the college and university libraries
represented in Bolton's catalog join in a lending system at

least as liberal as that which prevails among European libraries, on the basis of a definitely prepared list of books,
of which each library shall furnish a portion, and according
to its means.   This could be done, if necessary, on the
strictest basis of self-interest, but we might perhaps rise
to extending its benefits to non-contributing colleges.

I have said that at the present time the great objection
to the system is the extra burden which it throws on a few
of the large libraries, and an authorised general system of
exchange would increase that burden.   As a matter of fact,
under the present conditions, one naturally writes to the
largest library as being the one most likely to contain the
book sought.   In the case of the periodicals contained in Bolton's catalog and a few other matters, however, there is a
certain tendency towards equalization.

The considerate librarian, if he wishes to borrow one
of the Bolton's bibliography periodicals, would choose to ask
the favor of one of the smaller libraries having a set wherever possible.   Now on the same principle if the committee
of librarians of co-operating libraries should take this list
and indicate the lending copy or copies of each periodical, it
would be easily adjusted so that Harvard, Columbia and the
other great libraries should have no more than their share
of the burden.

There are, in fact, only 81 periodicals in the case of
Harvard and 79 in the case of Columbia which are not owned
by some other institution, and it is conceivable that in the
case of a general combination their burden should be reduced
to the loan of these and these only, whereas the sets that
each would be entitled to borrow would exceed 2000 each--
that is, they would stand to get 20 times what they give.

On the other hand, there are few institutions that
would not contribute something--and as a matter of fact, the
small college, with a faculty of half a dozen, if it contributes
little also uses little compared with one having a faculty of
several hundred, and what is more it uses the few standard
sets that it does own so much less that it can contribute
these as lending copies where the larger institutions must
keep them for reference.

I would propose further, therefore, that a definite beginning of co-operation should be made in just this way: That
a circle of co-operating libraries be formed, authorized by

their trustees to interchange, and that a committee of the librarians should take Bolton's catalog and decide on lending
copies--perhaps assigning three or four lending copies, geo-
graphically distributed.   By using the Bolton numbers and
letters the cost of printing would be insignificant, and a good
start could be made at once.   This start might be followed
up by taking, say, the list of historical periodicals, etc., in
Chevalier, and forming a check list of these with similar assignment.   This might perhaps soon be extended to a joint
list of the periodicals in the American libraries in all classes,
not of scientific periodicals only, but of all periodicals and
important sets of great publications.   The committee of co-
operating libraries, with such a list before it, could assign
lending responsibility in such way (1) That the larger libraries should be relieved of the strain of doing more than their
share of lending and (2) so that even the smallest library participating should be able to do something in the work.

If such a list were prepared for co-operation in lending it would naturally and inevitably extend to co-operation in
purchase.   The committee editing the list would discover
where the weakest spots in our joint American supply were
to be found, and would naturally distribute among themselves
the responsibility of filling the gaps in some common sense
judgment of which one was best suited to assume each periodical.   This would tend in time to definitize and extend co-
operation by specialization.   All this would result in direct
and immediate advantage in use, in an immense saving of
capital, in the removing of the unnecessary competition which
is raising the cost of scientific periodicals to fabulous proportions, and in a general systematization of the work of
building up the college and reference libraries.

In conclusion, there are two or three things which
somebody will think should be mentioned, and which may be
gathered up in anticlimax as a sort of miscellany.   In the
first place, the expense of this lending would be borne, as
it is now, by the borrower.   In the dim futurity, perhaps, a
paternal government may step in and help the matter by light-
ening still farther the expense of sending such books by mail.
For the present, the expense, though considerable, is not to
be compared with the expense of travelling to the books, and
for a conservative beginning the check of this amount of expense may not be altogether an evil.

In the second place, it should be said that this plan
would not need, in any sense, to destroy the right of indi-

vidual initiative.   Every institution will still be free to duplicate what it chooses, and to judge what new material it is
for its best interest to acquire.   It will simply extend the
privilege which it already gives to every scholar to use its
books if he will come to the books, to a privilege of having
the books taken to him at his expense.

In the third place, and for the benefit of those members of our association who look at the matter from the standpoint of the dealer, let me say that this need in no wise reduce the business or the profits of the book dealers.   American libraries, for a long time to come, are going to use with
eagerness every dollar that they can get for the purchase of
books.   This plan will merely save the dealer a good deal of
trouble in the hunting up of unnecessary copies of rare sets,
while not reducing the volume of his business in the least.

Finally, we must not close without recognizing more
explicitly the fine contributions to our problem of co-operation in lending which are being made by many libraries.   The
work of the library of the Surgeon-General's office comes
very near the ideal, both as to the localization of the supply
for need through cataloging and the actual supply by lending.
If there were a Surgeon-General's library for every branch
of knowledge this little tale might not have been told.

THE DIVISION OF A LIBRARY INTO BOOKS IN USE,
AND BOOKS NOT IN USE, With Different Storage
Methods for the Two Classes of Books*

Charles William Eliot

Before this assembly of experts it is proper that I
should describe the past experiences and present conditions
which have lately led me to study the library question anew,
and have caused me, who am not an expert, to venture to
write on the subject.

When Gore Hall was built in 1840, my predecessor,
President Josiah Quincy, supposed that the building had sufficient capacity to hold the probable accumulation of books
during the remainder of the century; yet within thirty-five
years it was necessary to construct an extension which held
many more books than the original building. Within twenty
years more it became necessary to reconstruct the interior
of the original Gore Hall in such a manner as greatly to increase its book capacity; and now, within six years of the
last enlargement, a further enlargement, more considerable
than either of the preceding, is declared to be absolutely
necessary. The city of Boston erected about forty years ago
what was then considered a very large library building on
Boylston Street. Within less than forty years that building
had to be replaced by a building of vastly greater capacity at
the cost of several millions of dollars; and this new building
is so placed with reference to the surrounding streets that it
will be almost impossible in time to come to more than double its capacity. Only thirteen years ago Cambridge built a
public library; but the city has already been obliged to make
a considerable extension of the building. In the meantime
many new public libraries have been erected in the various

_____

*Reprinted from Library Journal 27 (Conf. No.):51-56 (1902).

cities and towns which constitute the metropolitan district of
Boston. I have, therefore, witnessed a very extraordinary
increase in the number of books kept accessible to readers
in the communities which fall under my immediate observation; and I have also witnessed frequent enlargements of the
buildings used for storing these collections, enlargements repeated at always diminishing intervals. All over the country,
but especially in Massachusetts, local public libraries have
been rapidly established within a single generation; so that
the centres from which books are distributed, or at which
books are read, have multiplied extraordinarily. Since Gore
Hall was planned--that is, quite within the life-time of many
persons here present--the production of books and other
printed matter has increased at an unprecedented rate; until
now there is no library, however rich, which pretends to
keep pace with the annual publications of the world; and all
libraries, large and small alike, are compelled to exercise
close selection in the purchasing and acceptance of books.
No existing library can dream of providing two miles and
more of new shelving every year. Completeness can no longer be the ideal of any library. Judicious selection for local
and present use is the ideal.

At a university which employs a large number of specialists as teachers, the books selected for purchase will be
those which the university specialists decide are most needed
at the passing moment by themselves or their pupils; and
since these specialists change somewhat rapidly by death or
transfer to other fields of labor, the direction of purchases
in a given university library will probably change considerably from generation to generation; so that even in a university library the selection of the books must be called variable
and almost casual, unless an unchanging policy of purchasing
only in certain specified departments of knowledge be adopted
and persistently maintained. I know no instance of the long
maintenance of such a policy for a public collection not professional.

The prodigious annual output of books and magazines
is by no means all original matter. A large proportion of it
is matter which has only been revised or recast. Each generation makes its own treatises, gazeteers, bibliographies,
indices, dictionaries, and cyclopaedias, re-edits the famous
books come down from preceding generations, and writes its
own biographies of the heroic personages of the past. It is
impossible to discern any limit to this portentous flood of reproduction. Yet in each generation this immense mass of re-

vised or recast matter invalidates much of the printed work of former generations or throws it out of use. Moreover, all signs indicate that the flood of printed matter has by no means reached its height. Indeed there is every reason to suppose that printing and publishing will become cheaper and cheaper, and the facilities for authorship and the number of authors greater and greater. The ease with which books are made has altered the character of the printed book. It is plain that great masses of new books have only an ephemeral interest, like the monthly magazines and the weekly papers.

Under these conditions the great need of means of discriminating between books which may fairly be said to be in use and books which may fairly be said to be not in use has been forced on me, and on many other persons nearly concerned with the largest, readiest, and most profitable use of libraries, and with the promotion of sound reading among pupils at school, students at college or university, and the people at large. The problem is essentially an economic one. It is not a good use of the precious educational resources of a community, or an institution, to enlarge at frequent intervals its library building, if the new space needed for books in use can be secured by discarding books not in use; and it is not frugal policy to permit the presence of thousands or millions of dead books to increase the cost of service, care, and cleaning in a much-frequented library.

I admit at once that the means of just discrimination between books in use and books not in use are not easy to discern or to apply; but I maintain, nevertheless, that the search for these means should be diligently prosecuted, and that every reasonable suggestion of means of discrimination deserves careful attention. It is obvious that no one man is competent to discriminate, on principles of judgment which his own mind elaborates, between a dead book and a living book in all departments of learning. The only satisfactory test is the actual demand or absence of demand for the book in question. Thus, it might naturally be suspected that a book which had not been called for in a university library for twenty years possessed but a faint vitality; whereas a book that was called for every year would certainly be considered alive. The fact of disuse seems to me an effective criterion, and the question for librarians is how to determine that fact of disuse. In libraries where no person has access to the shelves except the librarian and his assistants, so that every book used is ordered by a written slip, and passes the delivery desk, the fact of disuse can certainly be satisfactorily

determined.   In libraries where some thousands of books,
say from five thousand to a hundred thousand, are kept on
open shelves, accessible to all users or all privileged users
of the library, there must be some principle of selection
which assigns books to those open shelves.   No judicious librarian will keep on open shelves books which are never
touched.   There already exists, therefore, a satisfactory criterion for large numbers of live books.   The real difficulty
in determining disuse arises in libraries which permit access
to all their shelves to a considerable number of readers who
may handle the books at their pleasure, and remove any of
them temporarily to neighboring tables where they can be
conveniently read.   This permission has no value except in
a classified library, or, rather, except in those parts of a
library which are classified.   There are many libraries in
which the "browsing" process is not permitted, and in them
this difficulty in determining the disuse of a book does not
exist.   Moreover, where the difficulty exists now it would be
removed by enforcing the simple rule that the reader admitted to the shelves may take a book down, but shall not put
it up; and this rule would have other obvious advantages.   I
shall have something to say later concerning the value of the
process of browsing in a library.

I have found on inquiry that the discrimination between
books in use and books not in use has already been made in
some libraries of widely different character as regards size,
rate of growth, and general purpose.   Thus the British Museum has already made large discriminations.   The Medical
Library of Boston, although it has lately procured a new
building much larger than its first, has still large numbers of
books stored in the suburbs of Boston.   The Harvard Library
has been forced to box thousands of books, and store them in
the cellars of other buildings--a very inconvenient method.
The Boston Athenaeum has for some years put its most used
books in its lower stories, and its least used in the upper,
for the convenience of its attendants, and of its proprietors
who have access to the shelves.   Many town libraries have
found no difficulty in deciding upon those books which are so
seldom called for that they may be put in out-of-the-way
places.

But what should be done with disused books, when
once the means of discrimination between the used and the
disused have been found?   It seems to me clear that a book
which is worth keeping at all ought to be kept accessible;
that is, where it can be found, on demand, with a reasonable

expenditure of time and labor. The problem, then, is to devise a mode of storing disused books, so that they may be kept safe and accessible, and yet at a low cost for shelter and annual care. The most obvious considerations of economy demand that disused books, or books very seldom used, should be stored in inexpensive buildings on cheap land. There is frightful waste in storing little-used books on land worth a million dollars an acre, if land worth a hundred dollars an acre would answer all reasonable purposes. Next, no unnecessary number of copies should be stored for one and the same community. If, for instance, there are thirty public or semi-public libraries within twelve miles of the State House in Boston, it is wasteful for each of those libraries to be storing disused books, for many of the books so preserved would be duplicates. There should be one store-house for disused books for the entire district, wherein not more than two copies of any book should be preserved. Thirdly, the interior construction of such a building should differ in important respects from the construction of the ordinary bookstack in use to-day. A stack like that of the Harvard Library, which was the first stack constructed of the type now common, or that of the Congressional Library, a more recent and far more costly type, provides a passageway between each two rows of books; and in order to get good daylight into the middle of these narrow aisles or passageways, the lengths of the rows are very moderate, and there are often passageways along the ends of the rows of books between these ends and the walls. The result of this arrangement is that not more than one-fifth of the cubical contents of the building which covers the stack is really occupied by books. In order to secure compact stowage, all books in such a store-house as we are contemplating should, in the first place, be assorted by size. They should next be marked by a label at the top of the back to receive only a serial letter and number. No classification of the books should be permitted; for a classified library occupies more space than one which is not classified. The books having been assorted by size should be placed three deep on the shelves, and on the edge of each shelf should stand fixed-location shelf-marks bearing the numbers of the three books behind each mark. The serial number once assigned to a book should never be changed, and the place of each book once fixed should never be changed. The passage-ways should be long, and should end against the walls, and only one passage-way down the middle of the stack should afford access to the passage-ways between the rows of books. In this way nearly two-thirds of the building might be actually occupied by books. The roof should be flat, and so constructed

as to defend the upper stories from the heat of the summer
sun. All windows should be double, to exclude dust and cold.
In winter the temperature of the entire building should be
kept low, and by the use of gratings for floors the whole
building should be treated as one room for purposes of heating
and ventilating. None but the attendants should ever be allowed in the stacks. They would find the books called for by
their serial numbers only, and would bring them to the reading-room and studies which should be attached to the building. It ought, of course, to be possible for any student who
desired a large number of books to have them brought to him
in a separate room where he could examine them at his leisure, and retain the use of them for a definite period. It
should also be possible for any library in the district which
used this store-house to procure any books from the store-
house on written or telephoned orders, the cards corresponding to all the books in the store-house being kept at all the
libraries which were large enough to accommodate such a
catalogue. Such a building could be a regular polygon, like
a square, and so have a shorter perimeter than any irregu-
lar polygon of the same area, like a long rectangle, for instance.

The books in such a store-house would be reasonably
accessible to real students. They would no longer encumber
the libraries from which they had been dismissed. They need
no longer encumber the card catalogues in ordinary use at
the libraries from which they had been dismissed. The discharge of disused books from the thirty or more libraries of
the whole district into this common receptacle would be inter-
mittent, perhaps, by weeks or months, but fairly continuous
by long periods, such as five-year or ten-year periods. The
libraries of books in use would themselves be more economically and effectively administered if relieved of the burden
of the dead books; and they would be under no necessity of
extending their buildings at short intervals over new areas of
more and more expensive land.

The treatment of the library catalogue under these new
conditions would deserve careful consideration and experimentation. In libraries which contained a well-classified subject
catalogue, it might, or might not, be best to keep in the
classified catalogue the titles of disused books. By retaining
all the titles which had ever found place in the classified catalogue, a student unacquainted with the literature of his subject would be supplied with an important bibliographical guide;
but on the other hand by keeping in the catalogue the titles of

disused books the bulk of the catalogue would be increased
in a progressive measure, and the daily use of the catalogue
would therefore be made more difficult and more time-consuming for everybody resorting to it.

These last considerations lead naturally to the interesting subject of "browsing." There can be no doubt that the
inexperienced student gets some advantage from looking over
the books in a classified library on a subject in which he has
an intelligent interest; but of course his chief advantage is
procured from those books which have still so much life in
them as to be sometimes read. Browsing on good books is
often helpful, but browsing on poor books, and particularly on
books which have been so replaced by better ones as to have
gone out of use, is a very questionable advantage for the ordinary student. I am not suggesting that browsing on live
books should be prevented, but only that browsing on dead
books might be made less convenient than it now is requiring
that the dead books to be examined should be ordered and
brought together for the browser in a reading-room or study.
For the advanced student, who wishes to make a really thorough study of the literature of a given subject, the examination of the books on that subject which happen to stand on
the shelves of a given library ought not to be satisfactory.
He may be quite certain that the collection is not complete,
and that it may even be described as casual. He ought to
make acquaintance with a thorough bibliography of his subject,
or he ought at least to examine thoroughly several classified
catalogues of books on his subject. He should never be content with the selection of books which happens to have been
made in a single library, but should examine the contents of
several libraries. In short, he ought to regard browsing in
one collection not as thorough study at all, but only as a
pleasing gratification of curiosity in comparatively leisure
moments.

It is obvious that the economical advantages of the
division of books which has been here suggested would be
numerous. In the first place, the trustees of libraries would
not have to hold vacant large pieces of expensive land all
about their present library buildings, in order to provide for
enlargements of those buildings in successive generations.
In the second place, they would not be put to the expense of
building these successive enlargements, but would always keep
in a sufficient building that number of books for which it had
originally been designed, the older books which had proved to
be disused being constantly replaced by newer books which

are to be put to the test of use, and the whole collection
being actually alive.   Again, the maintenance of the store-
house for disused books would be far less costly than the
maintenance of the building for the active library as regards
heat, light, number of attendants, and cleaning.   Finally,
the handling of the catalogues and the delivery of books at the
active library would be quicker and easier, and the service
of that library would, therefore, be less expensive and more
efficient.   Every hundred thousand books in a much-used library and every million cards in its catalogue increase the
cost of service and care, because they add to the difficulties
of the service, and the extent of the care-taking.

        It seems to me that emphasis should be laid hence-
forth not on the number of volumes which a library contains,
but on the wise selection of its books, and on the facilities
for the daily use of its treasures.   It is much more important that adequate provision of reading-rooms, large and small,
should be made, than that browsing be permitted, or that
every book owned by the library should be obtainable on demand within a few minutes.   It is not unreasonable that an
interval of twenty-four hours should elapse between the receipt
of an order for a book and its delivery.   Commercial circulating libraries both in England and in this country are highly
successful, although they often require a much longer interval
than this between the receipt of an order and the delivery.
As the facilities for the safe delivery of books by mail, parcel deliveries, or expresses increase, the habit of borrowing
books from a distance ought likewise to become common.
The student and the general reader alike should be willing to
await the delivery of the book he wants for hours or even
days, just as a naturalist waits for the season at which his
particular material is to be found, or for the time of year
when his plant flowers, or his moths escape from the chry-
salis, or his chickens or his trout hatch.   The real student
ought to be capable of some forelooking, and of a certain deliberation in reading.

        Whenever the distinction between books in use and
books out of use, and between a library of live books and a
store-house for dead books, comes to be admitted and applied,
it will be possible to return to spacious and handsome halls
and rooms for the permanent active library.   The modern
steel stack is not a decorative or inspiring structure, and
we should all be glad to advocate with a good conscience
more beautiful and interesting forms of construction for the
library of books in use.

It is an interesting but not an urgent question how many depositories of dead books might reasonably be provided in the United States. If the general conception should be accepted, the interests of different localities will in time determine the number of places of deposit for books out of use. In my report on Harvard University for the year 1900-01, I mentioned three appropriate places of deposit--Washington, New York, and Chicago; but I can see great convenience in having one place of deposit for Eastern Massachusetts; and doubtless the Pacific coast and the eastern slopes of the Rocky Mountains would some day need others.

It has been said that the present generation cannot determine the taste in books which any future generation will manifest, and therefore that present disuse of a book is not to be accepted as evidence that it is dead outright and forever. This suggestion has some truth in it, but it does not go far. There are few books now in use which have been resurrected after long burial; but if there were such books, their temporary storage in the house of disused books would not prevent their restoration to some of the active libraries when the new generation had discovered or rediscovered their merits. I am not proposing a crematory for dead books, but only a receiving-tomb. Neither am I proposing that the bibliophile or the antiquarian should be absolutely deprived of his idols, but only that his access to them should be made somewhat less convenient and attractive.

Another mode of selection in the purchase and holding of books by different libraries within some territory of moderate extent has often been suggested,--namely, the assignment to different libraries of different subjects to which they shall severally confine themselves in the purchase of their books. There is a great deal to be said for this mode of selection, if the interests of a large community like the Boston metropolitan district, for example, rather than those of a single town or city, or a single university, are to be considered. But it ought to be observed that this method of selecting the books which any given library shall own involves the same willingness on the part of readers to wait a reasonable time for the books they want, as must be assumed if the line of division in any one library shall be between books in use and books not in use. If European history were assigned as one of its subjects to the Boston Public Library and American history to the Harvard Library, the historical student in Cambridge might have to wait for his book until it could be brought from Boston, and vice versa. No principle

of selection can be applied to a group of libraries, which
does not involve, though infrequently, some reasonable delay
in the delivery to the reader of the book he wants; yet it is
indispensable that some principle of selection or other shall
be adopted.   It is also to be observed that books will inevitably come to be disused in the several departments assigned
to each coparate library.

What I have wished, and still wish, to urge upon the
attention of professional librarians--solely in the interest of
the best use of the best books--is the need of determining
beforehand the general policy which is to be adopted with regard to the storage and most convenient use of the overwhelming masses of books which are pouring forth at all the large
centres of bookmaking in the world, masses which each decade bids fair to double.   At present most of the libraries of
the country are vaguely contemplating an indefinite enlargement of their buildings, and an indefinite increase in the cost
of maintaining, caring for, and serving out their growing collections of books.   The present buildings of many libraries
may now look adequate for years to come; but surprisingly
soon their vacant shelves will be filled, and the pinch we
have felt three times within sixty years at the Harvard Library will afflict them also.   There seems to me to be an
urgent need of settling soon on a clear and feasible policy
for the future; and I know no body of persons more competent
than that I now address to discover and promulgate such a
policy.

PROPOSAL FOR A DIVISION OF RESPONSIBILITY
AMONG AMERICAN LIBRARIES IN THE
ACQUISITION AND RECORDING
OF LIBRARY MATERIALS*

Keyes D. Metcalf and Edwin E. Williams

Money can be saved by reducing duplication of work
and materials. Library resources can be made more widely
and more readily available by centralizing information and
they can be increased by coordinating the efforts of research
libraries. One or another of these general propositions, or
a combination of them, has been involved in every cooperative plan that librarians have undertaken or discussed.

If the discussions have been more numerous than the
achievements, the latter are far from insignificant. Many
possibilities have long been evident, and the American Library Association, in its charter, gave as one of its purposes
the inducing of "cooperation in all departments of bibliothecal
science and economy." A plan for expansion of Poole's Index by cooperative indexing of periodicals was unanimously
adopted at the first meeting of the Association in 1876; this
first great periodical index is then, in part, a product of library cooperation.

Still earlier, nearly a century ago, Charles Coffin
Jewett, then librarian of the Smithsonian Institution in Washington, proposed a plan for centralized cataloging that, if it
had been carried out successfully, might have saved the libraries of the country millions of dollars. The scheme
failed, partly because of mechanical difficulties with the ster-

---

*Reprinted by permission of the American Library Associa-
tion from College and Research Libraries 5:105-109 (March
1944).

eotype plates that he hoped to use for master copy and partly
because he was ahead of his time.   But, after Herbert Putnam became Librarian of Congress, the distribution of printed
cards was begun and centralized cataloging became a reality
on a large scale.   There have been various other efforts toward cooperative cataloging, and the project begun ten years
ago to supply cards for books not acquired by the Library of
Congress will, it is hoped, expand considerably in the immediate future under Mr. MacLeish's administration.

Perhaps the most recent realization of a means of securing economies by cooperation is the New England Deposit
Library, the first building to be erected for cooperative storage of little-used library materials.

In the field of making resources available, interlibrary
loans have been advocated from the beginning and have grown
steadily.   But interlibrary loan--or its most recent adjunct,
microphotographic reproduction--is possibly only after the materials to be borrowed or filmed have been located; union
lists and union catalogs are prerequisites.

Early accomplishments in this direction included lists
of specialized material, such as the Census of Incunabula and
Sabin's Dictionary of Books Relating to America.   The most
important achievements in this group are, of course, the works
edited by Winifred Gregory (Mrs. James T. Gerould)--two editions of the Union List of Serials and the union lists of newspapers, of foreign documents, and of international congresses.

Development of union catalogs and bibliographical centers has seemed to be the best way to make it possible to
locate individual books.   Regional catalogs have been established in recent years, but the Union Catalog at the Library
of Congress is the major development.   With an estimated
11,500,000 locations for 7,500,000 different titles and edi-
tions--about 60 per cent of the titles in American research
libraries--it is extremely useful.   Plans for expansion as proposed by Robert B. Downs should be encouraged.

A good deal, then, has been done to make resources
accessible, but very little, comparatively, has been accomplished toward increasing resources by cooperative acquisition.
Surveys of localities and regions have been made and there
have been agreements covering specific fields in certain areas
such as New York City, Chicago, and between the universities
of North Carolina and Duke.   The relative lack of progress in

cooperation of this sort undoubtedly results from the difficulties involved--the responsibilities of individual libraries,
legal restrictions on their freedom of action, and obstacles
to changing established practices.   The problem is complex
and, as in most other cooperative efforts, an initial investment is required.

Cooperation Is Desirable

There is, however, general agreement that cooperation
through library specialization in the different fields of research is desirable and this agreement has been expressed at
many meetings of the American Library Association and the
Association of Research Libraries; in reports received by the
director of the Experimental Division of Library Cooperation
at the Library of Congress as a result of his meetings with
librarians in the year 1941-42; and in the hearty approval
given by presidents, deans, and library committees of educational institutions throughout the country to the proposal that
is to be described in this article.

Indeed, the advantages of cooperation are so obvious
that everyone believes in it theoretically, at least, just as
everyone believes in world peace.   The difficulty is to determine a practicable first step.   And, in suggesting such a
step, it must be emphasized that regimentation is not wanted.
The library resources of the country ought to be made as
nearly complete as possible, resources should become more
readily available, and it should not be necessary to invest in
the research needed to catalog a book every time another copy
of that book is acquired by another library.

A possible solution is offered by a "Proposal for a
Division of Responsibility among American Libraries in the
Acquisition and Recording of Library Materials," which was
drawn up by a committee* of the Librarian's Council, a group
of librarians invited to advise the Librarian of Congress concerning the relation of the Library of Congress to other libraries.   This was placed in the hands of librarians of many
of the larger libraries of the country some months ago and
was approved by authorized representatives of the American
Library Association, the Association of Research Libraries,
and the Council of National Library Associations, as well as

---

*Consisting of Messrs. MacLeish, Boyd, and Metcalf.

by the American Council of Learned Societies.   The essential features of this proposal are as follows:

A

It is proposed that libraries having research collections join in a cooperative undertaking limited for the time
being to current materials in the Latin alphabet.   (It is
hoped that Slavic materials in the Cyrillic alphabet can be
added in the not too distant future.)   The term "materials"
refers for the time being only to books and pamphlets in the
regular book trade, but plans will be prepared later to include public documents, serials, periodicals, and at least a
selection of newspapers.

As to these current materials in the Latin alphabet,
the cooperating institutions would agree upon a common policy
with the following aims:

1.   That at least one copy of every book and pamphlet,
published anywhere in the world following the effective
date of the agreement which might reasonable be expected
to have interest to a research worker in America, shall
be acquired and made available promptly after publication
by some one of the cooperating libraries.

2.   That each item so acquired shall be promptly cataloged (if possible by centralized or cooperative cataloging),
listed promptly in the Union Catalog at the Library of
Congress and also in a new classed union catalog to be
established at the Library of Congress, from which subject
catalogs of limited fields may later be published in book
form or otherwise, as demand suggests.

B

To carry out these policies, it is proposed that a competent staff be employed to make possible the following preliminary steps at the earliest possible moment after money
has become available for the purpose.   It is hoped that steps
(1) through (6) below will be completed promptly enough so that
the plan can be put into operation immediately after the close
of the war.

1.   The staff will prepare for submission to cooperating

libraries a plan subdividing human knowledge into carefully
defined units, each as distinct as possible. It is suggested that the Library of Congress system of classification
might serve as a basis for most of this work.

2.   The staff will make a survey of existing special collections as a basis for the allocation of responsibility.

3.   The staff will make a survey of world book production
by country and by subject and estimate the adequacy of
present purchases and the probable additional expense involved in making current acquisitions complete instead of
selective.

4.   Each cooperating library will then be asked to name
the fields of its particular interest in which it would be
willing to specialize and to assume responsibility for a
comprehensive (not a selective) coverage within the terms
of Section A.

5.   On the basis of these offers of specialization, the
headquarters staff will try to arrange for the allocation of
fields for which no offer has been made and will suggest,
in cases where several offers have been made for the
same field, the allocation which seems to it most practicable.

6.   After the presidents, deans, trustees, committees,
and librarians of each cooperating institution have reached
agreement, each library will announce the fields for which
it is ready to accept formal responsibility.

7.   Nothing in the proposed arrangement will limit in any
way the freedom of any cooperating institution to purchase
any materials it desires to secure.   Librarians accepting
this proposal will merely accept affirmative responsibility
for the completion of certain fields, retaining the right to
abandon any field after reasonable notice of an intention
to do so.   In other fields, including those assigned for
complete coverage to others, libraries will of course be
free to purchase as their needs indicate.

8.   As soon as the allocation of fields is completed, the
headquarters staff will publish in appropriate professional
journals the list of allocations made and accepted, in order
that the responsibilities of each library under the plan may
be known to all librarians and all interested users of libraries.

C

In practical operation, this proposal would require the following action by each subscribing library:

1.   The prompt acquisition of all current publications in its allotted fields by ordering all titles of research interest listed in the national trade bibliographies and also those in standard reviews.   This may be done by each library ordering directly the books within the field for which it assumes responsibility or with the aid of agents, particularly in the smaller countries, who may collect and ship all books for their country to a central office in the United States for distribution.

2.   The prompt transmission to the Library of Congress of
a.   A catalog card for each title in a form suitable for use as copy for cooperative cataloging as well as for insertion in the Union Catalog;
b.   A card suitable for filing in a new classed catalog to be maintained in the Library of Congress, from which printed subject bibliographies may later be drawn if the demand requires.

It may prove wise to arrange for centralized cataloging of some books, particularly those in minor languages.

D

It is proposed that the program outlined in section C be put into effect as soon after the close of the war as possible.

E

In addition to carrying through the steps enumerated in section B above, the headquarters staff of this project would make plans and prepare a budget for future operations, including

1.   Acquisition abroad.   It is anticipated that it may prove desirable for the central office of the project to conduct correspondence with agencies in many, if not all, foreign countries, and the central office may even have to take

charge of the buying from certain countries and of materials in certain languages.

2.   Cataloging.   In the same way it may prove desirable for the central office to act as the representative of the participating libraries in the cooperative cataloging of books in certain languages.   If these books are purchased through a central office, an opportunity for centralized cataloging will be offered or the office might farm out such materials to properly equipped libraries for cooperative cataloging.

3.   Classed Union Catalog.   Here the central office would have no very serious role to play but might have to supervise the provision of cards to the Library of Congress.

4.   Change in assignments as they become desirable or necessary.

The cost of the central office after the first two years cannot be estimated at this time, but it should be organized in such a way that it can become self-supporting in not less than five years.

Two major criticisms of the foregoing proposal have been made.   First, it has been asserted that the plan is too large to be carried out and that the attempt is useless.   The sponsors do not hesitate to admit the magnitude of the project and the difficulties that are sure to arise but they are convinced that the results will justify a real effort along these lines and that information and experience of great value for future planning will be gained.

Second is the objection that inclusive acquisition of the sort proposed ignores the fact that selection is fundamental in the philosophy of librarianship.   Here the sponsors reply that they agree as to the importance of selection but that no librarian or group of librarians is wise enough to be sure of just what will and will not be needed at some future date, while a relatively slight addition to--or reallocation of--the funds now expended by American research libraries will insure us against errors of judgment by preserving at least one copy of each book somewhere in the country.   When they know that this safeguard is being taken, then librarians, except in the field or fields for which they have taken inclusive responsibility, should be free to buy selectively without misgivings.

Funds Not Yet Available

As has been noted, the foregoing proposal was approved by the American Council of Learned Societies and by the appropriate library organizations.   Efforts to obtain funds for putting it into operation have not, however, been successful.

The sponsors of the proposal are unwilling to give up. They are continuing their attempts to obtain foundation support but immediate success does not appear likely and valuable time is being lost.   It is of great importance that the preliminary steps be completed before the war is over.

It is possible that the money might be raised among interested libraries.   If each member of the Association of Research Libraries would give four hundred dollars per year, or perhaps somewhat less for two years, and if a little help could be obtained elsewhere, it should be possible to proceed.

Finally, an alternative would be to concentrate on certain phases of the plan or to deal only with material from Latin America, some of the minor European countries, Russia, or China, as representing areas where present acquisitions are most inadequate.   In this way a good deal might be learned at small expense and librarians would later be in a better position to develop the proposal on a broad scale. With this in mind, a special session of the Association of Research Libraries was held recently, and proposals were made for action in the areas mentioned.

It is hoped, however, that it need not be long before the comprehensive program can be attempted.   There seems to be little question of the desirability of the ends in view. American research libraries will not be contributing to scholarship as adequately and as economically as they ought until every book needed by research workers is acquired by some American library soon after publication, is listed in central union author and subject catalogs, is made available to other institutions by interlibrary loan or microfilm, and need be cataloged only once.

PART VI

AUTOMATION AND THE
FUTURE OF LIBRARIES

Introduction to Part VI

AUTOMATION AND THE FUTURE OF LIBRARIES

(To the Bodleian Library) You, having built
an ark to save learning from deluge, deserve
propriety in any new instrument or engine
whereby learning should be improved or advanced.
                              --Francis Bacon

There is much that is now going on in the world of
libraries that is new and challenging. If we have fixed ideas
of our worth as a profession and a commitment to provide
library service, we know perhaps too little, despite the sound
technical base on which we have to build and despite projec-
tions that have been made, about how that professional commitment will be put into practice in the years to come. The
tremendous output of print and non-print material, electronic
data processing and computer technology, and, more recently,
the development of computer-based library networks are only
a few of the developments of the past few years that seem
certain to profoundly affect, in one way or another, the future
of libraries. The services which we have developed so extensively over the past one hundred years will not be changed
overnight. The concerns that have been with us for the last
one hundred years may be modified somewhat but the services
provided to the public and the integration of technology into
our operations to improve and strengthen those services will
continue to be our major concern.

Although automation has been a real factor in librarianship for less than one-third of the period, because of its present impact and its potential for the future it must be considered here.

If technology is not the golden apple that writers such
as Vannevar Bush, Kemeney, and Licklider have held it out
to be, neither is it the demon that Ellsworth Mason and oth-

485

ers have suggested.   We have tried to include here articles
reflecting both of those points of view as well as ones that
take a more realistic view of our future and how technology
might be best integrated into libraries.

It is useful as we look towards the future to have a
sound historical perspective.   Hopefully this anthology will
help provide that perspective as we attempt to ascertain the
reality of the future.   Whatever does happen, it seems clear
that the articles included here will continue to play a significant role in shaping our thoughts and our actions.   As clearly and as concisely as those whose work we have included
here have addressed the concerns of the profession in their
time, the issues raised by them remain with us in many
ways and will continue to challenge us.

FROM FRIGHT TO FRANKENSTEIN*

Ralph R. Shaw

The problem of increasing size of the world's bibliography and the world's libraries, and of the steps which are alleged to be required to control, manage, or combat them is not new. The tempo of the arguments has stepped up so much in the last two decades, however, that the various schools of thought involved, and the implications of this problem, appear to merit serious study.

These arguments revolve around the indications that the volume of literature is increasing at a faster and faster rate and the allegation that radical innovations are essential if we are to remain, or become, masters of man's knowledge.

By and large these can be termed arguments from fright to frenzy. Whether either the fright or the frenzy is justifiable remains to be seen.

While solutions are commonly offered, this is not always the case and a considerable group starts with the argument that the mass is getting too large for handling--and stops there. This group divided into two sub-groups, one of which simply stops with a cliche about the all-engulfing black tide of print. The other sub-group would go a little farther, arguing that since it is not possible to keep up with everything we might as well give up--thus arguing from fright to lethargy (or perhaps from lethargy to fright) rather than from fright to frenzy. This latter group is not too far different from the many people and groups who for generations have avoided the effort of using recorded knowledge by arguing that consulting

---

*Reprinted with permission from D. C. Libraries 24:6-10 (January 1953).

what is known tends to chain the creative spirit.

But going on from these passive groups, we find a number of groups who, like the former, accept the prime assumption that the mass of literature is or is becoming so great as to require radical action; then go on to present panaceas or ameliorants.

Probably first among these numerically are those who tend to garble a song recently popular in certain quarters to read: "Let's make them throw it away." These range from professors who write articles like the "Last Canute" to librarians who write about the crisis in cataloging, the crisis in bibliography, etc. This presents a common form of argument from the assumption that mass requires manhandling. The argument here is never on the basis of whether big libraries or big catalogs, etc., are good or bad for the purposes of the group that they are to serve. It merely skips from "too big" to "something has to be done about this." Of course it would be difficult to get professors to agree on the books that are to be thrown away. For example, the Royal Society at its Scientific Information Conference came to grips with its preliminary recommendation that the way to handle the great mass of literature was to stop third-rate writing at its source. In the later stages of this conference, when it was attempted to determine how to tell what should be published and what should be kept from cluttering the literature, the net result was that only this recommendation itself was kept from cluttering the literature. This group is more disturbing than many of the others in that it shows an unhealthy willingness in those who live by intellectual processes to substitute slogans for thinking in this field.

Still another group hopefully looks forward to a solution of all these problems by machines of one description or another. By and large this group, as will be noted below, skips from the fact that machines are doing wonderful things in certain other fields, to the conclusion that they will solve our problems. The thing which these people tend to overlook is that machines, like people in this respect, must not only be good; they must be good for something--and the something that they are good for must bear some relationship to the job which we have to perform in storing, organizing, handling and supplying the knowledge contained in man's record of achievement.

This leads us to the more sophisticated enthusiasts

for mechanical devices, who have machines or mechanical devices to recommend. Each of these argues from mass to his particular solution, whether it be microfilm, microcards, electronic machines, or sawing books in half to make them smaller--without much regard for the immediate data. Also, substantially all of these base their arguments on the exponential curve of growth of libraries, which, with the inevitable charm of a half-truth, has worked its way so deeply into the gospel that it is generally quoted without question by scientists and librarians alike. This is the group which argues directly from fright, as imposed by the implications of the exponential chart, to Frankenstein, as exemplified by the particular mechanical solution put forth at the moment.

But in all of these cases the original argument is arithmetic. It is a matter of size and of allegedly increasing size and of allegedly exponentially increasing size that provides the alleged crisis which calls for each alleged solution. That being the case, if the premise is not sound then much of the argument which follows from it must be open to serious question--and in the case of the exponents of the exponential the basic premise rests upon partial data and upon obviously erroneous conclusions derived therefrom.

Let us analyze the implications, therefore, of this exponential curve. As you know, an exponential rate of growth is one which shows doubling in size in regular intervals of time. Mr. Rider drew his much-reproduced curve for the average holdings of ten selected university libraries, showing that they increased in size at a rate such that their average holdings have substantially doubled in size each 16 years, from 1820 through 1940. This line, like all exponential growth lines, is substantially a straight line, and the implication with which we are left is that it can be projected into the future thus predicting prodigious and fantastic growth of certain if not all libraries. From this horrible picture we have in the past leapt directly to panaceas. But this time, instead of leaping to a conclusion, let us see whether any conclusion can be drawn from the graph as presented. If, as is indicated, these libraries were to continue to double in size every sixteen years, then by the year 2090, which is just about as far ahead as the chart goes back, these libraries will have doubled nine more times. At the end of that period they will then average something over 1,228,000,000 volumes each, and will have to be adding books at the rate of 90 million volumes a year to continue this exponential growth. This does not appear very likely in view of the fact

that something less than 20 million books total have been published from the beginning of time to date.

But if this is not adequate, since it is not entirely impossible that we will be publishing 90 million books a year
for these libraries to add in the year 2100, let's take the case
of automobiles, where we can get a better check on this exponential curve. A chart showing registration of passenger
automobiles from 1900 through 1921 shows that they doubled
about once every two years throughout that period. Now, if
we follow that by doubling every two years from 1921 through
1951, in 1951 we should have had somewhat more than 157
billion passenger cars registered in the United States. Accordingly, last year there should have been registered 1,000
passenger cars for every man, woman, and child in the
country.

Another example of the foolishness of carrying extrap-
olation of the exponential curve too far is that of patent applications. For a 26-year period from 1844 to 1870 patent
applications substantially doubled every six years. Extrapolat-
ing that rate to the present would call for filing of about 270
million patents a year (when in fact the total number of patent
applications filed each year is now only around 70,000.)

And if further evidence about the habits of exponential
growth rates is needed, let's turn to another object which
shows an exponential curve of growth for a known period. An
infant doubles its weight during its first six months, and its
prenatal growth rate is much greater than that. So we can
draw an exponential growth curve for a period in which the
doubling of weight occurs faster than once each six months.
However, if instead of weighing the baby, we extrapolated the
doubling of weight in six months for just a few cycles, the
little monster, weighing only seven pounds at birth, should
weigh just under a ton by the time he reaches four years of
age.

All of which merely indicates that the straight-line
portion of an exponential rate of growth, while common to
many forms of life and of human endeavor, never lasts very
long, and the rapid tailing off of the climb is just as characteristic as is the rapid growth for a relatively brief period.

As a matter of fact, an exponential curve is always a
section of a larger curve, and it never stands alone. While
substantially all worth-while things have exponential growth

for a period, they always show non-exponential growth for at
least two periods.   No new invention is accepted the day it is
placed on the market.   Take the electric light bulb for example.   It is reported that three years after Edison placed
the electric lamp on the market he had 57 customers.   The
sales curve for this period was very flat indeed.   Then when
the lamp caught on, the sales skyrocketed in typical exponential fashion.   After a while, the market was substantially
saturated, and except for new installations, which now became
a relatively small figure as compared with the number of
bulbs in existence, and replacements, also a small number
as compared with the total, the market was saturated, and
the curve flattened off sharply again.   The flat start and the
flat end are just as characteristic of any growth curve as is
the steep, exponential, straight-line portion, and presentation
of the one without the other two is likely to be very misleading indeed.

While we librarians may be forgiven for ignorance of
the normal behavior of exponential growth rates, that would
hardly serve as an excuse for our more scientific brethren
who have taken the straight-line portion of this curve to their
hearts and argue from this curve in two directions to prove
the need for electronic controls.   Scientific American for
September of this year presents Rider's curve as the "Bibliographical Crisis" and calls for the development of electronic machines for solution of this problem.   On the other
hand, in another fairly recent publication, Bibliography in an
Age of Science, an eminent physicist recognizes that the rate
of growth of the larger libraries is already showing signs of
slowing down from the straight line exponential rate, but, instead of accepting that as the normal result at the end of all
periods of exponential growth, interprets it as evidence that
library techniques are incapable of coping with the rapidly increasing amount of literature and goes on, of course, to
recommend the development of electronic machines for this
purpose.

So much for the argument from fright.   Let us now
look at the Frankenstein.   The creatures which are proposed
as solving the bibliographical problems thus created range all
the way from the American Documentation Institute which was
founded upon the argument that the literature was too great
to be handled so new techniques had to be developed to handle
it--with the classic example of the failure of the International
Catalog of Scientific Literature as the prime argument in
point.   Here, too, the argument from fright was invalid and

the solution fell somewhat short of providing a solution. This
is commonly the case, and we ought to be able to expect
validating data for the claims for the new machines and techniques whether they be microfilms, microcards or electronic
machines.

As shown in a paper delivered before the University of
Chicago Institute on Bibliographical Management, the book,
the printed page in general, is a remarkably efficient storage
device. In its more condensed forms, such as handbooks,
the book stores more information in less space than any known
non-alphabetic device. But lest we be charged with a static
concept--that of storage--when the needs are dynamic, let us
look at the book as a finding device as compared with the
electronic substitutes proposed.

First it must be noted that there is no such thing as
an electronic machine. All the so-called electronic devices
have mechanical appurtenances which are bulky and limit the
speed at which the electronic parts can operate to that at
which the magnetic wires, punched cards, tapes, or the like,
can insert instructions, and at which results can be interpreted into intelligible form. The data are, and are likely
for a long time to be, stored mechanically rather than electronically. The nature of this storage for electronic machines
is such that it places narrow limits on their potential usefulness in our fields of work.

The Encyclopaedia Britannica stores about 227 million
alphabetic characters (figuring the picture areas as straight
text, which gives an advantage to the electronic machine since
it cannot read pictures and a larger area of words would be
required to translate the total pictures into a form which the
electronic machine could handle.) Since there are some 63
upper- and lower-case characters and punctuation marks in
the English language, and additional space has to be provided
for non-Roman alphabets such as Greek which appear in the
encyclopedia, at least 10 binary units (bits) will be required
to write each letter magnetically or electronically. This would
give us a total of 2 billion, 270 million bits. Assuming that
we could use bits only 10 thousands of an inch long (100 per
inch) this would mean a magnetic wire 22. 7 million inches
long. If we ran that at 100 inches per second, which is fast,
it would require 227,000 seconds or 63 hours to go through
the Encyclopaedia "electronically. " Or, if the wire were divided into 24 parts, just as the book is divided into 24 volumes, it would require 2 hours and 40 minutes per volume.

Even if we used a tape with 8 channels instead of a wire, we should still have a searching time of about 8 hours for the whole set or about 20 minutes per volume. That cannot compete with the old fashioned hand searching in the "antiquated" book form.

The moral of this is that before we can accept the solutions they will have to be presented on a more factual basis than that something desperate must be done--particularly when the most cursory examination thus shows that the book is a more efficient tool, both for storage of alphabetical intelligence and for finding alphabetic intelligence, than any other mechanical device so far presented or hinted at.   This is true primarily because the other mechanical and electronic devices are all single or two dimensional.   They require beginning at one end of a tape or wire and running straight through to the other.   Books on the other hand are three dimensional.   We can open a book, and by using indexes start the detailed searching very close to the answer.   This is apparently faster than any random unidirectional, linear process no matter how fast its machinery may run.

This leads to several conclusions: First the fright may be greater than the facts warrant and the Frankensteins proposed are not supported by evidence that they will serve acceptably as substitutes for existent tools, in terms of efficiency in handling the load.

Second, any device which is to compete with the book will need to utilize a multi-directional approach rather than a linear approach, if it is to have any chance whatever of success.   Some essays in this direction have been taken, and we are approaching understanding of the nature of the problem and understanding of the nature and attributes of the various tools, including the book.

A third thing which is becoming clear is that the problems of mass take care of themselves in all libraries except those few which attempt all-inclusiveness in a wide range of knowledge, whether the material with which they are concerned is in conventional book form or in less conventional forms, or both.   Only in the field of organization of intellectual content of literature is the mass involved of significance to any appreciable number of libraries or people.   To make this a little clearer, how many million-volume libraries are there as against the number with less than 100,000?   The college library, or the public library which does not aim at inclusion

of substantially everything printed in a wide range of subject
fields is not going to grow as large as many libraries already
have.   And having libraries which do operate with collections
of several million volumes (a size that only a few hundred
libraries at most are likely ever to achieve), it is difficult
to prove that the world will come to an end if two or three
or a dozen more libraries get to the million or even the five-
million-volume size.   Several of the largest libraries have
already slowed their rate of growth, and the sixteenth-century
forecast of Gesner that libraries will eventually grow bigger
than cities (recently reinvented by many others) has yet to
become a serious problem.   So the physical aspect of the size
of the collections is not of very general import.

    So let us think kindly of those who would frighten us
by slogans and catchwords about the great and growing mass
of the world's literature, and of those who take pity upon our
benighted state to solve all our problems with machines they
have not yet thought about, and let's get on with the part of
the job that is important.

    The organization of the ideas contained in literature is
a more difficult problem.   In this area the need for total recall is just as great in the smallest library which is faced
with a problem of research caliber as it is in the largest library, and it is as important in the research station in the
back country of Bolivia as it is in great centers of literature
in England, France, the United States, or elsewhere.   The
job which faces us is a large one.   It is a job of organizing
and communicating the intellectual content of man's recorded
knowledge.   The tools at hand have always determined in
large measure the extent to which this can be done, and they
always will.   So developing improved tools will always be a
part of our jobs.   If they are to be electronic, well and good.
If not, well and good.   But each will have to justify itself by
more than catchwords and will have to serve as more than a
development project.   If they do not they are gadgets rather
than tools--and with a job as big as the one we are faced
with we do not have time for gadgets for gadgets' sake.   Certain new developments in film recording, which maintain the
true compactness of storage of the alphabet in condensed
form, together with high-speed finding, constitute a step in
the direction of more compact storage and more rapid finding
and reproduction.   But even that will not compete with the
quick reference tool in the latter's field.

    So we are faced by an exciting job over the next few

decades (and for many decades thereafter). The extent to
which it will be achieved will depend in large measure on
librarians, whether they work in what is called special libraries, college libraries, or public libraries, who apply
concentrated thought to the true nature and scope of the bibliographical problem.

THE GREAT GAS BUBBLE PRICK'T;
OR, COMPUTERS REVEALED*

--by a Gentleman of Quality[1]

> In which are Exposed the delicious Delusions
> of those will-o-the-wisps; the Echoes in com-
> puterization of Phrenology, Haruspication, and
> other discredited Ancient sciences; and the
> moral and Mental decline of our Profession.
>
> "If it costs you twenty-five percent more,
> will you stop it?"
> "No."
> "Why not?"
> "Because we believe that sooner or later
> all libraries will automate."
>   --From a real-life, absurd conversation.

On an evaluation visit last spring to a small college
(collection 175,000 volumes, peak daily circulation 700), I
found the library automating its circulation records, an action tantamount to renting a Boeing 747 to deliver a bonbon
across town. Everyone felt great about it; it was a Good
Thing! In a college sorely pressed for funds, wasting this
amount of money was actually a serious crime against the
common weal.

This situation nicely characterizes the fatuousness of
one of the most curious periods in our nation's history--the
period that began with a rebound off Sputnik, which seemed

*Reprinted by permission of the American Library Associa-
tion from College and Research Libraries 32:183-196 (May
1971).

for a moment to snatch a tip from our crown of world leadership, to strip us of our masculinity, as it were.   In this
period, which has now passed its peak, money meant nothing,
the world of formal education was endowed with magical properties, and technology became an unquestioned God (If we can
put a man on the moon we can ...).   This decade boasted of
its technical potency with the false bravado of a male virgin,
and if the moon rocket in the Sea of Tranquility was its sexual symbol, the computer, choked in its navel cord of programs, was its abortion.

     This fact has yet to be generally absorbed.   It has
already become painfully clear that technology is a two-edged
sword of Damocles.   Grave doubt has been raised that the
computer has done even major industries much good. [2]   But,
oblivious to the signs of change, librarians are proceeding in
a kind of stunned momentum like a poleaxed steer, because
the computer industry and its public handmaidens have polluted our intellects.   In one of the most massive public manipulations in history, the computer has been joined to Mother-
hood, the True, the Good, and the Beautiful.   Operational
considerations have been stripped to a stark choice between
"the old hand-method" (ugh!) and THE COMPUTER.   The effect has been to obscure a whole range of machine and machine-manual alternatives. [3]   Technology has been set back
many years and intelligence has been uprooted.   Any fool
who does anything with a computer for any reason (we all
know at least one) is automatically a genius; anyone who does
not is the last of the dinosaurs.

     During a period of study sponsored by a Council on
Library Resources (CLR) fellowship which allowed me to study
problems in ten major research libraries last spring, my observations convinced me that the high costs of computerization
make it unfeasible for library operations and that it will become increasingly expensive in the future. [4]   The computer
feeds on libraries.   We actually devote large amounts of talent and massive amounts of money (perhaps $25 million dol-
lars a year in academic libraries alone) to diminish collections and reduce services, exactly at a time when libraries
are starved for both, by channeling money into extravagant
computerization projects which have little or no library benefits.   While my original expectations were entirely in the opposite direction, after talking at length with some of the finest
computer experts in the library world and probing the thinking behind more than forty computerized library operations, it
became clear that the application of computers to library pro-

cesses is a disaster, and that no one is willing to admit
it.

The reasons for its adoption are governed by a range
of irresponsible, irrational, and totally unmanaged factors,
both within the library and in the university, that cannot fail
to disgust anyone seriously concerned about the academic
world.   This article intends to analyze how we learn to stop
thinking and love the machine, and to make possible the return of intellect and managerial methods to an area of library
practice from which both have been driven.

The Rough Beast With Three Breasts

Unlike most other machines, the computer is not subject to reasonable surveillance at any level of operation. [5]
A college president or the manager of industrial research
cannot judge with any reasonable degree of accuracy how
much computer capacity is required for his needs, nor can
his subordinates.   This means that basically he must accept
his computer configuration on faith and on the urgings of computer industry representatives.

This condition in which the computer wanders free
from quality checks extends right down the line of a computer
operation to the head of programming, who cannot judge with
any degree of precision the quality of the programs written
for him. [6] He can tell whether they run (indeed, the principal struggle is to get them to run trouble-free at all), but he
cannot tell how they rate in comparison with the range of
other alternatives.   This free-form condition of control, which
is inherent in the occult nature of the computer, accounts for
the great range of loose work and random performance ob-
servable in computer operations.

Moreover, a computer operation is incapable of becoming stabilized on its own terms.   No matter what level
of performance is achieved, if a later generation computer is
marketed, it is necessary to shift as soon as possible to the
new generation, with all the agonies, dislocations, and set-
backs involved in the change, and with no assurance that the
same level of results can be achieved.   There is no choice
of remaining as you are if reasonably satisfied with your results because it is extremely difficult to recruit a systems
and programming staff (doubly difficult for libraries, which
lack the glamor and loose money that have characterized in-

dustry until recently). A good staff will abandon a super-
seded model computer, since to remain would make them professionally obsolescent.

These two floating conditions make computer operations
basically uncontrollable. In managerial terms, these facts
alone would argue for discarding out of hand any other machine in existence, until it was amenable to quality control.
But we have been conditioned to suspend completely the requirements that apply to all other equipment, and automatically accept the computer as Good, without questioning. We accept the computer as the pot of gold at the end of the rain-
bow, the touchstone that turns dross into gold. Glittering
with spangles, draped seductively in the fluff of unreason, it
really has sex appeal, and who applies reason while gulping
the lures of a floozie like Myra Breckenridge?[7]

The New Bloomusalem

When Leopold Bloom, Joyce's common man in Ulysses,
proclaims, while playing God in an hallucination, "the golden
city which is to be," thirty-two workmen wearing rosettes
construct "The New Bloomusalem," a megastructure in the
shape of a huge pork kidney. Something like this debased
miracle happened in library computerization in the decade of
the sixties, when computers rode tall in the industrial saddle
and librarians flung themselves at the horse's tail. During
that decade, our large problems were operational (whereas
now they are desperately financial) and we looked for a pan-
acea. Noting us sniffing around the computer, the industry
perked up and assured us they were the answer.

A kind of syllogistic thinking followed--we have problems; the computer says it can solve them; therefore, using
the computer solves our problems. [8] It's all simple enough
and clear enough if you just have Faith, and of course, Reason is the enemy of Faith; in fact, it gets in the way of cer-
tainty. In our awe at the wonders of technology, we forgot
the deadly threat of Dr. Strangelove's mechanical hand. Like
lemmings moving toward the sea, we surged to get with it,
became scientists, became industrialists, and practiced the
best that was known and felt in the business world. [9] In the
whole range of the academic world, we forgot one of our
traditional functions--to suspect the beguilement and evanes-
cence of the moment and "to keep clean our sense of difference between the temporarily and the permanently significant."[10]

In short, we embraced with fervor all the sins of the commercial world. Now, look at the commercial world and at
the academic world and wonder how it is that student rebels
connect the two.

The fascination of the computer, like that of a hooded
cobra, lies in its exotic beauty, which fixes its victim for
the spurt of poison.   On the surface it seems to have many
answers.   It looks effortless, is pleasantly mysterious, it
makes pleasing sounds, it promises great speed, and it has
a reputation for performing miracles.   Despite its beginnings
in 1942 (long before Xerox), it is considered the latest technological development.   So we got with the new and the tech-
nologically best by adopting the computer.   We did so to
solve simple and clearly defined problems--to save staff (or
substitute for staff that we couldn't hire), to speed processing,
and to save money.   Information retrieval was seen in the
distant mist, but these were the clear and central targets.

But when we used the computer, it didn't save staff,
and it didn't speed processing, and it cost a great deal more
to do the same things we were doing by hand.   Our reaction
was to computerize more.   Although we lost money on every
operation we computerized, the theory grew that if you knit
enough losses together, obviously you would save money.   In
Orwellian doublethink, if you waste money in an attempt to
save it, save better by wasting more.   We still didn't save
staff, and we didn't speed processing, and it cost us even
more money.   Our latest answer is to use newer and bigger
and more expensive computers; it still is not saving us staff
or speeding processing, and we are now spending extravagant
amounts of money.   We bombed library problems with the
computer, and the strategy didn't work.   So we bombed even
more problems with the computer and it still didn't work, so
we are bombing even more.

Just Like General Motors

At this point, the third strange fact about the computer
becomes clear.   It is a half-baked machine.   Every other kind
of equipment we use is bought for specific purposes, to perform defined tasks, at a known cost.   Even highly automated
equipment like the MT/ST comes with a simple program to
perform known tasks after a modicum of training.   A wholly
baked computer, nicely browned, would be ordered to specifications, and would come ready to dust off, to insert the

program provided by the manufacturer to do what we wanted
to be done, and to begin our computerized operation.   Only
under such conditions would we consider any other machine.
But we have been brainwashed not to apply the same reasonable standards to the computer.   The cobra has us hypnotized.

When it is dumped on your dock, it can do nothing for
you; like, Ford delivers you a Continental and deposits it in
your yard.   You leap with joy and shout to the neighbors who
come to admire.   You puff with pride, as we do for computers.   "Let's go for a ride," they say.   Somewhat sheep-
ishly, you explain that it is a new proto-electric Continental,
with a wonderful fume-free motor, but that there is no battery known strong enough to power it.   When they say, "Why
did you buy it?" do you reply, "Oh, I'll do my own Research
and Development to produce the battery"?

Such an answer would be insane, but this is exactly
what we do for computers. 11   We assume the responsibility,
the elaborate costs, and the human agonies involved in programming to make the machine do what we knew we wanted
it to do before we bought it.   In one project now underway,
it will take a staff of ten, three years to make anything happen.   Libraries really are getting important when they can
play junior GM (without GM's budget) and launch amateur research and development operations, which is what programming really consists of.   No matter how good our systems
staff, such research and development must remain amateur.
We don't know enough about technology even to know which
field we should work in to solve our problems, let alone
which machine we should encourage.   We haven't the meager-
est grasp of the perspective required by industrial R & D.
But we have enthusiasm, we have suspended our brains, and
we've come to love the computer.

We spend millions making the computer work for library activities, with a guarantee that it will produce a built-
in deficit and with only a vague chance that it will improve
anything.   We simply can't wait for the finished machine,
for the one that really works, the one which when it comes
will make computers useless.   We must develop it ourselves,
even if we have to sell our libraries (which we are doing) to
do so.

How We Are Covered With Locusts
and How the Invasion Began

How did we get into this mess? There are precedents
in human history. The mountebank pulls up at the crossroads
and the yokels throng the tailgate to buy snake-oil guaranteed
to cure any disorder of libraries. Gullibility accounts for
part of it; pressures account for the rest. The physical scientists and mathematicians brought the computer on campus for
its computational facility. [12] Engineering, which quickly was
seized by electronics specialists, burgeoned later. From
these three groups came large demands for computer time in
the universities. Administrators, naive and uninformed, began pressures to have all the computer time on campus used
because of its heavy cost. They began by offering "free"
computer time (an interesting concept at current prices) to
any department that would use it. This free offer sprang
from the prestige value inherent in using the computer (the
industry did supply the prestige) and from a conviction on the
part of administrators (also supplied by the industry) that use
of the computer saved money for any operation it touched.

As this free time was used, the demand for computer
time overran that available, and bigger, better, and much
more expensive computers were brought on campus. With
even greater increases in expense, administrative pressure
(as brainless as all other pressures involved in computerization) intensified, and in some instances became downright
nasty to departments that dragged their feet either through
lethargy or knowledge. They were joined by the computer
engineering faculty, which in recent INTREXed years, has
become self-deluded to an extreme degree. [13]

Librarians, most of whom are humanistically trained,
are especially sensitive to accusations by technologists and
administrators of refusing the best that is known to business
and technology. Even when they know better, consistent pressures unsettle their confidence. To cool the hot breath of the
president's office, one university made a list of special materials by computer when they knew in advance they could do
it considerably cheaper by more than one noncomputer method. To appease the demands of a renowned and totally im-
practical engineer, one university went to a computerized
circulation system as the least wasteful operation they could
run on the computer. The fatuous self-confidence of computer experts is considerably jolted when they have to cope
with the demands of library operations, which are far more

complex than anything else they tackle in terms of their machine.   But so long as they can throw stones from a comfortable theoretical distance their pressures are compelling
indeed.

The Electronic Calf

In a time of waning personal confidence, it takes a
very strong man to stand up to a university president and
tell him he's wrong when he is convinced by technologists
that inertia springs from ignorance.   There are only a few
men left these days.   Therefore, with the prod in our rear,
or approaching, we adapted to the new campus ecology, now
polluted by technologists.   Although some librarians seized
the computer for its public relations value (Look, mommy:
no catalogers!), the more sober members of the fraternity
went along with a better conscience by adopting a mystique
about the computer that grew partly outside and partly inside
librarianship.

This mystique generated, and in turn was generated
by, a group of librarians whose livelihood depended on the
computer, and whose reason for being depended largely on
their ability to believe the computer industry's claims laid
out before them.   The emergence of this Faith and the band
of True Believers have been responsible for the rapidity with
which we have gotten into computerization despite all evidence
that the fantastic claims for the computer are completely
false.   This group of the faithful was abetted by enormous
sums of government and foundation money that flowed, like
Niagaras of champagne (Lucius Beebe's phrase), into computerized projects for a five-year period.   With this ampli-
tude of fuel, these neo-Zoroastrians began to burn up the
world.

The Revelation

Blazoned across the dark benighted sky of conventional
librarianship were the following Truths:

The First Truth--Come to the computer all ye who
are heavy laden and It will make everything effortless. [14]

The Facts--The computer has involved librarians in
greater and more prolonged agonies than anything in recent

history short of the Florence flood.   Agonies of campus politics (flipped from computer to computer), agonies of financing
(since the golden angels have gone), agonies of programming,
patching programs, reprogramming, re-debugging programs,
agonies of lengthy machine breakdowns, agonies of deception
by computer experts (both in industry and in other campus
units) have left deep scars on every library computer expert
I have known.[15]   While I was on campus one university was
executing the second major cutback of computer capacity within three years, each causing major upheavals and changes in
staffs and procedures and the bitterest kind of infighting to
control the nature of the computer configuration.   The most
efficient road to ulcers on a college campus, short of the
president's office, is through library computerization.

       The Second Truth--Thou shalt do everything with the
speed of light, if thou butst computerize.

       The Facts--Response time of computers, which is in-
credibly fast (as fast as the movement of an electron), is not
to be confused with the response time of computerized processes.[16]   It is common knowledge that computerized class
schedules take weeks longer to produce than the old hand method.   In librarianship, these are some of the commonplace delays found strewn all along the trail: Circulation, a delay of
one day in the ability of the circulation file to account for the
location of a charged book (in one case, the costs of paper
led to updating the file only once every three days).   On-line
circulation, the alternative to batching, is so astronomically
expensive that anyone who adopts it should be summarily condemned as a public malefactor.   Acquisitions--consistently
slower in placing orders.   Acquisitions was so slow the spring
that I was on campus that, in one case, 20 percent of their
periodical subscriptions were cancelled due to slow placement
of orders.   Book catalogs--longer and longer delays in cumu-
lations because of the costs involved.   In the case of one university, an operation highly touted while in action had left a
liberal arts college with its book catalog in four (repeat, four)
parts.   They were at the point of doing what they were sure
would be, forever, their last total cumulation because of its
cost, while their future lies in a book catalog always in two
and three parts.   They would like to go to a card catalog,
but at 100,000 volumes, cannot afford to.   One circulation
operation, where the students were cleared faster than previously at the charge-out point, claimed this advantage, without noting that the new system involved the use of book cards

in lieu of user-written cards, and that the computer charging console takes longer than most simple charging machines.

The Third Truth--The computer will save you money.

The Facts--Computer experts laughed when I suggested economy as a motive for adopting the computer. No one claimed to have saved any money doing anything by computer, and although the analysis of computer costs is, to be charitable, hair-raisingly casual, estimates of costs of doing by computer exactly the same things that had previously been done manually were extremely high (in one case, five times the cost). We now know there is no clear evidence that the computer has saved industry money "even in routine clerical operations."17

The Fourth Truth--Well, anyway, once you have done it, thou shalt have economies in future programming by having programs convertible to later generation computers.

The Facts--Absolutely false! About half of the third-generation computers in major industries are in an emulation mode that makes them perform as second-generation computers because industry, having been hooked on the enormous programming costs for the second generation, is unwilling to absorb even higher costs to program for the third generation, which leads to an interesting view of our economy (like our libraries), buying the latest to get with it to avoid losing face. 18

The Fifth Truth--Well, anyway, once someone has done it, programs can be converted from location to location, so you save the expense of programming for yourself.

The Facts--This initially was one of the most appealing lures of the computer industry. A few years ago, in a correspondence with Robert Hayes of the University of California, I asked why we all had to make the computer repeat on machine the motions we were doing by hand. Since we all need about the same end products at the same key points in a serials operation, why couldn't one library program it and present the program in modules, each of which could accomplish one thing, for us to choose those we preferred? At length, in a series of letters, I learned the elaborate and

complex reasons why this could not be done. All the library
computerators I questioned agree that transferability of programs is completely unfeasible at present and in the future.[19]

        The Sixth Truth--Thou shalt have cheap computeriza-
tion by sharing computers with others.

        The Facts--This, again, was one of the bright prom-
ises laid out by the computer industry, but the deeper we get
into library computerization, the more evident it becomes that
sharing computers to reduce costs is a chimera. Yet within
the month, an eminent professor of industrial management
who read my CLR report trotted out the old turkey that, with
remote access consoles, sharing computers would soon make
them economical.

        The Seventh Truth--Thou shalt save money as you mul-
tiply the separate operations that you computerize if you combine them by a systems approach.

        The Facts--Though a common belief among the aborig-
ines of Computeria and sustained by a well-developed theology, there is no evidence whatsoever to support this belief.[20]

        The Eighth Truth--Thou shalt have greater service for
the public by computerizing library operations.

        The Facts--Most of the libraries computerized seem to
have no interest in improving service, as we can see from
such things as their average line-staff salaries (mostly at the
peonage level), the size of their cataloging backlog (in one
case about 300,000 volumes), and the staffing of their campus
branch libraries (about half of the staff needed). Money
wasted in computerization could greatly improve service if
applied to these areas. Also, processes that delay placement
of orders, delay accountability of circulation records, and
split the card catalog in multiple parts would not seem to be
aimed directly at improving service to the public.

The Credo

        Throughout the land, the priesthood, with no exception,
recited to me "The Credo of Automatic Automators":

I believe in the increasing cost of labor and the decreasing cost of computers.

I believe that in ten years (the time span was standardized) the cost curves will cross in favor of computers.

I believe that even if it isn't cheaper, the by-products
of computerization make it worthwhile.

Since my pilgrimage, I have had the same Credo recited by others who were not specifically computerators, so
there must be international specifications for its writing. It
requires some examination.

First: there really is no "decreasing cost of computers. " It is true that, on paper, the unit rental cost of new
generations of computers decreases, but in sounding out what
actually happens in practical applications, it is evident that
the cost of applying the machines has increased due to various factors, one being the difficulty of keeping the computer
fed without interruption. [21] But the central fact is that the
overwhelming costs in computerization are labor costs (machine costs run about 20 percent of the total), and the salaries of systems analysts and programmers go up even faster
than library staff salaries. Even after initial development
costs are absorbed, the repeated costs of reprogramming and
program adjustment are very high. Since the costs of computerized library operations are far higher than manual alternatives now, and the costs of computer labor are increasing faster than library labor costs, computerization will become increasingly expensive in the future.

Second: we are willing to accept any machine that
will save us money at any time, [22] but if that is ten years
from now, then 1981 is the time to adopt the machine. What
kind of folly wastes money for ten years on a machine that
it hopes will eventually save money? Within ten years new
machines, now unseen, will emerge in competition with the
computer.

Third: the matter of by-products is the smelliest red
herring of all those dragged across our path by computerators. The word is invoked with a kind of awe, as though it
descends from heaven to banish all the disabilities of the computer. As Melcher put it: "we find ourselves invited to ap-
plaud computer applications that are somewhat in a class with
the dog who played the violin--not that it was done well, but

rather than it was done at all." [23] I keep having draped before me as accomplishments by-products that either are of no
use whatsoever for a library operation, or that have a very
low incidence of use, or that can easily be done by hand or
by other machines faster and at a lower cost. The questions
that are ignored must be asked--what by-products are worthwhile, for what library purposes, at what costs, and for what
incidence of use? In sum, I find the Credo, like all matters
of dogma, an excuse for suspending the intellect on the part
of librarians and managers.

The Miracles

       At the very peak of library computerization we are
breeding a group of extremely able librarians, whose otherwise fine intelligence is completely blown when they evaluate
their machine. They analyze their daily operations with command and critical brilliance, but when they talk about their
future, like a sun-crazed prospector dribbling fool's gold
through his fingers, a dull film covers their eyes, and they
babble about miracles to come that are just around the corn-
er, with not a shred of evidence to support their beliefs.
Their faith is the exact equivalent of a witch's faith in flying
ointment. Unfortunately, we have long passed the stage in
which we could run a library from a broomstick.

       Nevertheless, one can respect the priesthood. It's
the acolytes, and at their fringe, the sycophants that make us
feel unclean. Here we are in a range of oneupmanship and
pretentiousness straight from Madison Avenue. [24] Responses
to questionnaires about computerized operations produce amaz-
ing answers, if you know what is really going on in libraries.
If someone lays down a transistor on a typewriter, the department is likely to respond that it has automated. The
computer is used to cover up weaknesses as cowdung was to
plaster frontier log cabins. If catalogers are low producers,
if circulation is in chaos, the tendency is to computerize instead of reviewing or revising operations, both of which require thinking.

       So, the rules of thumb are clear--if you start a library
from scratch, computerize and you're fifty years old. [25] If
you're upgrading an Ag college, the computer will liberalize
cows. If you're a frustrated junior college, computerize and
it makes you Ph.D. If your faculty is lousy, computerize
and you'll be Harvard. If you're bush league, computerize

and you'll win the Series. If you're stupid, computerize and
you'll feel great. Instant achievement by machine and cheap
attempts to invoke a false sheen of glory have replaced an intelligent confrontation of the problems in a large number of
weak libraries.

Run, Rabbit, Run

In view of the irrationality of the forces that led to library computerization, and the subsequent aggravation of this
situation by self-seekers, it should come as no surprise that
managerial practice has entirely left this field.[26] Of the
forty-odd computer projects reviewed on my leave in ten major libraries, not one was begun on the basis of a managerial
decision, after carefully reviewing and costing the operation
to be converted, costing other machine or machine-manual
alternatives (which were obviously available for many of them),
or carefully projecting the costs of the computer operation
after development costs (which one should be willing to absorb if retrievable over a period of time). Since most of
the projects were doing only what had been done manually,
price should have been the major factor in making this decision, yet very little cost analysis was applied, although all
the libraries were hard pressed for funds. No computerators
were surprised when I reported lack of managerial decisions;
it was taken for granted that there were none in computerization. Like concupiscence, the desire to computerize simply
must be satisfied no matter what the cost, and this at a time
when most universities and libraries are bankrupt and facing
an even bleaker financial future.

Downhill All the Way

My discussions of this problem have produced a number of oppositions over the past few months, the most interesting of which is the concept of comparative incompetence
advanced by a friend of mine. It makes no difference, the
argument goes, that no careful cost comparisons precede
computerization, because most librarians do not analyze costs
before making other changes in libraries. The premise, I
think, is false; but even if it were true, it is almost impossible to make even approximately as large a commitment in
any other way in a library as that involved in computerization, where a quarter of a million dollars is meager.

More harrowing than the enormous costs is the fact
that a computerized system is virtually irreversible, the
fourth distinctive disability of this machine. 27 Once you begin a systems approach to computerizing operations, you are
hung by the gills on the computer industry's fishstringer for
good.   Once applied, the computer acts as a powerful agent
against change.   The dynamics here are interesting.   One library began to computerize by hiring a systems librarian
who hired one programmer when they began to convert their
circulation operation.   Two years later, when the agonies of
this conversion had subsided (and the circulation costs were
fantastically more expensive than the manual system, and they
were cumulating circulation records only every three days),
the staff of this department was five, and, having been blooded,
was eager to begin computerizing another operation.   Even if
you could prove that further computerization was diabolically
evil, you still could not stop this momentum.

In addition, once computerization begins, the campus
pressures on the library to get with it have been assuaged,
the operation has been tapped for its public relations value,
and personal and institutional egos are heavily invested in
ploughing ahead to disaster.   This is especially true if the
computer project is the librarian's baby.   One highly touted
serials project began on "free" computer time, then later
was charged for the campus computer costs (which hurt, but
were not disabling).   When the campus changed its computer
and this operation had to use commercial firms for the computer configuration necessary to run its program, the cost
more than doubled previous costs.   After reprogramming for
over a year, this serials operation is still processed partly
off and partly on campus.   It is known as a disaster area
among computer experts, but this librarian stated recently
that he thought it had done his library a lot of good.

Inertia also results from sheer moral exhaustion.   The
prolonged agonies inflicted on any sane person during the process of converting to computerization push him to the extremes of human endurance.   After all the bugs are exter-
minated and the system is running, it is virtually impossible
for a survivor of the process to summon up the moral
strength to rethink, reorganize, redevise processes, and re-
staff.   In one case, where superficial cost comparisons convinced an acquisitions operation it was saving money, more
sober thought made clear that it was losing money and taking
longer by computer.   But the department head was very in-
dignant when I proposed that they could return to their former

system--"After going through all of that?" Another department head refused even to reconsider and attempt costs comparisons when, after three years, her computer system was
finally working.

Then, of course, there are enormous inflexibilities
imposed against change by finances. Development costs in
one case seem to be running over a million and a half dollars. You can be sure that it will take quite a jolt to make
a library abandon that large an investment. In other instances, the costs of changing to an alternative system require large amounts of money not in hand, as in the college
with the four-part book catalog that would prefer a card catalog. Until the totality of waste in operating by computer becomes so large that the figure really appalls, the library is
not likely to make the sensible move, especially in the face
of the beneficent connotation that (in libraries, at least) is
still attached to the computer.

The Brave New World

Anyone who computerizes at this point in time is hitch-
ing his wagon to a falling star. The honeymoon is over, if
our seduction by the computer can be so termed. We have
been sucked in by one of the most potent information control
powers in recent history. Computerizing library operations
at present and projected costs, and with foreseeable results,
is intellectually and fiscally irresponsible and managerially
incompetent. The proper answer to idiots who beamingly
dangle their computerized projects for our admiration is,
"Why don't you do something useful, instead."

The shrinking financial support of the academic world
will drive us to sense even against our will. On the campus
where I found forty-nine computers (four of them IBM 360's;
one, the largest capacity known), the president gave the blood-
iest state-of-the-university speech to date--dropping three
academic programs, cutting back the current budget forthwith
a million dollars, forecasting a further rollback of 3.5 million over the next three years, and even this predicated on
unusual success in fund raising.

This is no temporary condition tied to the recession.
More than two years ago, it was apparent that the public had
become disillusioned with technology and education. They expected miracles of both; yet it is clear that each is the an-

swer to only a part of our national problems. Public support
for technology, a keystone in education's expansion, will continue to decline. Alumni disillusionment with campus products
has seriously diminished alumni support. Foundations have
been turning from the academy to other social agencies. The
production of bachelor's, master's, and doctorate degrees has
overrun the market for their products. Elementary and secondary school populations continue to decline. Education has
costed itself out of sight, either in tuition costs or in the
total costs of public institutions. All of these factors guarantee us future curtailment of programs in higher education and
a continual decline in financial support, except for those programs immediately responsive to immediate problems that enjoy public favor. Make no mistake, we are about to shake
out the men from the boys, and the future in libraries (as in
other areas of university services) lies with the managers,
who can make the most out of every cent available. The
computer is the machine that evaporates money the fastest. [28]

In sum, our experience with the computer in library
operations has been one more replay of The Emperor's New
Clothes, and what we were led to believe were distant mountains laden with gold, available merely by boring a drift in
the slope, turn out, upon close inspection, to be the hairy
buttocks of the well-fed computer industry. And from such
a source we have gotten exactly what we should expect.

NOTES

1. Ellsworth Mason, Director of Library Services, Hofstra
    University.

2. Quite obviously, this kind of view is not encouraged by
    industry, but when it emerges, it is extremely re-
    vealing. In "Computers Can't Solve Everything,"
    Fortune (Oct. 1969, p. 126-29+, Tom Alexander
    reports the principal findings of a highly disenchant-
    ing survey by the Research Institute of America of
    computerization in 2,500 leading U.S. industrial
    companies. In "Automation: Rosy Prospects and
    Cold Facts," Library Journal (15 March 1968), p.
    1105-09, Daniel Melcher, president of the R. R.
    Bowker Company, indicates in detail that, although
    computerization is costing the publishing industry
    more than former processes, its effect has been to
    diminish performance.

Alexander contends: "But now, after buying or leasing some 60,000 computers during the past fifteen years, businessmen are less and less able to state with assurance that it's all worth it." (p. 126) "As the Research Institute of America survey revealed, most companies are unsure that there is a payoff from computers even in supposedly routine operations." (p. 128) "Relatively few companies have yet succeeded in devising nonclerical applications for the computer (because) programming and equipment costs are so high." (p. 127)

Melcher contends: "To be candid about it, however, I think we could have done all this if anybody had wanted it, even before the invention of the computer." (p. 1109) "Anything can be done (by computer), I guess, but that isn't the issue. What matters is whether anyone in his right mind would choose that way of doing it." (p. 1109) "They all hope for tangible economies in the future--though it is a bit puzzling to note that the $5 million companies seem to expect those economies when they reach $10 million, and the $10 million companies think there might be economies when they reach $20 million, etc." (p. 1105) "Computers have unmistakably lengthened the time it takes to fill an order, and have made it almost impossible to understand a royalty statement or get an intelligent answer to a complaint or a query." (p. 1105) "The near-term result often seems to be that information formerly available by means of a phone call to the order department is reported as unknowable until the computer makes its next periodic report." (p. 1106) "Batch processing ... can delay your orders, delay your deliveries, delay your payments, and cut you off from ready access to your own data." (p. 1109)

Victor Strauss, a consultant for printing management and contributing editor of Publisher's Weekly, states: "The computerization offered neither price advantages nor delivery advantages to book publishers." "The New Composition Technology: Promises and Realities," Publishers' Weekly 195: 62 (5 May 1969).

3. Circulation is one operation in which librarians seem to see nothing between a manual and a computerized system, whereas in reality, a large range of alter-

natives exists.   See also Melcher, p. 1106: "Other
machines also cost less or do more.   The cost of
offset printing plates drops from $1.50 a page to
$1 a page to ten cents a page, even to five cents
a page--in an almost unbelievable series of technical breakthroughs. "

4.   "The old idea that an automated system could be operated
     at a new lower cost than a manual system is dead,
     indeed. " [Allen Veaner, "The Application of Com-
     puters to Library Technical Processing," CRL 31:
     36 (Jan. 1970).]
          "Wishful thinking about present and future
     costs may give us librarians a black eye with the
     very administrators who are urging us to 'get with
     computers. '" [William Locke, "Computer Costs
     for Large Libraries," Datamation (Feb. 1970), p.
     74.]
          "I talked to one wholesaler who had really
     made his automation work, but who had wound up
     with costs a good deal higher than a competitor's.
     I asked whether he really thought he could get his
     costs down.   He said: 'No, but I think the other
     fellow's costs will rise--he's automating, too. '"
     (Melcher, p. 1107)
          See details of the high costs of computers
     in educational processes in Anthony G. Oettinger
     (of the Harvard University Program on Technology
     and Society), Run, Computer, Run (Cambridge,
     Mass.: Harvard University Press, 1969), p. 189-
     200.   This is the most penetrating analysis to date
     of the application of various technologies that are
     "force-fed, oversold, and prematurely applied. "
     See also the frank statement on the costs of com-
     puters, including limitations on the cost reductions
     possible in the longterm future, in Frederick G.
     Withington (of Arthur D. Little, Inc.), The Real
     Computer (Reading, Mass.: Addison-Wesley Pub-
     lishing Co., 1969), p. 37-41.
          The literature is riddled with irresponsible
     accounts of project costs that make no real attempt
     to include the full range of costs of computerization.

5.   This fact was called to my attention by a manager of
     an aerospace satellite systems division.

6.   "Programming is still very much an art and one in

which there seem to be no standards of performance. " (Alexander, p. 171)

7. Just compare. We are lured by the frills of computer-
    ization and forget its enormous basic costs. Myra,
    with her six-foot-seven escort, proposes to forget
    the six feet and concentrate on the inches. "The
    glamor, let's face it, is in the computers, but the
    breakthroughs are elsewhere. " (Melcher, p. 1107)

8. "They (computers) are creatures of their time, and they
    come because they are needed. " (Melcher, p. 1106)
    Melcher makes the common mistake of assuming
    that, because we needed something to help us in
    volume operations, the computer is what we needed.
    I contend that it is not. He states later, "It must
    be noted, however, that as yet the utilization of the
    computer to meet those changing needs has been
    massively disappointing. (p. 1107)

9. "The service bureau put out cards through its computer
    instead of through the far simpler card lister form-
    erly used. The result was no different, and they
    charged us three times as much--but it made us
    feel kind of big league. " (Melcher, p. 1109)

10. A phrase by one of our best poets of the 1930s, now
    reemerging, Laura Riding.

11. "In effect, each new task for a computer entails the de-
    sign, development, and fabrication of a unique ma-
    chine, assembled partly out of the boxful of hard-
    ware, partly out of software. " (Alexander, p. 171)

12. I still accept on faith the remarkable computational fa-
    cility of the computer, though cautioned by friends
    in industry that unless the computer is checked at
    each permutation point in a computation, they can-
    not be sure that the results are right, because of
    possible disorders in the machine. Since checking
    takes too much time, technologists accept the com-
    puter's results, fully aware that often they are work-
    ing with unreliable data!

13. This may have eased somewhat, since the extravagantly
    financed and well-publicized grunts of INTREX at
    M. I. T. have brought forth a mouse. The self-de-

lusion of electronics engineers is demonstrated in
the fact that, since they have taken over control of
the engineering schools, "insignificant" courses,
such as Power and Illumination, have been dropped
from all of them.   Maybe if we don't look, need
for such knowledge will go away.
        "When the new specialists were asked to un-
derstand before they criticized, some of them were
outraged.   'We should learn from you?   You've got
to be kidding.   Should we, the Knights of Systems
Analysis, soil our anointed hands with that old rub-
bish?   Learn about it?   We will simply sweep it
away in no time with our electronic broom.   We'll
put you out of business!'" [Victor Strauss, "Be-
twixt Cup and Lip," Publishers' Weekly (26 Jan.
1970), p. 263.]

14.   Similarities to Christian doctrine are due to the fact
        that Computer theology is vaguely Christian in ori-
        entation.

15.   The most extreme deception encountered involved a
        campus computer unit which contracted with the cen-
        tral library (apparently to get access to its grant
        money) to handle a library operation, one of whose
        basic requirements was the integrity of the informa-
        tion stored in the computer (an IBM 360/67).
        Months after programming began, the library dis-
        covered that the chances of this machine wiping out
        its storage file are high, a fact known to the ex-
        perts from the beginning.

16.   See Melcher's statements in footnotes two and four.

17.   Alexander, p. 126.

18.   "One knowledgeable consultant estimates that about half
        the System/360's now installed are still operating
        in the 'emulation' mode (i. e., are acting as second
        instead of third generation computers) ... at least
        a billion dollars worth of new machine capacity is,
        in effect, wasted." (Alexander, p. 129) If we can
        brainwash people to be so stupid, why can't we
        brainwash them to be virtuous?

19.   Allen Veaner discusses this problem in full in "Major
        Decision Points in Library Automation," CRL 31:
        308-09 (Sept. 1970).

20. "Within limits, the more of our processes we get com-
    puterized, the better chance we have of matching
    the costs of the manual system." [William Locke,
    "Computer Costs for Large Libraries," Datamation
    (Feb. 1970), p. 72.] When pursued by mail, Locke
    admitted that he has no evidence to support this con-
    tention.

21. "Despite the fact that, on a capacity basis, the IBM
    System/360, RCA Spectra 70, and GE 600 series
    are cheaper to lease or buy, they have been the
    hardest put to show a demonstrable payoff ... they
    are too costly to be sitting idle, but they also need
    more highly qualified--and more highly paid--per-
    sonnel to operate effectively." (Alexander, p. 129)

22. Hofstra is now running final cost estimates on an MT/
    ST card production system despite warnings against
    it. But we began with careful cost control of our
    manual production and will be able to compare
    costs to decide whether or not to continue.

23. (Melcher, p. 1107) His figure, of course, is stolen
    from Samuel Johnson.

24. "The rules of the computer game are that you talk only
    about what you are going to do, never about how it
    turned out. This is a science in which you publish
    the results of your experiments before you make
    them." (Melcher, p. 1105)

25. For what happens when computerization begins with the
    library, see Dan Mather, "Data Processing in an
    Academic Library," PNLA Quarterly 32:4-21 (July
    1968).

26. "In companies everywhere the reasons for buying com-
    puters were not thought out. From the top, the
    attitude was that you can't let the competition get
    ahead of you; if they buy computers we've got to buy
    computers. The result was great euphoria." (Al-
    exander, p. 126, quoting a GE internal consultant
    on computer usage.) "According to the survey,
    the majority of computer users believe they them-
    selves were to precipitous in acquiring their ma-
    chines." (Alexander, p. 127)

27. "Yet once in the grasp of an automated system, there
     is no turning back. Entering upon an automated
     system in any enterprise is practically an irrevers-
     ible step." [Veaner, "The Application of Comput-
     ers to Library Technical Processing," CRL 31:37
     (Jan. 1970).]

28. "But do people only want to save money?" plaintively
     writes a computerator to me. If at no other time,
     certainly when they are bankrupt.

A SELECTIVE SUBJECT INDEX